Labour Rights and the C Church

This book explores the extent of parallelism and cross-influence between Catholic Social Teaching and the work of the world's oldest human rights institution, the International Labour Organisation (ILO).

Sometimes there is a mutual attraction between seeming opposites who in fact share a common goal. This book is about just such an attraction between a secular organisation born of the political desire for peace and justice, and a metaphysical institution much older founded to bring peace and justice on earth. It examines the principles evident in the teachings of the Catholic Church and in the secular philosophy of the ILO; together with the theological basis of the relevant provisions of Catholic Social Teaching and of the socio-political origins and basis of the ILO. The spectrum of labour rights covered in the book extends from the right to press for rights, i.e., collective bargaining, to rights themselves – conditions in work – and on to post-employment rights in the form of social security and pensions. The extent of the parallelism and cross-influence is reviewed from the issue of the Papal Encyclical of Pope Leo XIII Rerum Novarum (1891) and from the founding of the ILO in 1919.

This book is intended to appeal to lay, professional and academic alike, and will be of interest to researchers and academics working in the areas of international human rights, theology, comparative philosophy, history and social and political studies.

On 4 January 2021 it was granted an Imprimatur by the Roman Catholic Archbishop of Liverpool, Malcolm P. McMahon O.P., meaning that the Catholic Church is satisfied that the book is free of doctrinal or moral error.

Paul Beckett has 40 years' experience both as an international commercial lawyer and as a human rights defender. He graduated from Worcester College, Oxford in 1978 with First Class honours in Jurisprudence. He also completed a Master of Studies in International Human Rights Law at New College, Oxford in 2014. Both a legal practitioner and an academic – a "pracademic" – he has been widely published and is often invited to take an active part in conferences, seminars and broadcasts. Married, with two grown sons, he lives and works in the Isle of Man.

Law and Religion

The practice of religion by individuals and groups, the rise of religious diversity, and the fear of religious extremism, raise profound questions for the interaction between law and religion in society. The regulatory systems involved, the religion laws of secular government (national and international) and the religious laws of faith communities, are valuable tools for our understanding of the dynamics of mutual accommodation and the analysis and resolution of issues in such areas as: religious freedom; discrimination; the autonomy of religious organisations; doctrine, worship and religious symbols; the property and finances of religion; religion, education and public institutions; and religion, marriage and children. In this series, scholars at the forefront of law and religion contribute to the debates in this area. The books in the series are analytical with a key target audience of scholars and practitioners, including lawyers, religious leaders and others with an interest in this rapidly developing discipline.

Series Editor
Professor Norman Doe, Director of the Centre for Law and Religion, Cardiff University, UK

Series Board

Carmen Asiaín, Professor, University of Montevideo, Uruguay
Paul Babie, Professor and Associate Dean (International), Adelaide Law School, Australia
Pieter Coertzen, Chairperson, Unit for the Study of Law and Religion, University of Stellenbosch, South Africa
Alison Mawhinney, Reader, Bangor University, UK
Michael John Perry, Senior Fellow, Center for the Study of Law and Religion, Emory University, USA

Titles in this series include:

Tax Law, Religion, and Justice
An Exploration of Theological Reflections on Taxation
Allen Calhoun

Labour Rights and the Catholic Church
The International Labour Organisation, the Holy See and Catholic Social Teaching
Paul Beckett

For more information about this series, please visit: www.routledge.com/Law-and-Religion/book-series/LAWRELIG

Acknowledgements

This book has been a difficult row to hoe, turning over land left fallow for the best part of a century, but I have not been alone.

My fellow lawyers and friends Roger Phillips and Terence McDonald set trains of thought in motion and have shown great resilience in the face of my preoccupation with this book over the past six months. Their patience is almost as great of that of my wife, Dr Lesley Stone: her loving understanding as I have written this my third book for Routledge in as many years, wiping evenings and weekends from the social calendar and monopolising dinner conversation, has not gone unnoticed, or unappreciated.

My thanks for their help go also to Alison Irvine-Moget at ILO Publishing and ILO Senior Researcher Dorothea Hoehtker, and to the team at Routledge whose passion for knowledge and its dissemination even in these most difficult of times is indefatigable.

This book is dedicated jointly to two people who have made an enormous difference to my professional and personal life. Neither has met the other, but I want to be there when one day they do. Professor Margaret Bedggood CNZM and I first met at Oxford University in 2013, to which I had returned after an absence of 35 years to read for a Masters in International Human Rights Law. It was in my conversations with Margaret that the ideas behind this book took shape and her constant support and encouragement powered their flight. Sir Julian Knowles (Mr Justice Julian Knowles) came into my life 15 years ago when he was still practising at the Bar in London. Julian's life-enhancing presence is a constant inspiration. It has been said of Albert Thomas, the first Director-General of the ILO, that he was "a game changer". That is true also of Margaret and Julian, and in all three cases it's a massive understatement.

My wish for this book is that it provoke and console in equal measure. It is a cliché to say that the shortcomings and mistakes are all my own. Well, they are.

Paul Beckett
All Saints Day 2020, Isle of Man

1 Introduction

The bond

What lies behind the title to this book? "Labour Rights and the Catholic Church" seems unambiguous enough, simply posing the question of what workers' rights are embedded in Catholic Social Teaching. But what of the International Labour Organisation paired with Catholic Social Teaching? What of the Holy See linked to the International Labour Organisation?

Sometimes there is a mutual attraction between seeming opposites, which turns out to be, in fact, an attraction between those who share a common goal, a common vision; those who walk on common pathways. It just does not appear that way to the casual observer who, imperfectly informed, attributes communality to mere coincidence. Perhaps that observer may stretch a point and say that what the two have in common is their identical but independently crafted solution to a puzzle: simple synchronicity. That observer would probably not go as far as to say that the attraction lies in each being aware of what the other has to offer and in the mutual benefit of the attraction itself: of symbiosis.

This book is about just such an attraction, between a secular organisation born of the political desire for peace and justice in the lawless chaos of 1919 and a metaphysical institution so very much older founded to bring peace and justice on earth. It shows how the principles of workers' rights in Catholic Social Teaching played a seminal role as a moral force in the formation and development of the International Labour Organisation, and how in turn the principles formed and promoted by that organisation have influenced and enriched Catholic Social Teaching itself to become part of the Magisterium of the Catholic Church.

It is the story of a special bond as historic as the ILO itself; though for most of the last century it has been hiding in plain sight.

Secularism has dominated the historiography of the ILO from the beginning. The first comprehensive account of the formation of the ILO was that of J T Shotwell in his *Origins of the International Labor Organization*[1] published in

---

1 J T Shotwell, *Origins of the International Labor Organization*, Volumes I and II (Columbia University Press, New York, 1934).

1934, and which remains a rich source of documentation contemporary to the negotiations of the Treaty of Versailles, which concerned the creation of the ILO. It makes no reference at all to any confessional, religious contribution. Four decades later, Antony Alcock produced his *History of the International Labour Organisation*[2] in 1971, which in its turn became the definitive text and which too is devoid of any confessional content. The tide has only very recently begun to turn. Daniel Maul in *The International Labour Organization: 100 Years of Global Social Policy*[3] published in 2019 examines the initiatives of ILO's first Director-General Albert Thomas who sought to establish relations with the Holy See. Yet Reiner Tosstorff in *Ursprünge de ILO*[4] [Origins of the ILO] published in 2020 also abides by the purely secularist historiographic tradition, focussing solely on the contribution of socialist trade unions.

Writing in 2008 ILO historian Jasmien Van Daele wrote:

> Within the broader network of transnational actors a lot has been said about labour and to a lesser extent liberal internationalism. On the side of Catholic social organizations, research on the ILO and the Christian working class is far less popular. One reason is the dominance of the socialist International Federation of Trade Unions in the ILO's Workers' Group in the first half of the twentieth century. In this light it would be interesting to know more about the (development of the) relationship between the ILO and the Catholic Church, after all both universal–international organizations.[5]

The challenge this poses is obvious; the solution perhaps less so.

Reinterpretation and hindsight

This is a secular age in which faith has faded and our understanding of the religious and social context of past measures – which were fuelled by hope and optimism for new beginnings – is distorted by what we know was to come. A note of caution has to be sounded when reviewing such material from a 21st-century perspective, with the benefit of over a century's hindsight:

2 Antony Alcock, *History of the International Labour Organisation* (Macmillan, Basingstoke, 1971).
3 Daniel Maul, *The International Labour Organization: 100 Years of Global Social Policy* (Walter de Grutyer GmbH, Berlin, 2019).
4 Reiner Tosstorff, *Ursprünge der ILO: Die Gründung der Internationalen Arbeitsorganisation und die Rolle der Gewerkshaften* (VSA Verlag, Hamburg, 2020).
5 A comprehensive historiography of the ILO from a multidisciplinary perspective is found in Jasmien Van Daele, "The International Labour Organization (ILO) in Past and Present Research" in *International Review of Social History* Vol. 53, No. 3 (December 2008) 485, 510.

When one compares the social encyclicals written in the century after the Encyclical of Pope Leo XIII *Rerum Novarum (On Capital and Labour)* (1891), it is possible to discern an evolution in the Church's view on political-economic systems and its postulated social solutions. Such a comparison must be conducted very carefully, however, since the authors of these encyclicals [...] never aspired to write a study that would encompass the whole problem, and this lack of a comprehensive solution iinevitably opens the field to deductive and inductive reasoning.[6]

After all, we are prone to see patterns in everything, from stars in the heavens to grains of sand on a beach. For us it is comforting to perceive order and method where perhaps in reality the random and the chaotic dominate. It is tempting to regard the synchronous as more than merely serendipitous.

There is also the seductive nature of hindsight.

Historiography cannot avoid a degree of backwards projection. The past is a foreign country, its language dead. We read the past from our position in the present and we write history, consciously or unconsciously, with current interests and concerns in mind. Anachronism is not a defect; it is an unavoidable virtue which becomes problematic only when it hides behind a smoke-screen of objectivity and detachment.[7]

That process of reinterpretation, founded on a predisposition to secularism in this undeniably secular first quarter of the 21st century, endures. Michel Godicheau, representing the International Association of Free Thought,[8] addressed the International Labour Conference which marked the centenary of the ILO in June 2019 and saw no place for religion at the ILO:

The trade union movement at the international level is reflected in the ILO, which was established in 1919 in the wake of the First World War of 1914 and international pressure from workers and also the fear of the October Revolution becoming widespread as a decision stemming from the Treaty of Versailles. From the get-go, the form was tripartite: governments, representatives of employer organizations and representatives of trade union organizations of workers. Now this structural form stemmed from a principle which recognized the different interests of the three components. *This entails managing a conflict of interests which are products of the class struggle. It is also to say that the very nature of the ILO, then the International Labour*

---

6 Maciej Zięba, *Papal Economics* (ISI Books, Wilmington, Delaware, 2013) 55.
7 Costas Douzinas, *The End of Human Rights* (Hart Publishing, Oxford, 2000) 376.
8 An International Organisation Formed in 2011 to Promote an Atheist Viewpoint <www.internationalfreethought.org/manifeste-pour-la-liberte-de-conscience/> (accessed 16 October 2020).

Office, was far removed from the social doctrine of the Catholic Church and its common good leading towards collaboration of class. [quoting Marc Blondel, former President of the National Federation of Free Thought] *Therefore, the ILO does not seek to engage in institutional dialogue with religions in order to bring them into the mix of tripartite dialogue.* Regardless of political, philosophical or religious references, the working class is made up on the basis of its own interests as part of a national context of its own organizations. These trade union organizations are the only ones who are allowed to represent their constituents.[9] [Emphasis added]

Yet amongst those trade unions there was from the beginning a substantial contribution to the development of the ILO made by the International Federation of Christian Trade Unions (themselves predominantly Catholic), diplomatic overtures were opened with the Holy See and since 1926 there has been without interruption a Jesuit in residence, acting as special advisor to the ILO Director-General on social and religious matters.[10] These facts and Marc Blondel's assertion cannot both be true.

But is "truth" a constant? Time distinguishes what is true from what is false. The first Director-General of the ILO, Albert Thomas (1919 to 1932), was aware from its earliest years that the ILO attracted relationships which may have lacked substance or staying power. In his Report to the 12th Session of the International Labour Conference in 1929 he made this plain:

In some quarters the Office may possibly be criticised for being too ready to welcome any manifestations of sympathy, and not enquiring in a sufficiently critical spirit whether the principles of the religious or social institutions which are attracted towards it are, in their origin and essence, really in harmony with the ideas of social justice represented by the Labour Charter. It may happen that some are honestly misled by superficial analogies, and that others may turn back, becoming uneasy at the possible consequences of their participation in the Office's work. Yet how can the Office, at this early stage of the great work in which most of the sovereign States of the world have consented to take part, reject any help which is sincerely offered? Why should it not give free play to all sympathy, even though it may not last, even though it may sometimes be superficial, if it helps in attaining practical results? Time will distinguish what is true from what is false.[11]

---

9 Record of the Proceedings of the 108th Session of the ILC 2019 162. <www.ilo.org/wcm sp5/groups/public/---ed_norm/---relconf/documents/meetingdocument/wcms_7262 21.pdf> (accessed 16 October 2020).

10 See Chapter 5.

11 Albert Thomas, Report to the 12th Session of the ILC 1929 91 <www.ilo.org/public/l ibdoc/ilo/P/09383/09383(1929-12).pdf> (accessed 16 October 2020) © ILO.

Cutting through the fog of hindsight, inductive reasoning and reinterpretation, this book adopts a diachronic approach. The Catholic Church, just as the ILO, is part of an evolutionary process when it comes to labour rights.[12]

How the fundamental principles of the ILO and of Catholic Social Teaching on labour rights evolved is examined using contemporary records wherever possible, listening to the voices of the time. For us, a century has passed, but the thoughts of those who were actors in and witnesses to these events, some of whose voices are stilled, can still be read. The time that was continues to tick inside the time that is.[13]

Work – an essential dimension of social life

There is a natural affinity between the Catholic Church and the ILO, based on a common concern for work and workers – seen from a Catholic perspective as "the moral obligation of work". Dominique Peccoud[14] writes:

> In the Catholic understanding, work has an immense ethical value, since through work a person earns his daily bread. In the Book of Genesis, the Church finds its conviction that work is a fundamental dimension of human existence on earth. The human being is made in the image and likeness of God and is placed in the universe in order to subdue the earth. [...]
>
> Through work a person also honours the Creator's gifts and talents received from Him. Work is thus a stewardship of talents, since in the design of God, every human being is called upon to develop and fulfil himself. Through education, but also through work, man is responsible for bringing to fruition latent talents and aptitudes granted to him. Thus man grows in humanity, enhances his personal worth and comes closer to being 'in the image and likeness of God'. In the words of Pope John Paul II in his Encyclical letter *Laborem exercens*:

> Man has to subdue the earth and dominate it, because as the "image of God" he is a person, that is to say, a subjective being capable of acting in a planned and rational way, capable of deciding about himself, and with a tendency to self-realization. *As a person, man is therefore the subject of work.* As a person he works, he performs various actions belonging to the work process; independently of their objective content, these actions must all serve to realize

12 "Although the idea of rights has figured prominently in Catholic thought since the writing of *Rerum Novarum*, it would be an exaggeration to claim that Catholic social thought contains a finished, comprehensive theory of rights". Kenneth L Grasso, "Reintegrating Rights: Catholicism, Social Ontology, and Contemporary Rights Discourse" in Bruce Frohnen and Kenneth Grasso, eds, *Rethinking Rights* (University of Missouri Press, 2009) 204. And see generally, Giorgio Filibeck, ed, *Les droits de l'homme dans l'enseignement de l'Eglise: de Jean XXIII à Jean-Paul II* (Libreria Editrice Vaticana, Cité du Vatican, 1992) and Robert Calderisi, *Earthly Mission: The Catholic Church and World Development* (Yale University Press, New Haven, 2013) chapter 3.
13 Eduardo Galeano, *Upside Down* (Mark Fried tr, Picador, New York, 1998) 210.
14 Jesuit in residence at the ILO 1997–2008.

his humanity, to fulfil the calling to be a person that is his by reason of his very humanity.[15]

In his Encyclical *Fratelli tutti (On Fraternity and Social Friendship)* (2020) Pope Francis writes:

> In a genuinely developed society, work is an essential dimension of social life, for it is not only a means of earning one's daily bread, but also of personal growth, the building of healthy relationships, self-expression and the exchange of gifts. Work gives us a sense of shared responsibility for the development of the world, and ultimately, for our life as a people.[16]

Other expressions of faith

The special bond between the Holy See and the ILO has lasted a century, but the impression must not be derived from this that the ILO in the early 21st century is in any way exclusive in its dealings with religious organisations and communities:

> [W]e have been continuing our journey of dialogue with religious organizations and communities. We have had a longstanding and ongoing interaction with the World Council of Churches (WCC) and the Catholic Church through the Pontifical Council for Justice and Peace. The Islamic Educational, Scientific and Cultural Organization (ISESCO), an organization of the Islamic Conference and Muslim scholars, has also joined the dialogue. Quite naturally, together we have been discussing our fundamental values: questions of human dignity, solidarity and security, peace, and social – values enshrined in the Decent Work Agenda.[17]

Nevertheless, evidence of the pre-eminent contribution of Catholic Social Teaching to the constitution and development of the ILO throughout the 20th and early 21st centuries is compelling, and is the focus of this book. The pan-religious dimension of the ILO as it moves through the 21st century is a history as yet incomplete and a book waiting to be written.

Chapter summaries

Chapter 2: Catholic Social Teaching in context

A book dealing with labour rights and the Catholic Church must first make clear what "rights" are referred to. Before this, however, the basis upon which such rights are formulated and acknowledged by the Holy See must be established.

15 Dominique Peccoud, "Decent Work: A Catholic Perspective" in Dominique Peccoud, ed, *Philosophical and Spiritual Perspectives on Decent Work* (ILO, World Council of Churches, ILO International Institute for Labour Studies, Geneva, 2004) 129–130.
16 Pope Francis, *Fratelli tutti* (2020) s 162 © Copyright – Libreria Editrice Vaticana.
17 *Convergences: Decent Work and Social Justice in Religious Traditions – A Handbook* (Pierre Martinot Lagarde, ILO, Geneva, 2012) 2 <www.ilo.org/pardev/partnerships/civil-society/religious/WCMS_172371/lang--en/index.htm> (accessed 16 October 2020).

This chapter therefore examines the concept and status of Catholic Social Teaching (CST) within the Magisterium of the Catholic Church and also compares CST to secular human rights, showing how much the two concepts differ one from another. Chapter 3 then examines labour rights within CST.

CST is found in a series of Papal Encyclicals (often referred to as the Social Encyclicals) and Apostolic Letters and Exhortations beginning with *Rerum novarum* in 1891, many marking an anniversary of that seminal work, and culminating most recently in *Fratelli tutti* (2020).

The continuing relevance and evolutionary potential of CST is highlighted, as is the fact that CST does not claim authority over the State in the secular realm.

Perhaps counter-intuitively, given its wide social dimension, what CST most certainly is not is socialism (or communism) in a cassock. Neither is it liberalism. The origin and basis within the Magisterium of this opposition is reviewed. Unlike the political creeds, CST does not propose a blueprint for a model society. It is a means of social orientation, and not intended to be a Utopian reconfiguring of society and human nature.

In dealing with human rights, the focus is on secular human rights and their interaction with CST. To what extent do the Social Encyclicals indicate that secular human rights in the early 21st century have become part of the Magisterium of the Catholic Church? Does the Catholic Church display characteristics of a human rights organisation?

These issues are relevant to the relationship between the Catholic Church and the ILO because understanding the nature of the bond between the Catholic Church and the ILO, and why it endures, requires an examination of where the boundaries between them lie, and from which complementary characteristics of the other each benefits. Were the Catholic Church itself a human rights institution, with the Holy See as its secretariat, then that bond between it and the ILO would consist of a mere relationship between parallel organisations whose similarities would prove, on closer examination, to be no more than synchronised responses to contemporary rights issues. There would have been no need for cross-fertilisation, no separation of functions, no symbiosis.

The fundamental differences between CST and secular human rights theory are set out, and how human rights at the heart of CST is charted, through inclusion in the Social Encyclicals, beginning with Pope St John XXIII's *Pacem in terris* in 1963 and through the role of the Pontifical Commission Justitia et Pax, one of the goals of which is the pursuit of human rights.

Chapter 3: Catholic Social Teaching and labour rights

This chapter examines the origins and evolution of labour rights in Catholic Social Teaching, beginning with the issue of *Rerum novarum* (1891).

The 19th-century origins of Social Catholicism are reviewed, highlighting forerunners and pioneers such as the Bishop of Mainz, Wilhelm Emmanuel von Ketteler and Bishop Mermillod of Fribourg in Switzerland.

The considerable contemporary significance and the modern continuing relevance of *Rerum novarum* is assessed, as are the consequences (almost certainly unintended by Pope Leo XIII – conservative and patrician – when it was issued) of its adaptation and reinterpretation over the following 130 years.

So as to enable a direct comparison with the labour rights articulated and promoted by the ILO to be made, this chapter uses the same classification as that established by the ILO in its fundamental principles (which are themselves covered in Chapter 4). In adopting this classification, care is taken to present CST in its own terms, and not to superimpose a secular political and philosophical interpretation. That classification covers i) Association and collective bargaining; ii) Wages and conditions in work; iii) Social Security; iv) Child labour; and v) Forced labour and slavery.

To what extent the Social Encyclicals hold common ground with the ILO, and whether this is more than mere coincidence or synchronicity, whether there is an actual symbiosis between the Holy See and the ILO, is explored in Chapters 5 and 6, after the ILO fundamental principles themselves are examined in Chapter 4.

Chapter 4: ILO – fundamental principles: Conventions and recommendations

Before turning to examine the fundamental principles of the ILO, this chapter recalls that labour rights articulated by the Holy See are by their very nature theologically based and not intended to provide either a framework for the application of the principles espoused or the means of monitoring their effectiveness. These are not within its areas of claimed expertise. The Catholic Church does not offer technical solutions. Such a framework and monitoring must be undertaken by an institution which, in the words of André Arnou, provides to the soul which is the Church a body living "in this tangible world".[18]

This chapter therefore examines the technical detail of the fundamental principles of the ILO. Endorsed by the Holy See not merely as principles but, by extension, as labour rights delivery systems, *these have themselves become an integral part of Catholic Social Teaching*. Those fundamental principles, as also adopted when in Chapter 3 classifying labour rights in CST, are: (i) Association and collective bargaining; (ii) Wages and conditions in work; (iii) Social Security; (iv) Child labour; and (v) Forced labour and slavery.

Each of the fundamental principles of the ILO finds its counterpoint in Catholic Social Teaching, the bass notes resounding from *Rerum novarum*.

Chapter 5: The International Labour Organisation: Origins and Social Catholicism 1919 to 1944

This chapter looks at the origins of the International Labour Organisation and at its Constitution at its dawn in 1919. It follows its development in the inter-War

---

18 A Arnou, *L'Organisation internationale du Travail et les Catholiques* (Éditions Spes, Paris, 1933) 20.

period, culminating in the Declaration of Philadelphia in 1944. It examines the role of Christianity in the foundation and development of the ILO and specifically the part played by Social Catholicism.

The enormous contribution made to that development by the ILO's first Director-General Albert Thomas, widely regarded as a game changer in the relationship between the Holy See and the ILO, is prominent in this account of gifted and highly motivated individual pioneers within the new organisation, of the contribution of the Catholic trade union movement, the role within the ILO of the Jesuit in residence and of a real, though publicly unacknowledged, diplomatic relationship between the ILO and the Holy See in the years leading up to World War Two.

The foundation of the ILO in 1919, regarded as a beacon of hope by contemporary commentators, is set in its social, economic and political context.

The chapter lays out the background to the ILO Constitution 1919 and to the Declaration of Philadelphia 1944 and assesses the striking parallels with CST in the adoption in the Constitution of a tripartite structure comprising representatives of Government, employers and workers; not least the rejection in CST of the idea of a class struggle and its advocating co-operation between the wealthy and the working population.

Due credit is given to what Albert Thomas described as the "movement of ideas", calling for the drawing up of international labour legislation which reached a focal point at the end of World War One.

Although during the course of its first decade this was to evolve rapidly, at the time of its formation the ILO as an institution had no formal association with the Holy See. The history is told of what gave rise to Albert Thomas' diplomatic initiatives with Rome and with international Catholic organisations in the years leading up to his early death in office in 1932, including the creation in 1926 of the post of Jesuit in residence at the ILO, why he believed this to be essential and how this provided the moral imperative, the "*force morale*" behind the ILO. Also told is how following Albert Thomas' death, and under his successor Harold Butler, the initiatives appeared to have ceased, at least as reflected in the Reports of the Directors-General and in the Proceedings of the ILO, as if a curtain had fallen.

The chapter looks at the struggles of Christian (predominantly Catholic) trade unions as a minority presence at the ILO and, their minority status notwithstanding, at their ability to present a united front and an alternative to the socialist narrative; though being generally regarded as never having been appropriately rewarded by the ILO and their contribution never having been acknowledged in the manner it deserved.

The chapter assesses the importance from the perspective of Catholic Social Teaching and its influence on the ILO of the series of appointments beginning in 1926 of a Jesuit in residence as special ecclesiastical adviser to the Director-General; something which has lost none of its early significance into the 21st century (as Chapter 6 examines).

The period covered in this chapter is a time of profound harmony between the Holy See and the ILO, as well as a convergence between their policies and goals on social issues. The secular histories of the formation and early evolution of the ILO are numerous and by sheer weight of those numbers have tended to dominate the narrative. The historical records, however, are far broader than the secular narrative will admit and are unambiguous. The secular approach far from tells the whole story.

Chapter 6: The Holy See and the ILO 1946 to 2020

In the wake of World War Two the balance in the relationship between the ILO and the Holy See itself began to shift, and, at the same time, what from the point of view of the Holy See had in the years between the wars been under the political radar and unstated now began to be expressed, at first tentatively and then by the reign of Pope Francis with unreserved and very public support.

If the period following World War One had been a time when Catholic Social Teaching exerted a strong influence on the work of the ILO and the colour and scope of its Conventions and Recommendations, then the period following World War Two saw the flow reversed. Labour rights in Catholic Social Teaching themselves began to absorb and so be augmented by the principles adopted by the ILO.

At the same time, the ILO's moral imperative, that "*force morale*" which in the years leading to World War Two had been Catholic Social Teaching, now began to be articulated within the organisation using the language of international human rights. Until the late 1960s neither the Records of Proceedings of the International Labour Conferences nor the Reports of the Directors-General made any reference to Catholic Social Teaching.

This chapter traces that shifting balance, beginning with the immediate post-War years 1946 to 1963, which saw Pope Pius XII crossing a threshold. On 19 November 1954, while receiving an ILO delegation in Rome, he became the first Pope publicly to acknowledge the work of the ILO, of which he said the ILO could be justly proud and on which he gave his apostolic blessing. In his Encyclical *Mater et magistra* (1961) Pope St John XXIII, who had succeeded Pope Pius XII in 1958, introduced the ILO into the Magisterium expressing his heartfelt appreciation of the ILO and its promotion of justice and humanity.

The pre-War difficulties of the Catholic trade unions in obtaining anything more than a minority presence at the ILO were resolved in 1948 when they were granted observer status at International Labour Conferences.

Milestones were reached when the International Labour Conference was addressed first by Pope St Paul VI in 1969[19] declaring himself a "fervent admirer", "collaborator" and "friend" of the ILO and then Pope St John Paul II in 1982,[20]

---

19 Record of the Proceedings of the 53rd Session of the ILC 1969 77–81 <www.ilo.org/public /libdoc/ilo/P/09616/09616(1969-53).pdf> © ILO (accessed 16 October 2020).

20 Record of the Proceedings of the 68th Session of the ILC 1982 21/1/-21/6 <www.ilo.org /public/libdoc/ilo/P/09616/09616(1982-68).pdf> © ILO (accessed 16 October 2020).

having already mentioned the ILO in his Encyclical *Laborem exercens* (1981), giving the ILO his unqualified, unlimited endorsement for its "tremendous record of achievements".

In 1991 the ILO formally commemorated the centenary of the seminal social Encyclical *Rerum novarum.*

The chapter listens to the voice of the Holy See expressed from the time of their first accreditation to the International Labour Conference in 1967 by its Observers. They represent a running assessment and, as such, are amongst the clearest indications of the Holy See's thinking on the development of labour rights. More than this, they subject those seemingly silent Reports of the Directors-General to an exegesis based on the principles of Catholic Social Teaching and, in so doing, identify what on a purely secular reading are hidden similarities in philosophy and approach. Their commentaries include not only general endorsement of the role and work of the ILO but specific observations on the necessity for dialogue, on poverty, on the plight of rural workers and migrants, on employment, on the need for vocational training, on child labour and on environmental issues.

The messages of Pope Francis to the ILO are set out, showing that the integration of the principles promoted by ILO into Catholic Social Teaching had by his reign become axiomatic.

Chapter 7: Common pathways

This chapter considers the two overarching policies introduced by the ILO on the quality of work itself and on the future evolution of work as a concept. Those policies are the Decent Work Agenda and the Future of Work Initiative.

The "common pathways" of the title of this chapter are those on which the Holy See and the ILO have found themselves when weighing those policies. Over the past 20 years, each has openly acknowledged their shared ethical values which, even if not always explicitly documented, show a convergence between the principles espoused by the ILO and the social teaching of the Catholic Church.

It examines the endorsement of the Decent Work Agenda by Pope St John Paul II in his Homily and Greeting After Mass on Rome on 1 May 2000 on the occasion of the Jubilee of Workers.[21] It shows how principles found in his Encyclical *Laborem exercens* (1981) correspond with the four fundamental principles of decent work: (i) freedom of association and the effective recognition of the right to collective bargaining; (ii) the elimination of all forms of forced or compulsory labour; (iii) the effective abolition of child labour; and (iv) the elimination of discrimination in respect of employment and occupation. It sets out the

---

21 *Jubilee of Workers, Greeting of the Holy Father John Paul II after Mass 1 May 2000* <www .vatican.va/content/john-paul-ii/en/speeches/2000/apr-jun/documents/hf_jp-ii_spe_2 0000501_jub-workers.html> (accessed 16 October 2020) © Copyright – Libreria Editrice Vaticana.

comments on the Decent Work Agenda made by the Holy See's Observers to the International Labour Conference.

In his Encyclical *Caritas in veritate* Pope Benedict XVI embodies the concept of decent work, drawing expressly on the work of Pope St John Paul II in *Laborem exercens* and the Jubilee of Workers, Greeting after Mass.

The Future of Work Initiative is examined. It was in his first Report as Director-General to the 102nd Session of the ILC in 2013[22] that Guy Ryder introduced seven ideas for ILO centenary initiatives, the seventh of which was "the future of work". On 18 November 2013 ILO Pope Francis received him in a private audience at the Vatican, the joint press release which followed stating that the dignity of work is a common concern for the ILO and the Catholic Church, particularly the situation of the most vulnerable, child labourers, domestic workers and migrants.

By May 2016, in Rome, Cardinal Turkson was able to say in his opening address to a conference "Sustainable Development and the Future of Work in the Context of the Jubilee of Mercy"[23] held under the auspices of the ILO, the Pontifical Council for Justice and Peace and Caritas International, that the Constitution of the ILO and the social teaching of the Church coincide in linking development, justice, sustainability and peace with decent work. Guy Ryder spoke of the community of values between the Catholic Church and the ILO. Their joint declared intent was "to search for alternative models of socio-economic integration based on the principles underlying the Social Doctrine of the Catholic Church and the standards set in ILO Conventions and Recommendations".

Although the ILO Centenary Declaration for the Future of Work 2019[24] makes no express connection with Catholic Social Teaching, perhaps at this point in time its principles are so embedded that no conscious effort to do so seems necessary.

It was in 2005 that Director-General Juan Somavia first spoke of working with the Holy See over a period of what was then 85 years. He said that they would continue their work "along what is clearly a common path";[25] and this image continues to resonate.

22 Report of the Director-General to the 102nd Session of the ILC 2013, *Towards the ILO Centenary: Realities, Renewal and Tripartite Commitment* <www.ilo.org/public/libdoc/ ilo/P/09383/09383(2013-102-1A).pdf> © ILO (accessed 16 October 2020).

23 Cardinal Turkson, "Opening Address" to the Conference "Sustainable Development and the Future of Work in the Context of the Jubilee of Mercy" (Rome, 2 May 2016) <www .iustitiaetpax.va/content/giustiziaepace/en/attivita1/presidente/2016/_sustainable-deve lopment-and-the-future-of-work--in-the-context-.html> (accessed 16 October 2020).

24 *ILO Centenary Declaration for the Future of Work 2019* <www.ilo.org/wcmsp5/groups /public/@ed_norm/@relconf/documents/meetingdocument/wcms_711674.pdf> (accessed 16 October 2020) © ILO.

25 Juan Somavia, *The Challenge of a Fair Globalization*, Presentation at the Pontifical Lateran University on the Report of the World Commission on the Social Dimension of Globalization (Rome, 25 February 2005) <www.ilo.org/public/english/bureau/dgo/speeches/som avia/2005/rome.pdf> © ILO (accessed 16 October 2020).

The chapter demonstrates that the promotion of two overarching policies by the ILO, the Decent Work Agenda and the Future of Work Initiative, caused the fog of collective amnesia which had descended on the ILO for decades, blanking out debate on the early foundational contribution made by Catholic Social Teaching and on its continuing influence, to lift. A wholly refreshed dialogue began, with a newly rediscovered awareness that the Holy See and the ILO were on common pathways.

A note on style and sources

References are, wherever the context allows, not gender specific. Non-inclusive language used by other authors and in Holy See and ILO historic sources reflects the social mores of their times and is found in many of the quoted passages. Those passages appear as originally written.

References are made both to "the Vatican" and to "the Holy See". Inherent in this is a certain anachronism: from the reunification of Italy in 1870 until the Lateran Accords signed on 11 February 1929 which recognised the Vatican City as a sovereign and independent Papal State, there was no such entity as "the Vatican".[26] The Holy See however never refers to itself as "the Vatican", and so references to the Vatican in this book indicate a physical location. This institutional transition itself, however, has no substantive bearing on the relationship between the ILO and the Catholic Church.

The term "Catholic Social Teaching" is used throughout, but references will be found in the text and in some quoted sources also to "Catholic social doctrine", "Catholic social justice" and the more generic "Social Catholicism". A body of teaching which constitutes doctrine is the means; the establishment of social justice is the end sought.

Sources not in English are quoted in their original languages with translations by the author. Where available and of sufficient quality, ILO materials are quoted in the ILO's own translation – but the earliest materials contain only short summaries in English of texts in other languages, something which did not go unremarked at the time:

> The ordinary translator is a kind of Charon, whose duty it is to transport ideas, which to him are dead, across the waters of Styx. He receives on the one bank gibbering ideas, and when he has ferried them across, it is to a land which to the translator is, after all, merely a land of shades. Only when the translator is an expert interested in his subject does translation cease to be material transportation and become spiritual transfiguration.[27]

---

26 The Editors of Encyclopaedia Britannica, *Lateran Treaty* <www.britannica.com/event/Lateran-Treaty> (accessed 16 October 2020).

27 G A Johnston, *International Social Progress: The Work of the International Labour Organisation of the League of Nations* (George Allen & Unwin Ltd., London, 1924) 197. Harold

On 26 January 1923 in his Encyclical *Rerum Omnium Pertubationem*,[28] Pope Pius XI declared St Francis de Sales to be the Heavenly Patron of all Writers, and told "those Catholics who as journalists and writers expound, spread, and defend the doctrines of the Church [...] in no uncertain manner precisely how they should write":

> 33. In the first place, and this the most important of all, each writer should endeavour in every way and as far as this may be possible to obtain a complete comprehension of the teachings of the Church. They should never compromise where the truth is involved, nor, because of fear of possibly offending an opponent, minimize or dissimulate it. They should pay particular attention to literary style and should try to express their thoughts clearly and in beautiful language so that their readers will the more readily come to love the truth. When it is necessary to enter into controversy, they should be prepared to refute error and to overcome the wiles of the wicked, but always in a way that will demonstrate clearly that they are animated by the highest principles and moved only by Christian charity.

The author has tried to follow this advice with regard not only to Catholic Social Teaching but also to the secular work of the International Labour Organisation.

Context

This book was written during the Covid-19 Crisis in 2020. Disproportionate numbers of dead amongst the poor, the imposition of unreasonable working demands on those lucky enough to come out of it still having a job, massively increased long-term unemployment and social distress became the "new normal", with no end in sight. Despite global instances of self-sacrifice and common accord, in financial terms, it became apparent that only the fittest would survive. Such harsh social and economic consequences had not been unforeseen.

> Dazu kommen in unserer Gesellschaft sozialdarwinistische Tendenzen; für sie gilt das Recht des Stärkeren und die rücksichtslose Durchsetzung eigener und eigennütziger Interessen. Diejenigen, die nicht mithalten können, geraten leicht unter die Räder und zwischen die Mühlsteine. Vor allem im Zug der Globalisierung der Wirtschaft und die Finanzmärkte sind unkontrollierte

---

Butler (ILO Director-General 1932 to 1938) in his memoirs recalls similar difficulties when the ILO Constitution itself was being drafted in 1919 – "to render the pregnant French idiom with its inexorable simplicity and exactitude of meaning into equally terse and pithy English, and that without lapsing into those horrid gallicisms which are so seductive to the translator, was a brain-wearing exercise". Harold Butler, *Confident Morning* (Faber and Faber, London, 1950) 172.

28 Pope Pius XI, *Rerum Omnium Pertubationem* (1923) © Copyright – Libreria Editrice Vaticana.

entfesselte neokapitalistische Kräfte mächtig geworden, für die Menschen und ganze Völker oft ebarmungslos zum Spielball der eigenen Gier nach Geld geworden sind.[29]

The comparison with 1919, countries weakened by war, wracked with influenza and ruined financially, became in 2020 almost clichéd. In a time long passed, when our present was his distant future, Pope Leo XIII wrote: "It is not rash to conjecture the future from the past. Age gives way to age, but the events of one century are wonderfully like those of another".[30]

Paul Beckett
All Saints' Day 2020, Isle of Man

Bibliography

The Holy See

Encyclicals, Apostolic letters, Exhortations (in chronological order)

Pope Leo XIII, *Rerum novarum* (1891)
Pope Pius XI, *Rerum Omnium Pertubationem* (1923)
Pope Francis, *Fratelli tutti* (2020)

Other materials (in chronological order)

Jubilee of Workers, *Greeting of the Holy Father John Paul II after Mass*, 1 May 2000 <www.vatican.va/content/john-paul-ii/en/speeches/2000/apr-jun/documents /hf_jp-ii_spe_20000501_jub-workers.html>
Cardinal Turkson, 'Opening Address' to the Conference "Sustainable Development and the Future of Work in the Context of the Jubilee of Mercy" (Rome, 2 May

---

29 Walter Kardinal Kasper, *Barmherzigkeit: Grundbegriff des Evangeliums – Schlüssel christlichen Lebens* (Freiburg im Breisgau: Verlag Herder GmbH, 2012) 24. [In addition, Social Darwinist leanings are now appearing in our society, for whom what counts is the right of the stronger and the unheeding implementation of one's own self-serving interests. Those who cannot keep up simply fall beneath the wheels and between the millstones. Above all, as a consequence of the globalisation of financial markets and of the economy, unregulated and unrestricted neo-capitalist powers have assumed control, for whom individuals and whole peoples are frequently and pitilessly reduced to the status of pawns in their lust for money.] How this will impact the work and effectiveness of the ILO remains a matter for speculation. The ILO on 29 June 2020 published its first response, looking back over its 100-year history to examine how it had dealt with earlier global crises, as a template for combatting that of Covid-19, citing the Great Depression of 1929, World War Two, the fight against HIV/ AIDS, the 2008 financial crisis, and regional crises such as SARS in Asia (2003) and Ebola in Africa (2014): Kari Tapiola, *An ILO for All Seasons: The International Labour Organization's Ways Out of Crisis* (ILO, Geneva, 2020) <www.ilo.org/actrav/info/pubs/WCMS_749391 /lang--en/index.htm> (accessed 16 October 2020).
30 Pope Leo XIII, *Rerum novarum* (1891) s 59 © Copyright – Libreria Editrice Vaticana.

2016)   <www.iustitiaetpax.va/content/giustiziaepace/en/attivita1/presidente
/2016/_sustainable-development-and-the-future-of-work--in-the-context-.html>

International Labour Organisation

International Labour Conferences

Record of the Proceedings of the 53rd Session of the ILC 1969 77–81 <www.ilo.org
/public/libdoc/ilo/P/09616/09616(1969–53).pdf>
Record of the Proceedings of the 68th Session of the ILC 1982 21/1/- 21/6 <www
.ilo.org/public/libdoc/ilo/P/09616/09616(1982–68).pdf>
Record of the Proceedings of the 108th Session of the ILC 2019 162 <www.ilo.org/
wcmsp5/groups/public/---ed_norm/---relconf/documents/meetingdocument
/wcms_726221.pdf>

Reports (in chronological order)

Albert Thomas, Report to the 12th Session of the ILC 1929 91 <www.ilo.org/public
/libdoc/ilo/P/09383/09383(1929–12).pdf>
Report of the Director-General to the 102nd Session of the ILC 2013, *Towards the
ILO Centenary: Realities, Renewal and Tripartite Commitment* <www.ilo.org/
public/libdoc/ilo/P/09383/09383(2013-102-1A).pdf>

Other materials (in chronological order)

Somavia, Juan, *The Challenge of a Fair Globalization*, Presentation at the Pontifical
Lateran University on the Report of the World Commission on the Social
Dimension of Globalization (Rome, 25 February 2005) <www.ilo.org/public/e
nglish/bureau/dgo/speeches/somavia/2005/rome.pdf>
Convergences: Decent Work and Social Justice in Religious Traditions – A Handbook
(ILO, Geneva, 2012) 2 <www.ilo.org/pardev/partnerships/civil-society/reli
gious/WCMS_172371/lang--en/index.htm>
ILO Centenary Declaration for the Future of Work 2019 <www.ilo.org/wcmsp5/g
roups/public/@ed_norm/@relconf/documents/meetingdocument/wcms_7116
74.pdf>

Secondary sources

Alcock, Antony, *History of the International Labour Organisation* (Macmillan,
Basingstoke, 1971).
Arnou, André, *L'Organisation internationale du Travail et les Catholiques* (Éditions
Spes, Paris, 1933).
Butler, Harold, *Confident Morning* (Faber and Faber, London, 1950).
Calderisi, Robert, *Earthly Mission: The Catholic Church and World Development* (Yale
University Press, New Haven, 2013) chapter 3.
Douzinas, Costas, *The End of Human Rights* (Hart Publishing, Oxford, 2000).
The Editors of Encyclopaedia Britannica, *Lateran Treaty* <www.britannica.com/
event/Lateran-Treaty>

Filibeck, Giorgio, ed, *Les droits de l'homme dans l'enseignement de l'Eglise: de Jean XXIII à Jean-Paul II* (Libreria Editrice Vaticana, Cité du Vatican, 1992).

Galeano, Eduardo, *Upside Down* (Mark Fried tr, Picador 1998).

Grasso, Kenneth L "Reintegrating Rights: Catholicism, Social Ontology, and Contemporary Rights Discourse" in Bruce Frohnen and Kenneth Grasso, eds, *Rethinking Rights* (University of Missouri Press, 2009) 204.

Johnston, G A, *International Social Progress: The Work of the International Labour Organisation of the League of Nations* (George Allen & Unwin Ltd., London, 1924).

Kasper, Walter Kardinal, *Barmherzigkeit: Grundbegriff des Evangeliums – Schlüssel christlichen Lebens* (Verlag Herder GmbH, Freiburg im Breisgau, 2012).

Maul, Daniel, *The International Labour Organization: 100 Years of Global Social Policy* (Walter de Grutyer GmbH, Berlin, 2019).

Peccoud, Dominique, "Decent Work: A Catholic Perspective" in Dominique Peccoud, ed, *Philosophical and Spiritual Perspectives on Decent Work* (ILO, World Council of Churches, ILO International Institute for Labour Studies, Geneva, 2004) 129.

Shotwell, J T, *Origins of the International Labor Organization*, Volumes I and II (Columbia University Press, New York, 1934).

Tapiola, Kari, *An ILO for All Seasons: The International Labour Organization's Ways out of Crisis* (ILO, Geneva, 2020) <www.ilo.org/actrav/info/pubs/WCMS_749391/lang--en/index.htm>

Tosstorff, Reiner, *Ursprünge der ILO: Die Gründung der Internationalen Arbeitsorganisation und die Rolle der Gewerkshaften* (VSA Verlag, Hamburg, 2020).

Van Daele, Jasmien, "The International Labour Organization (ILO) in Past and Present Research" in *International Review of Social History* Vol. 53, No. 3 (December 2008) 485.

Zięba, Maciej, *Papal Economics* (ISI Books, Wilmington, DE, 2013).

2 Catholic Social Teaching in context

Introduction

A book dealing with labour rights and the Catholic Church must first make clear what "rights" are referred to. Before this, however, the basis upon which such rights are formulated and acknowledged by the Holy See must be established.

This chapter therefore examines the concept and status of Catholic Social Teaching (CST)[1] within the Magisterium of the Catholic Church. The following chapter then examines labour rights within CST.

This chapter also compares CST to secular human rights, showing how much the two concepts differ one from another. Human rights began to infiltrate CST following World War Two, to the point where, in the reign of Pope Francis, human rights are seen unquestioningly as a fundamental component of CST itself.

From a contemporary standpoint it is attractive to reimagine all advances in social conditions as having been a conscious expression of the desire to implement a human rights agenda, but this is not necessarily the case. As examined in later chapters in this book, one of the dominant influences in the formation of the ILO in 1919 and its subsequent evolution was CST. There is no mention of "human rights" in the ILO records and contemporary accounts of its activities in the period between the two World Wars, for the simple reason that even the language of human rights still lay far into the future.

It was a common appreciation and understanding of CST which formed the bond between the Holy See and the ILO.

A word of restraint is in order. Writing in 1991, Gordon C Zahn provided a salutary reminder, lest critical enthusiasm run riot and a consideration of CST find itself in an ecclesiastical bubble, that CST is not at the forefront of everyone's thoughts. There has been

> a serious decline in the extent to which religion and utterances of religious leaders are considered relevant to social practices and policy. Or authoritative. Today it is clear, even among loyal and committed Catholics, when a

---

1 Also often referred to as Catholic Social Doctrine/Justice.

pope speaks on matters of public or even private behaviour, fewer are ready to listen and not all of those who do are ready to accept what they hear.[2]

Catholic Social Teaching – An outline[3]

CST forms part of the Magisterium of the Catholic Church.[4] Pope Pius XI put it simply: it is "the influence of ideas in the realm of facts".[5] In his Encyclical *Mater et magistra* (1961) Pope St John XXIII proclaimed the timelessness and fundamentals of CST:

> 218. The permanent validity of the Catholic Church's social teaching admits of no doubt.
>
> 219. This teaching rests on one basic principle: individual human beings are the foundation, the cause and the end of every social institution. That is necessarily so, for men are by nature social beings. This fact must be recognized, as also the fact that they are raised in the plan of Providence to an order of reality which is above nature.
>
> 220. On this basic principle, which guarantees the sacred dignity of the individual, the Church constructs her social teaching. She has formulated, particularly over the past hundred years, and through the efforts of a very well informed body of priests and laymen, a social doctrine which points out with

---

2 Gordon C Zahn, "Social Movements and Catholic Social Thought" in John A Coleman, ed, *One Hundred Years of Catholic Social Thought: Celebration and Challenge* (Orbis Books, New York, 1991) 53.

3 A broad exploration of CST beyond the field of labour rights is outside the scope of this book. The literature is vast. Three recently published accessible introductions to CST are Kenneth R Himes, ed, *Modern Catholic Social Teaching* (Second edition) (Georgetown University Press, Washington, DC, 2018); Thomas Storck, *An Economics of Justice & Charity: Catholic Social Teaching, Its Development and Contemporary Relevance* (Angelico Press, Kettering, OH, 2017); and Thomas Massaro S J, *Living Justice: Catholic Social Teaching in Action* (Third edition) (Rowman and Littlefield, Lanham, MD, 2016). The Catholic Charities of St Paul and Minneapolis provide a comprehensive online guide to Catholic Social Teaching at <www.cctwincities.org/education-advocacy/catholic-social-teaching/> (accessed 16 October 2020).

4 "Magisterium: The living teaching office of the Church, whose task it is to give as authentic an interpretation of the Word of God, whether in its written form (Sacred Scripture) or in the form of Tradition. The Magisterium ensures the Church's fidelity to the teaching of the Apostles in matters of faith and morals" *Catechism of the Catholic Church* (Second edition) (Libreria Editrice Vaticana, Citta del Vaticano, 2000) 887. And see Thomas Storck, *An Economics of Justice & Charity: Catholic Social Teaching, Its Development and Contemporary Relevance* (Angelico Press, Kettering, OH, 2017) chapter 7 "The Authority of the Church's Social Teaching" which expounds the concepts of the extraordinary, the ordinary and the universal Magisterium.

5 "Even today the authority of this Church doctrine is greater than it seems; for the influence of ideas in the realm of facts, though invisible and not easily measured, is surely of predominant importance". Pope Pius XI, *Divini redemptoris* (1937) s 37 © Copyright – Libreria Editrice Vaticana.

clarity the sure way to social reconstruction. The principles she gives are of universal application, for they take human nature into account, and the varying conditions in which man's life is lived. They also take into account the principal characteristics of contemporary society, and are thus acceptable to all.[6]

In his Encyclical *Centesimus annus* (1991) Pope St John Paul II had pulled these threads together:

> 59. [...] [CST] has an important interdisciplinary dimension. In order better to incarnate the one truth about man in different and constantly changing social, economic and political contexts, this teaching enters into dialogue with the various disciplines concerned with man. It assimilates what these disciplines have to contribute, and helps them to open themselves to a broader horizon, aimed at serving the individual person who is acknowledged and loved in the fullness of his or her vocation.[7]

You do not have to be a theologian to understand social Catholicism. Being human is enough. That said, there is something of the Cheshire Cat about CST: the more systematically it is studied, the more it tends to disappear from view, leaving only its smile hanging in the air. As Clifford Longley has written:

> The coherence of Catholic Social Teaching consists in the way its various principles seem to merge into and arise out of each other, almost as if each concept contains all the others. Thus is we were to lose one of the principles of Catholic Social Teaching, from some sort of theological amnesia, we could construct it from the others. We would be able to say what it consisted of, so to speak, from the hole it left behind, just as we would be able to reconstruct a missing piece of a jigsaw. This is one of the reasons that Catholic Social Teaching seems to resist being organised into lists, and why it is so difficult to break it up into sub-headings. [...] [T]here is a circular quality to these related concepts – they fade into each other. They are non-linear, and not even two dimensional. Were we to try to reproduce a diagram, I think we would have to work in three dimensions to begin to show the various concepts in relation to one another.[8]

6 Pope St John XXIII, *Mater et magistra* (1961) 218–220 © Copyright – Libreria Editrice Vaticana.
7 Pope St John Paul II, *Centesimus annus* (1991) s 59 © Copyright – Libreria Editrice Vaticana.
8 Clifford Longley, "Structures of Sin and the Free Market: John Paul II on Capitalism" in Paul Vallely, ed, *The New Politics: Catholic Social Teaching for the Twenty-First Century* (SCM Press, London, 1998) 98.

Addressing the 14th Session of the Pontifical Academy of Social Sciences on 3 May 2008, Pope Benedict XVI referred to the four fundamental principles of CST as the dignity of the human person, the common good, subsidiarity and solidarity.[9] These he described as "linked organically to one another and [...] mutually supportive of one another". He too acknowledged their complexity and multi-dimensionality:

> We can initially sketch the interconnections between these four principles by placing the dignity of the person at the intersection of two axes: one horizontal, representing "solidarity" and "subsidiarity", and one vertical, representing the "common good". This creates a field upon which we can plot the various points of Catholic social teaching that give shape to the common good.
>
> Though this graphic analogy gives us a rudimentary picture of how these fundamental principles imply one another and are necessarily interwoven, we know that the reality is much more complex. Indeed, the unfathomable depths of the human person and mankind's marvellous capacity for spiritual communion – realities which are fully disclosed only through divine revelation – far exceed the capacity of schematic representation.[10]

The indivisibility of CST is something to which Pope Benedict XVI returned in his Encyclical *Caritas in veritate* (2009):

> 12. [...] [C]larity is not served by certain abstract subdivisions of the Church's social doctrine, [...] there is a single teaching, consistent and at the same time ever new. It is one thing to draw attention to the particular characteristics of one Encyclical or another, of the teaching of one Pope or another, but quite another to lose sight of the coherence of the overall doctrinal corpus.[11]

He also stressed the interdisciplinary nature of CST and the need for assimilation and co-operation:

> 30. [...] [T]he theme of integral human development takes on an even broader range of meanings: the correlation between its multiple elements

9 See *Compendium of the Social Doctrine of the Church 2004*, chapter 4, "Principles of the Church's Social Doctrine, I. Meaning and Duty" 160–163 (Pontifical Council for Justice and Peace) <www.vatican.va/roman_curia/pontifical_councils/justpeace/documents/rc_pc_justpeace_doc_20060526_compendio-dott-soc_en.html> (accessed 16 October 2020).

10 Pope Benedict XVI, *Address to the 14th Session of the Pontifical Academy of Social Sciences* (Rome, 3 May 2008) <www.vatican.va/content/benedict-xvi/en/speeches/2008/may/documents/hf_ben-xvi_spe_20080503_social-sciences.html> (accessed 16 October 2020).

11 Pope Benedict XVI, *Caritas in veritate* (2009) s 12 © Copyright – Libreria Editrice Vaticana.

requires a commitment to foster the interaction of the different levels of human knowledge in order to promote the authentic development of peoples. [...] In view of the complexity of the issues, it is obvious that the various disciplines have to work together through an orderly interdisciplinary exchange.

31. [...] The Church's social doctrine, which has "an important interdisciplinary dimension", can exercise, in this perspective, a function of extraordinary effectiveness. It allows faith, theology, metaphysics and science to come together in a collaborative effort in the service of humanity. It is here above all that the Church's social doctrine displays its dimension of wisdom.[12]

How Catholic social thought compares to contemporary social and political discourse is explained by Kenneth L Grasso:

Catholic social thought [...] begins from an ontology of social life that differs fundamentally from those that inform the dominant traditions in both modern and classical thought. It offers us a thick vision of social life that does not absorb the individual into society or the social into the political, and an affirmation of the dignity of the individual human person that does not denigrate into a sterile and corrosive individualism. [...] [F]or Catholic social thought, a human being is neither a monad nor an unencumbered self, free to make of itself and the world whatever it chooses. On the contrary, Catholic thought maintains the existence of an order of human and social ends inscribed on the very structure of human nature that obligates the person prior to, and independently of, his or her consent, an order of ends inscribed on the very structure of human freedom and in which this freedom finds its fulfilment.[13]

Sources

CST is found in a series of Papal Encyclicals[14] (often referred to as the Social Encyclicals) and Apostolic Letters and Exhortations beginning with *Rerum*

---

12 Pope Benedict XVI, *Caritas in veritate* (2009) ss 30, 31 © Copyright – Libreria Editrice Vaticana.

13 Kenneth L Grasso, "Reintegrating Rights: Catholicism, Social Ontology, and Contemporary Rights Discourse" in Bruce Frohnen and Kenneth Grasso, eds, *Rethinking Rights* (University of Missouri Press, Columbia, Missouri, 2009) 198, 205.

14 "Encyclical: A pastoral letter written by the Pope and sent to the whole Church and even to the whole world, to express Church teaching on some important matter. Encyclicals are expressions of the ordinary papal Magisterium". Ordinary papal Magisterium is "when, without arriving at an infallible definition and without pronouncing in a 'definitive manner', [the Popes] propose [...] a teaching that leads to better understanding of Revelation in matters of faith and morals. To this ordinary teaching the faithful 'are to adhere to it with

novarum (On Capital and Labour), issued by Pope Leo XIII in 1891, many marking an anniversary of that seminal work and culminating most recently in *Fratelli tutti (On Fraternity and Social Friendship)*, issued by Pope Francis in 2020.[15]

Some contemporary Catholic scholars reject the long-standing convention that CST is delivered "top down" in this way. John A Coleman disagrees that CST is found solely in the pronouncements of Popes and cites the proposition of Gordon C Zahn that Catholic social thought can come "from below". Coleman writes that the Papal Social Encyclicals could be regarded "as a kind of 'background music', spiritual reading or motivational starters essentially, to evoke sufficient ecclesial justification to become involved in [catholic inspired social movements]". Citing Zahn, Coleman advocates "that we read 'official teaching' as primarily a response to earlier Catholic social movements for reform, justice and social betterment and then see the official encyclical documents as, substantively, charter documents for subsequent Catholic-based social action."[16]

In this chapter, CST is exhibited using primarily the orthodox "top down" approach, but acknowledging the interpretive application of CST (in Zahn's words "from below") employed by the emerging Catholic Democratic moment in Europe and by the ILO itself as part of that movement spanning the close of the 19th and the dawn of the 20th centuries.

Continuing relevance

Kenneth Grasso suggests that from the start of the 21st century there has been a resurgent interest in CST on the part of rights theorists:

> By laying the foundation for a theory of rights untainted by the shallow, atomistic model of social life that undergirds contemporary rights talk, Catholic social thought can help assure that this idea continues to bear good fruit, that it continues in the new millennium, as it did in the last, to contribute to the improvement of the human condition.[17]

For Richard Garnett, CST […] is about the person – about who we are and why it matters. Beneath, and supporting, the various statements and suggestions

---

religious assent' which, though distinct from the assent of faith, is nonetheless an extension of it". *Catechism of the Catholic Church* (Second edition) (Libreria Editrice Vaticana, Citta del Vaticano, 2000) 236, 876.

15 See the appendix to this chapter, which includes hyperlinks to all materials cited.

16 John A Coleman, "The Future of Catholic Social Thought" in Kenneth R Himes, ed, *Modern Catholic Social Teaching* (Second edition) (Georgetown University Press, Washington, DC, 2018) 611–612.

17 Kenneth L Grasso, "Reintegrating Rights: Catholicism, Social Ontology, and Contemporary Rights Discourse" in Bruce Frohnen and Kenneth Grasso, eds, *Rethinking Rights* (University of Missouri Press, Columbia, Missouri, 2009) 211.

regarding specific policy questions is the bedrock of Christian moral anthropology, of the good news about the dignity, vocation and destiny of man.[18]

Writing at the turn of the 21st century, Paul Vallely saw CST, developed over a century of thinking, as the one viable position from which to develop a critique of "unbridled capitalism" and "the total rigidity of communism" when compared with failed socialist and communist initiatives and what was then regarded as an underdeveloped green and environmental movement:[19]

> [T]he twenty-first century – a world in which unprecedented ferocity in global economic competition is predicted of an extent that it will not leave any child, woman or man untouched anywhere across the globe. That world – the hard reality of it in the present era, and the spectre of a more cruel version in the decades to come – is one which has prompted electorates all over the world to search for some new techniques or philosophies to cushion or mitigate the effects of the new post-historic capitalism. Uniquely Catholic Social Teaching offers insights whose appeal is far from restricted to Catholics or even Christians.[20]

Pope Benedict XVI reflected on the continuing relevance and evolutionary potential of CST in his Encyclical *Deus caritas est* (2005):

> 27. It must be admitted that the Church's leadership was slow to realize that the issue of the just structuring of society needed to be approached in a new way. [...] In today's complex situation, not least because of the growth

18 Richard Garnett, quoted in Maciej Zięba, *Papal Economics* (ISI Books, Wilmington, DE, 2013) 177.
19 Environmental concern was indeed soon to be added to the body of the Catholic Church's Social Teaching by Pope Francis, showing that CST its itself an evolutionary process: "13. [...] Particular appreciation is owed to those who tirelessly seek to resolve the tragic effects of environmental degradation on the lives of the world's poorest. Young people demand change. They wonder how anyone can claim to be building a better future without thinking of the environmental crisis and the sufferings of the excluded. 14. I urgently appeal, then, for a new dialogue about how we are shaping the future of our planet. We need a conversation which includes everyone, since the environmental challenge we are undergoing, and its human roots, concern and affect us all. The worldwide ecological movement has already made considerable progress and led to the establishment of numerous organizations committed to raising awareness of these challenges. Regrettably, many efforts to seek concrete solutions to the environmental crisis have proved ineffective, not only because of powerful opposition but also because of a more general lack of interest. Obstructionist attitudes, even on the part of believers, can range from denial of the problem to indifference, nonchalant resignation or blind confidence in technical solutions. We require a new and universal solidarity". Pope Francis, *Laudato Si'* (2015) 13, 14 © Copyright – Libreria Editrice Vaticana.
20 Paul Vallely, "Introduction" in Paul Vallely, ed, *The New Politics: Catholic Social Teaching for the Twenty-First Century* (SCM Press, London, 1998) 2. The capacity of CST to mitigate the impact of the global economic recession and consequent blood-letting in the wake of the Coronavirus Crisis of 2020 has empirically still to be determined.

of a globalized economy, the Church's social doctrine has become a set of fundamental guidelines offering approaches that are valid even beyond the confines of the Church: in the face of ongoing development these guidelines need to be addressed in the context of dialogue with all those seriously concerned for humanity and for the world in which we live.[21]

Nevertheless, sight ought never to be lost of the self-imposed boundaries of CST. The three defining principles of CST are *the common good* – shared values which transcend the rights of individuals; *solidarity* – mutual responsibility; and *subsidiarity* – political and social decisions should be taken at the lowest level possible consonant with good governance.

The key insight is that all three concepts are necessary and inter-related: without solidarity, the horizontal dimension of social structure, subsidiarity, the vertical dimension, can easily become selfish insularity. Subsidiarity and solidarity have often to be held in a necessary kind of tension.[22]

CST and the State

CST does not claim authority over the State in the secular realm. Pope Benedict XVI in his Encyclical *Deus caritas est* (2005) explored the pursuit of justice at the boundary of politics and religion:

28. […] Justice is both the aim and the intrinsic criterion of all politics. Politics is more than a mere mechanism for defining the rules of public life: its origin and its goal are found in justice, which by its very nature has to do with ethics. The State must inevitably face the question of how justice can be achieved here and now. But this presupposes an even more radical question: what is justice? The problem is one of practical reason; but if reason is to be exercised properly, it must undergo constant purification, since it can never be completely free of the danger of a certain ethical blindness caused by the dazzling effect of power and special interests.

21 Pope Benedict XVI, *Deus caritas est* (2005) s 27 © Copyright – Libreria Editrice Vaticana.
22 Clifford Longley, "Structures of Sin and the Free Market: John Paul II on Capitalism" in Paul Vallely, ed, *The New Politics: Catholic Social Teaching for the Twenty-First Century* (SCM Press, London, 1998) 99. Subsidiarity is a guiding principle of the ILO: "The ILO has always been very keen on that principle since the international legal instruments adopted by the International Labour Conference are not imposed on anybody. They become an international commitment through national ratification. They constitute guiding criteria that help structure the drafting of local laws and regulations". Juan Somavia, *The Challenge of a Fair Globalization*, Presentation at the Pontifical Lateran University on the Report of the World Commission on the Social Dimension of Globalization (Rome, 25 February 2005) <www.ilo.org/public/english/bureau/dgo/speeches/somavia/2005/rome.pdf> © ILO.

Here politics and faith meet. [...] Faith enables reason to do its work more effectively and to see its proper object more clearly. *This is where Catholic social doctrine has its place: it has no intention of giving the Church power over the State. Even less is it an attempt to impose on those who do not share the faith ways of thinking and modes of conduct proper to faith. Its aim is simply to help purify reason and to contribute, here and now, to the acknowledgment and attainment of what is just.* [Emphasis added]

[...] [T]he Church wishes to help form consciences in political life and to stimulate greater insight into the authentic requirements of justice as well as greater readiness to act accordingly, even when this might involve conflict with situations of personal interest. *Building a just social and civil order, wherein each person receives what is his or her due, is an essential task which every generation must take up anew. As a political task, this cannot be the Church's immediate responsibility.* Yet, since it is also a most important human responsibility, the Church is duty-bound to offer, through the purification of reason and through ethical formation, her own specific contribution towards understanding the requirements of justice and achieving them politically.[23] [Emphasis added]

Opposition to socialism and communism

Perhaps counter-intuitively, given its wide social dimension, what CST most certainly is not is socialism (or communism) in a cassock. Neither is it liberalism. In 1991, marking the centenary of *Rerum novarum*, John A Coleman wrote:

Despite many shifts and changes in Catholic social teaching during the past one hundred years, *Catholic social teaching remains a distinct and original social ideology*, with a sort of unity based on its Janus-faced opposition to both liberalism and socialism. [...] As these [...] have changed, over time, so has social Catholicism. Selectively, it has incorporated elements from these other two competing modern ideologies, yet generally based them on uniquely Catholic philosophical and theological grounds.[24] [Emphasis added]

---

23 Pope Benedict XVI, *Deus caritas est* (2005) s 28 © Copyright – Libreria Editrice Vaticana.
24 John A Coleman, "Neither Liberal nor Socialist: The Originality of Catholic Social Teaching" in John A Coleman, ed, *One Hundred Years of Catholic Social Thought: Celebration and Challenge* (Orbis Books, New York, 1991) 25. The application to CST of the term "ideology" is not undisputed. Michael J Schuck argues that "ideology" can be interpreted benignly and pejoratively; it may exist to conceal real world truths or to reveal them and the insistence by the Catholic Church that CST is not an ideology "is blurred by the equivocal interpretation given to the concept 'ideology' in church documents". Michael J Schuck, "The Ideological Uses of Catholic Social Teaching" in John A Coleman and Gregory Baum, eds, *Rerum Novarum: One Hundred Years of Catholic Social Teaching* (Concilium 1991/5 SCM Press, London, 1991) 47.

With the passage of time the term "liberalism" has shifted, and having a liberal attitude has come to signify a progressive open-mindedness. Viewed in this light, the opposition to liberalism on the part of the Catholic Church in the late 19th century may to us seem strange. The key is in that definitional shift. Albert Le Roy (Jesuit in residence at the ILO 1936–1955) explained:

> In 1891 Liberalism was in full swing. Economic laws were believed to act with the strictness and precision of physical laws. The State had to take good care not to intervene except in order to secure the normal working of the system, since any other action might upset the whole machinery. That human beings consequently had to suffer and become innocent victims of the system by no means disturbed the calm assurance of the advocates of *laissez faire*. The suffering was in the nature of things; any temporary disturbance would cure itself, and everything would come right of its own accord.

> The Church could not accept these inhuman theories, which made of economics an end in themselves and of man a mere tool. Economics are made for man and not man for economics.[25]

Throughout what Catherine Ruth Pakaluk has called "the Leonine era" (the period spanning the reigns of Pope Pius IX to Pope Pius XII, roughly 1850 to 1950) socialism was anathema to the Catholic Church. "Altogether, socialism and communism appear so often in the papal texts of the Leonine era, and with such importance, that they might be described as central foils over and against which the Church is defined and refined over time." [26]

In his Encyclical *Quadragesimo anno* (1931) Pope Pius XI noted that Pope Leo XIII had "sought no help from either Liberalism or Socialism, for the one had proved that it was utterly unable to solve the social problem aright, and the other, proposing a remedy far worse than the evil itself, would have plunged human society into great dangers":

> 117. We make this pronouncement: Whether considered as a doctrine, or an historical fact, or a movement, Socialism, if it remains truly Socialism, [...] cannot be reconciled with the teachings of the Catholic Church because its concept of society itself is utterly foreign to Christian truth.

---

25 Albert Le Roy, "The Fiftieth Anniversary of the Rerum Novarum" in *International Labour Review* Vol. XLIV, No. 4 (1941) 369, 386–7. For the role of the Jesuit in residence at the ILO see Chapter 5.

26 Catherine Ruth Pakaluk, "Socialism and Capitalism in Catholic Social Thought" in Gerard V Bradley and E Christian Brugger, eds, *Catholic Social Teaching: A Volume of Scholarly Essays* (Cambridge University Press, Cambridge, 2019) chapter 18, 436. And from a mid-20th-century perspective see Richard L Camp, *The Papal Ideology of Social Reform: A Study in Historical Development 1878–1967* (E J Brill, Leiden, 1969) chapter 3 "The Errors of Socialism and Communism".

120. If Socialism, like all errors, contains some truth (which, moreover, the Supreme Pontiffs have never denied), it is based nevertheless on a theory of human society peculiar to itself and irreconcilable with true Christianity. Religious socialism, Christian socialism, are contradictory terms; no one can be at the same time a good Catholic and a true socialist. [27]

This is not to paint Pope Pius XI as hankering after the *ancien régime* in the manner of the conservative Pope Pius X: "On the contrary, he seemed less bound to tradition and more willing to accept social change than any of his predecessors. He appeared in particular to be more able than they were to envision social institutions as dynamic and fluid".[28] It was to Pope Pius XI that Albert Thomas, Director-General of the ILO, turned in 1926 when asking for the appointment of a permanent representative of the Catholic Church at the ILO (in the form of the Jesuit in residence) to which Pope Pius XI had readily agreed.[29] Pope Pius XI's hostility to socialism and communism was founded on *Realpolitik*. He had served under Pope Benedict XV as the first Nuncio to Poland following the restoration of that country in the aftermath of World War One, where he was engaged in struggles with a rising socialist and communist political base which was tending towards totalitarianism. Both as Nuncio and later as Pope he had in the early 1920s been active (with only limited success) in trying to save the lives of imprisoned Catholic clergy and lay people in Stalin's newly established Soviet Union.[30] His assessment of communism was, understandably, one of raw emotion:

112. [...] Communism teaches and seeks two objectives: Unrelenting class warfare and absolute extermination of private ownership. Not secretly or by hidden methods does it do this, but publicly, openly, and by employing every and all means, even the most violent. To achieve these objectives there is nothing which it does not dare, nothing for which it has respect or

27 Pope Pius XI, *Quadragesimo anno* (1931) ss 10, 117, 120 © Copyright – Libreria Editrice Vaticana. Charles E Curran comments: "In the concepts of moral theology, socialism is intrinsically evil because it contravenes basic Christian teachings on private property and class relations, whereas capitalism is not intrinsically evil but often leads to abuses. Thus the condemnation is not symmetrical. Socialism alone is intrinsically evil". Charles E Curran, *Catholic Social Teaching 1891 – Present: A Historical, Theological and Ethical Analysis* (Georgetown University Press, Washington, DC, 2002) 200.
28 Richard L Camp, *The Papal Ideology of Social Reform: A Study in Historical Development 1878–1967* (E J Brill, Leiden, 1969) 37.
29 See Chapter 5.
30 For a contemporary account written during his reign and without the benefit of hindsight of what worse was yet to come, see William Teeling, *The Pope in Politics: The Life and Work of Pope Pius XI* (Lovat Dickson Limited, London, 1937). A retrospective assessment of the same events is in Robin Anderson, *Between Two Wars: The Story of Pope Pius XI* (Franciscan Herald Press, Chicago, IL, 1977).

reverence; and when it has come to power, it is incredible and portentlike in its cruelty and inhumanity.[31]

58. [...] Communism is intrinsically wrong, and no one who would save Christian civilization may collaborate with it in any undertaking whatsoever.[32]

That socialism continues to be such an anathema was most succinctly articulated by Pope St John Paul II in his Encyclical *Centesimus annus* (1991):

13. [...] [T]he fundamental error of socialism is anthropological in nature. *Socialism considers the individual person simply as an element, a molecule within the social organism, so that the good of the individual is completely subordinated to the functioning of the socio-economic mechanism.* Socialism likewise maintains that the good of the individual can be realized without reference to his free choice, to the unique and exclusive responsibility which he exercises in the face of good or evil. Man is thus reduced to a series of social relationships, and the concept of the person as the autonomous subject of moral decision disappears, the very subject whose decisions build the social order. [Emphasis added]

[...] In contrast, from the Christian vision of the human person there necessarily follows a correct picture of society. According to *Rerum novarum* and the whole social doctrine of the Church, the social nature of man is not completely fulfilled in the State, but is realized in various intermediary groups, beginning with the family and including economic, social, political and cultural groups which stem from human nature itself and have their own autonomy, always with a view to the common good.

48. [Referring to the Welfare State as a malfunctioning and defective model] [...] Here again the principle of subsidiarity must be respected: a community of a higher order should not interfere in the internal life of a community of a lower order, depriving the latter of its functions, but rather should support it in case of need and help to coordinate its activity with the activities of the rest of society, always with a view to the common good. [33]

Neither ideology nor blueprint

CST does not propose a blueprint for a model society. It is a means of social orientation, and not intended to be a Utopian reconfiguring of society and human nature. Pope Francis in his Apostolic Exhortation *Evangelii gaudium* (24 November 2013) acknowledged:

31 Pope Pius XI, *Quadragesimo anno* (1931) s 112 © Copyright – Libreria Editrice Vaticana.
32 Pope Pius XI, D*ivini redemptoris* (1937) s 58 © Copyright – Libreria Editrice Vaticana.
33 Pope St John Paul II, *Centesimus annus* (1991) ss 13, 48 © Copyright – Libreria Editrice Vaticana.

241. In her dialogue with the State and with society, the Church does not have solutions for every particular issue. Together with the various sectors of society, she supports those programmes which best respond to the dignity of each person and the common good. In doing this, she proposes in a clear way the fundamental values of human life and convictions which can then find expression in political activity.[34]

On 18 April 2018, speaking in the Vatican at a press conference held to present the activity of the "Centesimus Annus – Pro Pontifice" Foundation (to promote awareness of the Social Doctrine of the Catholic Church)[35] on the occasion of its 25th Anniversary, Archbishop Diarmuid Martin of Dublin noted that "the social teaching of the Church is by its nature always a work in progress [the application of which] can vary in the face of the different social and political conditions of the times", and observed: "The social teaching of the Church is part of the discipline of moral theology, *but moral theology cannot produce a handbook with all the answers to the social challenges of the times.*"[36][Emphasis added]

In his Encyclical *Sollicitudo rei socialis* (1987) Pope St John Paul II had already set the parameters:

41. The church's social doctrine is not a "third way" between liberal capitalism and Marxist collectivism, nor even a possible alternative to other solutions less radically opposed to one another: rather, it constitutes a category of its own. Nor is it an ideology, but rather the accurate formulation of the results of a careful reflection on the complex realities of human existence, in society and in the international order, in the light of faith and of the Church's Tradition. Its main aim is to interpret these realities, determining their conformity with or divergence from the lines of the Gospel teaching on man and his vocation, a vocation which is at once earthly and transcendent; its aim is thus to guide Christian behaviour. *It therefore belongs to the field, not of ideology, but of theology and particularly of moral theology.*[37] [Emphasis added]

This absence of an ideology is something to which Pope St John Paul II returned in his Encyclical *Centesimus annus* (1991):

46. [...] Nor does the Church close her eyes to the danger of fanaticism or fundamentalism among those who, in the name of an ideology which

34 *Evangelii gaudium* (2013) *Apostolic Exhortation of Pope Francis on the Proclamation of the Gospel in Today's World* s 241 © Copyright – Libreria Editrice Vaticana.
35 <www.centesimusannus.org/en/> (accessed 16 October 2020).
36 <www.catholicculture.org/culture/library/view.cfm?recnum=11851> (accessed 16 October 2020) © Copyright – Libreria Editrice Vaticana.
37 Pope St John Paul II, *Sollicitudo rei socialis* (1987) s 41 © Copyright – Libreria Editrice Vaticana.

purports to be scientific or religious, claim the right to impose on others their own concept of what is true and good. Christian truth is not of this kind. *Since it is not an ideology, the Christian faith does not presume to imprison changing socio-political realities in a rigid schema,* and it recognizes that human life is realized in history in conditions that are diverse and imperfect. Furthermore, in constantly reaffirming the transcendent dignity of the person, the Church's method is always that of respect for freedom.[38] [Emphasis added]

Rejecting any accusation that the Church's concern for the condition of workers "Considered superficially [...] could seem extraneous to the legitimate concern of the Church seen as a religious institution" Pope St John Paul II in his Encyclical *Sollicitudo rei socialis* (1987) stated:

> 8. [T]he social doctrine of the Church has once more demonstrated its character as an application of the word of God to people's lives and the life of society, as well as to the earthly realities connected with them, offering "principles for reflection", "criteria of judgment" and "directives for action".[39]

And in his Encyclical *Centesimus annus* (1991) Pope St John Paul II again stressed:

> 43. The Church has no models to present; models that are real and truly effective can only arise within the framework of different historical situations, through the efforts of all those who responsibly confront concrete problems in all their social, economic, political and cultural aspects, as these interact with one another. For such a task the Church offers her social teaching as an indispensable and ideal orientation, [40]

CST and Human Rights[41]

The questions posed in this section focus on secular human rights and their interaction with CST. To what extent do the Social Encyclicals indicate that secular

38 Pope St John Paul II, *Centesimus annus* (1991) s 46 © Copyright – Libreria Editrice Vaticana.
39 Pope St John Paul II, *Sollicitudo rei socialis* (1987) s 8 © Copyright – Libreria Editrice Vaticana.
40 Pope St John Paul II, *Centesimus annus* (1991) s 43 © Copyright – Libreria Editrice Vaticana.
41 For an accessible introduction to this dense topic see J Bryan Hehir, "The Modern Catholic Church and Human Rights" in John Witte, Jr. and Frank S Alexander, eds, *Christianity and Human Rights: An Introduction* (Cambridge University Press, Cambridge, 2010). See also Giorgio Filibeck, ed, *Les droits de l'homme dans l'enseignement de l'Eglise: de Jean XXIII à Jean-Paul II* (Libreria Editrice Vaticana, Cité du Vatican, 1992) and David Hollenbach,

human rights in the early 21st century have become part of the Magisterium of the Catholic Church? Does the Catholic Church display characteristics of a human rights organisation?

Writing in 1979, David Hollenbach identified the challenge facing the analyst:

> The history of modern Catholicism's understanding of the ethical foundation of human rights has been a complex one. It has developed under the crisscrossing historical pressures of political events, economic realities, ideological conflicts, and the institutional interests of the Church itself. Thus the Church's teaching on human rights has not been set forth with the lean lines of a rigorous moral argument.[42]

Why are these issues relevant to the relationship between the Catholic Church and the ILO? Understanding the nature of the bond between the Catholic Church and the ILO, and why it endures, requires an examination of where the boundaries between them lie, and from which complementary characteristics of the other each benefits.

The ILO has been retrospectively branded a human rights institution, though this terminology was certainly not present when it was founded in 1919, and both its foundation and its work in its early years were characterised by a strong affinity with CST.[43] Underpinning and increasingly defining the bond between the Catholic Church and the ILO after World War Two has been the attitude of the Holy See towards, and its engagement with, human rights. Were the Catholic Church itself a human rights institution, with the Holy See as its secretariat, then that bond between it and the ILO would consist of a mere relationship between parallel organisations whose similarities would prove on closer examination to be no more than synchronised responses to contemporary rights issues. There would have been no need for cross-fertilisation, no separation of functions, no symbiosis.

Fundamental differences between CST and secular human rights theory

Throughout the 19th century and well into the 20th, the Catholic Church not merely distanced itself from concepts which we now characterise as human rights, but actively opposed them.

Claims in Conflict: Retrieving and Renewing the Catholic Human Rights Tradition (Paulist Press, New York, 1979) chapter 2 "The Development of the Roman Catholic Rights Theory".

42 David Hollenbach, *Claims in Conflict: Retrieving and Renewing the Catholic Human Rights Tradition* (Paulist Press, New York, 1979) 89.

43 See Chapter 5.

Nineteenth-century Roman Catholicism strongly opposed the concept of human rights. Human rights were identified with the Enlightenment in the philosophical realm and with the call for democracy in the political realm. [...] The Enlightenment grounded human rights in the freedom and autonomy of the individual person, which Catholicism strongly opposed. [...] Freedom is not an absolute; it must always be considered in relationship to truth and other values. [...] Catholic moral theology insisted on duties and not on rights.[44]

A major transition [...] occurred in the twentieth century. Catholicism moved from a position of scepticism and opposition to the concept of human rights to an endorsement and appropriation of the concept in its teaching and ministry in the last fifty years of the century.[45]

As the vocabulary of human rights developed from the mid-20th century onwards and became common currency, the Catholic Church began to articulate in human rights terms, having however at all times proclaimed a universality akin to, but predating by centuries, that espoused in the Universal Declaration of Human Rights (1948) (UDHR).[46]

It is however far too easy to make a false comparison, and to see CST and human rights as two sides of the same coin. The Catholic concept of universal rights arising under the natural law is at odds with liberal human rights thinking which sets an atomised individual, claiming their rights, against the State and against all others claiming similar or conflicting rights. CST requires that a claimed right must, if it is to be fulfilled, first be weighed in the balance against the *common good* of the community. If there is a *right* there has to be a corresponding *duty*.

---

44 Charles E Curran, *Catholic Social Teaching 1891 – Present: A Historical, Theological and Ethical Analysis* (Georgetown University Press, Washington, DC, 2002) 215.

45 J Bryan Hehir, "The Modern Catholic Church and Human Rights" in John Witte, Jr. and Frank S Alexander, eds, *Christianity and Human Rights: An Introduction* (Cambridge University Press, Cambridge, 2010) 114. This is not a viewpoint which goes unchallenged, however: "There is no doubt that a very significant change occurred in the twentieth century as Catholic social teaching came to a greater appreciation of the freedom, dignity, and rights of the individual person. Yet although Catholic social teaching did learn from philosophical liberalism and human experience, it cannot and will not accept liberalism's individualistic understanding of the human person". Charles E Curran, *Catholic Social Teaching 1891 – Present: A Historical, Theological and Ethical Analysis* (Georgetown University Press, Washington, DC, 2002) 221.

46 <www.un.org/en/universal-declaration-human-rights/> (accessed 16 October 2020). An examination of the role and influence of the Catholic Church in and the application of the principles of Catholic Social Teaching to the coming into being and final form of the UDHR is outside the scope of this book, but see Philippe de la Chapelle, *La Déclaration Universelle des Droits de l'Homme et le Catholicisme* (Libraire Générale de Droit et de Jurisprudence, R Pichon et R Durand-Auzias, Paris, 1967).

Catholicism maintains neither that all political issues can be adequately con-
ceptualised as simple clashes of rights nor that all social and political goods
can be adequately articulated in the language of rights. If liberalism tends to
reduce the language of politics to the language of rights, in Catholic thought
rights language is but one element in a richer, more subtle vocabulary that
brings into play concepts such as the common good, solidarity, subsidiarity,
the public order and welfare, obligation, social ecology, and so on. [...]
Incorporating a range of goods foreign to the hyperindividualistic anthropology that undergirds so much of contemporary rights talk, Catholic social
thought points toward a more balanced form of rights discourse, a form of
rights discourse that provides for the claims of individuality together with
the claims of social obligation. [...] Catholic thinking about rights unfolds
against the backdrop of a pluralist understanding of the proper organization
of social life. In this view, a society is not a collection of atomized individuals,
but a *communitas communitatum.* [a community of communities][47]

CST and human rights each have their own distinct character:

S'il est vrai que tout l'enseignement social de l'Eglise est comme aimanté par
le respect de l'homme tel que Dieu l'a créé à son image, il faut cependant
veiller à garder aux droits de l'homme leur caractère propre [...]. Il s'agit
d'un grand arbre sur lequel on découvre de plus en plus de branches mais
dont les racines plongent dans le mystère de l'homme.[48]

Therefore, applying human rights norms to any analysis of Catholic Social
Teaching, if it is to be done, must be done conscious of the danger that this
ought only to be by way of analogy. Catholic Social Teaching is not rooted in
mere legalism. Cold legalism hardens hearts:

Human rights – cold rights – do not provide warmth, belonging, fitting, significance, do not exclude need for love, friendship, family, charity, sympathy,
devotion, sanctity, or for expiation, atonement, forgiveness.[49]

---

47 Kenneth L Grasso, "Reintegrating Rights: Catholicism, Social Ontology, and Contemporary
   Rights Discourse" in Bruce Frohnen and Kenneth Grasso, eds, *Rethinking Rights* (University of Missouri Press, 2009) 207–209.
48 Roger Cardinal Etchegaray, "Preface" in Giorgio Filibeck, ed, *Les droits de l'homme dans
   l'enseignement de l'Eglise: de Jean XXIII à Jean-Paul II* (Libreria Editrice Vaticana, Cité du
   Vatican, 1992). [If it is the case that all the social teaching of the Church is motivated by a
   respect for man created in God's image, it is nevertheless appropriate to accord to human
   rights their distinct character. [...] It is like discovering more and more branches of a great
   tree, whose the roots dive deep into the mystery of humanity.]
49 Louis Henken, "Religion, Religions and Human Rights" in Elizabeth Bucar and Barbara
   Barnett, eds, *Does Human Rights Need God?* (William B Eerdmans Publishing Company,
   Michigan, 2005) 154.

Human rights in the Social Encyclicals

Pope St John XXIII, who had served as the Papal Nuncio resident in Paris[50] and in that capacity was active and influential in promoting the UDHR (on the drafting of which he had worked "behind the scenes"[51]) and UNESCO, was the first of the Popes to express himself in human rights terms, but without omitting corresponding *duties*. Writing in a world which was by then familiar with the UDHR he affirmed in his Encyclical *Mater et magistra* (1961):

> 157. The solidarity which binds all men together as members of a common family makes it impossible for wealthy nations to look with indifference upon the hunger, misery and poverty of other nations whose citizens are unable to enjoy even elementary human rights.

> 211. Men, too, are becoming more and more conscious of their rights as human beings, rights which are universal and inviolable, and they are aspiring to more just and more human relations with their fellows.[52]

These rights Pope St John XXIII set out in his Encyclical *Pacem in terris* (1963), published a few weeks before his death – "an authentic charter of human rights"[53] and long-regarded as "the most systematic statement of Catholic teaching on human rights we have from the papacy."[54] In the spirit of the human rights it addressed, its opening lines were a radical departure from past Papal practice, and now embraced universality, for this was the first Encyclical to be addressed not solely to "the entire Catholic World" but also to "all Men of Good Will". Within Catholic Social Teaching rights *and duties* are indivisible:

> 9. Any well-regulated and productive association of men in society demands the acceptance of one fundamental principle: that each individual man is

---

50 For his own account of his mission, in the form of his correspondence, see Angelo Giuseppe Roncalli (Pope John XXIII), *Mission to France 1944–1953* (Loris Capovilla, ed, Dorothy White, trans) (Geoffrey Chapman, London, 1966).
51 "The Universal Declaration remained almost a dead letter for twenty years; but the involvement of prominent Catholics in drafting it, and the Church's promotion of the dignity of the human person, raised the importance of human rights in Catholic seminaries, religious communities, and papal documents, deeply affecting the way Catholic and other opinion leaders thought about these issues around the globe". Robert Calderisi, *Earthly Mission: The Catholic Church and World Development* (Yale University Press, New Haven, 2013) 65, 66.
52 Pope St John XXIII, *Mater et magistrata* (1961) ss 157, 211 © Copyright – Libreria Editrice Vaticana.
53 Synod of Bishops, *Justice in the World* (1971) s 56 <www.cctwincities.org/wp-content/uploads/2015/10/Justicia-in-Mundo.pdf> (accessed 16 October 2020) © Copyright – Libreria Editrice Vaticana.
54 J Bryan Hehir, "The Modern Catholic Church and Human Rights" in John Witte, Jr. and Frank S Alexander, eds, *Christianity and Human Rights: An Introduction* (Cambridge University Press, Cambridge, 2010) 120.

truly a person. His is a nature that is endowed with intelligence and free will. As such he has rights and duties, which together flow as a direct consequence from his nature. These rights and duties are universal and inviolable, and therefore altogether inalienable.

28. *The natural rights of which We have so far been speaking are inextricably bound up with as many duties, all applying to one and the same person. These rights and duties derive their origin, their sustenance, and their indestructibility from the natural law, which in conferring the one imposes the other.*

30. Once this is admitted, it follows that in human society one man's natural right gives rise to a corresponding duty in other men; the duty, that is, of recognizing and respecting that right. *Every basic human right draws its authoritative force from the natural law, which confers it and attaches to it its respective duty.* Hence, to claim one's rights and ignore one's duties, or only half fulfill them, is like building a house with one hand and tearing it down with the other.

63. In addition, heads of States must make a positive contribution to the creation of an overall climate in which the individual can both safeguard his own rights and fulfill his duties, and can do so readily. For if there is one thing we have learned in the school of experience, it is surely this: that, in the modern world especially, political, economic and cultural inequities among citizens become more and more widespread when public authorities fail to take appropriate action in these spheres. *And the consequence is that human rights and duties are thus rendered totally ineffective.*

75. There is every indication at the present time that these aims and ideals are giving rise to various demands concerning the juridical organization of States. The first is this: *that a clear and precisely worded charter of fundamental human rights be formulated and incorporated into the State's general constitutions.*[55] [Emphasis added]

With this in mind, he lauded the United Nations and its specialised agencies, described as having "highly important international functions in the economics, social, cultural, educational and health fields" and praised the UDHR and expressly the provisions of the Preamble in which

---

55 Pope St John XXIII, *Pacem in terris* (1963) ss 9 , 28, 30, 63, 75 © Copyright – Libreria Editrice Vaticana "*Pacem in terris* [...] makes no direct equation of natural law with human rights. Rather, human rights discourse is integrated into Roman Catholic social teaching to the extent that it facilitates the kind of order and relations between persons that are consistent with what we know of God's purposes for all creation". Esther D Reed, *Theology for International Law* (Bloomsbury, London, 2013) 262.

[…] the genuine recognition and complete observance of all the rights and freedoms outlined in the declaration is a goal to be sought by all peoples and all nations. […] It is therefore Our earnest wish that the United Nations Organization may be able progressively to adapt its structure and methods of operation to the magnitude and nobility of its tasks. May the day be not long delayed when every human being can find in this organization an effective safeguard of his personal rights; those rights, that is, which derive directly from his dignity as a human person, and which are therefore universal, inviolable and inalienable.[56]

Pacem in terris is not without its critics, one of whose principal concerns it that the Encyclical expressly encompasses economic, social and cultural rights which

> do not easily translate into tangible forms of human assistance. Furthermore, the text of the Encyclical does not suggest how these rights – encompassing each inhabitant of the planet – might be implemented or the desired state of affairs at least approximated.[57]

Such criticism reflects confusion and misplaced expectations on the part of rights activists, who see the absence of human rights delivery mechanisms on the part of the Catholic Church as a failing. They overlook the fact that the Catholic Church is not itself a human rights institution. It *interacts* with human rights institutions.

This interaction with human rights and human rights institutions was acknowledged during the reign of Pope St Paul VI in *Gaudium et spes* (1965), though only indirectly – the phrase "human rights" itself does not appear, though there are frequent mentions of "personal rights" and "rights of man". The importance of a metaphysical element, absent from secular human rights, is stressed:

---

56 Pope St John XXIII, *Pacem in terris* (1963) ss 143, 145 © Copyright – Libreria Editrice Vaticana. Pope St John Paul II in his Address to the United Nations on 2 October 1979 described the UDHR as embodying "the rights of the human being as a concrete individual and of the human being in his universal value. This document is a milestone on the long and difficult path of the human race. The progress of humanity must be measured not only by *the progress of science and technology*, which shows man's uniqueness with regard to nature, but also and chiefly by *the primacy given to spiritual values* and by *the progress of moral life*". [His emphasis] <www.vatican.va/content/john-paul-ii/en/speeches/1979/october/documents/hf_jp-ii_spe_19791002_general-assembly-onu.html> (accessed 16 October 2020) © Copyright – Libreria Editrice Vaticana.

57 Maciej Zięba, *Papal Economics* (ISI Books, Wilmington, DE, 2013) 34. This is a criticism not unique to *Pacem in terris* and which has also been made of the formulation of CST in the Encyclicals of Pope Pius XI in the 1930s: "The difficulty of [CST] was this: it could fly so high in the stratosphere of principles that, from above, the whole landscape was flattened out and no details could be perceived or – more–rarely – it could hew so close to the ground that its particular statement was too localized to be applicable elsewhere". Peter Hebblethwaite, "The Popes and Politics: Shifting Patterns in Catholic Social Doctrine" in Charles E Curran and R McCormick, eds, *Official Catholic Social Teaching* (Paulist Press, Mahwah, NJ, 1986) 268.

26. [T]here is a growing awareness of the exalted dignity proper to the human person, since he stands above all things, and his rights and duties are universal and inviolable."

41. [...] The Church, therefore, by virtue of the Gospel committed to her, proclaims the rights of man; she acknowledges and greatly esteems the dynamic movements of today by which these rights are everywhere fostered. Yet these movements must be penetrated by the spirit of the Gospel and protected against any kind of false autonomy. For we are tempted to think that our personal rights are fully ensured only when we are exempt from every requirement of divine law. But this way lies not the maintenance of the dignity of the human person, but its annihilation.

42. [...] The Church recognizes that worthy elements are found in today's social movements, especially an evolution toward unity, a process of whole-some socialization and of association in civic and economic realms. [...]

Moreover, since in virtue of her mission and nature she is *bound to no particular form of human culture, nor to any political, economic or social system, the Church by her very universality can be a very close bond between diverse human communities and nations,* provided these trust her and truly acknowledge her right to true freedom in fulfilling her mission. [...]

With great respect, therefore, this council regards all the true, good and just elements inherent in the very wide variety of institutions which the human race has established for itself and constantly continues to establish. The council affirms, moreover, that *the Church is willing to assist and promote all these institutions to the extent that such a service depends on her and can be associated with her mission.* [...]

43. This council exhorts Christians, as citizens of two cities, to strive to discharge their earthly duties conscientiously and in response to the Gospel spirit. [...] *Therefore, let there be no false opposition between professional and social activities on the one part, and religious life on the other.*[58] [Emphasis added]

Though not part of the Magisterium, the message sent by Pope St Paul VI for the Celebration of the Day of Peace on 1 January 1969 *The Promotion of Human Rights, the Way to Peace* addressed "To all men of good will, to all those responsible for the development of history today and tomorrow" emphasised the fundamental importance of human rights and their interdependence with peace:

---

58 Second Vatican Council, Pastoral Constitution on the Church in the Modern World *Gaudium et spes* (1965) ss 26, 41, 42, 43 © Copyright – Libreria Editrice Vaticana.

This year a special circumstance recommends Our proposal to all: *there has just been celebrated the twenty-fifth anniversary of the Declaration of Human Rights. This event interests all men, individuals, families, groups, associations and nations. No one must forget or neglect it, for it calls all to the fundamental recognition of the full dignified citizenship of every man on earth.* From such recognition springs the original title of Peace; in fact, the theme of World Peace Day is precisely this: "The promotion of Human Rights, the way to Peace". In order that man may be guaranteed the right to life, to liberty, to equality, to culture, to the enjoyment of the benefits of civilization, to personal and social dignity, Peace is necessary: *when Peace loses its equilibrium and efficiency, Human Rights become precarious and are compromised; when there is no Peace, right loses its human stature.* Moreover, *where Human Rights are not respected, defended and promoted, where violence or fraud is done to man's inalienable freedoms, where his personality is ignored or degraded, where discrimination, slavery or intolerance prevail, there true Peace cannot be.* Peace and Rights are reciprocally cause and effect, the one of the other: Peace favours Rights, and Rights in their turn favour Peace.[59] [Emphasis added]

In 1971 the Synod of Bishops in *Justitia in mundo* addressing human rights gave due weight to the secular, thereby affirming Pope St Paul VI's pronouncement that there is "no false opposition" between human rights and CST:

63. [...] Let recognition be given to the fact that international order is rooted in the inalienable rights and dignity of the human being. Let the UDHR be ratified by all Governments who have not yet adhered to it, and let it be fully observed by all.[60]

The election of Pope St John Paul II "had a profound human rights impact throughout the church."[61] At the beginning of his reign he issued his Encyclical

59 Pope St Paul VI, "Message for the Celebration of the Day of Peace on 1 January 1969" *The Promotion of Human Rights, the Way to Peace* <www.vatican.va/content/paul-vi/en/messag es/peace/documents/hf_p-vi_mes_19681208_ii-world-day-for-peace.html> (accessed 16 October 2020) © Copyright – Libreria Editrice Vaticana.
60 Synod of Bishops, *Justitia in mundo* (1971) s 64 www.cctwincities.org/wp-content/upl oads/2015/10/Justicia-in-Mundo.pdf (accessed 16 October 2020) © Copyright – Libreria Editrice Vaticana. Noting that *Justicia in mundo* addresses what he refers to as "interlocking" rights, David Hollenbach comments that there is "a recognition that human dignity implies a constellation of rights which must be understood, not singly, but in dynamic interrelation with each other". David Hollenbach, *Claims in Conflict: Retrieving and Renewing the Catholic Human Rights Tradition* (Paulist Press, New York, 1979) 85.
61 J Bryan Hehir, "The Modern Catholic Church and Human Rights" in John Witte, Jr. and Frank S Alexander, eds, *Christianity and Human Rights: An Introduction* (Cambridge University Press, Cambridge, 2010) 132.

Redemptor hominis (1979). Reflecting on the calamities of the 20th century, he saw hope in the form of a growing human rights movement:

> 17. [...] [W]e cannot fail to recall at this point, with esteem and profound hope for the future, the magnificent effort made to give life to the United Nations Organization, an effort conducive to the definition and establishment of man's objective and inviolable rights, with the member States obliging each other to observe them rigorously. This commitment has been accepted and ratified by almost all present-day States, and *this should constitute a guarantee that human rights will become throughout the world a fundamental principle of work for man's welfare. There is no need for the Church to confirm how closely this problem is linked with her mission in the modern world.* [...] The common good that authority in the State serves is brought to full realization only when all the citizens are sure of their rights. The lack of this leads to the dissolution of society, opposition by citizens to authority, or a situation of oppression, intimidation, violence, and terrorism, of which many examples have been provided by the totalitarianisms of this century. *Thus the principle of human rights is of profound concern to the area of social justice and is the measure by which it can be tested in the life of political bodies.*[62] [Emphasis added]

For Roger Ruston this passage represented a watershed: "It would be difficult to find more positive statements on rights in all papal literature." In Ruston's view, Pope St John Paul II "believes that advocacy and practice of human rights is *the* way" in which to promote social and international peace:

> The Church's post-World War II espousal of human rights then was not merely the admission that they were a good thing after all. [...] It was much more ambitious than that: human rights were adopted as the common currency between persons of good will in all cultures, through which the Church could exert a positive influence on the world as a whole, not merely in order to promote the advance of Catholicism.[63]

---

62   Pope St John Paul II, *Redemptor hominis* (1979) s 17 © Copyright – Libreria Editrice Vaticana.

63   Roger Ruston, *Human Rights and the Image of God* (SCM Press, London, 2004) 23 and see generally chapter 2 "An Awkward Embrace: Human Rights and the Church" in that work. A note of caution must however be sounded. In 1990 the Sacred Congregation for the Doctrine of the Faith (formerly referred to as the Office of the Holy Inquisition) issued *Instructions on the Ecclesial Vocation of the Theologian* which, in paragraph 36, states: "One cannot then appeal to these rights of man in order to oppose the interventions of the Magesterium. Such behaviour fails to recognise the nature and mission of the Church which has received from the Lord the task to proclaim the truth of salvation to all men [...] knowing that 'truth can impose itself on the mind only by virtue of its own truth [...]'" Cardinal Joseph Ratzinger was Prefect of the Sacred Congregation from 1981 until his election as Pope Benedict XVI in 2005 and so this caution is of the highest authority. <www.vatican.va/roman_curia

In his Encyclical *Laborem exercens* (1981) Pope St John Paul II stressed the "entirely positive and creative, educational and meritorious character of a man's work" as

> 11. [...] the basis for the judgments and decisions being made today in its regard in spheres that include human rights, as is evidenced by the international declarations on work and the many labour codes prepared either by the competent legislative institutions in the various countries or by organizations devoting their social, or scientific and social, activity to the problems of work. *One organization fostering such initiatives on the international level is the International Labour Organization, the oldest specialized agency of the United Nations Organization.*" [Emphasis added]

> 16. While work, in all its many senses, is an obligation, that is to say a duty, it is also a source of rights on the part of the worker. *These rights must be examined in the broad context of human rights as a whole, which are connatural with man, and many of which are proclaimed by various international organizations* [Emphasis added][64]

Laborem exercens has a particular resonance for the ILO, as it differentiates between "direct employers" and "indirect employers", amongst the latter being the ILO itself:

> 16. [...] [W]e must understand as *the indirect* employer many different factors, other than the direct employer, that exercise a determining influence on the shaping both of the work contract and, consequently, of just or unjust relationships in the field of human labour. [His emphasis]

> 17. The concept of indirect employer includes both persons and institutions of various kinds, and also collective labour contracts and the *principles* of conduct which are laid down by these persons and institutions and which determine the whole socioeconomic *system* or are its result. [His emphasis]

> [...] The attainment of the worker's rights cannot however be doomed to be merely a result of economic systems which on a larger or smaller scale are guided chiefly by the criterion of maximum profit. On the contrary, it is respect for the objective rights of the worker-every kind of worker: manual or intellectual, industrial or agricultural, etc.-that must constitute *the adequate and fundamental criterion* for shaping the whole economy, both on the level of the individual society and State and within the whole of the world

---

/congregations/cfaith/documents/rc_con_cfaith_doc_19900524_theologian-vocation_en.html> (accessed 16 October 2020) © Copyright – Libreria Editrice Vaticana.

64 Pope St John Paul II, *Laborem exercens* (1981) ss 11, 16 © Copyright – Libreria Editrice Vaticana.

economic policy and of the systems of international relationships that derive from it.

Influence in this direction should be exercised by all *the International Organizations* whose concern it is, beginning with the United Nations Organization. It appears that the International Labour Organization [has] fresh contributions to offer on this point in particular.[65] [His emphasis]

In his Encyclical *Sollicitudo rei socialis* (1987) Pope St John Paul II equated a constraint of human rights with poverty itself:

15. [...] We should add here that in today's world there are many other forms of poverty. For are there not certain privations or deprivations which deserve this name? The denial or the limitation of human rights – as for example the right to religious freedom, the right to share in the building of society, the freedom to organize and to form unions, or to take initiatives in economic matters – do these not impoverish the human person as much as, if not more than, the deprivation of material goods? And is development which does not take into account the full affirmation of these rights really development on the human level?

He saw as positive in the context of development:

26. [...] [T]he full awareness among large numbers of men and women of their own dignity and of that of every human being. This awareness is expressed, for example, in the more lively concern that human rights should be respected, and in the more vigorous rejection of their violation. [...] At this level one must acknowledge the influence exercised by the Declaration of Human Rights, promulgated some forty years ago by the United Nations Organization. Its very existence and gradual acceptance by the international community are signs of a growing awareness.

33. Nor would a type of development which did not respect and promote human rights – personal and social, economic and political, including the rights of nations and of peoples – be really worthy of man.

38. [...] The fact that men and women in various parts of the world feel personally affected by the injustices and violations of human rights committed in distant countries, countries which perhaps they will never visit, is a further sign of a reality transformed into awareness, thus acquiring a moral connotation.[66]

---

65 Pope St John Paul II, *Laborem exercens* (1981) ss 16, 17 © Copyright – Libreria Editrice Vaticana.
66 Pope St John Paul II, *Sollicitudo rei socialis* (1987) ss 15, 26, 33, 38 © Copyright – Libreria Editrice Vaticana.

In his Encyclical *Centesimus annus* (1991) to mark the centenary of *Rerum novarum*, Pope St John Paul II reflected on the events of 1989: "An important, even decisive, contribution was made by *the Church's commitment to defend and promote human rights.*"[67] [His emphasis] Considering the "crisis of Marxism" he saw the Catholic Church resurgent in the protection of workers' rights:

> 26. [...] In the crisis of Marxism, the natural dictates of the consciences of workers have re-emerged in a demand for justice and a recognition of the dignity of work, in conformity with the social doctrine of the Church. The worker movement is part of a more general movement among workers and other people of good will for the liberation of the human person *and for the affirmation of human rights.* It is a movement which today has spread to many countries, and which, far from opposing the Catholic Church, looks to her with interest.[68] [Emphasis added]

Pope Benedict XVI in his Encyclical *Caritas in veritate* (2009) placed the greater emphasis in Catholic Social Teaching not on *rights* but, as articulated in *Pacem in terris*, on *duties* – and in the early 21st century it is this which is the fundamental distinction between Catholic Social Teaching and the far narrower concepts found in almost all human rights doctrines:[69]

> 43. "The reality of human solidarity, which is a benefit for us, also imposes a duty" [quoting Pope St Paul VI *Populorum progressio s 17*].[70] Many people today would claim that they owe nothing to anyone, except to themselves. They are concerned only with their rights, and they often have great difficulty in taking responsibility for their own and other people's integral development. *Hence it is important to call for a renewed reflection on how rights presuppose duties, if they are not to become mere licence.* Nowadays we are witnessing a grave inconsistency. On the one hand, appeals are made to alleged rights, arbitrary and non-essential in nature, accompanied by the demand that they be recognized and promoted by public structures, while, on the other hand, elementary and basic rights remain unacknowledged and are violated in much of the world. [...] *[I]ndividual rights, when detached from a framework of duties which grants them their full meaning, can run wild, leading to an escalation of demands which is effectively unlimited and indiscriminate. An overemphasis on rights leads to a disregard for duties.*

---

67 Pope St John Paul II, *Centesimus annus* (1991) s 22 © Copyright – Libreria Editrice Vaticana.
68 Pope St John Paul II, *Centesimus annus* (1991) s 26 © Copyright – Libreria Editrice Vaticana.
69 A singular exception being found in the *African Charter on Human and Peoples' Rights* (the 'Banjul Charter') 1981 which in Part I Chapter II (Articles 27 to 29) sets out those *duties* to be performed by an individual towards their family, society and the international community as a quid pro quo for the *rights* enjoyed under the Charter. <www.achpr.org/legalinstruments/detail?id=49> (accessed 16 October 2020).
70 Pope St Paul VI, *Populorum progressio* (1967) © Copyright – Libreria Editrice Vaticana.

Duties set a limit on rights because they point to the anthropological and ethical framework of which rights are a part, in this way ensuring that they do not become licence. Duties thereby reinforce rights and call for their defence and promotion as a task to be undertaken in the service of the common good. Otherwise, if the only basis of human rights is to be found in the deliberations of [...] *The sharing of reciprocal duties is a more powerful incentive to action than the mere assertion of rights.*[71] [Emphasis added]

In his Address to the European Parliament in Strasbourg on 25 November 2014, Pope Francis criticised the misuse of the concept of human rights when severed from the concept of the common good:

At the same time, however, care must be taken not to fall into certain errors which can arise from a misunderstanding of the concept of human rights and from its misuse. Today there is a tendency to claim ever broader individual rights – I am tempted to say individualistic; underlying this is a conception of the human person as detached from all social and anthropological contexts, as if the person were a "monad" (μονάς), increasingly unconcerned with other surrounding "monads". The equally essential and complementary concept of duty no longer seems to be linked to such a concept of rights. As a result, the rights of the individual are upheld, without regard for the fact that each human being is part of a social context wherein his or her rights and duties are bound up with those of others and with the common good of society itself.

I believe, therefore, that it is vital to develop a culture of human rights which wisely links the individual, or better, the personal aspect, to that of the common good, of the "all of us" made up of individuals, families and intermediate groups who together constitute society. In fact, unless the rights of each individual are harmoniously ordered to the greater good, those rights will end up being considered limitless and consequently will become a source of conflicts and violence.[72]

In his Apostolic Exhortation *Gaudete et exsultate* (2018) Pope Francis has made his point more bluntly. Christianity should not become "a sort of NGO stripped of the luminous mysticism so evident in the lives of [the saints]" yet equally:

---

71 Pope Benedict XVI, *Caritas in veritate* (2009) s 43 © Copyright – Libreria Editrice Vaticana And see his earlier statement made in 1990 on necessarily limited recourse to "rights of man" made in his capacity as Prefect of the Sacred Congregation for the Doctrine of the Faith. See n 63.
72 *Address of Pope Francis to the European Parliament* (Strasbourg, 25 November 2014) <www.vatican.va/content/francesco/en/speeches/2014/november/documents/papa-francesco_20141125_strasburgo-parlamento-europeo.html> (accessed 16 October 2020) © Copyright – Libreria Editrice Vaticana.

101. The other harmful ideological error is found in those who find suspect the social engagement of others, seeing it as superficial, worldly, secular, materialist, communist or populist. Or they relativize it, as if there are other more important matters, or the only thing that counts is one particular ethical issue or cause that they themselves defend. [...] We cannot uphold an ideal of holiness that would ignore injustice in a world where some revel, spend with abandon and live only for the latest consumer goods, even as others look on from afar, living their entire lives in abject poverty.[73]

Nevertheless, the respect to be given to human rights on the one hand and the contrast to be made between an atomised right and the common good on the other has begun to blur. Pope Francis has gone even further than his predecessors and has begun to weave human rights into the fabric of Catholic Social Teaching. In doing so, he is departing from the approach of Pope Benedict XVI and from his own earlier pronouncements in 2014. Pope Francis does not address the issue of comparing the "sharing of reciprocal duties" with "the mere assertion of rights". He simply and plainly regards human rights as such as being axiomatically and unquestionably of fundamental importance.

On 10 December 2018 he addressed in Rome an international religious conference "Human Rights in the Contemporary World: Achievements, Omissions, Negations"[74] and incorporated parts of that Address, expressing his concern for what he terms "insufficiently universal human rights" in his Encyclical *Fratelli tutti* (2020):

22. It frequently becomes clear that, in practice, human rights are not equal for all. Respect for those rights "is the preliminary condition for a country's social and economic development. When the dignity of the human person is respected, and his or her rights recognized and guaranteed, creativity and interdependence thrive, and the creativity of the human personality is released through actions that further the common good". Yet, "by closely observing our contemporary societies, we see numerous contradictions that

73 Pope Francis, *Gaudete et exsultate: Apostolic Exhortation to the Call to Holiness in Today's World* (2018) s 100, 101 © Copyright – Libreria Editrice Vaticana. Pope Francis in his engagement with CST divides opinion and is not without his critics: "There is an element of the *bien-pensant* (of fashionable or politically correct thinking) in Francis's papacy. His utterances and self-presentation tend to affirm positions internal to Catholic theology widely held by dissenting Catholic scholars and opinions about politics and the world widely held by left-leaning elites. Francis's frequent ill-disciplined, off-the-cuff remarks are treated with more seriousness than they deserve [...]" Daniel J Mahoney, "The Social Teaching of Pope Francis" in Gerard V Bradley and E Christian Brugger, eds, *Catholic Social Teaching: A Volume of Scholarly Essays* (Cambridge University Press, Cambridge, 2019) chapter 9, 217.
74 Pope Francis, *Human Rights in the Contemporary World: Achievements, Omissions, Negations* (Rome, 10 December 2018) <https://w2.vatican.va/content/francesco/en/messages/pont-messages/2018/documents/papa-francesco_20181210_messaggio-diritti-umani.html> (accessed 16 October 2020) © Copyright – Libreria Editrice Vaticana.

lead us to wonder whether the equal dignity of all human beings, solemnly proclaimed seventy years ago, is truly recognized, respected, protected and promoted in every situation. In today's world, many forms of injustice persist, fed by reductive anthropological visions and by a profit-based economic model that does not hesitate to exploit, discard and even kill human beings. While one part of humanity lives in opulence, another part sees its own dignity denied, scorned or trampled upon, and its fundamental rights discarded or violated". What does this tell us about the equality of rights grounded in innate human dignity?[75]

He calls for a "sure defence of fundamental human rights", recognising "the urgent need to combat all that threatens or violates fundamental human rights" and that "We are still far from a globalization of the most basic of human rights".[76]

Justitia et Pax

Pope St Paul VI had already established the Pontifical Commission Justitia et Pax in January 1967 and had referred to its mission in his Encyclical *Populorum progressio* (1967):[77]

> 5. Even more recently, We sought to fulfil the wishes of the [Vatican] Council and to demonstrate the Holy See's concern for the developing nations. To do this, We felt it was necessary to add another pontifical commission to the Church's central administration. The purpose of this commission is "to awaken in the People of God full awareness of their mission today. In this way they can further the progress of poorer nations and international social justice, as well as help less developed nations to contribute to their own development".
>
> The name of this commission, Justice and Peace, aptly describes its program and its goal. We are sure that all men of good will want to join Our fellow Catholics and fellow Christians in carrying out this program. So today We earnestly urge all men to pool their ideas and their activities for man's complete development and the development of all mankind.

In June 1988 the Commission was renamed a Pontifical Council by Pope St John Paul II in the *Apostolic Constitution Pastor Bonus*, and retains from among its original goals the pursuit of human rights:

---

75 Pope Francis, *Fratelli tutti* (2020) s 22 © Copyright – Libreria Editrice Vaticana.
76 Pope Francis, *Fratelli tutti* (2020) ss 172, 187, 189 © Copyright – Libreria Editrice Vaticana.
77 Pope St Paul VI, *Populorum progressio* (1967) © Copyright – Libreria Editrice Vaticana.

Art. 142 The goal of the Pontifical Council for Justice and Peace is to promote justice and peace in the world in accordance with the Gospel and the social teaching of the Church.

Art. 143 §1. The Council makes a thorough study of the social teaching of the Church and ensures that this teaching is widely spread and put into practice among people and communities, *especially regarding the relations between workers and management, relations that must come to be more and more imbued with the spirit of the Gospel.* [Emphasis added]

§2. It collects information and research on justice and peace, about human development and violations of human rights; it ponders all this, and, when appropriate, shares its conclusions with the groupings of bishops. *It cultivates relationships with Catholic international organizations and other institutions, even ones outside the Catholic Church, which sincerely strive to achieve peace and justice in the world.*[78] [Emphasis added]

As the Pontifical Council Justitia et Pax itself observes, the question of human rights:

> has assumed increasing importance in the mission of the Church and consequently in the work of the Pontifical Council. Pope John Paul II consistently stresses that the dignity of the human person is the foundation of the promotion and defense of his or her inalienable rights. The Council deals with the subject from three perspectives: deepening the doctrinal aspect, dealing with questions under discussion in international organizations, showing concern for the victims of the violation of human rights.[79]

Conclusions

Although therefore the Catholic Church is committed to defend and promote human rights, from the perspective of CST, human *rights* is only one half of the equation: *duties* and the *common good* must also be factored in. Human rights are at most a component within CST, and do not represent its totality. As is also the case in its dynamic with socialism, liberalism and communism, CST retains its own identity and authority. The Catholic Church is neither a human rights nor a secular political institution.

David Hollenbach sums up:

---

78 *Apostolic Constitution Pastor Bonus* (1988) Articles 142 to 144 <www.vatican.va/content/ john-paul-ii/en/apost_constitutions/documents/hf_jp-ii_apc_19880628_pastor-bonus.h tml≥ (accessed 16 October 2020) © Copyright – Libreria Editrice Vaticana.
79 Pontifical Council for Justice and Peace <www.vatican.va/roman_curia/pontifical_council s/justpeace/documents/rc_pc_justpeace_pro_20011004_en.html> (accessed 16 October 2020).

Catholic rights theory is far removed from individualist or libertarian social philosophy. The theory presented in the encyclicals is personalist, not individualist, and it recognizes that persons are essentially social and institution building beings. Because of this fact the personal rights which belong to every human being in an unmediated way create duties which bind other persons, society and the state.[80]

The consequences for the interaction of the Catholic Church and the ILO have flowed from this. The ILO has looked to the Holy See and specifically to CST to provide a "*force morale*", a moral imperative to underpin its work. The Catholic Church has no need to function as an NGO for labour rights or as an autonomous labour rights delivery system. Indeed, it lacks the capacity to do so. The ILO serves it well. The DNA of CST is embedded in the ILO, and increasingly the concerns addressed by the ILO are being reflected in CST. In that shared DNA is the bond between them. This is explored in the following chapters.

Appendix

Reigning Pope	*Title*	*Date*	*Web*
Leo XIII (20 February 1878–20 July 1903)	Rerum Novarum (On Capital and Labour)	Encyclical Letter 15 May 1891	www.vatican.va/ content/leo-xiii /en/encyclicals/ documents/hf_ l-xiii_enc_1505 1891_rerum-nova rum.html
	Graves de Communi Re (On Christian Democracy)	Encyclical Letter 18 January 1901	www.vatican.va/ content/leo-xiii /en/encyclicals/ documents/hf_ l-xiii_enc_1801 1901_graves-de- communi-re.html
Pius XI (6 February 1922– 10 February 1939)	Quadragesimo Anno (Reconstruction of the Social Order)	Encyclical Letter 15 May 1931	www.vatican.va/ content/pius-xi /en/encyclicals/ documents/hf_p -xi_enc_1931051 5_quadragesimo- anno.html

(*Continued*)

---

80 David Hollenbach, *Claims in Conflict: Retrieving and Renewing the Catholic Human Rights Tradition* (Paulist Press, New York, 1979) 97.

Reigning Pope	Title	Date	Web
	Divini Redemptoris (On Atheistic Communism)	Encyclical Letter 19 March 1937	www.vatican.va/ content/pius-xi /en/encyclicals/ documents/hf_p -xi_enc_1937031 9_divini-redemp toris.html
St John XIII (28 October 1958–3 June 1963)	Mater et Magistra (Church as Mother and Teacher of All Nations)	Encyclical Letter 15 May 1961	www.vatican.va/ content/john-xx iii/en/encyclic als/documents/ hf_j-xxiii_enc_1 5051961_mater .html
	Pacem in Terris (Peace on Earth)	Encyclical Letter 11 April 1963	www.vatican.va/ content/john-xx iii/en/encyclic als/documents/ hf_j-xxiii_enc_1 1041963_pacem .html
St Paul VI (21 June 1963–6 August 1978)	Gaudium et Spes (On the Church in the Modern World)	Pastoral Constitution 7 December 1965	www.vatican.va/ archive/hist_co uncils/ii_vatic an_council/docu ments/vat-ii_co nst_19651207_ga udium-et-spes_e n.html
	Populorum Progressio (On the redemption of Peoples)	Encyclical Letter 26 March 1967	http://w2.vatican .va/content/paul -vi/en/encyclical s/documents/hf_ p-vi_enc_260319 67_populorum .html
	Octogesima Adveniens – The Eightieth Anniversary of "Rerum Novarum" (A call to Action)	Apostolic Letter: 14 May 1971	www.vatican.va/ content/paul-vi/ en/apost_letters /documents/hf _p-vi_apl_19710 514_octogesima- adveniens.html

(Continued)

Reigning Pope	Title	Date	Web
	Justitia in Mundo (Justice in the World) (Synod of Bishops)	30 September–6 November 1971	www.cctwincities .org/wp-content /uploads/2015/ 10/Justicia-in-Mundo.pdf and www.synod.va/co ntent/synod/en/ synodal_assembl ies/1971-second -ordinary-gener al-assembly--the -ministerial-priest hoo.html
St John Paul II (16 October 1978–2 April 2005)	Redemptor Hominis (The Redeemer of Man)	Encyclical Letter 4 March 1979	www.vatican.va/ content/john-pa ul-ii/en/encycl icals/documents /hf_jp-ii_enc _04031979_re demptor-hominis .html
	Laborem Exercens (On Human Work)	Encyclical Letter 14 September 1981	www.vatican.va/ content/john-pa ul-ii/en/encycl icals/documents /hf_jp-ii_enc _14091981_la borem-exercens. html
	Sollicitudo Rei Socialis (On Social Concerns)	Encyclical Letter 30 December 1987	www.vatican.va/ content/john-pa ul-ii/en/encycl icals/documents /hf_jp-ii_enc_3 0121987_sollici tudo-rei-socialis .html
	Centesimus Annus (On the 100th anniversary of Pope Leo XIII's Rerum Novarum)	Encyclical Letter 1 May 1991	www.vatican.va/ content/john-pa ul-ii/en/encycl icals/documents /hf_jp-ii_enc_0 1051991_centesi mus-annus.html

(Continued)

Reigning Pope	Title	Date	Web
Benedict XVI (19 April 2005–28 February 2013)	Deus Caritas Est (On Christian Love – God is Love)	Encyclical Letter 25 December 2005	www.vatican.va/ content/benedic t-xvi/en/encycl icals/documents /hf_ben-xvi_enc _20051225_deus-caritas-est.html
	Caritas in veritate (Charity in Truth)	Encyclical Letter 29 June 2009	www.vatican.va/ content/benedic t-xvi/en/encycl icals/documents /hf_ben-xvi_enc _20090629_carit as-in-veritate.html
Francis (13 March 2013–present)	Evangelii Gaudium: Apostolic Exhortation on the Proclamation of the Gospel in Today's World	Apostolic Exhortation 24 November 2013	http://w2.vatican.va /content/france sco/en/apost_ex hortations/docu ments/papa-fran cesco_esortazio ne-ap_20131124 _evangelii-gaudi um.html
	Laudato si' (Praise be to you – On Care For Our Common Home)	Encyclical Letter 24 May 2015	www.vatican.va/ content/frances co/en/encyclica ls/documents/pa pa-francesco_20 150524_enciclica -laudato-si.html
	Gaudete et exsultate: Apostolic Exhortation on the call to holiness in today's world	Apostolic Exhortation 19 March 2018	http://w2.vatican.va /content/france sco/en/apost_ex hortations/docu ments/papa-fran cesco_esortazione -ap_20180319_ gaudete-et-exsu ltate.htm
	Fratelli tutti (On Fraternity and Social Friendship)	Encyclical Letter 3 October 2020	www.vatican.va/ content/frances co/en/encyclica ls/documents/pa pa-francesco_20 201003_enciclica -fratelli-tutti.html

Bibliography

The Holy See

Encyclicals, Apostolic letters, Exhortations (in chronological order)

Pope Pius XI, *Quadragesimo anno* (1931).
____, *Divini redemptoris* (1937).
Pope St John XXIII, *Mater et magistra* (1961).
____, *Pacem in terris* (1963).
Second Vatican Council, Pastoral Constitution on the Church in the Modern World *Gaudium et spes* (1965).
Pope St Paul VI, *Populorum progressio* (1967).
Pope St John Paul II, *Redemptor hominis* (1979).
____, *Laborem exercens* (1981).
____, *Sollicitudo rei socialis* (1987).
____, *Centesimus annus* (1991).
Pope Benedict XVI, *Deus caritas est* (2005).
____, *Caritas in veritate* (2009).
Pope Francis, *Evangelii gaudium* (2013) Apostolic Exhortation on the Proclamation of the Gospel in Today's World.
____, *Laudato Si'* (2015).
____, *Gaudete et exsultate: Apostolic Exhortation to the call to holiness in today's world* (2018).
____, *Fratelli tutti* (2020).

Other materials (in chronological order)

Pope St Paul VI, "Speech for the Celebration of the Day of Peace on 1 January 1969" *The Promotion of Human Rights, the Way to Peace* <www.vatican.va/content/paul-vi/en/messages/peace/documents/hf_p-vi_mes_19681208_ii-world-day-for-peace.html> (accessed 16 October 2020).
Synod of Bishops, *Justice in the World* (1971) s 56 <www.cctwincities.org/wp-content/uploads/2015/10/Justicia-in-Mundo.pdf> (accessed 16 October 2020).
Pope St John Paul II, Address to the United Nations (New York, 2 October 1979) <www.vatican.va/content/john-paul-ii/en/speeches/1979/october/documents/hf_jp-ii_spe_19791002_general-assembly-onu.html> (accessed 16 October 2020)
Catechism of the Catholic Church (Second edition) (Libreria Editrice Vaticana, Citta del Vaticano, 2000).
Apostolic Constitution Pastor Bonus Pope St John Paul II, (1988) Articles 142 to 144 <www.vatican.va/content/john-paul-ii/en/apost_constitutions/documents/hf_jp-ii_apc_19880628_pastor-bonus.html> (accessed 16 October 2020).
Sacred Congregation for the Doctrine of the Faith, *Instructions on the Ecclesial Vocation of the Theologian* (1990) <www.vatican.va/roman_curia/congregations/cfaith/documents/rc_con_cfaith_doc_19900524_theologian-vocation_en.html> (accessed 16 October 2020).
Compendium of the Social Doctrine of the Church Pontifical Council for Justice and Peace, (2004) <www.vatican.va/roman_curia/pontifical_councils/justpeace/documents/rc_pc_justpeace_doc_20060526_compendio-dott-soc_en.html> (accessed 16 October 2020).

Pope Benedict XVI, *Address to the 14th Session of the Pontifical Academy of Social Sciences* (Rome, 3 May 2008) <www.vatican.va/content/benedict-xvi/en/speech es/2008/may/documents/hf_ben-xvi_spe_20080503_social-sciences.html> (accessed 16 October 2020).

Archbishop Diarmuid Martin, *Press Conference to Present the Activity of the "Centesimus Annus – Pro Pontifice" Foundation* (Rome, 18 April 2018) <www.catholiccul ture.org/culture/library/view.cfm?recnum=11851> (accessed 16 October 2020).

Pope Francis, *Address of Pope Francis to the European Parliament* (Strasbourg, 25 November 2014) <www.vatican.va/content/francesco/en/speeches/2014/ november/documents/papa-francesco_20141125_strasburgo-parlamento-europ eo.html> (accessed 16 October 2020).

Pope Francis, *Human Rights in the Contemporary World: Achievements, Omissions, Negations* (Rome, 10 December 2018) <https://w2.vatican.va/content/franc esco/en/messages/pont-messages/2018/documents/papa-francesco_2018 1210_messaggio-diritti-umani.html> (accessed 16 October 2020).

International Labour Organisation

Somavia, Juan, *The Challenge of a Fair Globalization*, Presentation at the Pontifical Lateran University on the Report of the World Commission on the Social Dimension of Globalization (Rome, 25 February 2005) <www.ilo.org/public/english/bureau /dgo/speeches/somavia/2005/rome.pdf> (accessed 16 October 2020)

International documents

Universal Declaration of Human Rights (1948).

African Charter on Human and Peoples' Rights (the "Banjul Charter") 1981 <www.a chpr.org/legalinstruments/detail?id=49> (accessed 16 October 2020).

Secondary sources

Anderson, Robin, *Between Two Wars: The Story of Pope Pius XI* (Franciscan Herald Press, Chicago, 1977).

Calderisi, Robert, *Earthly Mission: The Catholic Church and World Development* (Yale University Press, New Haven, 2013).

Camp, Richard L, *The Papal Ideology of Social Reform: A Study in Historical Development 1878–1967* (E J Brill, Leiden, 1969) ch 3 "The Errors of Socialism and Communism".

Cardinal Etchegaray, R, "Preface" in Giorgio Filibeck, ed, *Les droits de l'homme dans l'enseignement de l'Eglise: de Jean XXIII à Jean-Paul II* (Libreria Editrice Vaticana, Cité du Vatican, 1992).

The Catholic Charities of St Paul and Minneapolis, "Catholic Social Teaching" <www.cctwincities.org/education-advocacy/catholic-social-teaching/> (accessed 16 October 2020).

de la Chapelle, Philippe, *La Déclaration Universelle des Droits de l'Homme et le Catholicisme* (*Libraire Générale de Droit et de Jurisprudence*, R Pichon et R Durand-Auzias, Paris, 1967).

Coleman, John A, "Neither Liberal nor Socialist: The Originality of Catholic Social Teaching" in John A Coleman, ed, *One Hundred Years of Catholic Social Thought: Celebration and Challenge* (Orbis Books, New York, 1991) 25.

____, "The Future of Catholic Social Thought" in Kenneth R Himes, ed, *Modern Catholic Social Teaching* (Second edition) (Georgetown University Press, Washington, DC, 2018) 611.

Curran, Charles E, *Catholic Social Teaching 1891 – Present: A Historical, Theological and Ethical Analysis* (Georgetown University Press, Washington, DC, 2002).

Filibeck, Giorgio (ed), *Les droits de l'homme dans l'enseignement de l'Eglise: de Jean XXIII à Jean-Paul II* (Libreria Editrice Vaticana, Cité du Vatican, 1992).

Grasso, Kenneth L, "Reintegrating Rights: Catholicism, Social Ontology, and Contemporary Rights Discourse" in Bruce Frohnen and Kenneth Grasso, eds, *Rethinking Rights* (University of Missouri Press, Columbia, Missouri, 2009) 198.

Hebblethwaite, Peter, "The Popes and Politics: Shifting Patterns in Catholic Social Doctrine" in Charles E Curran and R McCormick, eds, *Official Catholic Social Teaching* (Paulist Press, Mahwah, NJ, 1986) 268.

Hehir, J Bryan, "The modern Catholic Church and Human Rights" in John Witte, Jr. and Frank S Alexander, eds, *Christianity and Human Rights: An Introduction* (Cambridge University Press, Cambridge, 2010) 113.

Henken, Louis, "Religion, Religions and Human Rights" in Elizabeth Bucar and Barbara Barnett, eds, *Does Human Rights Need God?* (William B Eerdmans Publishing Company, Michigan, 2005) 154.

Himes, Kenneth R (ed), *Modern Catholic Social Teaching* (Second edition) (Georgetown University Press, Washington, DC, 2018).

Hollenbach, David, *Claims in Conflict: Retrieving and Renewing the Catholic Human Rights Tradition* (Paulist Press, New York, 1979).

Le Roy, Albert, "The Fiftieth Anniversary of the Rerum Novarum" in *International Labour Review*, Vol XLIV, No. 4, October 1941 369.

Longley, Clifford, "Structures of Sin and the Free Market: John Paul II on Capitalism" in Paul Vallely, ed, *The New Politics: Catholic Social Teaching for the Twenty-First Century* (SCM Press, London, 1998) 98.

Mahoney, Daniel J, "The Social Teaching of Pope Francis" in Gerard V Bradley and E Christian Brugger, eds, *Catholic Social Teaching: A Volume of Scholarly Essays* (Cambridge University Press, Cambridge, 2019) 217.

Massaro SJ, Thomas, *Living Justice: Catholic Social Teaching in Action* (Third edition) (Rowman and Littlefield, Lanham, MD, 2016).

Pakaluk, Catherine Ruth, "Socialism and Capitalism in Catholic Social Thought" in Gerard V Bradley and E Christian Brugger, eds, *Catholic Social Teaching: A Volume of Scholarly Essays* (Cambridge University Press, Cambridge, 2019) ch 18, 436.

Roncalli, Angelo Giuseppe (Pope John XXIII), *Mission to France 1944–1953* (Loris Capovilla, ed, Dorothy White, trans) (Geoffrey Chapman, London, 1966).

Ruston, Roger, *Human Rights and the Image of God* (SCM Press, London, 2004).

Schuck, Michael J, "The Ideological Uses of Catholic Social Teaching" in John A Coleman and Gregory Baum, eds, *Rerum Novarum: One Hundred Years of Catholic Social Teaching* (Concilium 1991/5 SCM Press, London, 1991) 47.

Storck, Thomas, *An Economics of Justice & Charity: Catholic Social Teaching, Its Development and Contemporary Relevance* (Angelico Press, Kettering, OH, 2017).

Teeling, William, *The Pope in Politics: The Life and Work of Pope Pius XI* (Lovat Dickson Limited, London, 1937).

Vallely, Paul, "Introduction" in Paul Vallely, ed, *The New Politics: Catholic Social Teaching for the Twenty-First Century* (SCM Press, London, 1998) 1.

Zahn, Gordon C, "Social Movements and Catholic Social Thought" in John A Coleman, ed, *One Hundred Years of Catholic Social Thought: Celebration and Challenge* (Orbis Books, New York, 1991) 53.

Zięba, Maciej, *Papal Economics* (ISI Books, Wilmington, DE, 2013).

3 Catholic Social Teaching and labour rights

Introduction

The importance of work within CST is fundamental. In his Encyclical *Fratelli tutti* (2020) Pope Francis writes:

> In a genuinely developed society, work is an essential dimension of social life, for it is not only a means of earning one's daily bread, but also of personal growth, the building of healthy relationships, self-expression and the exchange of gifts. Work gives us a sense of shared responsibility for the development of the world, and ultimately, for our life as a people.[1]

In a more relaxed moment, on a Pastoral Visit to the Ilva factory in Genoa on 27 May 2017, Pope Francis took part in a question-and-answer session, and spoke of the importance of work:

> It must be clear that the real goal to reach is not that of 'income for all' but rather, 'work for all'. Because without work, without work for all, there will be no dignity for all. The work of today and that of tomorrow will be different, perhaps very different – we think of the industrial revolution, there has been a change; here too there will be a revolution – it will be different from yesterday's work, but it will have to be work, not pension, not retirement: work. [...] Without work, you can survive; but to live, you need work. The choice is between surviving and living.[2]

As is explored in later chapters in this book, the influence of secular trade unionism, liberal and socialist politics and even of communism on the development of the ILO was considerable – and in many histories of the ILO dominates the narrative

1 Pope Francis, *Fratelli tutti* (2020) s 162 © Copyright – Libreria Editrice Vaticana.
2 Pastoral Visit of His Holiness Pope Francis to Genoa; Encounter with Representatives of the World of Work, 27 May 2017 <www.vatican.va/content/francesco/en/speeches/2017/may/documents/papa-francesco_20170527_lavoratori-genova.html> (accessed 17 October 2020) © Copyright – Libreria Editrice Vaticana.

to the total exclusion of any confessional element: that CST played a key role in that development does not mean that labour rights within CST were a reflection of those political philosophies or indebted to them. This chapter sets out why.

In this chapter CST is analysed in the context of labour rights, using the same classification as that established by the ILO in its fundamental principles.[3] In adopting this classification, care is taken to present CST in its own terms, and not to superimpose a secular political and philosophical interpretation. As John Cronin wrote:

> If [someone] combs through [the Social Encyclicals], only taking passages that seem to support his position and ignoring those that appear to contradict his thinking, then his approach is wrong. He is not seeking to learn. He is merely using the popes, and misusing their teaching, to confirm his preconceptions.[4]

Writing in 1941 to mark the fiftieth anniversary of *Rerum novarum*, Albert Le Roy, who was Jesuit in residence at the ILO from 1936 to 1955, set the Encyclicals in context:

> It would therefore be mistaken to look on the Encyclicals as a source of ready-made formulae giving an answer to every question, and to believe that they only need to be copied word-for-word to bring about an economic and social order infused at once with the breath of life. Their aim is at once more modest and more elevated. They lay no claim to form a complete system and to give an answer in technical matters, since these lie outside the competence of religious authority. Even though the Church claims the right to survey all human actions, and even though she can very truly say that nought that is human is alien to her, this does not mean that she proposes to exceed her own proper domain. Economic and social affairs concern her only because they are closely bound up with the moral and spiritual side of things.[5]

CST and labour rights – the beginning: *Pope Leo XIII and Rerum novarum (1891)*

The wellspring of CST and labour rights is the radical and prescient Papal Encyclical of Pope Leo XIII[6] *Rerum novarum* (On Capital and Labour) (1891).

---

3 See Chapter 4.
4 John F Cronin, *Christianity and Social Progress: A Commentary on Mater et Magistra* (Helicon, Baltimore, 1965) 20–21.
5 Albert Le Roy, "The Fiftieth Anniversary of the Rerum Novarum" in *International Labour Review* Vol XLIV, No. 4 (October 1941) 369, 371.
6 Pope Leo XIII bridged traditionalism and modernity in unexpected ways – he was the first Pope to appear on film, in 1896 <www.youtube.com/watch?v=cMbmF0vHhFw> (accessed 17 October 2020).

In it, he addressed the mutual rights and duties of labourers and employers, setting out fundamental principles governing the relationship of capital and labour. As David Hollenbach wrote: "It was with Leo XIII that the Church began to move from a stance of adamant resistance to modern Western developments in political and social life to a stance of critical participation in them".[7] Cardinal Walter Kasper sets this in context:

> Die katholische Kirche hat seit den durch die industrielle Revolution im 19. Jahrhundert aufkommenden sozialen Problemen und himmelschreienden Ungerechtigkeiten ihre Soziallehre entwickelt. [...] Nach Vorlaüfern und Vorkämpfern wie Bischof Wilhelm Emmanuel von Ketteler von Mainz haben sich die Päpste seit der Enzyklika *Rerum novarum* von Papst Leo XIII (1891) an die Spitze dieser katholischen sozialen Bewegung gestellt. Sie haben soziale Ungerechtigkeit gebrandmarkt und die Entwicklung des modernen Sozialstaates gefördert.[8]

Rerum novarum was born of Pope Leo XIII's wish to reintegrate traditional Catholic values of the rights of the working classes in the current political debate and to forestall what he believed to be their exploitation through opportunistic revolutionary forces. As Philippe de la Chapelle wrote:

> Léon XIII (1878–1903) ne voulut cependant pas accepter cette situation de divorce qui s'installait progressivement entre le monde et l'Eglise. Il s'employa dès lors à dissiper les malentendus, et à réinsérer les vérités traditionelles due "droit des gens" au sein des préoccupations politiques de l'heure. Il désirait voir le Catholicisme se réjouir et s'attrister des joies et des peines de ce monde.[9]

---

7 David Hollenbach, *Claims in Conflict: Retrieving and Renewing the Catholic Human Rights Tradition* (Paulist Press, New York, 1979) 43. And see Richard L Camp, *The Papal Ideology of Social Reform: A Study in Historical Development 1878–1967* (E J Brill, Leiden, 1969) chapter 4 "The Rights and Duties of Labor and Capital".

8 Walter Kardinal Kasper, *Barmherzigkeit: Grundbegriff des Evangeliums – Schlüssel christlichen Lebens* (Verlag Herder GmbH, Freiburg im Breisgau, 2012) 184 [The Catholic Church has developed its social teaching since the emergence during the Industrial Revolution of the 19th century of social problems and injustices which cried out to heaven. The Popes, in the footsteps of forerunners and pioneer activists such as the Bishop of Mainz Wilhelm Emmanuel von Ketteler, have since Pope Leo XIII's Encyclical *Rerum novarum* (1891) placed themselves at the forefront of this Catholic social movement. They have excoriated social injustice and promoted the development of the modern welfare State.]

9 [Leo XIII (1878–1903) was not prepared to accept this growing trend of division between the world and the Church. From that moment on he set himself to dispel misunderstandings and to reintegrate within the contemporary political debate traditional truths regarding the rights of the people. His wish was to see Catholicism rejoice in the joys and share in the sorrows of this world.] Philippe de la Chapelle, *La Déclaration Universelle des Droits de l'Homme et le Catholicisme* (Librairie Générale de Droit et de Jurisprudence, R Pichon et R Durand-Auzias, Paris, 1967) 337.

The thunderous opening of the Encyclical bears this out:

1. That the spirit of revolutionary change, which has long been disturb-
    ing the nations of the world, should have passed beyond the sphere of
    politics and made its influence felt in the cognate sphere of practical
    economics is not surprising. The elements of the conflict now raging are
    unmistakable, in the vast expansion of industrial pursuits and the mar-
    vellous discoveries of science; in the changed relations between masters
    and workmen; in the enormous fortunes of some few individuals, and
    the utter poverty of the masses; the increased self-reliance and closer
    mutual combination of the working classes; as also, finally, in the pre-
    vailing moral degeneracy. [...] [T]here is no question which has taken
    deeper hold on the public mind.
2. [...] The discussion is not easy, nor is it void of danger. It is no easy
    matter to define the relative rights and mutual duties of the rich and of
    the poor, of capital and of labor. And the danger lies in this, that crafty
    agitators are intent on making use of these differences of opinion to
    pervert men's judgments and to stir up the people to revolt.
3. [...] [W]orking men have been surrendered, isolated and helpless, to the
    hardheartedness of employers and the greed of unchecked competition.
    The mischief has been increased by rapacious usury. [...] To this must
    be added that the hiring of labour and the conduct of trade are concen-
    trated in the hands of comparatively few; so that a small number of very
    rich men have been able to lay upon the teeming masses of the labouring
    poor a yoke little better than that of slavery itself.
4. To remedy these wrongs the socialists, working on the poor man's envy
    of the rich, are striving to do away with private property, and contend
    that individual possessions should become the common property of all,
    to be administered by the State or by municipal bodies. [...] But their
    contentions are so clearly powerless to end the controversy that were
    they carried into effect the working man himself would be among the
    first to suffer. They are, moreover, emphatically unjust, for they would
    rob the lawful possessor, distort the functions of the State, and create
    utter confusion in the community.[10]

It is to this Encyclical that the opening debates of the International Labour
Conference in the earliest years of the ILO repeatedly appealed, and it has continued to be an ILO point of reference.[11]

10 Pope Leo XIII, *Rerum novarum* (1891) ss 1, 2, 3, 4 © Copyright – Libreria Editrice Vaticana.
11 See Chapter 5.

19th-century origins of Social Catholicism: Forerunners and pioneers

Rerum novarum is today widely regarded as being the seminal social Encyclical and, as such, the point of origin of labour rights in Catholic social teaching. As a comprehensive exposition it did – and still does – function as a milestone, yet as with milestones, marks not a point of origin but a measure of distance already travelled.

The Bishop of Mainz, Wilhelm Emmanuel von Ketteler (1811–1877), in response to the publication in 1848 of the *Communist Manifesto* of Karl Marx, began a hearts and minds campaign which engendered a European and specifically German Catholic movement addressing the "social question". In September 1869 an assembly of German bishops promoted the prohibition of child labour in factories, the limitation of working hours of factory workers, the separation of the sexes in the workshops, the closing of unsanitary workshops, Sunday rest, the obligation to care for workers who were temporarily or permanently disabled and the appointment by the State of factory inspectors. Further parallels in the writings of von Ketteler with what half a century later was to become the Constitution of the ILO are striking: he called for an increase in workers' wages to match the actual value of their work; and affirmed that religion required that work not be treated as a commodity or recompensed simply on the basis of supply and demand, that it was a crime against the working class to abuse a worker and treat them as a machine until their strength was exhausted, to work them for such long hours that their strength failed, to employ children and to compromise the morality of employed young girls.[12]

Bishop Mermillod of Fribourg in Switzerland called a succession of Catholic social conferences (the International Federation of Catholic Social Workers, the "Fribourg Union", formed in 1884 and lasting until his death in 1892). The Fribourg Union

> espoused a more radical reconstruction of the social order along corporate lines – bringing together capital, owners, workers and "consumers" into occupational groups that would work together for the good of the industry under the direction of a broader corporation and thus overcome the division between capital and labour.[13]

It proposed, amongst other suggested reforms, a "just wage" sufficient for a labourer's family: Pope Leo XIII "was deeply interested in their work" and in

---

12 Albert Le Roy, *Catholicisme social et organisation internationale du travail* (Éditions Spes, Paris, 1937) 25–26.

13 Charles E Curran, *Catholic Social Teaching 1891–Present: A Historical, Theological and Ethical Analysis* (Georgetown University Press, Washington, DC, 2002) 9. This is precisely the "Tripartite" template of State, employer and workers representatives found in the ILO Constitution 1919.

1888 asked the Fribourg Union for a report on this.[14] In England, rights pioneer Cardinal Manning's public and unqualified support of those involved in the London Dock Strike in 1889 was also ground-breaking. [15]

As Richard L Camp observed, *Rerum novarum* was followed by:

> the rapid development of a left wing in the social catholic movement which was a direct outgrowth of the school of social reform inspired by Ketteler and Leo XIII and which was known as "Christian democracy". Its followers were strong in Italy, France and Belgium by the end of Leo XIII's reign and were actively pursuing their own particular social and political program.[16]

Paul Misner points to the political developments in Christian democracy of the 1890s in Belgium and France, and draws "a nuanced conclusion":

> [...] *Rerum novarum*, firm in its principles and orientations, was both prudent and open as to the applications and the solutions, none of which are imposed. The encyclical itself did not make social Catholicism, properly speaking, into

---

14 Richard L Camp, *The Papal Ideology of Social Reform: A Study in Historical Development 1878–1967* (E J Brill, Leiden, 1969) 80. For a detailed account of the interaction of the Fribourg Union with Pope Leo XIII during the period immediately preceding the proclamation of *Rerum Novarum*, see Joseph Joblin, "L'Appel de l'Union de Fribourg à Léon XIII en Faveur d'une Legislation International du Travail: Son Lien avec 'Rerum Novarum'" in *Archivum Historiae Pontificiae* Vol. 28 (1990) 357–372.

15 See Gavan Duffy, *Labour and Justice: The Worker in Catholic Social Teaching* (Freedom Publishing Pty Ltd., Melbourne, 2008) chapter 5 "The rise of the proletariat" and Thomas C Behr, "The Nineteenth-Century Historical and Intellectual Context of Catholic Social Teaching" in Gerard V Bradley and E Christian Brugger, eds, *Catholic Social Teaching: A Volume of Scholarly Essays* (Cambridge University Press, Cambridge, 2019) chapter 2. Writing just at the outbreak of World War One, Father Lambert McKenna S J reflected on the roll call of activists who had preceded the Encyclical: "Some thirty or forty years ago, there arose all over the Catholic world an extraordinary movement of mind and action. Her pastors such as Manning in England, Korum and Ketteler in Germany, Langenieux and Pie in France, Gibbons and Ireland in America, and a brilliant band of Catholic laymen such as Mun and de la Tour du Pin in France, Windthorst in Germany, Descurtins in Switzerland, Vogelsang in Austria, raised their voices in eloquent pleading for the rights of the poor". Lambert McKenna S J, *The Church and Labour: A Series of Six Tracts* (Irish Messenger Office, Dublin, 1914) 16. For an account of what he describes as "the spectrum of Catholic social movements" originating in 19th-century France, see John A Coleman, "Neither Liberal nor Socialist: The Originality of Catholic Social Teaching" in John A Coleman, ed, *One Hundred Years of Catholic Social Thought: Celebration and Challenge* (Orbis Books, New York, 1991) 28–35. For the corresponding development in the German states in the 19th century and the direct contribution which German lay activists made to the debate on the social question see Michael Schäfers (trans John Bowden), "Rerum Novarum – The Result of Christian Social Movements 'From Below'" in John A Coleman and Gregory Baum, eds, *Rerum Novarum: One Hundred Years of Catholic Social Teaching* (Concilium 1991/5 SCM Press, London, 1991) 3.

16 Richard L Camp, *The Papal Ideology of Social Reform: A Study in Historical Development 1878–1967* (E J Brill, Leiden, 1969) 32.

an ideological system between socialism and liberalism. However, the manner in which the encyclical and the church's social teaching were presented did contribute *to make it an ideology*. [Emphasis added][17]

It is this ideology which so strongly influenced those charged with the task of bringing the ILO into being in 1919, rooted as they were in the Christian social democratic traditions of northern Europe.[18] The political impact on the subsequent development of the ILO of the Christian democratic tradition in Europe must not be underestimated. The growth of the Christian democrat movement in Italy, Germany, Austria and Belgium and, to a more modest extent, in France and the Netherlands, was exponential after 1945 – "In all of these nations, they made striking progress in infusing into society their own interpretation of Catholic social teaching".[19]

The practical implementation of the principles in *Rerum novarum* was to follow soon, when *l'Association internationale pour la protection légale des travailleurs*[20] was founded in Basle in 1900: the Holy See ensured that it was officially represented, paying its membership dues and sending a delegate to its conventions. This organisation was a prefiguring of the ILO, though with the more limited function of reviewing national labour legislation and creating a central database.[21]

Rerum novarum: *Significance and continuing influence*

For the Catholic Church, the publication of *Rerum novarum* marked "the spectacular re-entry of the Church in an arena from which it had been excluded as a major player by the great intellectual and political events of the Enlightenment and its aftermath". [22]

---

17 Paul Misner, *Social Catholicism in Europe from the Onset of Industrialization to the First World War* (Darton, Longman and Todd, London, 1991) 222. It must however be acknowledged that classifying CSJ as an "ideology" has not received papal approval. Pope St John Paul II in his Encyclical Sollicitudo rei Socialis (1987) s 41 says that CSJ belongs to the realm not of ideology but of moral theology.

18 See Chapter 5.

19 Richard L Camp, *The Papal Ideology of Social Reform: A Study in Historical Development 1878–1967* (E J Brill, Leiden, 1969) 41.

20 [The International Association for the Legal Protection of Workers].

21 Albert Le Roy, *Catholicisme social et organisation internationale due travail* (Éditions Spes, Paris, 1937) 13. See also Nadjib Souamaa, "Les origines de l'OIT (1890–1950): élaboration et premières expérimentations d'un modèle d' 'Europe sociale'" in *La Revue de l'Ires* Vol. 2015/4 No. 87, (2015) 63–88 which from an exclusively secular viewpoint examines the composite role of *l'Association internationale pour la protection légale des travailleurs* and a number of other late 19th century European associations for the protection of workers in promoting what was to become the ILO. Available online at www.cairn.info/revue-de-l-ires -2015-4-page-63.htm (accessed 17 October 2020).

22 Ernest A Fortin, "'Sacred and Inviolable': Rerum Novarum and Natural Rights" in *Theological Studies* Vol. 53 (1992) 209.

Writing in 1941 on the fiftieth anniversary of *Rerum novarum*, Albert Le Roy (who was Jesuit in residence at the ILO from 1936 to 1955) placed the Encyclical in its historical context:

> At the time when the *Rerum Novarum* appeared, the situation of the workers was indeed lamentable, and fifty years of efforts and of progress cannot make us forget it. Millions of human beings had no horizon beyond the factory gates, which closed about them pitilessly every day, even on Sundays, leaving them face to face for ten to twelve hours with machinery working at an ever increasing speed. The right of association and freedom to combine in trade unions had only just been recognised in the most advanced countries. There was no security for the morrow in the event of accident or sickness, and the worker had to toil until the end for fear of dying of starvation or becoming a burden on members of his family who were themselves barely able to earn their own living.[23]

As Paul Misner writes:

> The encyclical, as the first major statement by one of the old established forces of order in nineteenth-century society to take up and endorse the grievances of the working class against their betters, could be expected to make waves. It did, despite the efforts of some liberal conservative commentators to downplay any new departures that a reading of the encyclical might suggest.

> Up to this point the Vatican had been increasingly isolated and allied only with retrograde institutions and monarchies. Many, Catholics and non-Catholics, used the term "Christian socialists" for those who set about putting *Rerum novarum* into practice. Apparently the church was breaking its old ties and looking to the masses to find a new legitimacy. Thus contemporaries saw a significance in the encyclical going well beyond "social teaching".[24]

For Eamon Duffy "*Rerum Novarum* is one of those historic documents whose importance is now hard to grasp":

> The Pope's social analysis was elementary, and what he had to say about the unions was timid, and wrapped up in romantic tosh about medieval craft guilds. [...] Many Christians, many Catholics, in the 1880s and 1890s were saying more penetrating and more challenging things. For the successor of

---

23 Albert Le Roy, "The Fiftieth Anniversary of the Rerum Novarum" in *International Labour Review* Vol. XLIV, No. 4 (1941) 369–388, at 380.
24 Paul Misner, *Social Catholicism in Europe from the Onset of Industrialization to the First World War* (Darton, Longman and Todd, London, 1991) 214, 218.

64 Catholic Social Teaching and labour rights

Pio Nono to say these things, however, was *truly revolutionary*. Leo's attack on unrestricted capitalism, his insistence on the duty of state intervention on behalf of the worker, his assertion of the right to a living wage and the rights of organised labour, *changed the terms of all future Catholic discussion on social questions, and gave weight and authority to more adventurous advocates of Social Catholicism*. Without being either a democrat or a liberal himself, *Leo opened the door to the evolution of Catholic democracy*.[25] [Emphasis added]

A near contemporary commentator, Rev. Henry Parkinson, writing in 1912, was amongst those who regarded it as a triumph:

[T]he great "Charter of the Workman", as it has been justly called, came at a time when the world was unripe for its Gospel teaching. Perhaps it was part of its providential mission to hasten the ripening. It was received at first with apathy and reluctance in some quarters, and was certainly slow in its effect upon society; but its triumph is now assured, though its conquest is not yet complete. It is much more than a letter on social and economic subjects; it is the opening out of the economic system of the Church in human society.[26]

Apathy was a reaction amongst Catholics to something which Pope Pius XI was later to describe in his Encyclical *Quadragesimo Anno* (1931) as "so noble and lofty and so utterly new to worldly ears", "in advance of its time beyond all expectation" but as a result of which "the slow of heart disdained to study this new social philosophy and the timid feared to scale so lofty a height. There were some also who stood, indeed, in awe at its splendour, but regarded it as a kind of imaginary ideal of perfection more desirable then attainable".[27]

Reluctance was based in a misapprehension; that the Encyclical had its roots in socialism. Whilst "The appearance of Rerum Novarum in 1891 manifested an awakening on the part of the nineteenth-century papacy to the social and religious cataclysm resulting from the Industrial Revolution"[28] that awakening was

25 Eamon Duffy, *Saints & Sinners: A History of the Popes* (Third Edition) (Yale University Press, New Haven, 2006) 312.
26 Henry Parkinson, *The Pope and the People: Select Encyclicals of Leo XIII* (Catholic Truth Society, London, 1912) Preface (quoted in J W Poynter, *The Popes and Social Problems* (Watts & Co., London, 1949) 21). "The whole world listened to the voice of the man who spoke as the Vicar of Christ, the founder of society. His voice was listened to by sovereigns, by statesmen, by men of every calling, of every rank, of every degree of culture, of every school of thought, by those outside the Church, as well as by those within, with a reverent attention, never before perhaps accorded to any Pontifical utterance". Lambert McKenna S J, *The Church and Labour: A Series of Six Tracts* (Irish Messenger Office, Dublin, 1914) 17.
27 Pope Pius XI, *Quadragesimo anno* (1931) s 14 © Copyright – Libreria Editrice Vaticana.
28 Roger Ruston, *Human Rights and the Image of God* (SCM Press, London, 2004) 271.

not triggered by a sudden swing towards liberalism.[29] Rather, "it was essentially a plea to the common sense of the ruling classes".[30]

For Pope Pius XI, looking back over 40 years in his Encyclical *Quadragesimo Anno* (1931), Pope Leo XIII's initiative was innovatory (which is a forgivable exaggeration):

> 28. *A new branch of law, wholly unknown to the earlier time, has arisen* from this continuous and unwearied labour to protect vigorously the sacred rights of the workers that flow from their dignity as men and as Christians. These laws undertake the protection of life, health, strength, family, homes, workshops, wages and labour hazards, in fine, everything which pertains to the condition of wage workers, with special concern for women and children. *Even though these laws do not conform exactly everywhere and in all respects to Leo's recommendations, still it is undeniable that much in them savours of the Encyclical,* On the Condition of Workers, to which great credit must be given for whatever improvement has been achieved in the workers' condition.[31] [Emphasis added]

Pope St John Paul II, in his Encyclical *Centesimus annus* (1991)[32] marking the centenary of *Rerum novarum*, ranked its socioeconomic significance behind its character as an instrument of evangelisation:

> 54. [...] The Encyclical Rerum novarum can be read as a valid contribution to socioeconomic analysis at the end of the nineteenth century, but its specific value derives from the fact that it is a document of the Magisterium and is fully a part of the Church's evangelizing mission, together with many other documents of this nature. Thus the Church's *social teaching* is itself a valid *instrument of evangelization.* As such, it proclaims God and his mystery of salvation in Christ to every human being, and for that very reason reveals man to himself. In this light, and only in this light, does it concern itself with everything else: the human rights of the individual, and in particular of the 'working class', the family and education, the duties of the State, the ordering of national and international society, economic life, culture, war and peace, and respect for life from the moment of conception until death.

29 See the treatment of the Encyclical, with particular reference to its stance on real property rights, of 19th-century political economist Henry George, *The Condition of Labour: An Open Letter to Pope Leo XIII* (Swann Sonnenschein & Co, London, 1892), in which he compares and contrasts the principles promoted in the Encyclical with those of socialism, communism, protectionism and trade unions.

30 "Yet for all the vigour of its language – and the fact that it was condemned as a socialist document at the time – it was essentially a plea to the common sense of the ruling classes: 'The condition of the workers is the question of the hour. It will be answered one way or another, rationally or irrationally, and which way it goes is of the greatest importance to the state'". [Rerum novarum s 58.1] Paul Vallely, "Introduction" in Paul Vallely, ed, *The New Politics: Catholic Social Teaching for the Twenty-First Century* (SCM Press, London, 1998) 4.

31 Pope Pius XI, *Quadragesimo anno* (1931) s 28 © Copyright – Libreria Editrice Vaticana.

32 Pope St John Paul II, *Centesimus annus* (1991) s 54 © Copyright – Libreria Editrice Vaticana.

Unintended consequences?

Pope Leo XIII, conservative, patrician and "no friend of the modern freedoms",[33] had released from its lamp a genie whose evolutionary spirit could not be reconfined. For this was not just the point of origin of the articulation of labour rights within Catholic social justice, but the beginning of a political process which would unfold steadily and which would include the formation of the ILO three decades later, when the world addressed by Pope Leo XIII had changed beyond recognition.

As Gordon C Zahn comments, the growth of Catholic social movements in the wake of *Rerum novarum* was not only unanticipated by Pope Leo XIII; it was almost certainly unintended:

> [T]oday's more activist Catholic social movements would be regarded by Leo XIII as too radical, even dangerous departures from his principal themes and intentions, and the policies and programs they promote would be for him a source of serious concern meriting disapproval or even condemnation. Consider, if you will, a few contemporary examples: ecumenism, feminism; the familiar clutch of movements for social justice as defined by demands for racial, social and economic equality. To trace these back to Leo and his encyclical would require a generous exercise of imaginative extrapolation.

Nevertheless:

> This unanticipated extension of papal social thought turned out to be the major and most lasting contribution of *Rerum Novarum*. Whether so intended or not, it legitimized and even *invited* open criticism of the established social order and, without spelling out specific guidelines, encouraged activity designed to translate that criticism into corrective reform and social betterment.[34]

CST and the fundamental principles of the ILO

Association and collective bargaining[35]

As Pope Pius XI remarked in his Encyclical *Quadragesimo anno* (1931), Pope Leo XIII had in his Encyclical *Rerum novarum* (1891) anticipated by decades the recognition in many nations of trade unions:

33 Charles E Curran, *Catholic Social Teaching 1891–Present: A Historical, Theological and Ethical Analysis* (Georgetown University Press, Washington, DC, 2002) 68.
34 Gordon C Zahn, "Social Movements and Catholic Social Thought" in John A Coleman, ed, *One Hundred Years of Catholic Social Thought: Celebration and Challenge* (Orbis Books, New York, 1991) 44, 50.
35 A concise overview is given by Joe Holland, *100 Years of Catholic Social Teaching Defending Workers & Their Unions* (Pax Romana, Washington, DC, 2012).

30. […] For at that time in many nations those at the helm of State, plainly imbued with Liberalism, were showing little favour to workers' associations of this type; nay, rather they openly opposed them, and while going out of their way to recognize similar organisations of other classes and show favour to them, they were with criminal injustice denying the natural right to form associations to those who needed it most to defend themselves from ill treatment at the hands of the powerful. There were even some Catholics who looked askance at the efforts of workers to form associations of this type as if they smacked of a socialistic or revolutionary spirit.[36]

Looking back with a degree of unconcealed historical romanticism to the Medieval Guild system which bound master and servant together, Pope Leo XIII applauded

48. […] such associations and organizations as afford opportune aid to those who are in distress, and which draw the two classes more closely together. Among these may be enumerated societies for mutual help; various benevolent foundations established by private persons to provide for the workman, and for his widow or his orphans, in case of sudden calamity, in sickness, and in the event of death; and institutions for the welfare of boys and girls, young people, and those more advanced in years.

49. […] Such unions should be suited to the requirements of this our age – an age of wider education, of different habits and of far more numerous requirements in daily life. It is gratifying to know that there are actually in existence not a few associations of this nature, consisting either of workmen alone, or of workmen and employers together, but it were greatly to be desired that they should become more numerous and more efficient.

50. The consciousness of his own weakness urges man to call in aid from without. […] It is this natural impulse which binds men together in civil society; and it is likewise this which leads them to join together in associations which are, it is true, lesser and not independent societies, but, nevertheless, real societies.[37]

---

36 Pope Pius XI, *Quadragesimo anno* (1931) s 30 © Copyright – Libreria Editrice Vaticana. Not all nations, however, had withheld recognition: in the United Kingdom, for example, trade unions were first legalised under the Trade Union Act 1871 (34 & 35 Vict c 31). A copy of that Act is available online from the ILO at https://www.ilo.org/dyn/natlex/docs /ELECTRONIC/98373/117044/F1671923749/IRL98373.pdf (accessed 16 October 2020).

37 Pope Leo XIII, *Rerum novarum* (1891) ss 48 to 50 © Copyright – Libreria Editrice Vaticana. A detailed review of the terminological evolution of the concept of "trade union" from *Rerum novarum* to *Mater et magistra*, which highlights uncertainties resulting from the early inconsistency in vocabulary, made worse by a plethora of terms employed in the Latin originals of the Encyclicals prior to standardisation in *Mater et magistrata*, is found in

He acknowledged that some associations could be suppressed on the grounds of being "evidently bad, unlawful or dangerous to the State" but cautioned that "[...] every precaution should be taken not to violate the rights of individuals and not to impose unreasonable regulations under pretence of public benefit"[38] and urged the formation of Christian trade unions.[39] He favoured a light touch on the part of the State:

> The State should watch over these societies of citizens banded together in accordance with their rights, but it should not thrust itself into their peculiar concerns and their organisation, for things move and live by the spirit inspiring them, and may be killed by the rough grasp of a hand from without.[40]

The trade unions should be accorded internal constitutional freedom.[41]

Pope Leo XIII did not regard workers and employers as naturally hostile to each other:

> 19. The great mistake made in regard to the matter now under consideration is to take up with the notion that class is naturally hostile to class, and that the wealthy and the working men are intended by nature to live in mutual conflict. So irrational and so false is this view that the direct contrary is the truth. Just as the symmetry of the human frame is the result of the suitable arrangement of the different parts of the body, so in a State is it ordained by nature that these two classes should dwell in harmony and agreement, so as to maintain the balance of the body politic. Each needs the other: capital cannot do without labour, nor labour without capital. Mutual agreement results in the beauty of good order, while perpetual conflict necessarily produces confusion and savage barbarity.[42]

In his Encyclical *Graves de Communi Re* (On Christian Democracy)[43] issued on 18 January 1901, Pope Leo XIII in referred back to *Rerum novarum* and reacted

---

Kevin Quinn, "Trade Unions in 'Mater et Magistra'" in *Gregorianum* Vol. 43, No. 2 (1962) 268–294.

38 Pope Leo XIII, *Rerum novarum* (1891) s 52 © Copyright – Libreria Editrice Vaticana.

39 Pope Leo XIII, *Rerum novarum* (1891) s 54 © Copyright – Libreria Editrice Vaticana (a call echoed by Pope Pius XI in calling for Catholic unions – *Quadragesimo anno* (1931) s 35 © Copyright – Libreria Editrice Vaticana).

40 Pope Leo XIII, *Rerum novarum* (1891) s 55 © Copyright – Libreria Editrice Vaticana.

41 Pope Leo XIII, *Rerum novarum* (1891) s 56 © Copyright – Libreria Editrice Vaticana (a precept endorsed by Pope Pius XI in *Quadragesimo anno* (1931) s 87 © Copyright – Libreria Editrice Vaticana).

42 Pope Leo XIII, *Rerum novarum* (1891) s 19 © Copyright – Libreria Editrice Vaticana. It is precisely this tripartite relationship of State, employers and workers which is at the heart of the ILO Constitution 1919. See Chapter 5.

43 Pope Leo XIII, *Graves de Communi Re* (1901) ss 2, 11, 21, 26 © Copyright – Libreria Editrice Vaticana.

to contemporary accusations against him that this had a political origin with socialist intentions.

> 11. For, it is the opinion of some, and the error is already very common, that the social question is merely an economic one, whereas in point of fact it is, above all, a moral and religious matter, and for that reason must be settled by the principles of morality and according to the dictates of religion.

He firmly reasserted his conservative credentials, rejecting political solutions in favour of the purely theological:

> 2. [W]e dwelt at length on the rights and duties which both classes of society – those namely, who control capital, and those who contribute labour – are bound in relation to each other; and at the same time, We made it evident that the remedies which are most useful to protect the cause of religion, and to terminate the contest between the different classes of society, were to be found in the precepts of the Gospel.

and in particular lambasting socialism "The harvest of misery is before our eyes, and the dreadful projects of the most disastrous national upheavals are threatening us from the growing power of the socialistic movement" (s 21) and insisting that social initiatives by individuals or associations "should be formed under episcopal authority. Let them not be led astray by an excessive zeal in the cause of charity". (s 26)

Paul Misner, commenting on *Graves de Communi Re*, writes:

> For how then could the church play its role as arbiter of economic morality, part of its mission to the world? How would such autonomous labour unions be any more beneficial to society than manufacturers' or bankers' associations, whose social consciousness and conscience left much to be desired? Was such autonomy a step forward? Not in Leo's eyes and still less so in those of his successor Pope Pius X![44]

It came too late: that *Graves de Communi Re* receives barely a mention in most accounts of the period is a measure of its lack of success, and it is usually omitted from the canon of CST documents.

On the fortieth anniversary of *Rerum novarum* Pope Pius XI in his Encyclical *Quadragesimo anno* (1931)[45] recorded with approval the spread of workers' associations, both those which were exclusively Catholic and (though with noticeable reluctance) those which were secular:

---

44 Paul Misner, *Social Catholicism in Europe from the Onset of Industrialization to the First World War* (Darton, Longman and Todd, London, 1991) 321.

45 Pope Pius XI, *Quadragesimo anno* (1931) s 35 © Copyright – Libreria Editrice Vaticana.

35. This second method has especially been adopted where either the laws of a country, or certain special economic institutions, or that deplorable dissension of minds and hearts so widespread in contemporary society and an urgent necessity of combating with united purpose and strength the massed ranks of revolutionarists, have prevented Catholics from founding purely Catholic labor unions. Under these conditions, Catholics seem almost forced to join secular labor unions. These unions, however, should always profess justice and equity and give Catholic members full freedom to care for their own conscience and obey the laws of the Church. It is clearly the office of bishops, when they know that these associations are on account of circumstances necessary and are not dangerous to religion, to approve of Catholic workers joining them [...] Side by side with these unions there should always be associations zealously engaged in imbuing and forming their members in the teaching of religion and morality so that they in turn may be able to permeate the unions with that good spirit which should direct them in all their activity. As a result, the religious associations will bear good fruit even beyond the circle of their own membership.

Seventy years after Pope Leo XIII's ground-breaking work, in a world starkly divided into Eastern and Western and post-colonial blocs, Pope St John XXIII in his Encyclical *Mater et magistra* (1961) recognised the evolved nature of trade unionism and its relationship with the State; it was:

> timely and imperative [...] that workers be given the opportunity to exert their influence through the State, and not just within the limits of the spheres of their own employment. [...] It is therefore very appropriate, or even necessary, that these public authorities and institutions bring the workers into their discussions, and those who represent the rights, demands and aspirations of the workingmen; and not confine their deliberations to those who merely represent the interests of management.[46]

The parallelism between his view and of the work of the ILO was expressly acknowledged:

> We must express here our heartfelt appreciation of the work that is being done by the ILO [...] For many years now it has been making an effective and valued contribution to the establishment in the world of an economic and social order marked by justice and humanity, an order which recognises and safeguards the lawful rights of the workingman.[47]

---

46 Pope St John XXIII, *Mater et magistra* (1961) ss 97, 99 © Copyright – Libreria Editrice Vaticana.
47 Pope St John XXIII, *Mater et magistra* (1961) s 103 © Copyright – Libreria Editrice Vaticana.

In his Encyclical *Pacem in terris* (1963) Pope St John XXIII made it clear that trade union rights were now embedded in CST:

23. Men are by nature social, and consequently they have the right to meet together and to form associations with their fellows. They have the right to confer on such associations the type of organization which they consider best calculated to achieve their objectives. They have also the right to exercise their own initiative and act on their own responsibility within these associations for the attainment of the desired results.

24. As We insisted in Our encyclical *Mater et Magistra*, the founding of a great many such intermediate groups or societies for the pursuit of aims which it is not within the competence of the individual to achieve efficiently, is a matter of great urgency. Such groups and societies must be considered absolutely essential for the safeguarding of man's personal freedom and dignity, while leaving intact a sense of responsibility.[48]

The Second Vatican Council in *Gaudium et spes* (1965) declared the founding of trade unions to be a basic right, though one to be exercised responsibly:

68. [...] Among the basic rights of the human person is to be numbered the right of freely founding unions for working people. These should be able truly to represent them and to contribute to the organizing of economic life in the right way. Included is the right of freely taking part in the activity of these unions without risk of reprisal. Through this orderly participation joined to progressive economic and social formation, all will grow day by day in the awareness of their own function and responsibility, and thus they will be brought to feel that they are comrades in the whole task of economic development and in the attainment of the universal common good according to their capacities and aptitudes.

When, however, socio-economic disputes arise, efforts must be made to come to a peaceful settlement. Although recourse must always be had first to a sincere dialogue between the parties, a strike, nevertheless, can remain even in present-day circumstances a necessary, though ultimate, aid for the defense of the workers' own rights and the fulfilment of their just desires. As soon as possible, however, ways should be sought to resume negotiation and the discussion of reconciliation.[49]

48 Pope St John XXIII, *Pacem in terris* (1963) ss 23, 24 © Copyright – Libreria Editrice Vaticana (reaffirmed by Second Vatican Council, Pastoral Constitution on the Church in the Modern World *Gaudium et spes* (1965) s 68 © Copyright – Libreria Editrice Vaticana).
49 Second Vatican Council, *Gaudium et spes* (1965) s 68 © Copyright – Libreria Editrice Vaticana.

Pope St Paul VI in his Apostolic Letter *Octogesima adveniens* (1971) again stressed that *responsible* trade unionism was the key:

> 14. [...] Although for the defense of these rights democratic societies accept today the principle of labor union rights, they are not always open to their exercise. The important role of union organizations must be admitted: their object is the representation of the various categories of workers, their lawful collaboration in the economic advance of society, and the development of the sense of their responsibility for the realization of the common good. Their activity, however, is not without its difficulties. Here and there the temptation can arise of profiting from a position of force to impose, particularly by strikes – the right to which as a final means of defense remains certainly recognized – conditions which are too burdensome for the overall economy and for the social body, or to desire to obtain in this way demands of a directly political nature. When it is a question of public service, required for the life of an entire nation, it is necessary to be able to assess the limit beyond which the harm caused to society become inadmissible.[50]

The treatment of trade union formation and membership in the Encyclicals does borrow the language of politics and the marketplace, but this is within the context of Catholic social justice and the spiritual dimension must therefore also be present, as Pope St Paul VI had previously observed in his Encyclical *Populorum progressio* (1967):

> 39. Every form of social action involves some doctrine; *and the Christian rejects that which is based on a materialistic and atheistic philosophy, namely one which shows no respect for a religious outlook on life,* for freedom or human dignity. So long as these higher values are preserved intact, however, the existence of a variety of professional organizations and trade unions is permissible. Variety may even help to preserve freedom and create friendly rivalry. We gladly commend those people who unselfishly serve their brothers by working in such organizations.[51] [Emphasis added]

Pope St John Paul II in his Encyclical *Laborem exercens* (1981) was equally emphatic: "The experience of history teaches that [trade unions] are an indispensable element of social life, especially in modern industrialised societies" and analysed this not as reflecting some "class" structure of society or class struggle,

---

50 Pope St Paul VI, *Octogesima adveniens* (1971) s 14 © Copyright – Libreria Editrice Vaticana (reaffirmed by Pope St John Paul II – "a strike remains, in a sense, an extreme means. It must not be abused; [...] especially for 'political' purposes". *Laborem exercens* (1981) s 20 © Copyright – Libreria Editrice Vaticana).

51 Pope St Paul VI, *Populorum progressio* (1967) s 39 © Copyright – Libreria Editrice Vaticana.

but as being "the struggle for social justice" with trade unions "a constructive factor of social order and solidarity, and it is impossible to ignore it".[52]

In his Encyclical *Centesimus annus* (1991), Pope St John Paul II, echoing his own address to the ILO given on 15 June 1982 and that of Pope Paul to the ILO on 10 June 1969[53] (both of which are referred to in the footnotes to the Encyclical at this point), emphasised the importance of trade unions:

> 15. [...] This is the place to mention once more the role of trade unions, not only in negotiating contracts, but also as 'places' where workers can express themselves. They serve the development of an authentic culture of work and help workers to share in a fully human way in the life of their place of employment.[54]

Globally, trade union rights are in the early 21st century under threat and the Church sounds the alarm. Pope Benedict XVI, in his Encyclical *Caritas in veritate* (2009), writes:

> 25. [...] Through the combination of social and economic change, trade union organisations experience greater difficulty in carrying out their task of representing the interests of workers, partly because Governments, for reasons of economic utility, often limit the freedom or the negotiating capacity of labour unions. Hence traditional networks of solidarity have more and more obstacles to overcome. The repeated calls issued within the Church's social doctrine, beginning with *Rerum Novarum* must therefore be honoured today even more than in the past, as a prompt and far-sighted response to the urgent need for new forms of co-operation at the international level, as well as the local level.[55]

Pope Benedict XVI advocated an evolutionary leap forward for trade unions in this century:

> 64. While reflecting on the theme of work, it is appropriate to recall how important it is that *labour unions* – which have always been encouraged and supported by the Church – should be open to the new perspectives that are emerging in the world of work. [...] The global context in which work takes place also demands that national labour unions, which tend to limit themselves to defending the interests of their registered members, should turn their attention to those outside their membership, and in particular to workers in developing countries where social rights are often violated. [...] [This]

---

52 Pope St John Paul II, *Laborem exercens* (1981) s 20 © Copyright – Libreria Editrice Vaticana.
53 See Chapter 6.
54 Pope St John Paul II, *Centesimus annus* (1991) s 15 © Copyright – Libreria Editrice Vaticana.
55 Pope Benedict XVI, *Caritas in veritate* (2009) s 25 © Copyright – Libreria Editrice Vaticana.

will enable trade unions to demonstrate the authentic ethical and cultural motivations that made it possible for them, in a different social and labour context, to play a decisive role in development. The Church's traditional teaching makes a valid distinction between the respective roles and functions of trade unions and politics. This distinction allows unions to identify civil society as the proper setting for their necessary activity of defending and promoting labour, especially on behalf of exploited and unrepresented workers, whose woeful condition is often ignored by the distracted eye of society.[56]

Wages and conditions in work[57]

Wages

In social terms, decades ahead of his time, but in theological terms the heir to a long Christian tradition, Pope Leo XIII in his Encyclical *Rerum novarum* (1891) wrote:

> Doubtless, before deciding whether wages are fair, many things have to be considered; but wealthy owners and all masters of labour should be mindful of this – that to exercise pressure upon the indigent and the destitute for the sake of gain, and to gather one's profit out of the need of another, is condemned by all laws, human and divine. To defraud anyone of wages that are his due is a great crime which cries to the avenging anger of Heaven.[58]

He stressed the practical necessities underlying wage negotiations – balancing a worker's ability to accept any wage he chose against his "natural right to procure what is required in order to live"[59] and concluded (in an age when State intervention in the realm of private contractual arrangements was largely unknown):

> Let the working man and the employer make free agreements, and in particular let them agree freely as to the wages; nevertheless, there underlies a dictate of natural justice more imperious and ancient than any bargain between man and man, namely, that wages ought not to be insufficient to support a frugal and well behaved wage-earner. If through necessity or fear of a worse evil the workman accepts harder conditions because an employer or contractor will afford him no better, he is made the victim of force and injustice.[60]

56 Pope Benedict XVI, *Caritas in veritate* (2009) s 64 © Copyright – Libreria Editrice Vaticana.
57 For a discussion on the interaction between the ILO and the Holy See with regard to the ILO's Decent Work Agenda and its Future Work Initiative see Chapter 7.
58 Pope Leo XIII, *Rerum novarum* (1891) s 20 © Copyright – Libreria Editrice Vaticana.
59 Pope Leo XIII, *Rerum novarum* (1891) s 44 © Copyright – Libreria Editrice Vaticana.
60 Pope Leo XIII, *Rerum novarum* (1891) s 45 © Copyright – Libreria Editrice Vaticana.

Forty years later, as the Great Depression was in full spate, Pope Pius XI in his Encyclical *Quadragesimo Anno* (1931) recognised the need for State intervention in the bargaining process and advocated worker participation in the ownership of the businesses which employed them – "Workers and other employees thus become sharers in ownership or management or participate in some fashion in the profits received"[61] and stressed "the social aspect also to be considered in addition to the personal or individual aspect [...] For man's productive effort cannot yield its fruits [...] unless a social and juridical order watches over the exercise of work",[62] and argued for the establishment of a minimum wage (reflecting the social norms of his times, this was to be a minimum wage for the father of the household, allowing mothers to concentrate on household duties and work primarily in the home or in its immediate vicinity). The threefold criteria were the needs of the worker and his family, the economic condition of the business concerned and the public economic good:

> 71. In the first place, the worker must be paid a wage sufficient to support him and his family. [...] Every effort must therefore be made that fathers of families receive a wage large enough to meet ordinary family needs adequately. But if this cannot always be done under existing circumstances, social justice demands that changes be introduced as soon as possible whereby such a wage will be assured to every adult workingman.

> 72. In determining the amount of the wage, the condition of a business and of the one carrying it on must also be taken into account; for it would be unjust to demand excessive wages which a business cannot stand without its ruin and consequent calamity to the workers.

> 74. Lastly, the amount of the pay must be adjusted to the public economic good. [...] Hence it is contrary to social justice when, for the sake of personal gain and without regard for the common good, wages and salaries are excessively lowered or raised; and this same social justice demands that wages and salaries be so managed [...] as to offer the greatest possible number the opportunity of getting work and obtaining suitable means of livelihood.[63]

In a changed world 20 years later, the same problems remained, and Pope St John XXIII in his Encyclical *Mater et magistra* (1961) set out the factors determining a just wage:

---

61 Pope Pius XI, *Quadragesimo anno* (1931) s 65 © Copyright – Libreria Editrice Vaticana.
62 Pope Pius XI, *Quadragesimo anno* (1931) s 69 © Copyright – Libreria Editrice Vaticana.
63 Pope Pius XI, *Quadragesimo anno* (1931) ss 71, 72, 74 © Copyright – Libreria Editrice Vaticana. See the analysis by Catherine Ruth Pakaluk of the treatment of just wages in *Quadragesimo anno* in Gerard V Bradley and E Christian Brugger, eds, *Socialism and Capitalism in Catholic Social Thought in Catholic Social Teaching: A Volume of Scholarly Essays* (Cambridge University Press, Cambridge, 2019) chapter 18, 447–456.

71. [T]he remuneration of work is not something that can be left to the laws of the marketplace; nor should it be a decision left to the will of the more powerful. It must be determined in accordance with justice and equity; which means that workers must be paid a wage which allows them to live a truly human life and to fulfil their family obligations in a worthy manner. Other factors too enter into the assessment of a just wage: namely, the effective contribution which each individual makes to the economic effort, the financial state of the company for which he works, the requirements of the general good of the particular country [...] and finally the requirements of the common good of the universal family of nations of every kind, both large and small.

72. The above principles are valid always and everywhere. So much is clear. But their degree of applicability to concrete cases cannot be determined without reference to the quantity and quality of available resources; and these can – and in fact do – vary from country to country, and even, from time to time, within the same country.[64]

He advocated shared ownership: "[W]orkers should be allocated shares in the firms for which they work, especially when they are paid no more than a minimum wage".[65] Wages should increase "within the limits of the common good" as economies expand.[66]

For Pope St John XIII the question of the demands of "the common good" applied not merely to a particular country but to the whole human family:

79. What are these demands? On the national level they include: employment of the greatest possible number of workers; care lest privileged classes arise, even among the workers; maintenance of equilibrium between wages and prices; the need to make goods and services accessible to the greatest number; elimination, or at least the restriction, of inequalities in the various branches of the economy – that is, between agriculture, industry and services; creation of a proper balance between economic expansion and the development of social services, especially through the activity of public authorities; the best possible adjustment of the means of production to the progress of science and technology; seeing to it that the benefits which make possible a more human way of life will be available not merely to the present generation but to the coming generations as well.

---

64 Pope St John XXIII, Mate*r et magistra* (1961) ss 71, 72 © Copyright – Libreria Editrice Vaticana.

65 Pope St John XXIII, *Mater et magistra* (1961) s 75 © Copyright – Libreria Editrice Vaticana.

66 Pope St John XXIII, *Mater et magistra* (1961) s 112 © Copyright – Libreria Editrice Vaticana.

80. The demands of the common good on the international level include: the avoidance of all forms of unfair competition between the economies of different countries; the fostering of mutual collaboration and good will; and effective co-operation in the development of economically less advanced communities.

81. These demands of the common good, both on a national and a world level, must also be borne in mind when assessing the rate of return due as compensation to the company's management, and as interest or dividends to investors.[67]

No-one should be excluded from the right to a just wage, a theme to which Pope St John XXIII returned in his Encyclical *Pacem in terris* (1963):

The government should make similarly effective efforts to see that those who are able to work can find employment in keeping with their aptitudes, and that each worker receives a wage in keeping with the laws of justice and equity.[68]

In reviewing principles governing socio-economic life as a whole, *Gaudium et spes* (1965) did not refer expressly to a just or living wage, but nevertheless addressed the issue:

[R]emuneration for labour is to be such that man may be furnished the means to cultivate worthily his own material, social, cultural and spiritual life and that of his dependents, in view of the function and productiveness of each one, the conditions of the factory or workshop, and the common good.[69]

For Pope St John Paul II, in his Encyclical *Laborem exercens* (1981), and in the context of wages and other social benefits,

The key problem of social ethics [...] is that of *just remuneration*[70] for work done. [...] Hence, in every case, a just wage is the concrete means of *verifying the justice*[71] of the whole socio-economic system and, in any case, of checking that it is functioning justly.

19. [...] This means of checking concerns above all the family. Just remuneration for the work of an adult who is responsible for a family means

---

67 Pope St John XXIII, *Mater et magistra* (1961) ss 79–81 © Copyright – Libreria Editrice Vaticana.
68 Pope St John XXIII, *Pacem in terris* (1963) s 64 © Copyright – Libreria Editrice Vaticana.
69 Second Vatican Council, *Gaudium et spes* (1965) s 67 © Copyright – Libreria Editrice Vaticana.
70 [His emphasis]
71 [His emphasis]

remuneration which will suffice for establishing and properly maintaining a family and for providing security for its future. Such remuneration can be given either through what is called a family wage – that is, a single salary given to the head of the family for his work, sufficient for the needs of the family without the other spouse having to take up gainful employment out-side the home-or through other social measures such as family allowances or grants to mothers devoting themselves exclusively to their families.[72]

Recalling that the Church is "the Church of the poor", he noted:

> 8. And the "poor" appear under various forms: they appear in various places and at various times; in many cases they appear as a *result of the violation of the dignity of human work*:[73] either because the opportunities for human work are limited as a result of the scourge of unemployment, or because a low value is put on work and the rights that flow from it, especially the right to a just wage and to the personal security of the worker and his or her family.[74]

On the centenary of *Rerum novarum*, in his Encyclical *Centesimus annus* (1991), Pope St John Paul II looked back to Pope Leo XIII's promotion of the need for a just wage and the worker's victimisation under "force and injustice", and noted how little had changed in the intervening 100 years:

> 8. [...] A workman's wages should be sufficient to enable him to support himself, his wife and his children. [...] Would that these words, written at a time when what has been called 'unbridled capitalism' was pressing forward, should not have to be repeated today with the same severity. Unfortunately, even today one finds instances of contracts between employers and employ-ees which lack reference to the most elementary justice regarding the employment of children or women, working hours, the hygienic condition of the work-place and fair pay; and this is the case despite the International Declarations and Conventions[75] on the subject and the internal laws of States.

> 15. [...] Furthermore, society and the State must ensure wage levels ade-quate for the maintenance of the worker and his family, including a certain amount for savings. This requires a continuous effort to improve workers' training and capability so that their work will be more skilled and productive,

---

72 Pope St John Paul II, *Laborem exercens* (1981) s 19 © Copyright – Libreria Editrice Vaticana.
73 [His emphasis]
74 Pope St John Paul II, *Laborem exercens* (1981) s 8 © Copyright – Libreria Editrice Vaticana.
75 In the footnote to the Encyclical, at this point there is a reference to the UDHR and although not specified, the reference to "Conventions" must be taken to include those promulgated by the ILO. Note also that the Holy See ratified in 1990 the *Convention on the Rights of the Child*, which came into force in 1990 <www.ohchr.org/en/professionalinterest/pages/crc .aspx> (accessed 17 October 2020).

as well as careful controls and adequate legislative measures to block shameful forms of exploitation, especially to the disadvantage of the most vulnerable workers, of immigrants and of those on the margins of society. The role of trade unions in negotiating minimum salaries and working conditions is decisive in this area.[76]

Working conditions

Pope Leo XIII's reservations about State interference in matters of private contract did not in his Encyclical *Rerum novarum* (1891) extend to questions of working conditions:

> 36. Whenever the general interest or any particular class suffers, or is threatened with harm, which can in no other way be met or prevented, the public authority must step in to deal with it. [...] [I]f health were endangered by excessive labour, or by work unsuited to sex or age – in such cases, there can be no question but that, within certain limits, it would be right to invoke the aid and authority of the law.

> 42. If we turn not to things external and material, the first thing of all to secure is to save unfortunate working people from the cruelty of men of greed, who use human beings as mere instruments for money-making. It is neither just nor human so to grind men down with excessive labour as to stupefy their minds and wear out their bodies. [...]. Daily labour, therefore should be so regulated as not to be protracted over longer hours than strength admits. How many and how long the intervals of rest should be must depend on the nature of the work, on circumstances of time and place, and on the health and strength of the workman. Those who work in mines and quarries, and extract coal, stone and metals from the bowels of the earth, should have shorter hours in proportion as their labor is more severe and trying to health. Then, again, the season of the year should be taken into account; for not unfrequently a kind of labor is easy at one time which at another is intolerable or exceedingly difficult.[77]

Pope Pius XI in his Encyclical *Quadragesimo anno* (1931) excoriated the approach of the "so-called Manchester Liberals", who advocated "[...] that all accumulation of capital falls by an absolutely insuperable economic law to the rich, and that by the same law the workers are given over and bound to perpetual want, to the scantiest of livelihoods".[78]

---

76 Pope St John Paul II, *Centesimus annus* (1991) ss 8, 15 © Copyright – Libreria Editrice Vaticana.
77 Pope Leo XIII, *Rerum novarum* (1891) ss 36, 42 © Copyright – Libreria Editrice Vaticana.
78 Pope Pius XI, *Quadragesimo anno* (1931) s 54 © Copyright – Libreria Editrice Vaticana.

Thirty years later, though reflecting the sensibilities of a slightly earlier period, Pope St John XXIII, in his Encyclical *Pacem in terris* (1963) stated:

> 18. In the economic sphere, it is evident that a man has the inherent right not only to be given the opportunity to work, but also to be allowed the exercise of personal initiative in the work he does.
>
> 19. The conditions in which a man works form a necessary corollary to these rights. They must not be such as to weaken his physical or moral fibre, or militate against the proper development of adolescents to manhood. Women must be accorded such conditions of work as are consistent with their needs and responsibilities as wives and mothers.[79]

Gaudium et spes (1965) decried "[…] disgraceful working conditions, where men are treated as mere tools for profit, rather than as free and responsible persons"[80] and the treatment of migrant workers as "mere tools of production".[81] "It happens too often, however, even in our days, that workers are reduced to the level of being slaves to their work. This is by no means justified by the so-called economic laws".[82]

Pope St John Paul II in his Encyclical *Laborem exercens* (1981) emphasised that among workers' rights "there should never be overlooked the right to a working environment and to manufacturing processes which are not harmful to the workers' physical health or to their moral integrity".[83] He was in 1982 to address the ILO,[84] a relationship thus established which lasted for the rest of his Pontificate. At the Workers' Jubilee in 2000, highlighting the need for a decent work agenda, he referred to the work of the ILO:

> The commitment to resolve these problems in all parts of the world involves everyone. It concerns you, owners and management, you, financiers, and you, craftsmen, tradespeople and workers. All must work so that the economic system in which we live does not upset the fundamental order of the priority of work over capital, of the common good over private interest. It is

---

79 Pope St John XXIII, *Pacem in terris* (1963) ss 18, 19 © Copyright – Libreria Editrice Vaticana.
80 Second Vatican Council, Pastoral Constitution on the Church in the Modern World *Gaudium et spes* (1965) s 27 © Copyright – Libreria Editrice Vaticana.
81 Second Vatican Council, Pastoral Constitution on the Church in the Modern World *Gaudium et spes* (1965) s 66 © Copyright – Libreria Editrice Vaticana.
82 Second Vatican Council, Pastoral Constitution on the Church in the Modern World *Gaudium et spes* (1965) s 67 © Copyright – Libreria Editrice Vaticana.
83 Pope St John Paul II, *Laborem exercens* (1981) s 19 © Copyright – Libreria Editrice Vaticana.
84 See Chapter 6.

ever more necessary, as Mr Juan Somavia[85] said a short while ago, to establish a global coalition in favour of "decent work".[86]

Pope Benedict XVI recalled this greeting and defined "decent" in regard to work:

> It means work that expresses the essential dignity of every man and woman in the context of their particular society: work that is freely chosen, effectively associating workers, both men and women, with the development of their community; work that enables the worker to be respected and free from any form of discrimination; work that makes it possible for families to meet their needs and provide schooling for their children, without the children themselves being forced into labour; work that permits the workers to organise themselves freely, and to make their voices heard; work that leaves enough room for rediscovering one's roots at a personal, familial and spiritual level; work that guarantees those who have retired a decent standard of living.[87]

Pope Francis has not been afraid to identify specific abuses. He concluded his *Regina Caeli* address on 28 April 2013 with the words:

> At this moment, a special moment, I wish to raise a prayer for the many victims caused by the tragic collapse of a factory in Bangladesh.[88] I express my solidarity with and deepest sympathies to the families who are mourning their loved ones, and I address a strong appeal from my heart that the dignity and safety of the worker always be protected.[89]

The Compendium of Social Doctrine of the Church 2004 identifies as a root cause the lack of regulation in developing countries:

> 316. In developing countries, moreover, there has been an expansion in recent years of 'informal' and 'hidden' economic activities. This represents a promising sign of economic growth and development, but it raises many ethical and legal problems. In fact, the significant increase in job opportunities

---

85 The then Director General of the ILO.
86 Pope St John Paul II, *Jubilee of Workers, Greeting of Pope John Paul II after Mass*, 1 May 2000 <www.vatican.va/holy_father/john_paul_ii/speeches/2000/apr-jun/documents/ hf_jp-ii_spe_20000501_jub-workers_en.html> (accessed 17 October 2020) © Copyright – Libreria Editrice Vaticana.
87 Pope Benedict XVI, *Caritas in veritate* (2009) s 63 © Copyright – Libreria Editrice Vaticana.
88 Pope Francis was referring to the collapse of the Rana Plaza building in Dhaka, Bangladesh on 24 April 2013, which killed at least 1,132 people and injured more than 2,500. See *The Rana Plaza Accident and Its Aftermath* published in 2018 by the ILO at <www.oit.org/glo bal/topics/geip/WCMS_614394/lang--en/index.htm>(accessed 17 October 2020).
89 Pope Francis, *Regina Caeli* address (Rome, 28 April 2013) <www.vatican.va/content/fr ancesco/en/angelus/2013/documents/papa-francesco_regina-coeli_20130428.html> (accessed 17 October 2020).

in the context of such activities is owed to the lack of in a large segment of the local work force and to disorderly growth in formal economic sectors. *Large numbers of people are thus forced to work under seriously distressing conditions and in situations that lack the rules necessary for safeguarding workers' dignity.* Levels of productivity, income and living standards are extremely low and often inadequate for guaranteeing to workers and their families the minimum level of subsistence.[90] [Emphasis added]

Social security

Pope Leo XIII in his Encyclical *Rerum novarum* (1891) raised those affluent Catholics who, as a private initiative, had "spent large sums in founding and widely spreading benefit and insurance societies"[91] and took this to the next level, that of State aid:

> Among the several purposes of a society, one should be to try to arrange for a continuous supply of work at all times and seasons; as well as to create a fund out of which the members may be effectually helped in their needs, not only in the cases of accident, but also in sickness, old age and distress.[92]

Seventy years later, Pope St John XXIII in his Encyclicals *Mater et magistra* (1961) and *Pacem in terris* (1963) linked this to the legitimate redistribution of wealth within society:

> Systems of social insurance and social security can make a most effective contribution to the overall distribution of national income in accordance with the principles of justice and equity. They can therefore be instrumental in reducing imbalances between the different classes of citizens.[93]

> The government must also see to the provision of insurance facilities, to obviate any likelihood of a citizen's being unable to maintain a decent standard of living in the event of some misfortune, or greatly increased family responsibilities.[94]

Twenty years later, Pope St John Paul II in his Encyclical *Laborem exercens* (1981) elevated this further to a question of fundamental moral principle:

---

90 *Compendium of the Social Doctrine of the Church* (Pontifical Council for Justice and Peace, 2004) Chapter VII *The "New Things" of the World of* Work, para 316 <www.vatican.va/roman_curia/pontifical_councils/justpeace/documents/rc_pc_justpeace_doc_20060526_compendio-dott-soc_en.html> (accessed 17 October 2020).

91 Pope Leo XIII, *Rerum novarum* (1891) s 55 © Copyright – Libreria Editrice Vaticana.

92 Pope Leo XIII, *Rerum novarum* (1891) s 58 © Copyright – Libreria Editrice Vaticana.

93 Pope St John XXIII, *Mater et magistra* (1961) s 136 © Copyright – Libreria Editrice Vaticana.

94 Pope St John XXIII, *Pacem in terris* (1963) s 64 © Copyright – Libreria Editrice Vaticana.

18. The obligation to provide unemployment benefits, that is to say, the duty to make suitable grants indispensable for the subsistence of unemployed workers and their families, is a duty springing from the fundamental principle of the moral order in this sphere, namely the principle of the common use of goods or, to put it another and still simpler way, the right to life and subsistence.[95]

He stressed the need for health care (especially in the case of work-related injuries), pension, old age and accident cover:

19. Besides wages, various *social benefits* intended to ensure the life and health of workers and their families play a part here. The expenses involved in health care, especially in the case of accidents at work, demand that medical assistance should be easily available for workers, and that as far as possible it should be cheap or even free of charge. Another sector regarding benefits is the sector associated with the *right to rest*. In the first place this involves a regular weekly rest comprising at least Sunday, and also a longer period of rest, namely the holiday or vacation taken once a year or possibly in several shorter periods during the year. A third sector concerns the right to a pension and to insurance for old age and in case of accidents at work. Within the sphere of these principal rights, there develops a whole system of particular rights which, together with remuneration for work, determine the correct relationship between worker and employer. Among these rights there should never be overlooked the right to a working environment and to manufacturing processes which are not harmful to the workers' physical health or to their moral integrity.[96] [His emphasis]

Recognising that in the early 21st century such rights are under grave threat, Pope Benedict XVI in his Encyclical *Caritas in veritate* (2009) sounded the alarm:

25. From the social point of view, systems of protection and welfare, already present in many countries in Paul VI's day, are finding it hard and could find it even harder in the future to pursue their goals of true social justice in today's profoundly changed environment. The global market has stimulated first and foremost, on the part of rich countries, a search for areas in which to outsource production at low cost with a view to reducing the prices of many goods, increasing purchasing power and thus accelerating the rate of development in terms of greater availability of consumer goods for the domestic market. Consequently, the market has prompted new forms of competition between States as they seek to attract foreign businesses to set up production centres, by means of a variety of instruments, including favourable fiscal

---

95 Pope St John Paul II, *Laborem exercens* (1981) s 18 © Copyright – Libreria Editrice Vaticana.
96 Pope St John Paul II, *Laborem exercens* (1981) s 19 © Copyright – Libreria Editrice Vaticana.

regimes and deregulation of the labour market. These processes have led to a *downsizing of social security systems* [his emphasis] as the price to be paid for seeking greater competitive advantage in the global market, with consequent grave danger for the rights of workers, for fundamental human rights and for the solidarity associated with the traditional forms of the social State.[97]

Child labour

Pope Leo XIII in his Encyclical *Rerum novarum* (1891) warned:

42. [...] Finally, work which is quite suitable for a strong man cannot rightly be required from a woman or a child. And, in regard to children, great care should be taken not to place them in workshops and factories until their bodies and minds are sufficiently developed. For, just as very rough weather destroys the buds of spring, so does too early an experience of life's hard toil blight the young promise of a child's faculties, and render any true education impossible.[98]

Reviewing the words of Pope Leo XIII 40 years later in his Encyclical *Quadragesimo Anno* (1931), Pope Pius XI commented "[T]o abuse the years of childhood and the limited strength of women is grossly wrong"[99] but added nothing further to the debate.

Throughout the succeeding decades, the emphasis in the Social Encyclicals has been on the education and mental development of children – the question of child labour and the exploitation of children was not touched upon at all until the promulgation on 3 October 2020 by Pope Francis of his Encyclical *Fratelli tutti*, which addressed this in the context of modern slavery: "children, women and men of all ages – are deprived of freedom and forced to live in conditions akin to slavery". Quoting his own Address to the United Nations Organisation on 25 September 2015,[100] he called for effective solutions to be found to "the phenomenon of social and economic exclusion", including "the sexual exploitation of boys and girls, slave labour, including prostitution".[101]

Beyond the Social Encyclicals, the Catholic Church is not silent on the exploitation of children. In his Message for the World Day of Peace 1996 Pope St John Paul II focussed on children:

---

97 Pope Benedict XVI, *Caritas in veritate* (2009) s 25 © Copyright – Libreria Editrice Vaticana.
98 Pope Leo XIII, *Rerum novarum* (1891) s 42 © Copyright – Libreria Editrice Vaticana.
99 Pope Pius XI, *Quadragesimo anno* (1931) s 71 © Copyright – Libreria Editrice Vaticana.
100 Pope Francis, "Address to the United Nations Organisation" (New York, 25 September 2015) <http://m.vatican.va/content/francesco/en/speeches/2015/september/documents/papa-francesco_20150925_onu-visita.html> (accessed 17 October 2020) © Copyright – Libreria Editrice Vaticana.
101 Pope Francis, *Fratelli tutti* (2020) ss 24, 188 © Copyright – Libreria Editrice Vaticana.

5. Millions of children suffer from other kinds of violence present both in poverty-stricken and in developed societies. These kinds of violence are often less obvious, but they are no less terrible. [...] Poverty is indeed the cause of inhuman living and working conditions. In some countries children are forced to work at a tender age and are often badly treated, harshly punished, and paid absurdly low wages. Because they have no way of asserting their rights, they are the easiest to blackmail and exploit. In other circumstances children are bought and sold, so that they can be used for begging or, even worse, forced into prostitution, as in the case of so-called 'sex tourism'. This utterly despicable trade degrades not only those who take part in it but also those who in any way promote it. Some do not hesitate to enlist children in criminal activities, especially the selling of narcotics, thus exposing them to the risk of personal involvement in drug use. Many children end up with the street as their only home. Having run away, or having been abandoned by their families, or never having known a family environment, these young people live by their wits and in a state of total neglect, and they are considered by many as refuse to be eliminated.[102]

The Compendium of the Social Doctrine of the Church 2004 addresses the issue:[103]

245. The situation of a vast number of the world's children is far from being satisfactory, due to the lack of favourable conditions for their integral development despite the existence of a specific international juridical instrument for protecting their rights.[104] [...] These are conditions connected with the lack of health care, or adequate food supply, little or no possibility of receiving a minimum of academic formation or inadequate shelter. Moreover, some serious problems remain unsolved: *trafficking in children, child labour, the phenomenon of 'street children', the use of children in armed conflicts, child marriage, the use of children for commerce in pornographic material*, also in the use of the most modern and sophisticated instruments of social communication. It is essential to engage in a battle, at the national and international levels, against the violations of the dignity of boys and girls caused by sexual

102 Pope St John Paul II, *Message for the 1996 World Day of Peace "Let Us Give Children a Future of Peace"* para 5 <https://w2.vatican.va/content/john-paul-ii/en/messages/peace/documents/hf_jp-ii_mes_08121995_xxix-world-day-for-peace.html> (accessed 17 October 2020) © Copyright – Libreria Editrice Vaticana.

103 *Compendium of the Social Doctrine of the Church* (Pontifical Council for Justice and Peace, 2004) paras 245, 296 <www.vatican.va/roman_curia/pontifical_councils/justpeace/documents/rc_pc_justpeace_doc_20060526_compendio-dott-soc_en.html> (accessed 17 October 2020) © Copyright – Libreria Editrice Vaticana.

104 *Convention on the Rights of the Child*, which came into force in 1990 and which the Holy See ratified in 1990 <www.ohchr.org/en/professionalinterest/pages/crc.aspx> (accessed 17 October 2020).

exploitation, by those caught up in paedophilia, and by every kind of violence directed against these most defenceless of human creatures.

296. [...] After more than a hundred years, the blight of child labour has not yet been overcome.

Even with the knowledge that, at least for now, in certain countries the contribution made by child labour to family income and the national economy is indispensable, and that in any event certain forms of part-time work can prove beneficial for children themselves, the Church's social doctrine condemns the increase in 'the exploitation of children in the workplace in conditions of veritable slavery'.[105] This exploitation represents a serious violation of human dignity, with which every person, 'no matter how small or how seemingly unimportant in utilitarian terms',[106] is endowed.

Forced labour and slavery

CST is not infrequently classified as Eurocentric, and the non-existence in Europe of slavery in its most broadly recognised form – the mass sale and purchase of humankind for unlimited unpaid labour – may account for an almost total absence of the discussion of slavery in the Social Encyclicals of the earlier 20th century. When used at all, the term was applied to political systems such as communism and harsh working conditions which, in the opinion of the Catholic Church, *equated* to slavery – what the Second Vatican Council referred to as "social and psychological slavery".

Forced labour and, its extreme counterpart, slavery remain a scourge in the 21st century – "the spreading on a virtual worldwide dimension of ever new forms of slavery such as trafficking in human beings, child soldiers, the exploitation of workers, illegal drug trafficking, prostitution".[107] It is these and other everevolving forms which slavery can take in a globalised, technologically advanced society which have towards the end of the 20th century and into the 21st begun to resonate and which the Catholic Church continues anew to address:

105 Pope St John Paul II, *Message for the 1998 World Day of Peace "From the Justice of Each Comes Peace for All"* para 6 <https://w2.vatican.va/content/john-paul-ii/en/messages/peace/documents/hf_jp-ii_mes_08121997_xxxi-world-day-for-peace.html > (accessed 17 October 2020) © Copyright – Libreria Editrice Vaticana.

106 Pope St John Paul II, *Letter to the Secretary-General of the United Nations on the Occasion of the World Summit for Children* (22 September 1990) <www.vatican.va/content/john-paul-ii/en/letters/1990/documents/hf_jp-ii_let_19900922_de-cuellar.html> (accessed 17 October 2020) © Copyright – Libreria Editrice Vaticana.

107 *Compendium of the Social Doctrine of the Church* (Pontifical Council for Justice and Peace, 2004) para 158 <www.vatican.va/roman_curia/pontifical_councils/justpeace/documents/rc_pc_justpeace_doc_20060526_compendio-dott-soc_en.html> (accessed 17 October 2020).

3. [...] The world of work, profoundly changed by the advances of modern technology, reveals extraordinary levels of quality, but unfortunately it must also acknowledge new forms of instability, exploitation and even slavery within the very societies that are considered affluent. In different areas of the planet the level of well-being continues to grow, but there is also a dangerous increase in the numbers of those who are becoming poor, and, for various reasons, the gap between less developed and rich countries is widening.[108]

There is a long provenance of attempted intervention. In his Encyclical *Sicut dudum (Against the Enslaving of Black Natives from the Canary Islands)* issued on 13 January 1435, Pope Eugene IV (reigned 4 March 1431–23 February 1447) demanded on pain of excommunication the freeing of enslaved baptised peoples in the Canary Islands.[109] Self-evidently, this did not prove to be an initiative which in many succeeding centuries under the pressure of colonial expansion had any great lasting effect. By the late 19th century, slavery was held in disrepute in the Western world, but Pope Leo XIII in his Encyclical *In plurimis* (On the Abolition of Slavery) (1888) addressed to the Bishops of Brazil (where in that year "large numbers of those who in that vast empire groan beneath the yoke of slavery, have been legally set free" although slavery itself had not at that point been abolished in Brazil) found it necessary once more to condemn the practice:

21. [...] It is, however, chiefly to be wished that this may be prosperously accomplished, which all desire, that slavery may be banished and blotted out without any injury to divine or human rights, with no political agitation, and so with the solid benefit of the slaves themselves, for whose sake it is undertaken.[110]

Christopher Dawson sets slavery in its modern context:

It is true that the worst results of modern industrialism cannot be compared with the horrors of the Roman slave system, but the existence of the modern ideals of humanity and liberty has caused the evils of the modern system to be far more strongly felt.[111]

In his Encyclical *Rerum novarum* (1891) Pope Leo XIII was the first of the Popes to equate the exploitation of labour and slavery:

108 *Compendium of the Social Doctrine of the Church* (Pontifical Council for Justice and Peace, 2004) para 3 <www.vatican.va/roman_curia/pontifical_councils/justpeace/documents /rc_pc_justpeace_doc_20060526_compendio-dott-soc_en.html> (accessed 17 October 2020).
109 Pope Eugene IV, *Sicut dudum* (1435). © Copyright – Libreria Editrice Vaticana.
110 Pope Leo XIII, *In plurimis* (1888) s 21 © Copyright – Libreria Editrice Vaticana.
111 Christopher Dawson, *Progress and Religion: An Historical Inquiry* (Catholic University Press, Washington, DC, 2001) 162.

3. [...] To this must be added that the hiring of labour and the conduct of trade are concentrated in the hands of comparatively few; so that a small number of very rich men have been able to lay upon the teeming masses of the labouring poor a yoke little better than that of slavery itself.[112]

In his Encyclical *Divini redemptoris* (1937) Pope Pius XI equated working conditions under a totalitarian regime in Russia with slavery itself, despite stirrings of material success in that new economy, and affirmed that Christianity and not communism represented "real and universal brotherhood":

23. [...] Nevertheless We know from reliable and even very recent testimony that not even there, in spite of slavery imposed on millions of men, has Communism reached its promised goal. After all, even the sphere of economics needs some morality, some moral sense of responsibility, which can find no place in a system so thoroughly materialistic as Communism.

36. [...] [I]t was Christianity that first affirmed the real and universal brotherhood of all men of whatever race and condition. This doctrine she proclaimed by a method, and with an amplitude and conviction, unknown to preceding centuries; and with it she potently contributed to the abolition of slavery.[113]

The Second Vatican Council in *Gaudium et spes* (1965) acknowledged and condemned the ever-evolving forms of slavery:

4. [...] Never has the human race enjoyed such an abundance of wealth, resources and economic power, and yet a huge proportion of the world's citizens are still tormented by hunger and poverty, while countless numbers suffer from total illiteracy. Never before has man had so keen an understanding of freedom, *yet at the same time new forms of social and psychological slavery make their appearance.*

27. [...] Furthermore, whatever is opposed to life itself, such as any type of murder, genocide, abortion, euthanasia or wilful self-destruction, whatever violates the integrity of the human person, such as mutilation, torments inflicted on body or mind, attempts to coerce the will itself; whatever insults human dignity, such as subhuman living conditions, arbitrary imprisonment, deportation, *slavery, prostitution, the selling of women and children*; as well as disgraceful working conditions, where men are treated as mere tools for profit, rather than as free and responsible persons; all these things and others of their like are infamies indeed.

---

112 Pope Leo XIII, *Rerum novarum* (1891) s 3 © Copyright – Libreria Editrice Vaticana.
113 Pope Pius XI, *Divini redemptoris* (1937) ss 4, 27 © Copyright – Libreria Editrice Vaticana.

29. [...] Human institutions, both private and public, must labour to minister to the dignity and purpose of man. *At the same time let them put up a stubborn fight against any kind of slavery, whether social or political, and safeguard the basic rights of man under every political system.*[114] [Emphasis added]

In his Encyclical *Redemptor hominis* (1979) Pope St John Paul II presents a reimagined form of slavery, born of naked materialism, which he condemns:

16. [...] Indeed there is already a real perceptible danger that, while man's dominion over the world of things is making enormous advances, he should lose the essential threads of his dominion and in various ways let his humanity be subjected to the world *and become himself something subject to manipulation in many ways* – even if the manipulation is often not perceptible directly – through the whole of the organization of community life, through the production system and through pressure from the means of social communication. *Man cannot relinquish himself or the place in the visible world that belongs to him; he cannot become the slave of things, the slave of economic systems, the slave of production, the slave of his own products.* A civilization purely materialistic in outline condemns man to such slavery, even if at times, no doubt, this occurs contrary to the intentions and the very premises of its pioneers.[115] [Emphasis added]

In his Encyclical *Sollicitudo rei socialis* (1987) Pope St John Paul II warned of the danger that purely economic development could of itself become a form of slavery:

28. At the same time, however, the 'economic' concept itself, linked to the word development, has entered into crisis. In fact there is a better understanding today that the mere accumulation of goods and services, even for the benefit of the majority, is not enough for the realization of human happiness. Nor, in consequence, does the availability of the many real benefits provided in recent times by science and technology, including the computer sciences, bring freedom from every form of slavery. On the contrary, the experience of recent years shows that *unless all the considerable body of resources and potential at man's disposal is guided by a moral understanding and by an orientation towards the true good of the human race, it easily turns against man to oppress him.*

46. [...] It is fitting to add that the aspiration to freedom from all forms of slavery affecting the individual and society is something noble and legitimate.

114 Second Vatican Council, Pastoral Constitution on the Church in the Modern World *Gaudium et spes* (1965) ss 4, 27, 29 © Copyright – Libreria Editrice Vaticana.
115 Pope St John Paul II, *Redemptor hominis* (1979) s 16 © Copyright – Libreria Editrice Vaticana.

This in fact is the purpose of development, or rather liberation and development, taking into account the intimate connection between the two.

Development which is merely economic is incapable of setting man free, on the contrary, it will end by enslaving him further. Development that does not include the cultural, transcendent and religious dimensions of man and society, to the extent that it does not recognize the existence of such dimensions and does not endeavour to direct its goals and priorities toward the same, is even less conducive to authentic liberation. Human beings are totally free only when they are completely themselves, in the fullness of their rights and duties. The same can be said about society as a whole.[116] [Emphasis added]

In his Encyclical *Centesimus annus* (1991) Pope St John Paul II echoed Pope Leo XIII in condemning those working practices which were indistinguishable from slavery:

61. [...] At the beginning of industrialized society, it was 'a yoke little better than that of slavery itself' which led my Predecessor to speak out in defence of man. [...] The Church has constantly repeated that the person and society need not only material goods but spiritual and religious values as well. Furthermore, as she has become more aware of the fact that too many people live, not in the prosperity of the Western world, but *in the poverty of the developing countries amid conditions which are still 'a yoke little better than that of slavery itself'*, she has felt and continues to feel obliged to denounce this fact with absolute clarity and frankness, although she knows that her call will not always win favour with everyone.[117] [Emphasis added]

Pope Francis, in his Apostolic Exhortation on the Proclamation of the Gospel in Today's World *Evangelii Gaudium* (2013), expressed anguish at modern slavery in the form of human trafficking:

75. We cannot ignore the fact that in cities human trafficking, the narcotics trade, the abuse and exploitation of minors, the abandonment of the elderly and infirm, and various forms of corruption and criminal activity take place. At the same time, what could be significant places of encounter and solidarity often become places of isolation and mutual distrust. Houses and neighbourhoods are more often built to isolate and protect than to connect and integrate. [...]

116 Pope St John Paul II, *Sollicitudo rei socialis* (1987) ss 28, 46 © Copyright – Libreria Editrice Vaticana.
117 Pope St John Paul II, *Centesimus annus* (1991) s 61 © Copyright – Libreria Editrice Vaticana.

211. I have always been distressed at the lot of those who are victims of various kinds of human trafficking. How I wish that all of us would hear God's cry: 'Where is your brother?' (Gen 4:9). Where is your brother or sister who is enslaved? Where is the brother and sister whom you are killing each day in clandestine warehouses, in rings of prostitution, in children used for begging, in exploiting undocumented labour? Let us not look the other way. There is greater complicity than we think. The issue involves everyone! This infamous network of crime is now well established in our cities, and many people have blood on their hands as a result of their comfortable and silent complicity.[118]

Pope Francis in his Encyclical *Laudato Si'* sees the "culture of relativism" which for him is "a relativism which sees everything as irrelevant unless it serves one's own immediate interests" as being the

disorder which drives one person to take advantage of another, to treat others as mere objects, imposing forced labour on them or enslaving them to pay their debts. The same kind of thinking leads to the sexual exploitation of children and abandonment of the elderly who no longer serve our interests.[119]

Pope Francis in his Apostolic Exhortation *Gaudete et exsultate* (2018) expressed his concern for those so impoverished as to be prone to slavery and exploitation:

101. [...] Equally sacred, however, are the lives of the poor, those already born, the destitute, the abandoned and the underprivileged, the vulnerable infirm and elderly exposed to covert euthanasia, the victims of human trafficking, new forms of slavery, and every form of rejection.

His most comprehensive and brutally frank condemnation of slavery is found in his Encyclical *Fratelli tutti* (2020), in which he quotes from his message for the 2015 World Day of Peace:[120]

24. We should also recognize that 'even though the international community has adopted numerous agreements aimed at ending slavery in all its forms, and has launched various strategies to combat this phenomenon, millions of people today – children, women and men of all ages – are deprived of freedom and forced to live in conditions akin to slavery [...] Today, as in

---

118 Pope Francis, *Evangelii Gaudium* (2013) ss 75, 211 © Copyright – Libreria Editrice Vaticana.

119 Pope Francis, *Laudato Si'* (2015) ss 122, 123 © Copyright – Libreria Editrice Vaticana.

120 *Message of His Holiness Pope Francis for the Celebration of the World Day of Peace* (Rome, 1 January 2015) (Libreria Editrice Vaticana) <www.vatican.va/content/francesco/en/messages/peace/documents/papa-francesco_20141208_messaggio-xlviii-giornata-mondiale-pace-2015.html> (accessed 17 October 2020) © Copyright – Libreria Editrice Vaticana.

the past, slavery is rooted in a notion of the human person that allows him or her to be treated as an object [...] Whether by coercion, or deception, or by physical or psychological duress, human persons created in the image and likeness of God are deprived of their freedom, sold and reduced to being the property of others. They are treated as means to an end [...] [Criminal networks] are skilled in using modern means of communication as a way of luring young men and women in various parts of the world'. A perversion that exceeds all limits when it subjugates women and then forces them to abort. An abomination that goes to the length of kidnapping persons for the sake of selling their organs. Trafficking in persons and other contemporary forms of enslavement are a worldwide problem that needs to be taken seriously by humanity as a whole: 'since criminal organizations employ global networks to achieve their goals, efforts to eliminate this phenomenon also demand a common and, indeed, a global effort on the part of various sectors of society'.[121]

Conclusions

The Social Encyclicals are not a blueprint for social change, but they are moral and spiritual guidance for those in the social and political arena who can bring about that change.

The Social Encyclicals address all five fundamental principles of the ILO – association and collective bargaining, wages and conditions in work, social security, child labour and forced labour and slavery.

Although not itself the origin of Social Catholicism, Pope Leo XIII's Encyclical *Rerum novarum* was a nodal point from which radiated a plethora of initiatives whose aim was the alleviation of suffering of the working population and (in the spirit of those early times) to place a restraint on revolutionary tendencies which threatened the status quo. The Encyclical has been glossed and reinterpreted for 130 years, which speaks not of its diminishing relevance but of its enduring truths. As Pope Francis in his Encyclical *Fratelli tutti* (2020) reminds us when speaking of poverty, this "must always be understood and gauged in the context of the actual opportunities available in each historical period".[122]

To what extent the Social Encyclicals hold common ground with the ILO, and whether this is more than mere coincidence or synchronicity, whether there is actual symbiosis between the Holy See and the ILO, is explored in Chapters 5 and 6.

121 Pope Francis, *Fratelli tutti* (2020) s 24 © Copyright – Libreria Editrice Vaticana.
122 Pope Francis, *Fratelli tutti* (2020) s 21 © Copyright – Libreria Editrice Vaticana.

Bibliography

The Holy See

Encyclicals, Apostolic letters, Exhortations (in chronological order)

Pope Eugene IV, *Sicut dudum* (1435).
Pope Leo XIII, *In plurimis* (1888).
____, *De rerum novarum* (1891).
____, *Graves de communi re* (1901).
Pope Pius XI, *Quadragesimo anno* (1931).
____, *Divini redemptoris* (1937).
Pope St John XXIII, *Mater et magistrata* (1961).
____, *Pacem in terris* (1963).
Second Vatican Council, Pastoral Constitution on the Church in the Modern World *Gaudium et spes* (1965).
Pope St Paul VI, *Populorum progressio* (1967).
____, *Octogesima adveniens* (1971).
Pope St John Paul II, *Redemptor hominis* (1979).
____, *Laborum exercens* (1981).
____, *Sollicitudo rei socialis* (1987).
____, *Centesimus annus* (1991).
Pope Benedict XVI, *Caritas in veritate* (2009).
Pope Francis, *Evangelii Gaudium* (2013).
____, *Laudato Si'* (2015).
____, *Fratelli tutti* (2020).

Other materials (in chronological order)

Pope St John Paul II, *Letter to the Secretary-General of the United Nations on the Occasion of the World Summit for Children* (22 September 1990) <http://www.vatican.va/content/john-paul-ii/en/letters/1990/documents/hf_jp-ii_let_199 00922_de-cuellar.html> (accessed 17 October 2020).
Pope St John Paul II, *Message for the 1996 World Day of Peace "Let Us Give Children a Future of Peace"* para 5 <https://w2.vatican.va/content/john-paul-ii/en/mess ages/peace/documents/hf_jp-ii_mes_08121995_xxix-world-day-for-peace.html > (accessed 17 October 2020).
Pope St John Paul II, *Message for the 1998 World Day of Peace "From the Justice of each Comes Peace for All"* para 6 <https://w2.vatican.va/content/john-paul-ii/en/ messages/peace/documents/hf_jp-ii_mes_08121997_xxxi-world-day-for-peace .html > (accessed 17 October 2020).
Jubilee of Workers, Greeting of Pope John Paul II after Mass, 1 May 2000 <http://www.vatican.va/holy_father/john_paul_ii/speeches/2000/apr-jun/documents/hf_jp-ii_spe_20000501_jub-workers_en.html> (accessed 17 October 2020).
Compendium of the Social Doctrine of the Church (2004) <http://www.vatican.va/roman_curia/pontifical_councils/justpeace/documents/rc_pc_justpeace_doc_2 0060526_compendio-dott-soc_en.html> (accessed 17 October 2020).
Pope Francis, *Regina Caeli Address* (Rome, 28 April 2013) <http://www.vatican.va/content/francesco/en/angelus/2013/documents/papa-francesco_regina-coeli _20130428.html> (accessed 17 October 2020).

Message of His Holiness Pope Francis for the Celebration of the World Day of Peace (Rome, 1 January 2015) <http://www.vatican.va/content/francesco/en/me ssages/peace/documents/papa-francesco_20141208_messaggio-xlviii-giornata -mondiale-pace-2015.html> (accessed 17 October 2020).

Pope Francis, 'Address to the United Nations Organisation' (New York, 25 September 2015) <http://m.vatican.va/content/francesco/en/speeches/2015/september /documents/papa-francesco_20150925_onu-visita.html> (accessed 17 October 2020).

'Pastoral Visit of His Holiness Pope Francis to Genoa; Encounter with Representatives of the World of Work 27' May 2017 <http://www.vatican.va/content/franc esco/en/speeches/2017/may/documents/papa-francesco_20170527_lavor atori-genova.html> (accessed 17 October 2020).

International Labour Organisation

The Rana Plaza Accident and Its Aftermath (2018) <http://www.oit.org/global /topics/geip/WCMS_614394/lang--en/index.htm>(accessed 17 October 2020).

International documents

UN Convention on the Rights of the Child 1990 <https://www.ohchr.org/en/profe ssionalinterest/pages/crc.aspx> (accessed 17 October 2020)

Secondary sources

Behr, Thomas C, 'The Nineteenth-Century Historical and Intellectual Context of Catholic Social Teaching' in Gerard V Bradley and E Christian Brugger, eds, *Catholic Social Teaching: A Volume of Scholarly Essays* (Cambridge University Press, Cambridge, 2019) ch 2.

Camp, Richard L, *The Papal Ideology of Social Reform: A Study in Historical Development 1878–1967* (E J Brill, Leiden, 1969).

Coleman, John A, 'Neither Liberal nor Socialist: The Originality of Catholic Social Teaching' in John A Coleman, ed, *One Hundred Years of Catholic Social Thought: Celebration and Challenge* (Orbis Books, New York, 1991).

Cronin, John F, *Christianity and Social Progress: A Commentary on Mater et Magistrata* (Helicon, Baltimore, MD, 1965).

Curran, Charles E, *Catholic Social Teaching 1891 – Present: A Historical, Theological and Ethical Analysis* (Georgetown University Press, Washington, DC, 2002).

Dawson, Christopher, *Progress and Religion: An Historical Inquiry* (Catholic University Press, Washington, DC, 2001).

de la Chapelle, Philippe, *La Déclaration Universelle des Droits de l'Homme et le Catholicisme* (Libraire Générale de Droit et de Jurisprudence, R Pichon et R Durand-Auzias, Paris, 1967).

Duffy, Eamon, *Saints & Sinners: A History of the Popes* (3rd edition) (Yale University Press, New Haven, CT, 2006).

Duffy, Gavan, *Labour and Justice: The Worker in Catholic Social Teaching* (Freedom Press Pty Ltd., Melbourne, 2008).

Fortin, Ernest A, "Sacred and Inviolable': Rerum Novarum and Natural Rights' in *Theological Studies* Vol. 53 (1992) 209.

George, Henry, *The Condition of Labour: An Open Letter to Pope Leo XIII* (Swann Sonnenschein & Co, London, 1892).

Holland, Joe, *100 Years of Catholic Social Teaching Defending Workers & Their Unions* (Pax Romana, Washington, DC, 2012).

Hollenbach, David, *Claims in Conflict: Retrieving and Renewing the Catholic Human Rights Tradition* (Paulist Press, New York, 1979).

Joblin, Joseph, 'L'Appel de l'Union de Fribourg à Léon XIII en Faveur d'une Legislation International du Travail: Son Lien avec "Rerum Novarum"' in *Archivum Historiae Pontificiae* Vol. 28 (1990) 357–372.

Kasper, Walter Kardinal, *Barmherzigkeit: Grundbegriff des Evangeliums – Schlüssel christtlichen Lebens* (Verlag Herder GmbH, Freiburg im Breisgau, 2012).

Le Roy, Albert, *Catholicisme social et organisation internationale du travail* (Éditions Spes, Paris, 1937).

____, 'The Fiftieth Anniversary of the Rerum Novarum' in *International Labour Review* Vol. XLIV(4) (October 1941) 369.

McKenna SJ, Lambert, *The Church and Labour: A Series of Six Tracts* (Irish Messenger Office, Dublin, 1914).

Misner, Paul, *Social Catholicism in Europe From the Onset of Industrialization to the First World War* (Darton, Longman and Todd, London, 1991).

Pakaluk, Catherine Ruth, 'Socialism and Capitalism in Catholic Social Thought' in Gerard V Bradley and E Christian Brugger, eds, *Catholic Social Teaching: A Volume of Scholarly Essays* (Cambridge University Press, Cambridge, 2019) ch 18, 436.

Parkinson, Henry, *The Pope and the People: Select Encyclicals of Leo XIII* (Catholic Truth Society, 1912).

Poynter, J W, *The Popes and Social Problems* (Watts & Co, London, 1949).

Quinn, Kevin, 'Trade Unions in "Mater et Magistrata"' in *Gregorianum* Vol. 43(2) (1962) 268.

Ruston, Roger, *Human Rights and the Image of God* (SCM Press, 2004).

Schäfers, Michael (trans John Bowden), 'Rerum Novarum – The Result of Christian Social Movements "From Below"' in John A Coleman and Gregory Baum, eds, *Rerum Novarum: One Hundred Years of Catholic Social Teaching* (Concilium 1991/5 SCM Press, London, 1991).

Souamaa, Nadjib, 'Les origines de l'OIT (1890–1950): élaboration et premières experimentations d'un modèle d'"Europe sociale"' in *La Revue de l'Ires* 4 (2015) 63.

Vallely, Paul, 'Introduction' in Paul Vallely, ed, *The New Politics: Catholic Social Teaching for the Twenty-First Century* (SCM Press, London, 1998).

Zahn, Gordon C, 'Social Movements and Catholic Social Thought' in John A Coleman, ed, *One Hundred Years of Catholic Social Thought: Celebration and Challenge* (Orbis Books, New York, 1991) 44.

4   ILO – Fundamental principles
Conventions and recommendations

Introduction

"Vivre en ce monde sensible"

Labour rights articulated by the Holy See are by their very nature theologically based and not intended to provide either a framework for the application of the principles espoused or the means of monitoring their effectiveness. These are not within its areas of claimed expertise.

André Arnou, the first Jesuit in residence at the ILO, writing in 1933 stressed the interdependence of the spiritual and the corporeal, finding in this analogy a compelling reason for the creation of the ILO:

> Car si pour vivre en ce monde sensible, l'âme a besoin d'un corps, l'esprit de justice et de charité agira-t-il sur la Société des hommes sans des lois, sans des organismes? Et c'est pourquoi a été créée, forgée, mise au point, une technique et une institution de la Paix sociale internationale: l'Organisation internationale du Travail.[1]

Based upon his own first-hand working experience at the ILO, André Arnou believed that one could not fail to be struck by the profound similarities between the objectives and principles of the ILO and the teachings found in the Papal Encyclicals, each seeking the establishment of truly humane systems of work through a blend of co-operation and State intervention on the basis of international legislation.[2]

Maurice Barbier notes that by virtue of its interest in international labour legislation the Holy See could not have been other than approving of the creation

---

1 [For just as in order to live in this tangible world, the soul needs a body, could the spirit of justice and of charity bring their influence to bear on mankind without laws, without institutions? And it is for this reason that there has been established, wrought, put in place, an engine and agency for international social Peace: the International Labour Organisation.] A Arnou, *L'Organisation internationale du Travail et les Catholiques* (Éditions Spes, Paris, 1933) 20.

2 A Arnou, *L'Organisation internationale du Travail et les Catholiques* (Éditions Spes, Paris, 1933) 104.

of the ILO, its moral support by 1931 having been given officially (albeit without mentioning the ILO by name). In Barbier's analysis, Pope Pius XI in his Encyclical *Quadragesimo anno* (1931):

> soulignait la concordance remarquable entre les principes de l'O.I.T et les directives de Léon XIII dans *Rerum Novarum*. C'était principalement à la constitution de l'Organisation et à ses conventions que faisait allusion le pape quand il écrivait:[3]

> 21. [...] [T]he teaching which On the Condition of Workers contains has gradually and imperceptibly worked its way into the minds of those outside Catholic unity who do not recognize the authority of the Church. Catholic principles on the social question have as a result, passed little by little into the patrimony of all human society, and We rejoice that the eternal truths which Our Predecessor of glorious memory proclaimed so impressively have been frequently invoked and defended not only in non-Catholic books and journals but in legislative halls also courts of justice.

> 22. Furthermore, after the terrible war, when the statesmen of the leading nations were attempting to restore peace on the basis of a thorough reform of social conditions, did not they, among the norms agreed upon to regulate in accordance with justice and equity the labour of the workers, give sanction to many points that so remarkably coincide with Leo's principles and instructions as to seem consciously taken therefrom?[4]

Addressing the 52nd Session of the ILC in 1968,[5] the first to be addressed by the newly created Observer of the Holy See, the Reverend Father Henri de Riedmatten described his new mission as having "set the seal on a tradition of mutual contacts going right back to the origins of your Organisation", and continued:

> The Holy See has constantly shown the highest esteem for the ILO. Here I need quote only two instances: first, the address given by Pope Pius XII at Castel Gandolfo when he received the members of the 127th Session of the Governing Body, and the second the express homage paid to the ILO. by Pope John XXIII in the Encyclical *Mater et Magistra*. In May last year

---

3 [underlined the astonishing concordance between the principles of the ILO and the statements of Pope Leo XIII in *Rerum Novarum*. It was primarily to the Constitution of the ILO and its Conventions to which the Pope was alluding when he wrote:] Maurice Barbier, 'Les Relations Entre l'Église Catholique et l'Organisation International du Travail' in *Politique étrangère*, Vol. 37, No. 3 (1972) (Institut Français des Relations Internationales) 351, 362–363.
4 Pope Pius XI, *Quadragesimo anno* (1931) ss 21, 22 © Copyright – Libreria Editrice Vaticana.
5 Henri de Riedmatten, Address to the 52nd Session of the ILC 1968 202–204 <www.ilo.org /public/libdoc/ilo/P/09616/09616(1968-52).pdf> (accessed 17 October 2020) © ILO.

the Director-General heard from Pope St Paul VI himself the expression of the hopes placed by the Church in the ILO. in the light of the joint prospects formulated and developed on our part in the Encyclical *Populorum Progressio.*

Do not your ideals and the very theme of your work reflect the statement in that Encyclical to the effect that the worker, in devoting his efforts to a material which demands his fullest attention, impresses his mark upon it, and thereby acquires tenacity, ingenuity and inventive spirit? [...]

Our experts and our resources have for a long time been deployed in different parts of the world. Several of them are to be found among the delegations present here. In some places they have combined their efforts with those of the ILO and they have in some cases requested the support of the Organisation or, in other cases, have themselves provided support. *This form of frank collaboration on the broadest possible basis and without any false calculatory spirit is something which the Holy See would like to see established on all possible occasions and in all possible places.* [...]

[W]e shall always be ready to offer our fraternal collaboration, respecting the convictions of all parties, in the fullest communion with the great volume of good will, which animates your meetings, your work, your Secretariat and your experts. We hope that this sincere offer will be accepted by you for what it is—our reply to your own invitation to associate ourselves more closely with your work, in conformity with the true nature of the Holy See. [Emphasis added]

The complimentary but different competences of the ILO and the Holy See were articulated by Archbishop Bertello representing the Holy See at the 71st Session of the ILC in 1985:

Naturally the Church has neither the competence nor the means to propose technical solutions in regard to structural change due to economic and technical innovations which over the last few years have thoroughly disturbed the composition and the very nature of manpower. However, bearing in mind the complexity of social life and the wide range of groups, tendencies and interests, the Church feels that an essential part of its mission is to indicate the ethical principles – and that is its specific contribution to the solution of economic problems – according to which such solutions should be contemplated, if they are to be in keeping with man's needs, to act not against man but for him.[6]

6 Record of Proceedings of the 71st Session of the ILC 1985 22/24 – 22/26 <www.ilo.org /public/libdoc/ilo/P/09616/09616(1985-71).pdf> © ILO (accessed 17 October 2020).

Archbishop Tauran addressing the 81st Session of the ILC in 1994 on the occasion of the 75th anniversary of the foundation of the ILO and of the 50th anniversary of the Declaration of Philadelphia made this same point:

> It is not for the Catholic Church to offer technical solutions to these serious problems, but all the children of the Church [...] are very much aware now more than ever before that God expects each one of them to show a spirit of solidarity to his brothers and sisters in humanity to ensure that selfishness, indifference and sometimes even hate, never have the final say.[7]

ILO: Fundamental principles

This chapter therefore examines the technical detail of the fundamental principles of the ILO. Endorsed by the Holy See not merely as principles but, by extension, as labour rights delivery systems, *these have themselves become an integral part of Catholic Social Teaching.*

What are these fundamental principles?

The International Labour Conference at its 86th Session 1998 issued a Declaration on Fundamental Principles and Rights at Work.[8] Its motivation is set out in the Preamble:

> Whereas the ILO was founded in the conviction that social justice is essential to universal and lasting peace;
> Whereas economic growth is essential but not sufficient to ensure equity, social progress and the eradication of poverty, confirming the need for the ILO to promote strong social policies, justice and democratic institutions;
> [...]

---

7 Record of Proceedings of the 81st Session of the ILC 1994 9/8 – 9/9 <www.ilo.org/public/libdoc/ilo/P/09616/09616(1994-81).pdf> © ILO (accessed 17 October 2020).
8 Declaration on Fundamental Principles and Rights at Work (ILO, Geneva, 1998) <www.ilo.org/wcmsp5/groups/public/---ed_norm/---declaration/documents/normativeinstrument/wcms_716594.pdf> (accessed 17 October 2020). The Apostolic Nuncio, Holy See, Archbishop Bertello (Permanent Observer to the UN organisations in Geneva) addressing the ILC in 2000 commented on increasing global wealth disparity and confirmed: "This situation shows very clearly the importance and the topicality of the Declaration on Fundamental Principles and Rights at Work and this is something which the Holy See has recognised". Record of Proceedings of the 88th Session of the ILC 2000 18/7 <www.ilo.org/public/libdoc/ilo/P/09616/09616(2000-88)V.1.pdf> © ILO (accessed 29 August 2020). And see Steve Hughes and Nigel Haworth, *The International Labour Organisation (ILO): Coming in from the Cold* (Routledge, London and New York, 2011) chapter 4 'The Declaration on Fundamental Principles and Rights at Work: A New Approach to Labour Standards?'

Whereas, in seeking to maintain the link between social progress and economic growth, the guarantee of fundamental principles and rights at work is of particular significance in that it enables the persons concerned, to claim freely and on the basis of equality of opportunity, their fair share of the wealth which they have helped to generate, and to achieve fully their human potential;

Whereas the ILO is the constitutionally mandated international organization and the competent body to set and deal with international labour standards, and enjoys universal support and acknowledgement in promoting Fundamental Rights at Work as the expression of its constitutional principles;

Whereas it is urgent, in a situation of growing economic interdependence, to reaffirm the immutable nature of the fundamental principles and rights embodied in the Constitution of the Organization and to promote their universal application;

The rallying cry to all Members, obliging them to respect these fundamental principles whether or not they have themselves ratified the Conventions in question[9], follows. The International Labour Conference:

1. Recalls:
   (a) that in freely joining the ILO, all Members have endorsed the principles and rights set out in its Constitution and in the Declaration of Philadelphia, and have undertaken to work towards attaining the overall objectives of the Organization to the best of their resources and fully in line with their specific circumstances;
   (b) that these principles and rights have been expressed and developed in the form of specific rights and obligations in Conventions recognized as fundamental both inside and outside the Organization.
2. Declares that all Members, even if they have not ratified the Conventions in question, have an obligation arising from the very fact of membership in the Organization to respect, to promote and to realize, in good faith and in accordance with the Constitution, the principles concerning the fundamental rights which are the subject of those Conventions, namely:
   (a) freedom of association and the effective recognition of the right to collective bargaining;

---

9 [The texts of the following Conventions is available at: <www.ilo.org/dyn/normlex/en/f ?p=1000:12000:::NO:::>] Forced Labour Convention 1930 (C29) and Protocol of 2014 to the Forced Labour Convention 1930 (P29); Freedom of Association and Protection of the Right to Organise Convention 1948 (C87); Right to Organise and Collective Bargaining Convention 1949 (C98); Equal Remuneration Convention 1951 (C100); Abolition of Forced Labour Convention 1957 (C105); Discrimination (Employment and Occupation) Convention 1958 (C111); Minimum Age Convention 1973 (C138); and Worst Forms of Child Labour Convention 1999 (C182).

(b) the elimination of all forms of forced or compulsory labour;

(c) the effective abolition of child labour; and

(d) the elimination of discrimination in respect of employment and occupation.

This chapter covers the following topics:

- association and collective bargaining
- wages and working conditions
- social security
- child labour
- forced labour

This chapter traces how those fundamental principles evolved and sets out to what extent, in the ILO's own estimation, they are working.

Association and collective bargaining[10]

The second General Principle within the ILO Constitution 1919 is: "The right of association for all lawful purposes by the employed as well as by the employers".[11] Yet almost no progress was made until after World War Two.[12]

The Declaration of Philadelphia 1944[13] recognises that "freedom of expression and of association are essential to sustained progress" and that the ILO is under a "solemn obligation" to promote programmes which will achieve "the effective recognition of the right of collective bargaining, the co-operation of

---

10 For a comprehensive review of collective bargaining from an ILO perspective, compared and contrasted with Article 8 of the International Covenant on Economic, Social and Cultural Rights 1966, see Ben Saul, David Kinley and Jaqueline Mowbray, *The International Convention on Economic, Social and Cultural Rights: Commentary, Cases and Materials* (Oxford University Press, Oxford, 2014) chapter 10. See also Gerry Rodgers, Eddy Lee, Lee Swepston and Jasmien Van Daele, *The ILO and the Quest for Social Justice, 1919–2009* (ILO, Geneva, 2009) 45–53, which includes details of on the ground investigations by the ILO of threats to trade union activities in Chile (1973), Poland (1978–1990), South Africa (1992) and Colombia (2006).

11 <www.ilo.org/public/libdoc/ilo/1920/20B09_18_engl.pdf> (accessed 17 October 2020).

12 The Right of Association (Agriculture) Convention 1921 (C11) in Article 1 stated: "Each Member of the International Labour Organisation which ratifies this Convention undertakes to secure to all those engaged in agriculture the same rights of association and combination as to industrial workers, and to repeal any statutory or other provisions restricting such rights in the case of those engaged in agriculture". <www.ilo.org/dyn/normlex/en/f?p=NORM LEXPUB:12100:0::NO:12100:P12100_INSTRUMENT_ID:312156:NO> (accessed 17 October 2020). This lacked precision, and in the years following, the ILO could not secure amongst its Members a substantive definition of the right to Freedom of Association or for what "lawful purposes" such association should serve.

13 Declaration of Philadelphia 1944 <www.ilo.org/public/libdoc/ilo/1944/44B09_10_e_f .pdf> (accessed 17 October 2020). This was incorporated as an annex to the ILO Constitution as amended in 1946.

management and labour in the continuous improvement of productive efficiency, and the collaboration of workers and employers in the preparation and application of social and economic measures". [14]

Respect for fundamental civil and political rights is transcendent:

> All appropriate measures should be taken to guarantee that, irrespective of trade union affiliation, trade union rights can be exercised in normal conditions with respect for basic human rights and in a climate free of violence, pressure, fear and threats of any kind.[15]

The report of the ILO Director General to the International Labour Conference (97th session) in 2008 *Freedom of Association in practice: Lessons learned* contains the following, which encapsulates the ILO's mission:

> Promotion and realization of freedom of association and the effective recognition of the right to organize are at the heart of the ILO mandate. They are both challenges and opportunities, as they are major means of finding solutions to other issues in the world work. They are essential to human rights, democracy and the social and economic development of countries. With the support and participation of its constituents, the ILO will continue to build on the progress made so far.[16]

Organisation and non-interference

Under the Freedom of Association and Protection of the Rights to Organise Convention 1948 (C087)[17] workers and employers have the right to establish and join (subject only to the rules of the organisation concerned) organisations of their own choosing without previous authorisation. These organisations have the right to draw up their constitutions and rules, to elect representatives in full freedom, to organise their administration and activities and to formulate

---

14 Declaration of Philadelphia 1944 Article I(b) and Article III(e) <www.ilo.org/public/libdoc /ilo/1944/44B09_10_e_f.pdf> (accessed 17 October 2020).

15 *Freedom of Association: Compilation of Decisions of the Committee on Freedom of Association* (Sixth edition) (ILO, Geneva, June 2018) paras 73, 18 <www.ilo.org/wcmsp5/groups/ public/---ed_norm/---normes/documents/publication/wcms_632659.pdf> (accessed 17 October 2020).

16 *Freedom of Association in Practice: Lessons Learned*, Report of the Director-General to the 97th Session of the ILC 2008, Report I(B) xiii <www.ilo.org/wcmsp5/groups/public/-- -dgreports/---dcomm/documents/publication/wcms_096122.pdf> (accessed 17 October 2020).

17 Freedom of Association and Protection of the Rights to Organise Convention 1948 (C087) Article 2 <www.ilo.org/dyn/normlex/en/f?p=NORMLEXPUB:12100:0::NO:12100:P 12100_INSTRUMENT_ID:312232:NO> (accessed 17 October 2020).

their programmes, and there must be no interference in this from the public authorities,[18] for though the law of the land must be respected, this must not be such as to impair the guarantees provided for in the Convention.[19]

The ILO sets limits to non-interference:

> 727. Trade union organizations should not engage in political activities in an abusive manner and go beyond their true functions by promoting essentially political interests.

> 730. It is only in so far as trade union organizations do not allow their occupational demands to assume a clearly political aspect that they can legitimately claim that there should be no interference in their activities. On the other hand, it is difficult to draw a clear distinction between what is political and what is, properly speaking, trade union in character. These two notions overlap and it is inevitable, and sometimes usual, for trade union publications to take a stand on questions having political aspects, as well as on strictly economic and social questions.[20]

Collective bargaining

To the right of association is added, under a combination of the Right to Organise and Collective Bargaining Convention 1949[21] and the Collective Bargaining Convention 1981,[22] the right of collective bargaining, workers to enjoy adequate protection against acts of anti-union discrimination in respect of their employment[23] and under which workers' organisations may negotiate with employers' organisations for (a) determining working conditions and terms of employment, (b) regulating relations between employers and workers and (c) regulating relations between employers' and workers' organisations.[24]

18 C087 Article 3.
19 C087 Article 8.
20 *Freedom of Association: Compilation of Decisions of the Committee on Freedom of Association* (Sixth edition) (ILO, Geneva, June 2018) paras 727 and 730, 137 <www.ilo.org/wcmsp5/groups/public/---ed_norm/---normes/documents/publication/wcms_632659.pdf> (accessed 17 October 2020). This begs the question whether religious issues can be categorised as "social questions". The document makes no express reference to religion.
21 Right to Organise and Collective Bargaining Convention 1949 (C098) <www.ilo.org/dyn/normlex/en/f?p=NORMLEXPUB:12100:0::NO:12100:P12100_INSTRUMENT_ID:312243:NO> (accessed 17 October 2020).
22 Collective Bargaining Convention 1981 (C154) <www.ilo.org/dyn/normlex/en/f?p=NORMLEXPUB:12100:0::NO:12100:P12100_INSTRUMENT_ID:312299:NO> (accessed 17 October 2020).
23 C098 Article 1.
24 C154 Article 2.

"Collective agreements" are defined in Article II.2 of the Collective Agreements Recommendation 1951[25] as:

2.(1) For the purpose of this Recommendation, the term *collective agreements* means all agreements in writing regarding working conditions and terms of employment concluded between an employer, a group of employers or one or more employers' organisations, on the one hand, and one or more representative workers' organisations, or, in the absence of such organisations, the representatives of the workers duly elected and authorised by them in accordance with national laws and regulations, on the other.

(2) Nothing in the present definition should be interpreted as implying the recognition of any association of workers established, dominated or financed by employers or their representatives.

Discrimination

Article 1 of Convention 98 addresses anti-union discrimination:[26]

1.1. Workers shall enjoy adequate protection against acts of anti-union discrimination in respect of their employment.

1.2. Such protection shall apply more particularly in respect of acts calculated to –

(a) make the employment of a worker subject to the condition that he shall not join a union or shall relinquish trade union membership;

(b) cause the dismissal of or otherwise prejudice a worker by reason of union membership or because of participation in union activities outside working hours or, with the consent of the employer, within working hours.

At the level of individual membership, workers' representatives are to enjoy effective protection against any act prejudicial to them, including dismissal, based on their status or activities as such, in so far as they act in conformity with existing laws or collective agreements.[27] For these purposes, a workers' representative is a trade union official or other elected representative.[28]

25 Collective Agreements Recommendation 1951 (R91) <www.ilo.org/dyn/normlex/en/f ?p=NORMLEXPUB:12100:0::NO:12100:P12100_INSTRUMENT_ID:312429:NO> (accessed 17 October 2020).

26 "Anti-union discrimination is one of the most serious violations of freedom of association, as it may jeopardize the very existence of trade unions". *Freedom of Association: Compilation of Decisions of the Committee on Freedom of Association* (Sixth edition) (ILO, Geneva, June 2018) para 1072, 201 <www.ilo.org/wcmsp5/groups/public/---ed_norm/---normes/d ocuments/publication/wcms_632659.pdf> (accessed 17 October 2020).

27 Workers Representatives Convention 1971 (C135) Article 1 <www.ilo.org/dyn/normlex/e n/f?p=NORMLEXPUB:12100:0::NO:12100:P12100_INSTRUMENT_ID:312280:NO> (accessed 17 October 2020).

28 C135 Article 3.

Committee on Freedom of Association

The ILO Committee on Freedom of Association, set up in 1951, has dealt with more than 3,200 cases. Its work does not constitute a body of jurisprudence as such, its decisions form no precedents and it has no sanctioning powers. It focusses instead on promoting dialogue:

2. The CFA is composed of nine regular members and nine deputies from the Government, Workers' and Employers' groups of the [Governing Body], and has an independent Chairperson. The CFA meets three times a year and, taking into account the observations transmitted by governments, carries out an examination of the complaints lodged against them and recommends to the [Governing Body], as appropriate, that a case requires no further examination (definitive report) or that it should draw the attention of the government concerned to the problems that have been found and invite it to take the appropriate measures to resolve them (interim or follow-up reports). Finally, the CFA may be called upon to ascertain whether it would be appropriate to endeavour to obtain the agreement of the government concerned for the case to be referred to a Fact-Finding and Conciliation Commission.

3. The conclusions issued by the CFA in specific cases are intended to guide the governments and national authorities for discussion and the action to be taken to follow-up on its recommendations in the field of freedom of association and the effective recognition of the right to collective bargaining. In making its conclusions and recommendations, the CFA is guided by the principles of freedom of association and the effective recognition of the right to collective bargaining as expressed above, as well as by the long-standing experience and expertise of its members in the field of industrial relations. *The object of the CFA complaint procedure is not to blame or punish anyone, but rather to engage in a constructive tripartite dialogue to promote respect for trade union rights in law and practice.* When doing so, the CFA is cognizant of different national realities and legal systems.[29] [Emphasis added]

The right to strike

Neither the Freedom of Association and Protection of the Rights to Organise Convention 1948 nor the Right to Organise and Collective Bargaining Convention 1949 refers to the right to strike. This has not impeded the evolution within the ILO of an extensive body of principles concerning the right to strike, determining that it derives from the right of workers' organisations to pursue

29 <www.ilo.org/global/standards/subjects-covered-by-international-labour-standards/freed om-of-association/WCMS_632659/lang--en/index.htm> (accessed 17 October 2020) and see *Freedom of Association: Compilation of Decisions of the Committee on Freedom of Association* (Sixth edition) (ILO, Geneva, June 2018) <www.ilo.org/wcmsp5/groups/public/---ed_n orm/---normes/documents/publication/wcms_632659.pdf> (accessed 17 October 2020).

their own programmes of activities to defend workers' economic and social interests. The ILO's Committee of Experts on the Application of Conventions and Recommendations has referred to the right to strike as an "intrinsic corollary" of Freedom of Association[30] and as "one of the essential means available to workers and to their organizations for furthering and defending their interests".[31]

In 2012 the Employers group at the International Labour Conference challenged the existence of an international right to strike,[32] and this prompted the International Trade Union Confederation (ITUC) to prepare its report *The Right to Strike and the ILO: The legal Foundations (March 2014)*. Amongst the many national and international statutory and judicial sources quoted in the report as evidence for the right to strike, the ITUC whilst expressly not arguing that the right to strike is an absolute right under customary law called in aid CSJ as signifying universal acceptance of the proposition:

> And, whilst no argument is made that papal encyclicals are binding sources of law, the recognition of the right to strike by the Catholic Church is further evidence of the universally accepted nature of the right. In Encyclical *Rerum Novarum – On the Rights and Duties of Capital and Labour* (1891), Pope Leo XIII explained:
>
> When work people have recourse to a strike and become voluntarily idle, it is frequently because the hours of labor are too long, or the work too hard, or because they consider their wages insufficient. The grave inconvenience

---

30 ILO, *Freedom of Association and Collective Bargaining* (ILO, Geneva, 1994) para 179 <http://www.ilo.org/public/libdoc/ilo/P/09661/09661(1994-81-4B).pdf> (accessed 17 October 2020). Para 179 nevertheless recognises that the right is not unlimited: "This right is not, however, absolute and may be restricted in exceptional circumstances or even prohibited for certain categories of workers, in particular certain public servants or for essential services in the strict sense of the term, on condition that compensatory guarantees are provided for. A negotiated minimum service might be established in other services which are of public utility ("services d'utilité publique") where a total prohibition of strike action cannot be justified". Further, Article I.4 of the Voluntary Conciliation and Arbitration Recommendation 1951 (R92) states: "If a dispute has been submitted to conciliation procedure with the consent of all the parties concerned, the latter should be encouraged to abstain from strikes and lockouts while conciliation is in progress". <www.ilo.org/dyn/normlex/en/f?p=NORMLEXPUB:12100:0::NO:12100:P12100_INSTRUMENT_ID:312430:NO> (accessed 17 October 2020). For further substantive restrictions on strike action in ILO practice, relating to emergencies, essential services, minimum operational services, and armed forces, police and state administration, see Ben Saul, David Kinley and Jaqueline Mowbray, *The International Convention on Economic, Social and Cultural Rights: Commentary, Cases and Materials* (Oxford University Press, Oxford, 2014) 584–588 and 595–597.

31 ILO, *Freedom of Association and Collective Bargaining* (ILO, Geneva, 1994) para 152 <http://www.ilo.org/public/libdoc/ilo/P/09661/09661(1994-81-4B).pdf> (accessed 17 October 2020).

32 Record of Proceedings of the 101st Session of the ILC 2012. Addresses by Daniel Funes de Rioja as Chairperson of the Employers' Group with a response from Luc Cortebeeck as Chairperson of the Workers' Group 7/6 to 7/9 <www.ilo.org/public/libdoc/ilo/P/09616/09616(2012-101).pdf> (accessed 17 October 2020).

of this not uncommon occurrence should be obviated by public remedial measures [...] The laws should forestall and prevent such troubles from arising; they should lend their influence and authority to the removal in good time of the causes which lead to conflicts between employers and employed.

Nearly 100 years later, John Paul II, in *Laborem Exercens* (1981), Section 20 "The Importance of Unions", explained:

> *One method* used by unions in pursuing the just rights of their members is *the strike* or work stoppage, as a kind of ultimatum to the competent bodies, especially the employers. This method is recognized by Catholic social teaching as legitimate in the proper conditions and within just limits. In this connection workers should be assured the *right to strike*, without being subjected to personal penal sanctions for taking part in a strike.[33]

Wages and working conditions[34]

Adequate living wage

The economic feasibility or even the appropriateness in a free market economy of an adequate living wage remains the subject of general debate in the early 21st century. Yet the phrase "the provision of an adequate living wage" has a long pedigree, included within Section I (Preamble) of the ILO Constitution in its original form in 1919 (Part XIII of the Treaty of Versailles).[35]

The Declaration of Philadelphia 1944[36] concerning the aims and purposes of the ILO reaffirmed this:

III. The Conference recognises the solemn obligation of the International Labour Organisation to further among the nations of the world programmes which will achieve:

[...]

(d) policies in regard to wages and earnings, hours and other conditions of work calculated to ensure a just share of the fruits of progress to all, and a minimum living wage to all employed and in need of such protection.

---

33 *The Right to Strike and the ILO: The Legal Foundations* (International Trade Union Confederation, March 2014) 94–95 <www.ituc-csi.org/IMG/pdf/ituc_final_brief_on_the_right_to_strike.pdf> (accessed 17 October 2020).
34 For a comprehensive review of just and favourable conditions of work from an ILO perspective, compared and contrasted with Article 7 of the International Covenant on Economic, Social and Cultural Rights 1966 see Ben Saul, David Kinley and Jaqueline Mowbray, *The International Convention on Economic, Social and Cultural Rights: Commentary, Cases and Materials* (Oxford University Press, Oxford, 2014) chapter 9.
35 Treaty of Versailles 1919, Part XIII <www.ilo.org/public/libdoc/ilo/1920/20B09_18_engl.pdf> (accessed 17 October 2020).
36 Declaration of Philadelphia 1944 <www.ilo.org/public/libdoc/ilo/1944/44B09_10_e_f.pdf> (accessed 17 October 2020).

The ILO's first steps regarding wages had nothing to do with their adequacy, but with protecting the worker from being paid merely in kind or in the form of promissory notes or coupons, from being paid at irregular intervals and from unwarranted deductions from whatever wage he earned, and from being forced to dispense his wages at his employer's behest in his employer's stores. Workers' wages were to be treated as preferred creditors on any insolvency[37] of the employer.[38]

Payment in kind was recognised as being standard practice in some industries, but only sanctioned when and if partially contributing to a wage. "The payment of wages in the form of liquor of high alcoholic content or of noxious drugs shall not be permitted in any circumstances". Payment was first and foremost to be in legal tender.[39]

Equal pay

Equal remuneration for men and women workers, for work of equal value, was first found in Article 427 of the Treaty of Versailles 1919, as the seventh General Principle: "The principle that men and women should receive equal remuneration for work of equal value".

Nevertheless, Although the new Organization did adopt progressive ideas such as equal remuneration for work of equal value, its first standards in this area were highly protective and followed the temper of the times in assigning women a secondary role in the economy – conferring international legitimacy on women's economic straitjacket that it took decades to unfasten.[40]

World War Two was the accelerator. Article II(a) of the Declaration of Philadelphia 1944[41] states:

> Believing that experience has full demonstrated the truth of the statement in the Constitution of the International Labour Organisation that lasting peace can be established only if it is based on social justice, the Conference affirms that:

37 As expanded upon in Protection of Workers' Claims (Employer's Insolvency) Convention 1992 (C173) <www.ilo.org/dyn/normlex/en/f?p=NORMLEXPUB:12100:0::NO:12100 :P12100_INSTRUMENT_ID:312318:NO> (accessed 17 October 2020).

38 Protection of Wages Convention 1949 (C95) <www.ilo.org/dyn/normlex/en/f?p=NORM LEXPUB:12100:0::NO:12100:P12100_INSTRUMENT_ID:312240:NO> (accessed 17 October 2020).

39 Protection of Wages Convention 1949 (C095) <www.ilo.org/dyn/normlex/en/f?p =NORMLEXPUB:12100:0::NO:12100:P12100_INSTRUMENT_ID:312240:NO> (accessed 17 October 2020).

40 Gerry Rodgers, Eddy Lee, Lee Swepston and Jasmien Van Daele, *The ILO and the Quest for Social Justice, 1919–2009* (ILO, Geneva, 2009) 57.

41 Declaration of Philadelphia 1944, Article II(a) <www.ilo.org/public/libdoc/ilo/1944/ 44B09_10_e_f.pdf> (accessed 17 October 2020).

(a) all human beings, irrespective or race, creed or sex, have the right to pursue both their material well-being and their spiritual development in conditions of freedom and dignity, of economic security and equal opportunity.

The seventh General Principle was eventually given full force in the Equal Remuneration Convention 1951:[42]

Article 1
For the purpose of this Convention--

(a) the term **remuneration** includes the ordinary, basic or minimum wage or salary and any additional emoluments whatsoever payable directly or indirectly, whether in cash or in kind, by the employer to the worker and arising out of the worker's employment;
(b) the term **equal remuneration for men and women workers for work of equal value** refers to rates of remuneration established without discrimination based on sex.

Article 2

1. Each Member shall, by means appropriate to the methods in operation for determining rates of remuneration, promote and, in so far as is consistent with such methods, ensure the application to all workers of the principle of equal remuneration for men and women workers for work of equal value.
2. This principle may be applied by means of –

   (a) national laws or regulations;
   (b) legally established or recognised machinery for wage determination;
   (c) collective agreements between employers and workers; or
   (d) a combination of these various means.

"Women had been on the front line of production during the war in many countries, and the myth that they could not do certain jobs or were not as productive as men could no longer be sustained".[43]

42 Equal Remuneration Convention 1951 (C100) <www.ilo.org/dyn/normlex/en/f?p =NORMLEXPUB:12100:0::NO:12100:P12100_INSTRUMENT_ID:312245:NO> (accessed 17 October 2020).
43 *Giving Globalization a Human Face,* International Labour Conference (101st Session) Report III9IB (Geneva, 2012) 272 <www.ilo.org/wcmsp5/groups/public/---ed_norm/---relconf/documents/meetingdocument/wcms_174846.pdf> (accessed 17 October 2020).

Minimum wage

The concept of a minimum wage was first addressed in the Minimum Wage-Fixing Machinery Convention 1926,[44] the recommended criteria for determining the minimum wage being:

> For the purpose of determining the minimum rates of wages to be fixed, the wage-fixing body should in any case take account of the necessity of enabling the workers concerned to maintain a suitable standard of living. For this purpose regard should primarily be had to the rates of wages being paid for similar work in trades where the workers are adequately organised and have concluded effective collective agreements, or, if no such standard of reference is available in the circumstances, to the general level of wages prevailing in the country or in the particular locality.[45]

In the Minimum Wage Fixing Convention 1970 the concept of a minimum wage was further developed.[46] Minimum wages were to have the force of law and not be subject to abatement, and the elements of a minimum wage to be the needs of workers and their families taking into account the general level of wages and benefits in the country, and economic factors including the requirements of economic development.[47]

The 79th Session of the International Labour Conference in 1992 provided the definition of "minimum wage":

> Minimum wage may be understood to mean the minimum sum payable to a worker for work performed or services rendered, within a given period, whether calculated on the basis of time or output, which may not be reduced either by individual or collective agreement, which is guaranteed by law and which may be fixed in such a way as to cover the minimum needs of the worker and his or her family, in the light of national economic and social conditions.[48]

---

44 Minimum Wage-Fixing Machinery Convention 1926 (C30) <www.ilo.org/dyn/normlex/en/f?p=NORMLEXPUB:12100:0::NO:12100:P12100_INSTRUMENT_ID:312171:NO> (accessed 17 October 2020). The position of workers in agriculture was addressed specifically in the Minimum Wage Fixing Machinery (Agriculture) Convention 1951 (C99) <www.ilo.org/dyn/normlex/en/f?p=NORMLEXPUB:12100:0::NO:12100:P12100_INSTRUMENT_ID:312244:NO> (accessed 17 October 2020).

45 Minimum Wage-Fixing Machinery Recommendation 1928 Paragraph III (R30) <www.ilo.org/dyn/normlex/en/f?p=NORMLEXPUB:12100:0::NO:12100:P12100_INSTRUMENT_ID:312368:NO> (accessed 17 October 2020).

46 Minimum Wage Fixing Convention 1970 (C131) <www.ilo.org/dyn/normlex/en/f?p=NORMLEXPUB:12100:0::NO:12100:P12100_INSTRUMENT_ID:312276:NO> (accessed 17 October 2020).

47 C131 Articles 2.1 and 3.

48 Minimum Wages: Wage-Fixing Machinery, Application and Supervision, Report III (Part 4B), International Labour Conference, 79th Session 1992 <www.ilo.org/public/libdoc/ilo/P/09661/09661%281992-79-4B%29.pdf> (accessed 17 October 2020).

Discrimination

The Discrimination (Employment and Occupation) Convention 1958 (C111)[49] (one of the ILO's fundamental principles) expanded the range of Convention 100 beyond remuneration by introducing a comprehensive definition of "discrimination":

> Article 1.1. For the purpose of this Convention the term *discrimination* includes –
>
> (a) any distinction, exclusion or preference made on the basis of race, colour, sex, religion, political opinion, national extraction or social origin, which has the effect of nullifying or impairing equality of opportunity or treatment in employment or occupation;
> (b) such other distinction, exclusion or preference which has the effect of nullifying or impairing equality of opportunity or treatment in employment or occupation as may be determined by the Member concerned after consultation with representative employers' and workers' organisations, where such exist, and with other appropriate bodies.

Working conditions: scope

The stated aim of the ILO is

> to create worldwide awareness of the dimensions and consequences of work-related accidents, injuries and diseases and to place the health and safety of all workers on the international agenda to stimulate and support practical action at all levels.[50]

According to ILO estimates, a worker dies from a work-related accident or disease every 15 seconds. Every day, some 6,300 workers die from occupational accidents or work-related diseases, amounting to more than 2.3 million deaths a year. Furthermore, over 313 million workers suffer non-fatal occupational injuries each year, or in other words 860,000 people are injured on the job every day. In addition to the tremendous human cost, estimates have identified the significant economic impact of inadequate occupational safety and health: 4 per cent of total global gross domestic product is lost annually (equivalent to US$2.8 trillion) by costs related to lost working time,

---

49 Discrimination (Employment and Occupation) Convention 1958 (C111) <www.ilo.org/dyn/normlex/en/f?p=NORMLEXPUB:12100:0::NO:12100:P12100_INSTRUMENT_ID:312256:NO> (accessed 17 October 2020).
50 ILO Topics: Safety and Health at Work <www.ilo.org/global/topics/safety-and-health-at-work/lang--en/index.htm> (accessed 17 October 2020). The ILO database on occupational safety and health is at: <www.ilo.org/inform/online-information-resources/databases/osh/lang--en/index.htm> (17 October 2020).

interruptions in production, treatment of occupational injuries and diseases, rehabilitation and compensation.[51]

Working environment

In assessing working conditions the ILO has concerned itself both with the working environment and the nature of the work itself. Environmental awareness began in 1960 and evolved ever greater specificity as health and safety awareness developed:

Convention	Number	Web reference (accessed 11 October 2020)
Radiation Protection Convention 1960	C115	www.ilo.org/dyn/normlex/en/f?p=NORM LEXPUB:12100:0::NO:12100:P12100 INSTRUMENT_ID:312260:NO
Hygiene (Commerce and Offices) Convention 1964	C120	www.ilo.org/dyn/normlex/en/f?p=NORM LEXPUB:12100:0::NO:12100:P12100 _INSTRUMENT_ID:312265:NO
Occupational Cancer Convention 1974	C139	www.ilo.org/dyn/normlex/en/f?p=NORM LEXPUB:12100:0::NO:12100:P12100 _INSTRUMENT_ID:312284:NO
Working Environment (Air pollution, Noise and Vibration) Convention 1977	C148	www.ilo.org/dyn/normlex/en/f?p=NORM LEXPUB:12100:0::NO:12100:P12100 _INSTRUMENT_ID:312293:NO
Occupational Safety and Health Convention 1981	C155	www.ilo.org/dyn/normlex/en/f?p=NORM LEXPUB:12100:0::NO:12100:P12100 _INSTRUMENT_ID:312300:NO
Protocol of 2002 to the Occupational Safety and Health Convention	P155	www.ilo.org/dyn/normlex/en/f?p=NORM LEXPUB:12100:0::NO:12100:P12100 _INSTRUMENT_ID:312338:NO
Occupational Health Services Convention 1985	C161	www.ilo.org/dyn/normlex/en/f?p=NORM LEXPUB:12100:0::NO:12100:P12100 _INSTRUMENT_ID:312306:NO
Asbestos Convention 1986	C162	www.ilo.org/dyn/normlex/en/f?p=NORM LEXPUB:12100:0::NO:12100:P12100 _INSTRUMENT_ID:312307:NO
Safety and Health in Construction Convention 1988	C167	www.ilo.org/dyn/normlex/en/f?p=NORM LEXPUB:12100:0::NO:12100:P12100 _INSTRUMENT_ID:312312:NO
Chemicals Convention 1990 (	C170	www.ilo.org/dyn/normlex/en/f?p=NORM LEXPUB:12100:0::NO:12100:P12100 _INSTRUMENT_ID:312315:NO

(Continued)

---

51 *Working Together to Promote a Safe and Healthy Working Environment*, International Labour Conference (106th session) Report III (Part 1B) 2 (Geneva, 2017) <www.ilo.org/wcmsp5 /groups/public/---ed_norm/---relconf/documents/meetingdocument/wcms_543647 .pdf> (accessed 17 October 2020).

Convention	Number	Web reference (accessed 11 October 2020)
Prevention of Major Industrial Accidents Convention 1993	C174	www.ilo.org/dyn/normlex/en/f?p=NORM LEXPUB:12100:0::NO:12100:P12100 _INSTRUMENT_ID:312319:NO
Health and Safety in Mines Convention 1995	C176	www.ilo.org/dyn/normlex/en/f?p=NORM LEXPUB:12100:0::NO:12100:P12100 _INSTRUMENT_ID:312321:NO
Safety and Health in Agriculture Convention 2001	C184	www.ilo.org/dyn/normlex/en/f?p=NORM LEXPUB:12100:0::NO:12100:P12100 _INSTRUMENT_ID:312329:NO
Promotional Framework for Occupational Safety and Health Convention 2006	C187	www.ilo.org/dyn/normlex/en/f?p=NORM LEXPUB:12100:0::NO:12100:P12100 _INSTRUMENT_ID:312332:NO

Vocational training

The need to promote development by means of vocational guidance and vocational training (by methods that are appropriate to national conditions rather than setting a global norm) had been recognised in the Human Resources Development Convention 1975.[52]

Violence and harassment

The 108th (Centenary) Session of the International Labour Conference in June 2019 adopted the Violence and Harassment Convention 2019 (C190),[53] a composite reconfiguring of other international human rights instruments concerned with civil, political, economic, social and cultural rights in general and racism, discrimination against women, protection of migrant workers and protection of persons with disabilities in particular.

The Preamble to the Convention recognises "that violence and harassment in the world of work can constitute a human rights violation or abuse, and that violence and harassment is a threat to equal opportunities, is unacceptable and incompatible with decent work" and "the importance of a work culture based on mutual respect and dignity of the human being to prevent violence and harassment". It recalls

52 Human Resources Development Convention 1975 (C142) <www.ilo.org/dyn/normlex/en/f?p=NORMLEXPUB:12100:0::NO:12100:P12100_INSTRUMENT_ID:312287:NO> (accessed 17 October 2020).
53 Violence and Harassment Convention 2019 (C190) <www.ilo.org/dyn/normlex/en/f?p=NORMLEXPUB:12100:0::NO:12100:P12100_INSTRUMENT_ID:3999810:NO> (accessed 17 October 2020).

that Members have an important responsibility to promote a general environ-ment of zero tolerance to violence and harassment in order to facilitate the prevention of such behaviours and practices, and that all actors in the world of work must refrain from, prevent and address violence and harassment.

"Violence and harassment" is defined in Article 1.1(a) as referring to "a range of unac-ceptable behaviours and practices, or threats thereof, whether a single occurrence or repeated, that aim at, result in, or are likely to result in physical, psychological, sexual or economic harm, and includes gender-based violence and harassment" and the meaning of "gender-based violence and harassment" in Article 1.1(b) is "violence and harassment directed at persons because of their sex or gender, or affecting per-sons of a particular sex or gender disproportionately, and includes sexual harassment."

What for the purposes of violence and harassment constitutes the scope of worker, workplace and working conditions in the second decade of the 21st century is immensely (though, it can be argued, justifiably) broad, as set out in Articles 2 and 3:

Article 2

1. This Convention protects workers and other persons in the world of work, including employees as defined by national law and practice, as well as persons working irrespective of their contractual status, persons in training, including interns and apprentices, workers whose employment has been terminated, volunteers, jobseekers and job applicants, and indi-viduals exercising the authority, duties or responsibilities of an employer.
2. This Convention applies to all sectors, whether private or public, both in the formal and informal economy, and whether in urban or rural areas.

Article 3

This Convention applies to violence and harassment in the world of work occurring in the course of, linked with or arising out of work:

(a) in the workplace, including public and private spaces where they are a place of work;
(b) in places where the worker is paid, takes a rest break or a meal, or uses sanitary, washing and changing facilities;
(c) during work-related trips, travel, training, events or social activities;
(d) through work-related communications, including those enabled by information and communication technologies;
(e) in employer-provided accommodation; and
(f) when commuting to and from work.

The implementation strategy is national-based. "Each Member which ratifies this Convention shall respect, promote and realize the right of everyone to a world of work free from violence and harassment". (Article 4.1), the provisions of the Convention to be applied by means of national laws and regulations, as well as through collective agreements or other measures consistent with national practice, including by extending or adapting existing occupational safety and health measures to cover violence and harassment and developing specific measures where necessary. (Article 12)

Social security[54]

The years 1919 to 1944

From its inception the ILO has had as a fundamental object the right to social security.[55] "By creating a 'social shield' against economic insecurity and hardship through the redistribution of income, social security has, from the beginning, been an essential part of the road to social justice for the ILO".[56] The ILO Constitution in its original form in 1919 (Part XIII of the Treaty of Versailles)[57] included within Section I:

> And whereas conditions of labour exist involving such injustice, hardship and privation to large numbers of people as to produce unrest so great that the peace and harmony of the world are imperilled; and an improvement of those conditions is urgently required: as, for example, by the regulation of the hours of work, including the establishment of a maximum working day and week, the regulation of the labour supply, the prevention of unemployment, the provision of an adequate living wage, the protection of the worker against sickness, disease and injury arising out of his employment, the protection of children, young persons and women, provision for old age and injury

By 1935, 15 Conventions relating to social security had been adopted covering the following social risks: sickness and medical care, unemployment, old age benefits, workers' compensation, invalidity, survivors and the pension rights of migrants:

---

54 For a comprehensive review of the right to social security from an ILO perspective, compared and contrasted with Article 9 of the International Covenant on Economic, Social and Cultural Rights 1966 see Ben Saul, David Kinley and Jaqueline Mowbray, *The International Convention on Economic, Social and Cultural Rights: Commentary, Cases and Materials* (Oxford University Press, Oxford, 2014) chapter 11. And see Gerry Rodgers, Eddy Lee, Lee Swepston and Jasmien Van Daele, *The ILO and the Quest for Social Justice, 1919–2009* (ILO, Geneva, 2009) chapter 4 'Social Protection'. The ILO Social Security database is at: <www.ilo.org/inform/online-information-resources/databases/social-security/lang--en/index.htm >(accessed 17 October 2020).

55 The ILO Social Protection Department provides ILO Member States with tools and assistance to achieve and maintain the human right to social protection. <www.ilo.org/secsoc/lang--en/index.htm> (accessed 17 October 2020).

56 Gerry Rodgers, Eddy Lee, Lee Swepston and Jasmien Van Daele, *The ILO and the Quest for Social Justice, 1919–2009* (ILO, Geneva, 2009) 140.

57 Treaty of Versailles 1919, Part XIII <www.ilo.org/public/libdoc/ilo/1920/20B09_18_e ngl.pdf> (accessed 17 October 2020).

Convention	Number	Web reference (accessed 11 October 2020)
Workmen's Compensation (Agriculture) Convention 1921	C12	www.ilo.org/dyn/normlex/en/f?p=NORMLEXPUB:12100:0::NO:12100:P12100_INSTRUMENT_ID:312157:NO
Workmen's Compensation (Accidents) Convention 1925	C17	www.ilo.org/dyn/normlex/en/f?p=NORMLEXPUB:12100:0::NO:12100:P12100_INSTRUMENT_ID:312162:NO
Workmen's Compensation (Occupational Diseases) Convention 1925	C18	www.ilo.org/dyn/normlex/en/f?p=NORMLEXPUB:12100:0::NO:12100:P12100_INSTRUMENT_ID:312163:NO
Equality of Treatment (Accident Compensation) Convention 1925	C19	www.ilo.org/dyn/normlex/en/f?p=NORMLEXPUB:12100:0::NO:12100:P12100_INSTRUMENT_ID:312164:NO
Sickness Insurance (Industry) Convention 1927	C24	www.ilo.org/dyn/normlex/en/f?p=NORMLEXPUB:12100:0::NO:12100:P12100_INSTRUMENT_ID:312169:NO
Sickness Insurance (Agriculture) Convention 1925	C25	www.ilo.org/dyn/normlex/en/f?p=NORMLEXPUB:12100:0::NO:12100:P12100_INSTRUMENT_ID:312170:NO
Old-Age Insurance (Industry, etc.) Convention 1933	C35	www.ilo.org/dyn/normlex/en/f?p=NORMLEXPUB:12100:0::NO:12100:P12100_INSTRUMENT_ID:312180:NO
Old-Age Insurance (Agriculture) Convention 1933	C36	www.ilo.org/dyn/normlex/en/f?p=NORMLEXPUB:12100:0::NO:12100:P12100_INSTRUMENT_ID:312181:NO
Invalidity Insurance (Industry, etc.) Convention 1933	C37	www.ilo.org/dyn/normlex/en/f?p=NORMLEXPUB:12100:0::NO:12100:P12100_INSTRUMENT_ID:312182:NO
Invalidity Insurance (Agriculture) Convention 1933	C38	www.ilo.org/dyn/normlex/en/f?p=NORMLEXPUB:12100:0::NO:12100:P12100_INSTRUMENT_ID:312183:NO
Survivors' Insurance (Industry, etc.) Convention 1933	C39	www.ilo.org/dyn/normlex/en/f?p=NORMLEXPUB:12100:0::NO:12100:P12100_INSTRUMENT_ID:312184:NO
Survivors' Insurance (Agriculture) Convention 1933	C40	www.ilo.org/dyn/normlex/en/f?p=NORMLEXPUB:12100:0::NO:12100:P12100_INSTRUMENT_ID:312185:NO
Workingmen's Compensation (Occupational Diseases) Convention (Revised) 1934	C42	www.ilo.org/dyn/normlex/en/f?p=NORMLEXPUB:12100:0::NO:12100:P12100_INSTRUMENT_ID:312187:NO
Unemployment Provisions Convention 1934	C44	www.ilo.org/dyn/normlex/en/f?p=NORMLEXPUB:12100:0::NO:12100:P12100_INSTRUMENT_ID:312189:NO
Maintenance of Migrants' Pension Rights Convention 1935	C48	www.ilo.org/dyn/normlex/en/f?p=NORMLEXPUB:12100:0::NO:12100:P12100_INSTRUMENT_ID:312193:NO

These prefigured by over a decade the Universal Declaration of Human Rights 1948, which in Article 25 includes (though only in very general terms) a right to social security.[58]

Measures taken in 1944

As with other areas of concern to the ILO, World War Two was the catalyst.

> A few years ago social security was little more than a slogan, a bare outline of an idea; today the slogan stands for a wide-visioned, constructive programme; and tomorrow the programme will have become an accomplished fact if humanity remains free and follows the road of progress. [...] Social insurance can and must remain an institution for civic education, the image and instrument of democracy in action.[59]

The Declaration of Philadelphia 1944[60] reaffirmed the importance of social security provision

I. The Conference reaffirms the fundamental principles on which the organisation is based and, in particular, that:
    [...]
(d) the war against want requires to be carried on with unrelenting vigour within each nation, and by continuous and concerted international effort in which the representatives of workers and employers, enjoying equal status with those of Governments, join with them in free discussion and democratic decision with a view to the promotion of the common welfare.

III. The Conference recognises the solemn obligation of the International Labour Organisation to further among the nations of the world programmes which will achieve:
    [...]
(f) the extension of social security measures to provide a basic income to all in need of such protection and comprehensive medical care;

---

58 Universal Declaration of Human Rights 1948 Article 25 www.un.org/en/universal-declaration-human-rights/ (accessed 17 October 2020): Article 25. (1) Everyone has the right to a standard of living adequate for the health and well-being of himself and of his family, including food, clothing, housing and medical care and necessary social services, and the right to security in the event of unemployment, sickness, disability, widowhood, old age or other lack of livelihood in circumstances beyond his control.

59 Oswald Stein, Head of the ILO Social Insurance Department, 'Building Social Security' in *International Labour Review* Vol. 44, No. 3 (ILO, Geneva, 1941) 248, 274.

60 Declaration of Philadelphia 1944 <www.ilo.org/public/libdoc/ilo/1944/44B09_10_e_f .pdf> (accessed 17 October 2020).

The ILO Income Security Recommendation 1944 (R67)[61] in its General Principles unambiguously endorsed the compulsory nature of social security:

1. Income security schemes should relieve want and prevent destitution by restoring, up to a reasonable level, income which is lost by reason of inability to work (including old age) or to obtain remunerative work or by reason of the death of a breadwinner.
2. Income security should be organised as far as possible on the basis of compulsory social insurance, whereby insured persons fulfilling prescribed qualifying conditions are entitled, in consideration of the contributions they have paid to an insurance institution, to benefits payable at rates, and in contingencies, defined by law.

In doing so it reflected a period of profound social change, from pre-War ideas of welfare (rooted in religious and charitable initiatives) to post-War assertions of legal rights – often human rights – and obligations.[62]

Social Security (Minimum Standards) Convention 1952 (C102)

The principal ILO Convention in the field of social security is the Social Security (Minimum Standards) Convention 1952 (C102).[63] The benefits are a combination of periodic payments and medical care, and may be limited in time and subject to the claimant having satisfied contribution requirements over a given period (and in certain cases to the claimant making a contribution towards the cost). There are nine defined areas:[64] *medical care* (including morbid conditions,

---

61 Income Security Recommendation 1944 (R67) <www.ilo.org/dyn/normlex/en/f?p =NORMLEXPUB:12100:0::NO:12100:P12100_INSTRUMENT_ID:312405:NO> (accessed 17 October 2020). And see also the Medical Care Recommendation 1944 (R69) <www.ilo.org/dyn/normlex/en/f?p=NORMLEXPUB:12100:0::NO:12100:P12100 _INSTRUMENT_ID:312407:NO> (accessed 17 October 2020).
62 Ben Saul, David Kinley and Jacqueline Mowbray, *The International Convention on Economic, Social and Cultural Rights: Commentary, Cases and Materials* (Oxford University Press, Oxford, 2014) 610–611.
63 Social Security (Minimum Standards) Convention 1952 (C102) <www.ilo.org/dyn/norm lex/en/f?p=NORMLEXPUB:12100:0::NO:12100:P12100_INSTRUMENT_ID:312247 :NO> (accessed 17 October 2020).
64 Though member States need only comply with three, which must include at least one of unemployment benefit, old-age benefit, employment injury benefit, invalidity benefit or survivors' benefit (C102 Article 2(a)(ii)). This was "a standard which is not so low that it represents no advance at all and not so high that it is really impossible of attainment by a majority of countries […] [the] text was about right, as steering between the extremes of unrealism on the one hand and inadequacy on the other". (ILO: Record of Proceedings of the 35th Session of the ILC 1952 318 – statement by Mr Dennys, Government Advisor, United Kingdom <www.ilo.org/public/libdoc/ilo/P/09616/09616(1952-35).pdf> (accessed 17 October 2020).

pregnancy and confinement,[65] *sickness benefit* (incapacity for work resulting from a morbid condition and involving suspension of earnings),[66] *unemployment benefit* (suspension of earnings due to inability to obtain suitable employment in the case of a person capable of and available for work),[67] *old-age benefit* (survival beyond a prescribed age),[68] *employment injury benefit* (a morbid condition, incapacity for work, total loss of earning capacity, loss of support suffered by widow or child),[69] *family benefit* (responsibility for the maintenance of children),[70] *maternity benefit* (pregnancy and confinement and their consequences, and suspension of earnings),[71] *invalidity benefit* (inability to engage in any gainful activity, which inability is likely to be permanent or persists after the exhaustion of sickness benefit)[72] and *survivors' benefit* (the loss of support suffered by the widow or child as the result of the death of the breadwinner, potentially limited to widows incapable of self-support).[73] The Convention (Articles 65 to 67) links the level of benefits to a percentage of between 40% and 50% of the former earnings of specified workers.

These minimum standards are to be applied by a Member to the nationals of any other Member within its territory to guarantee equality of treatment.[74] To ensure continuity of benefits, and that contributions and time periods made and complied with in the territory of one Member count towards benefit entitlement in the territory of another Member to which the worker may have moved,

---

65 C102 Article 8 as expanded upon in the Medical Care and Sickness Benefits Convention 1969 (C130) <www.ilo.org/dyn/normlex/en/f?p=NORMLEXPUB:12100:0::NO:12100 :P12100_INSTRUMENT_ID:312275:NO> (accessed 17 October 2020).

66 C102 Article 14 as expanded upon in C130 and the Employment Promotion and Protection against Unemployment Convention 1988 (C168) <www.ilo.org/dyn/normlex/e n/f?p=NORMLEXPUB:12100:0::NO:12100:P12100_INSTRUMENT_ID:312313:NO> (accessed 17 October 2020).

67 C102 Article 20.

68 C102 Article 26.1 as expanded upon in the Invalidity, Old-Age and Survivors' Benefits Convention 1967(C128) <www.ilo.org/dyn/normlex/en/f?p=NORMLEXPUB:12100 :0::NO:12100:P12100_INSTRUMENT_ID:312273:NO> (accessed 17 October 2020).

69 C102 Article 32, as expanded upon in the Employment Injury Benefits Convention 1964 (as amended) (C121) <www.ilo.org/dyn/normlex/en/f?p=NORMLEXPUB:12100:0:: NO:12100:P12100_INSTRUMENT_ID:312266:NO> (accessed 17 October 2020).

70 C102 Article 40.

71 C102 Article 47, as further articulated in the Maternity Protection Convention (Revised) 1952 (C103) <www.ilo.org/dyn/normlex/en/f?p=NORMLEXPUB:12100:0::NO:12100 :P12100_INSTRUMENT_ID:312248:NO> (accessed 17 October 2020), itself further revised in the Maternity Protection Convention 2000 (C183) <www.ilo.org/dyn/norm lex/en/f?p=NORMLEXPUB:12100:0::NO:12100:P12100_INSTRUMENT_ID:312328 :NO> (accessed 17 October 2020).

72 C102 Article 54, as expanded upon in C128.

73 C102 Article 60, as expanded upon in C128.

74 Equality of Treatment (Social Security) Convention 1962 (C118) Article 3 <www.ilo.org /dyn/normlex/en/f?p=NORMLEXPUB:12100:0::NO:12100:P12100_INSTRUMENT _ID:312263:NO> (accessed 17 October 2020).

the Maintenance of Social Security Rights Convention 1982 (C157)[75] sets out the structure of an international system for the maintenance of rights in social security.

In its Conclusions, the Report of the Committee on Social Security to the 89th Session of the International Labour Conference in 2001 states:

2. Social security is very important for the well-being of workers, their families and the entire community. It is a basic human right and a fundamental means for creating social cohesion, thereby helping to ensure social peace and social inclusion. It is an indispensable part of government social policy and an important tool to prevent and alleviate poverty. It can, through national solidarity and fair burden sharing, contribute to human dignity, equity and social justice. It is also important for political inclusion, empowerment and the development of democracy.

3. Social security, if properly managed, enhances productivity by providing health care, income security and social services. In conjunction with a growing economy and active labour market policies, it is an instrument for sustainable social and economic development. It facilitates structural and technological changes which require an adaptable and mobile labour force. It is noted that while social security is a cost for enterprises, it is also an investment in, or support for, people. With globalization and structural adjustment policies, social security becomes more necessary than ever.[76]

Rights-based approach

In Report VI *Social Security for Social Justice and Fair Globalization* presented to the 100th Session of the International Labour Conference in 2011, the ILO affirmed its rights-based approach to social security:

24. The universal need for social security has been recognized by the world community as a human right. Since the ILO was first set up in 1919, pursuing the achievement of social security has consistently been at the core of its mandate. The Organization's approach to social security reflects both the status of social security in international law and its own constitutional mandate. The approach is rights-based: i.e. in order to realize the right to social security, the ILO uses international legal instruments as the starting point, the main reference and the legal basis for the recognition of the existence of

75 Maintenance of Social Security Rights Convention 1982 (C157) <www.ilo.org/dyn/norm lex/en/f?p=NORMLEXPUB:12100:0::NO:12100:P12100_INSTRUMENT_ID:312302 :NO> (accessed 17 October 2020).
76 Report of the Committee on Social Security to the 89th Session of the International Labour Conference 2001 <www.ilo.org/public/english/standards/relm/ilc/ilc89/pdf/pr-16.pdf > 16/33 (accessed 17 October 2020).

this right, and seeks to anchor all assistance and policy advice in international social security standards.[77]

Report VI highlights that the ILO approach to human rights avoids the pitfall of abstraction and generalisation which so often undermines the implementation of human rights instruments:

> 435. While providing for the right to social security, the international human rights instruments and their supervisory mechanisms have remained mostly silent on the definition and specific content of this right. In the absence of such definition and given the ILO's mandate, it has been left to the ILO to establish the parameters and substantive provisions of the right to social security. In this respect, ILO social security standards, and more particularly Convention No. 102, have constituted the main reference for the interpretation and definition of this right, while providing guidance for its implementation in a very detailed way. As mentioned previously, they have always been regarded as playing a key role by providing substantive content to the right to social security; [...]

> 436. Moreover, international experience shows that the ILO social security Conventions, and particularly Convention No. 102, are a means of preventing the levelling-down of social security systems worldwide, as they constitute benchmarks to assess whether their requirements have been met and contribute to the creation of a level playing-field for social conditions across the world.

> 438. Convention No. 102, the ILO's flagship Convention on social security, embodies an internationally accepted definition of the principles of social security and has been recognized as a symbol of social progress. It plays a key role in defining the right to social security under international human rights instruments.[78]

Social protection floors

The Preamble to the Social Protection Floors Recommendation 2012 (R202)[79] reaffirms the importance of those ILO measures adopted seven decades earlier:

> Considering also ILO social security standards, in particular the Social Security (Minimum Standards) Convention, 1952 (No. 102), the Income Security

---

77 Report VI, *Social Security for Social Justice and Fair Globalization*, Presented to the 100th Session of the International Labour Conference 2011 para 24 <www.social-protection.org/gimi/gess/ShowWiki.action?wiki.wikiId=827> (accessed 17 October 2020).
78 Report VI, *Social Security for Social Justice and Fair Globalization*, Presented to the 100th Session of the International Labour Conference 2011 paras 435, 436, 438 <www.social-protection.org/gimi/gess/ShowWiki.action?wiki.wikiId=827> (accessed 17 October 2020).
79 Social Protection Floors Recommendation 2012 (R202) <www.ilo.org/dyn/normlex/en/f?p=NORMLEXPUB:12100:0::NO::P12100_INSTRUMENT_ID:3065524> (accessed 17 October 2020).

Recommendation, 1944 (No. 67), and the Medical Care Recommendation, 1944 (No. 69), and noting that these standards are of continuing relevance and continue to be important references for social security systems, and

Recalling that the ILO Declaration on Social Justice for a Fair Globalization recognizes that "the commitments and efforts of Members and the Organization to implement the ILO's constitutional mandate, including through international labour standards, and to place full and productive employment and decent work at the centre of economic and social policies, should be based on [...] (ii) developing and enhancing measures of social protection [...] which are sustainable and adapted to national circumstances, including [...] the extension of social security to all",

The Recommendation provides guidance to member States to:

(a) establish and maintain, as applicable, social protection floors as a fundamental element of their national social security systems; and
(b) implement social protection floors within strategies for the extension of social security that progressively ensure higher levels of social security to as many people as possible, guided by ILO social security standards.[80]

Child labour

The ILO states that as of September 2017, worldwide 218 million children between 5 and 17 years are in employment. Among them, 152 million are victims of child labour, and of those 73 million work in hazardous conditions.[81] Almost half of all 152 million children victims of child labour are aged 5 to 11 years. "Child labour is concentrated primarily in agriculture (71%), which includes fishing, forestry, livestock herding and aquaculture, and comprises both subsistence and commercial farming; 17% in Services; and 12% in the Industrial sector, including mining".[82]

The protection of children and young persons has been a fundamental principle of the ILO since its inception. Within Section II, General Principles, of

---

80 R202 Objectives, Scope and Principles I.1(a) and (b).
81 "[C]hildren's lives are being lost or shortened by being exposed to hazardous work. Many people simply do not realize how vulnerable children are to toxic chemicals, to extreme temperatures, to repetitive mind-numbing tasks, to isolation or to denigration, threats and violence". *Children in Hazardous Work* (ILO, Geneva, 2011) ix <www.ilo.org/wcmsp5/g roups/public/@dgreports/@dcomm/@publ/documents/publication/wcms_155428.pdf> (accessed 17 October 2020).
82 ILO, Child Labour <www.ilo.org/global/topics/child-labour/lang--en/index.htm> (accessed 17 October 2020) And see *Global Estimates of Child Labour: Results and Trends, 2012-2016* (ILO, Geneva, 2017) <www.ilo.org/wcmsp5/groups/public/---dgreports/---d comm/documents/publication/wcms_575499.pdf> (accessed 17 October 2020).

the ILO Constitution in its original form in 1919 (Part XIII of the Treaty of Versailles)[83] Article 427 provides:

> **Sixth** The abolition of child labour and the imposition of such limitations on the labour of young persons as shall permit the continuation of their education and assure their proper physical development.

The minimum age Conventions adopted between 1919 and 1921 were without precedent in the protection of the rights of children.[84] The ILO's response to the complexities of the exploitation of children then evolved over the following 80 years, culminating in the Worst Forms of Child Labour Convention 1999 (C182),[85] the members ratifying this being obliged to "take immediate and effective measures to secure the prohibition and elimination of the worst forms of child labour as a matter of urgency" (Article 1). Children are all persons under the age of 18 (Article 2). What "the worst forms of child labour" comprised in 1999 was massively wider than in 1919.

The Minimum Age (Industry) Convention 1919 (C05)[86] was adopted in the dawn of the ILO. A child was a person under 14 (or under 12 in Japan and India),[87] and the focus was on children working in any public or private "industrial undertaking":

1. For the purpose of this Convention, the term *industrial undertaking* includes particularly –

    (a) mines, quarries and other works for the extraction of minerals from the earth;

---

83 Treaty of Versailles 1919 Part XIII <www.ilo.org/public/libdoc/ilo/1920/20B09_18_e ngl.pdf> (accessed 17 October 2020).

84 See Gerry Rodgers, Eddy Lee, Lee Swepston and Jasmien Van Daele, *The ILO and the Quest for Social Justice, 1919–2009* (ILO, Geneva, 2009) 67–74.

85 Worst Forms of Child Labour Convention 1999 (C182) <www.ilo.org/dyn/normlex/en /f?p=NORMLEXPUB:12100:0::NO:12100:P12100_INSTRUMENT_ID:312327:NO> (accessed 17 October 2020).

86 Minimum Age (Industry) Convention 1919 (C05) <www.ilo.org/dyn/normlex/en/f ?p=NORMLEXPUB:12100:0::NO:12100:P12100_INSTRUMENT_ID:312150:NO> (accessed 17 October 2020).

87 As regards night work, between the hours of 10 pm and 5 am children were young persons under 18, though young persons over 16 could be employed at night in industries which by reason of the nature of the process were required to be carried on continuously day and night: Night Work of Young Persons (Industry) Convention 1919 (C06) Article 2(2) "(a) manufacture of iron and steel; processes in which reverberatory or regenerative furnaces are used, and galvanising of sheet metal or wire (except the pickling process); (b) glass works; (c) manufacture of paper; (d) manufacture of raw sugar; (e) gold mining reduction work". <www.ilo.org/dyn/normlex/en/f?p=NORMLEXPUB:12100:0::NO:12100:P 12100_INSTRUMENT_ID:312151:NO> (accessed 17 October 2020).

   (b) industries in which articles are manufactured, altered, cleaned, repaired, ornamented, finished, adapted for sale, broken up or demolished, or in which materials are transformed; including shipbuilding, and the generation, transformation, and transmission of electricity and motive power of any kind;

   (c) construction, reconstruction, maintenance, repair, alteration, or demolition of any building, railway, tramway, harbour, dock, pier, canal, inland waterway, road, tunnel, bridge, viaduct, sewer, drain, well, telegraphic or telephonic installation, electrical undertaking, gas work, water work, or other work of construction, as well as the preparation for or laying the foundations of any such work or structure;

   (d) transport of passengers or goods by road or rail or inland waterway, including the handling of goods at docks, quays, wharves, and warehouses, but excluding transport by hand.

The ILO Conventions which followed continued to concentrate on conditions in the workplace, be that agriculture, work at sea, fishing, working underground or non-industrial employment.[88] Absent was a generalised concept of child exploitation. In the Depression years of the 1930s, when a number of the Conventions dealing with child labour were revised, adopting a higher minimum age (15 years), wider economic factors were in play:

> Once again, there was a need to cope with widespread unemployment, and many believed that fewer young people should take on jobs that should go to adults. [...] The motivations behind the adoption of certain instruments, subsequently considered as promoting fundamental human rights, were not therefore as elevated as they might have seemed.[89]

The various, industry-specific minimum working age Conventions led to fragmentation, and in 1973 the Minimum Age Convention (C138)[90] took a globalised

---

88 The texts of the following are available at <www.ilo.org/dyn/normlex/en/f?p=1000 :12000:::NO:::> Minimum Age (Sea) Convention 1920 (C07); Minimum Age (Agriculture) Convention 1921 (C10); Minimum Age (Trimmers and Stokers) Convention 1921 (C15); Minimum Age (Non-Industrial Employment) Convention 1931 (C33); Minimum Age (Sea) Convention (Revised) 1936 (C58); Minimum Age (Industry) Convention (Revised) 1937 (C59); Minimum Age (Non-Industrial Employment) Convention (Revised) 1937 (C60); Medical Examination of Young Persons (Industry) Convention 1946 (C77); Medical Examination of Young Persons (Non-Industrial Occupations) Convention 1946 (C78); Night Work of Young Persons (Non-Industrial Occupations) Convention 1946 (C79); Night Work of Young Persons (Industry) Convention (Revised) 1948 (C90); Minimum Age (Fishermen) Convention 1959 (C112); Minimum Age (Underground Work) Convention 1965 (C123); Minimum Age Convention 1973 (C138) (accessed 17 October 2020).

89 Gerry Rodgers, Eddy Lee, Lee Swepston and Jasmien Van Daele, *The ILO and the Quest for Social Justice, 1919–2009* (ILO, Geneva, 2009) 71.

90 Minimum Age Convention (C138) <www.ilo.org/dyn/normlex/en/f?p=NORMLEXPU B:12100:0::NO:12100:P12100_INSTRUMENT_ID:312283:NO> (accessed 17 October

approach stating in Article 3(1): "The minimum age for admission to any type of employment or work which by its nature or the circumstances in which it is carried out is likely to jeopardise the health, safety or morals of young persons shall not be less than 18 years". What such work comprises is not defined and "shall be determined by national laws or regulations or by the competent authority, after consultation with the organisations of employers and workers concerned, where such exist" (Article 3(2)).[91] Further voice was given to this in the Minimum Age Recommendation 1973,[92] which in its Preamble recognised "that the effective abolition of child labour and the progressive raising of the minimum age for admission to employment constitute only one aspect of the protection and advancement of children and young persons". Articles I.2 and I.3 provide the wider context:

2. In this connection special attention should be given to such areas of planning and policy as the following:

   (a) firm national commitment to full employment, in accordance with the Employment Policy Convention and Recommendation, 1964, and the taking of measures designed to promote employment-oriented development in rural and urban areas;
   (b) the progressive extension of other economic and social measures to alleviate poverty wherever it exists and to ensure family living standards and

---

2020). C138 was not an immediate success: "[I]t is a highly technical instrument, and attracted few ratifications for over 25 years, both because many countries considered it too detailed, and because they were not ready to make a commitment to tackling child labour on a comprehensive basis". Gerry Rodgers, Eddy Lee, Lee Swepston and Jasmien Van Daele, *The ILO and the Quest for Social Justice, 1919–2009* (ILO, Geneva, 2009) 72. ILO Director-General Albert Thomas had from the outset recognised the limitations placed on the ILO by its inability to expedite ratification of its Conventions, and in the context of child welfare issues "stepped up the Office's contacts with other international networks working in related fields, both as potential sources of information and also for their ability to bring pressure to bear on this issue both nationally and internationally" including the newly formed International Association for Child Protection and International Save the Children. Droux makes no mention of contacts with any religious organisation. Joëlle Droux, 'From Inter-agency Competition to Transnational Cooperation: The ILO Contribution to Child Welfare Issues during the Interwar Years' in Sandrine Kott and Joëlle Droux, eds, *Globalizing Social Rights: The International Labour Organization and Beyond* (ILO and Palgrave Macmillan, Basingstoke, 2013) 262, 265.

91 With a further concession to the minimum age being made in Article 3(3): "Notwithstanding the provisions of paragraph 1 of this Article, national laws or regulations or the competent authority may, after consultation with the organisations of employers and workers concerned, where such exist, authorise employment or work as from the age of 16 years on condition that the health, safety and morals of the young persons concerned are fully protected and that the young persons have received adequate specific instruction or vocational training in the relevant branch of activity".

92 Minimum Age Recommendation 1973 (R146) <www.ilo.org/dyn/normlex/en/f?p=NORMLEXPUB:12100:0::NO:12100:P12100_INSTRUMENT_ID:312484:NO> (accessed 17 October 2020).

income which are such as to make it unnecessary to have recourse to the economic activity of children;

(c) the development and progressive extension, without any discrimination, of social security and family welfare measures aimed at ensuring child maintenance, including children's allowances;

(d) the development and progressive extension of adequate facilities for education and vocational orientation and training appropriate in form and content to the needs of the children and young persons concerned;

(e) the development and progressive extension of appropriate facilities for the protection and welfare of children and young persons, including employed young persons, and for the promotion of their development.

3. Particular account should as necessary be taken of the needs of children and young persons who do not have families or do not live with their own families and of migrant children and young persons who live and travel with their families. Measures taken to that end should include the provision of fellowships and vocational training

The world of 1999 was (as today) probably convinced of being very different in its treatment of children as a source of labour from the world of 1919, still reeling from the after effects of the Great War and the ensuing Influenza Pandemic. Resources in the 1920s and 1930s were scarce, and children were a resource. Yet in its breadth the evolved definition in the Worst Forms of Child Labour Convention 1999,[93] acknowledging contemporary abuses, has the power to shock:

3. For the purposes of this Convention, the term **the worst forms of child labour** comprises:

(a) all forms of slavery or practices similar to slavery, such as the sale and trafficking of children, debt bondage and serfdom and forced or compulsory labour, including forced or compulsory recruitment of children for use in armed conflict;

(b) the use, procuring or offering of a child for prostitution, for the production of pornography or for pornographic performances;

(c) the use, procuring or offering of a child for illicit activities, in particular for the production and trafficking of drugs as defined in the relevant international treaties;

(d) work which, by its nature or the circumstances in which it is carried out, is likely to harm the health, safety or morals of children.

---

93 Worst Forms of Child Labour Convention 1999 (C182) Article 3 <www.ilo.org/dyn/norm lex/en/f?p=NORMLEXPUB:12100:0::NO:12100:P12100_INSTRUMENT_ID:312327 :NO> (accessed 17 October 2020).

Looking back to the emphasis on education as a key to development found in the Sixth Principle from 1919, Convention 182 states in Article 7(2):

2. Each Member shall, taking into account the importance of education in eliminating child labour, take effective and time-bound measures to:

    (a) prevent the engagement of children in the worst forms of child labour;
    (b) provide the necessary and appropriate direct assistance for the removal of children from the worst forms of child labour and for their rehabilitation and social integration;
    (c) ensure access to free basic education, and, wherever possible and appropriate, vocational training, for all children removed from the worst forms of child labour;
    (d) identify and reach out to children at special risk; and
    (e) take account of the special situation of girls.

Although it is non-binding, the Worst Forms of Child Labour Recommendation 1999 (R190)[94] in Paragraph II 3 defines hazardous work:

3. In determining the types of work referred to under Article 3(d) of the Convention, and in identifying where they exist, consideration should be given, inter alia, to:

    (a) work which exposes children to physical, psychological or sexual abuse;
    (b) work underground, under water, at dangerous heights or in confined spaces;
    (c) work with dangerous machinery, equipment and tools, or which involves the manual handling or transport of heavy loads;
    (d) work in an unhealthy environment which may, for example, expose children to hazardous substances, agents or processes, or to temperatures, noise levels, or vibrations damaging to their health;
    (e) work under particularly difficult conditions such as work for long hours or during the night or work where the child is unreasonably confined to the premises of the employer.

Convention 182 was an immediate success: "The Convention quickly became the most rapidly ratified Convention in ILO history – and it began to pull ratifications of Convention No. 138 along with it".[95]

---

94 Worst Forms of Child Labour Recommendation 1999 (R190) <www.ilo.org/dyn/norm lex/en/f?p=NORMLEXPUB:12100:0::NO:12100:P12100_INSTRUMENT_ID:312528 :NO> (accessed 17 October 2020).
95 Gerry Rodgers, Eddy Lee, Lee Swepston and Jasmien Van Daele, *The ILO and the Quest for Social Justice, 1919–2009* (ILO, Geneva, 2009) 73.

In its report *Children in Hazardous Work*[96] a decade ago, the ILO was not bereft of optimism:

> This report has shown how serious the problem is. But it has also provided a picture of the array of tools that are now available to address it: wider awareness of the international labour standards, laws and regulations, education policies, enterprise policies and closer monitoring of supply chains, local regulations grounded in the "hazardous work lists", active worker associations even in rural areas, and most of all a growing sense worldwide that having children doing hazardous work can no longer be tolerated in a modernizing and globally connected society. The proof that such measures can have an effect is seen in the declining rates of hazardous work among younger children and girls.

Yet in the ILO Centenary Declaration for the Future of Work 2019[97] the International Labour Conference declares that:

A. In discharging its constitutional mandate, taking into account the profound transformations in the world of work, and further developing its human-centred approach to the future of work, the ILO must direct its efforts to:

   [...]

   (xiii) eradicating forced and child labour and promoting decent work for all and fostering cross-border cooperation, including in areas or sectors of high international integration;

The problem persists.

Forced labour

The ILO states that as of September 2017 an estimated 40.3 million people were in modern slavery, including 24.9 million in forced labour and 15.4 million in forced marriage. Out of the 24.9 million people trapped in forced labour, 16 million people are exploited in the private sector such as domestic work, construction or agriculture; 4.8 million persons in forced sexual exploitation and 4 million persons in forced labour imposed by state authorities. Women and girls

---

96 *Children in Hazardous Work* (ILO, Geneva, 2011) 67 <www.ilo.org/wcmsp5/groups/publ ic/@dgreports/@dcomm/@publ/documents/publication/wcms_155428.pdf> (accessed 17 October 2020).
97 ILO Centenary Declaration for the Future of Work 2019 <www.ilo.org/ilc/ILCSessions /108/reports/texts-adopted/WCMS_711674/lang--en/index.htm> (accessed 17 October 2020). And see Chapter 7.

are disproportionately affected by forced labour, accounting for 99% of victims in the commercial sex industry and 58% in other sectors.[98]

The morphing of slavery, which was regarded as passing into history, into forced labour was present in the thinking of the ILO from its earliest times. Writing in 1926 George Barnes observed:

> The recent enquiry [by the Mandates and Slavery Commissions of the League of Nations] into slavery has demonstrated that perhaps the worst evil of modern times is not slavery in the old sense of ownership, which has gradually been reduced if not eliminated from the modern civilised world, but the forced labour which is frequently imposed upon subject peoples, often without pay, and very frequently with so little attention to sanitary conditions that its effects upon the population are truly disastrous. [...] Here is a problem to which the International Labour Organisation must devote itself, and is now preparing to devote itself".[99]

Forced or compulsory labour (defined as all work or service which is exacted from any person under the menace of any penalty and for which that person has not offered himself voluntarily) was condemned in the Forced Labour Convention 1930.[100] J P Daughton describes the process of investigating, negotiating and drafting of this Convention as "one of the most wide-sweeping efforts to reform cases of brutality and injustice of European colonialism ever attempted" whilst at the same time noting that powerful colonial forces were at work whose critics were, despite the best efforts of the ILO to restrain such influence, "marginalized from the Convention proceedings and were allowed to voice only relatively benign statements of disapproval".[101]

Excluded from the definition of forced labour was military service; "normal civic obligations of the citizens of a full self-governing country"; work "as a

---

98 ILO, Forced Labour, Modern Slavery and Human Trafficking <www.ilo.org/global/topics /forced-labour/lang--en/index.htm> (accessed 17 October 2020). And see *Global Estimates of Modern Slavery: Forced Labour and Forced Marriage* (ILO, Geneva, 2017) <www .ilo.org/wcmsp5/groups/public/---dgreports/---dcomm/documents/publication/wcm s_575479.pdf> (accessed 17 October 2020).

99 George N Barnes, *History of the International Labour Office* (Williams and Norgate Limited, London, 1926) 71. In the Preface to this book, Émile Vandervelde describes George Barnes and the ILO's first Director-General Albert Thomas as "the two men who have played the most important part in the history of the International Labour Organisation".

100 Forced Labour Convention 1930 (C29) <www.ilo.org/dyn/normlex/en/f?p=NORM LEXPUB:12100:0::NO:12100:P12100_INSTRUMENT_ID:312174:NO> and see Protocol of 2014 to the Forced Labour Convention 1930 <www.ilo.org/dyn/normlex/en /f?p=NORMLEXPUB:12100:0::NO:12100:P12100_INSTRUMENT_ID:3174672:NO > (each accessed 17 October 2020).

101 J P Daughton, 'ILO Expertise and Colonial Violence in the Interwar Years' in Sandrine Kott and Joëlle Droux, eds, *Globalizing Social Rights: The International Labour Organization and Beyond* (ILO and Palgrave Macmillan, Basingstoke, 2013) 85, 86.

consequence of a conviction in a court of law" (though not to be "placed at the disposal of private individuals, companies or association");

> any work or service exacted in cases of emergency, that is to say, in the event of war or of a calamity or threatened calamity, such as fire, flood, famine, earthquake, violent epidemic or epizootic diseases, invasion by animal, insect or vegetable pests, and in general any circumstance that would endanger the existence or the well-being of the whole or part of the population;

and minor communal services if for the agreed benefit of the community. (Article 2(2)).

That forced labour could be used as a weapon of war was not in the minds of the draftspersons in 1930, but the atrocities of the World War Two had made this aspect of compulsion all too clear. The definition needed to be expanded. Under the Abolition of Forced Labour Convention 1957:

> 1. Each Member of the International Labour Organisation which ratifies this Convention undertakes to suppress and not to make use of any form of forced or compulsory labour –
>
>   (a) as a means of political coercion or education or as a punishment for holding or expressing political views or views ideologically opposed to the established political, social or economic system;
>   (b) as a method of mobilising and using labour for purposes of economic development;
>   (c) as a means of labour discipline;
>   (d) as a punishment for having participated in strikes;
>   (e) as a means of racial, social, national or religious discrimination.[102]

The Protocol of 2014 to the Forced Labour Convention 1930 (P029)[103] addresses gaps in the Convention regarding implementation strategies:

> Article 1.1. In giving effect to its obligations under the Convention to suppress forced or compulsory labour, each Member shall take effective measures

---

102 Abolition of Forced Labour Convention 1957 (C105) Article 1 <www.ilo.org/dyn/norm lex/en/f?p=NORMLEXPUB:12100:0::NO:12100:P12100_INSTRUMENT_ID:31225 0:NO> (accessed 17 October 2020).

103 Protocol of 2014 to the Forced Labour Convention 1930 (P029) <www.ilo.org/dyn/ normlex/en/f?p=NORMLEXPUB:12100:0::NO::P12100_ILO_CODE:P029> (accessed 17 October 2020). The Protocol also deleted from the Forced Labour Convention 1930 Articles 3 to 24 (considered long since to have ceased to be applicable) which had allowed the continuation of forced labour in European colonies for a transitional period pending its eventual abolition and limiting the use of these powers to exploit "native populations" in Africa and Asia.

to prevent and eliminate its use, to provide to victims protection and access to appropriate and effective remedies, such as compensation, and to sanction the perpetrators of forced or compulsory labour.

Article 2 The measures to be taken for the prevention of forced or compulsory labour shall include:

(a) educating and informing people, especially those considered to be particularly vulnerable, in order to prevent their becoming victims of forced or compulsory labour;
(b) educating and informing employers, in order to prevent their becoming involved in forced or compulsory labour practices;
(c) undertaking efforts to ensure that:
    (i) the coverage and enforcement of legislation relevant to the prevention of forced or compulsory labour, including labour law as appropriate, apply to all workers and all sectors of the economy; and
    (ii) labour inspection services and other services responsible for the implementation of this legislation are strengthened;
(d) protecting persons, particularly migrant workers, from possible abusive and fraudulent practices during the recruitment and placement process;
(e) supporting due diligence by both the public and private sectors to prevent and respond to risks of forced or compulsory labour; and
(f) addressing the root causes and factors that heighten the risks of forced or compulsory labour.

Conclusions

Each of the fundamental principles of the ILO finds its counterpoint in Catholic Social Teaching, the bass notes resounding from *Rerum novarum*.

This is not to claim that those fundamental principles owe their existence solely to an appreciation on the part of the founders of the ILO and of those who have framed its Conventions and Recommendations in succeeding decades to Catholic Social Teaching alone. To do so would be absurd in light of the huge contribution made to the work of the ILO, not only by secular bodies but also of other confessions. Yet as recently as 2012 in making a case for the right to strike *as embodied in ILO instruments* the ITUC was both comfortable with and confident in citing Encyclicals as "further evidence of the universally accepted nature of the right".

When comparing the principles of Catholic Social Teaching examined in the previous chapter with the fundamental principles of the ILO, there is no incompatibility: on the contrary, there are strong parallels. As will be shown in later chapters, the Holy See's relationship with the ILO has evolved to the point where approbation of the ILO fundamental principles is almost absolute. ILO Jesuit in residence André Arnou was stating a self-evident truth about the spiritual, apolitical role of the Holy See when he wrote that to live in a tangible world and to achieve justice and charity, institutions have to be in place; and in the field of labour rights that institution is the ILO.

Just as the influence of Catholic Social Teaching on the development of the fundamental principles of the ILO is apparent, so have those fundamental principles themselves become an integral part of Catholic Social Teaching. They are, from a Catholic perspective, both the articulation and the practical application of those labour rights proclaimed in the Social Encyclicals.

Bibliography

The Holy See

Encyclicals, Apostolic letters, Exhortations (in chronological order)

Pope Pius XI, *Quadragesimo anno* (1931).

International Labour Organisation

Conventions and recommendations

Minimum Age (Industry) Convention 1919 (C05)
Night Work of Young Persons (Industry) Convention 1919 (C06)
Minimum Age (Sea) Convention 1920 (C07)
Minimum Age (Agriculture) Convention 1921 (C10)
Right of Association (Agriculture) Convention 1921 (C11)
Workmen's Compensation (Agriculture) Convention 1921 (C12)
Minimum Age (Trimmers and Stokers) Convention 1921 (C15)
Workmen's Compensation (Accidents) Convention 1925 (C17)
Workmen's Compensation (Occupational Diseases) Convention 1925 (C18)
Equality of Treatment (Accident Compensation) Convention 1925 (C19)
Sickness Insurance (Industry) Convention 1927 (C24)
Sickness Insurance (Agriculture) Convention 1925 (C25)
Forced Labour Convention 1930 (C29) and Protocol of 2014 to the Forced Labour Convention 1930 (P29)
Minimum Wage-Fixing Machinery Convention 1926 (C30)
Minimum Wage-Fixing Machinery Recommendation 1928 para III (R30)
Minimum Age (Non-Industrial Employment) Convention 1931 (C33)
Old-Age Insurance (Industry, etc.) Convention 1933 (C35)
Old-Age Insurance (Agriculture) Convention 1933 (C36)
Invalidity Insurance (Industry, etc.) Convention 1933 (C37)
Invalidity Insurance (Agriculture) Convention 1933 (C38)
Survivors' Insurance (Industry, etc.) Convention 1933 (C39)
Survivors' Insurance (Agriculture) Convention 1933 (C40)
Workingmen's Compensation (Occupational Diseases) Convention (Revised) 1934 (C42)
Unemployment Provisions Convention 1934 (C44)
Maintenance of Migrants' Pension Rights Convention 1935 (C48)

Minimum Age (Sea) Convention (Revised) 1936 (C58)

Minimum Age (Industry) Convention (Revised) 1937 (C59)

Minimum Age (Non-Industrial Employment) Convention (Revised) 1937 (C60)

Medical Examination of Young Persons (Industry) Convention 1946 (C77)

Medical Examination of Young Persons (Non-Industrial Occupations) Convention 1946 (C78)

Night Work of Young Persons (Non-Industrial Occupations) Convention 1946 (C79)

Income Security Recommendation 1944 (R67)

Medical Care Recommendation 1944 (R69)

Freedom of Association and Protection of the Right to Organise Convention 1948 (C87)

Night Work of Young Persons (Industry) Convention (Revised) 1948 (C90)

Protection of Wages Convention 1949 (C95)

Right to Organise and Collective Bargaining Convention 1949 (C98)

Minimum Wage Fixing Machinery (Agriculture) Convention 1951 (C99)

Equal Remuneration Convention 1951 (C100)

Collective Agreements Recommendation 1951 (R91)

Voluntary Conciliation and Arbitration Recommendation 1951 (R92)

Social Security (Minimum Standards) Convention 1952 (C102)

Abolition of Forced Labour Convention 1957 (C105)

Discrimination (Employment and Occupation) Convention 1958 (C111)

Minimum Age (Fishermen) Convention 1959 (C112)

Radiation Protection Convention 1960 (C115)

Equality of Treatment (Social Security) Convention 1962 (C118)

Hygiene (Commerce and Offices) Convention 1964 (C120)

Employment Injury Benefits Convention 1964 (as amended) (C121)

Minimum Age (Underground Work) Convention 1965 (C123)

Invalidity, Old-Age and Survivors' Benefits Convention 1967(C128)

Medical Care and Sickness Benefits Convention 1969 (C130)

Minimum Wage Fixing Convention 1970 (C131)

Workers Representatives Convention 1971 (C135)

Minimum Age Recommendation 1973 (R146)

Minimum Age Convention 1973 (C138)

Occupational Cancer Convention 1974 (C139)

Human Resources Development Convention 1975 (C142)

Working Environment (Air pollution, Noise and Vibration) Convention 1977 (C148)

Collective Bargaining Convention 1981 (C154)

Occupational Safety and Health Convention 1981 (C155)

Maintenance of Social Security Rights Convention 1982 (C157)

Occupational Health Services Convention 1985 (C161)

Asbestos Convention 1986 (C162)

Safety and Health in Construction Convention 1988 (C167)

Employment Promotion and Protection against Unemployment Convention 1988 (C168)

Protection of Workers' Claims (Employer's Insolvency) Convention 1992 (C173)

Prevention of Major Industrial Accidents Convention 1993 (C174)

Health and Safety in Mines Convention 1995 (C176)

Worst Forms of Child Labour Recommendation 1999 (R190)

Worst Forms of Child Labour Convention 1999 (C182)
Maternity Protection Convention 2000 (C183)
Safety and Health in Agriculture Convention 2001 (C184)
Promotional Framework for Occupational Safety and Health Convention 2006 (C187)
Social Protection Floors Recommendation 2012 (R202)
Violence and Harassment Convention 2019 (C190)

International Labour Conferences (in chronological order)

Record of Proceedings of the 35th Session of the ILC 1952 318 – Statement by Mr Dennys, Government Advisor, United Kingdom <www.ilo.org/public/libdoc/ilo/P/09616/09616(1952–35).pdf> (accessed 17 October 2020).

Henri de Riedmatten, Address to the 52nd Session of the ILC 1968 202–204 <www.ilo.org/public/libdoc/ilo/P/09616/09616(1968–52).pdf> (accessed 17 October 2020).

Record of Proceedings of the 71st Session of the ILC 1985 22/24 – 22/26 <www.ilo.org/public/libdoc/ilo/P/09616/09616(1985–71).pdf>© ILO (accessed 17 October 2020).

Record of Proceedings of the 81st Session of the ILC 1994 9/8 – 9/9 <www.ilo.org/public/libdoc/ilo/P/09616/09616(1994–81).pdf> © ILO (accessed 17 October 2020).

Record of Proceedings of the 88th Session of the ILC 2000 18/7 <www.ilo.org/public/libdoc/ilo/P/09616/09616(2000–88)V.1.pdf> © ILO (accessed 29 August 2020).

Record of Proceedings of the 101st session of the ILC 2012. Addresses by Daniel Funes de Rioja as Chairperson of the Employers' Group with a response from Luc Cortebeeck as Chairperson of the Workers' Group 7/6 to 7/9 <www.ilo.org/public/libdoc/ilo/P/09616/09616(2012-101).pdf> (accessed 17 October 2020).

Reports (in chronological order)

Minimum Wages: Wage-Fixing Machinery, Application and Supervision, Report III (Part 4B), *International Labour Conference*, 79th Session 1992 <www.ilo.org/public/libdoc/ilo/P/09661/09661%281992-79-4B%29.pdf> (accessed 17 October 2020).

Report of the Committee on Social Security to the 89th Session of the International Labour Conference 2001 <www.ilo.org/public/english/standards/relm/ilc/ilc89/pdf/pr-16.pdf> 16/33 (accessed 17 October 2020).

Freedom of Association in Practice: Lessons Learned, Report of the Director-General to the 97th Session of the ILC 2008, Report I(B) xiii <www.ilo.org/wcmsp5/groups/public/---dgreports/---dcomm/documents/publication/wcms_096122.pdf> (accessed 17 October 2020).

Report VI, *Social Security for Social Justice and Fair Globalization*, presented to the 100th Session of the International Labour Conference 2011 para 24 <www.social-protection.org/gimi/gess/ShowWiki.action?wiki.wikiId=827> (accessed 17 October 2020).

Children in Hazardous Work (ILO, Geneva, 2011) ix <www.ilo.org/wcmsp5/groups/public/@dgreports/@dcomm/@publ/documents/publication/wcms_155428.pdf> (accessed 17 October 2020).

Giving Globalization a Human Face, International Labour Conference (101st session) Report III9IB) (Geneva, 2012) 272 <www.ilo.org/wcmsp5/groups/

public/---ed_norm/---relconf/documents/meetingdocument/wcms_174846
.pdf> (accessed 17 October 2020).

Working together to Promote a Safe and Healthy Working Environment, International
Labour Conference (106th session) Report III (Part 1B) 2 (Geneva, 2017) <www
.ilo.org/wcmsp5/groups/public/---ed_norm/---relconf/documents/meeti
ngdocument/wcms_543647.pdf> (accessed 17 October 2020).

Other materials (in chronological order)

Treaty of Versailles 1919, Part XIII <www.ilo.org/public/libdoc/ilo/1920/20B09
_18_engl.pdf>(accessed 17 October 2020).
Declaration of Philadelphia 1944 <www.ilo.ch/dyn/normlex/en/f?p=1000:62
:0::NO:62:P62_LIST_ENTRIE_ID:2453907:NO#declaration   >   (accessed
17 October 2020).
ILO, *Freedom of Association and Collective Bargaining* (ILO, Geneva, 1994) para 179
<www.ilo.org/public/libdoc/ilo/P/09661/09661(1994-81-4B).pdf> (accessed
17 October 2020).
Declaration on Fundamental Principles and Rights at Work (ILO, Geneva, 1998)
<www.ilo.org/wcmsp5/groups/public/---ed_norm/---declaration/documents/
normativeinstrument/wcms_716594.pdf> (accessed 17 October 2020).
Global Estimates of Child Labour: Results and Trends, 2012–2016 (ILO, Geneva,
2017) <www.ilo.org/wcmsp5/groups/public/---dgreports/---dcomm/docum
ents/publication/wcms_575499.pdf> (accessed 17 October 2020).
Global Estimates of Modern Slavery: Forced Labour and Forced Marriage (ILO, Geneva,
2017) <www.ilo.org/wcmsp5/groups/public/---dgreports/---dcomm/docum
ents/publication/wcms_575479.pdf> (accessed 17 October 2020).
*Freedom of Association: Compilation of Decisions of the Committee on Freedom of
Association* (Sixth edition) (ILO, June 2018) para 73, 18 <www.ilo.org/wcmsp5
/groups/public/---ed_norm/---normes/documents/publication/wcms_6326
59.pdf> (accessed 17 October 2020).
ILO, Centenary Declaration for the Future of Work 2019 <www.ilo.org/ilc/ILCS
essions/108/reports/texts-adopted/WCMS_711674/lang--en/index.htm>
(accessed 17 October 2020).
ILO, Topics: Safety and Health at Work <www.ilo.org/global/topics/safety-and-hea
lth-at-work/lang--en/index.htm> (accessed 17 October 2020).
ILO, Child Labour <www.ilo.org/global/topics/child-labour/lang--en/index.h
tm> (accessed 17 October 2020).
ILO, Forced Labour, Modern Slavery and Human Trafficking <www.ilo.org/global/
topics/forced-labour/lang--en/index.htm> (accessed 17 October 2020).

International documents

Universal Declaration of Human Rights 1948.

Secondary sources

Arnou, A, *L'Organisation internationale du Travail et les Catholiques* (Éditions Spes,
Paris, 1933).

Barbier, Maurice, "Les Relations Entre l'Église Catholique et l'Organisation International du Travail" in *Politique étrangère* Vol. 37(3) (1972) (Institut Français des Relations Internationales) 351.

Barnes, George N, *History of the International Labour Office* (Williams and Norgate Limited, London, 1926).

Daughton, J P, "ILO Expertise and Colonial Violence in the Interwar Years" in Sandrine Kott and Joëlle Droux, eds, *Globalizing Social Rights: The International Labour Organization and Beyond* (ILO and Palgrave Macmillan, Basingstoke, 2013) 85.

Droux, Joëlle, "From Inter-Agency Competition to Transnational Cooperation: The ILO Contribution to Child Welfare Issues during the Interwar Years" in Sandrine Kott and Joëlle Droux, eds, *Globalizing Social Rights: The International Labour Organization and Beyond* (ILO and Palgrave Macmillan, Basingstoke, 2013) 262.

Hughes, Steve and Haworth, Nigel, *The International Labour Organisation (ILO): Coming in from the Cold* (Routledge, London, 2011).

International Trade Union Confederation (ITUC), *The Right to Strike and the ILO: The legal Foundations* (March 2014) <www.ituc-csi.org/IMG/pdf/ituc_final_brief_on_the_right_to_strike.pdf > (accessed 17 October 2020).

Rodgers, Gerry, Lee, Eddy, Swepston, Lee and Van Diele, Jasmien, *The ILO and the Quest for Social Justice, 1919 – 2009* (ILO, Geneva, 2009).

Saul, Ben, Kinley, David, and Mowbray, Jaqueline, *The International Convention on Economic, Social and Cultural Rights: Commentary, Cases and Materials* (Oxford University Press, Oxford, 2014).

Stein, Oswald, "Building Social Security" in *International Labour Review* (ILO, Geneva), Vol. 44(3) (1941) 248.

5 The International Labour Organisation – Origins and Social Catholicism, 1919 to 1944

Introduction

This chapter looks at the origins of the International Labour Organisation and at its Constitution at its dawn in 1919. It follows its development in the inter-War period culminating in the Declaration of Philadelphia in 1944, seen firstly through the lens of secular histories (largely because barely a history of the ILO has ever more than touched upon anything other than a secular narrative). This secular approach far from tells the whole story, and so this chapter goes on to examine the role of Christianity in the birth and development of the ILO and specifically the part played by Social Catholicism.

Maurice Barbier writing soon after the ILO celebrated its half century commented:

> Les relations de l'Eglise avec l'O.I.T. sont particulièrement étroites, non seulement parce qu'elles remontent aux origines de l'Organisation et que les chrétiens ont préparé la création de celle-ci, mais parce qu'il y a une harmonie profonde entre les deux institutions et une convergence remarquable entre leur doctrine et leurs objectifs en matière sociale. [...]

> Les conditions historiques de la création de l'O.I.T, sa structure tripartite destinée à favoriser le dialogue entre patrons et ouvriers, et ses méthodes visant à développer la législation internationale du travail répondaient parfaitement aux aspirations des milieux catholiques, telles qu'elles s'exprimaient dans la doctrine sociale de l'Eglise et chez les syndicats chrétiens. C'est pourquoi ces milieux nouèrent des relations étroites avec l'O.I.T d'une double manière: d'une part, les syndicats chrétiens, en majorité catholiques et s'inspirant de la doctrine sociale de l'Eglise, participèrent directement aux activités de l'Organisation; d'autre part, l'Eglise catholique proprement dite manifesta son intérêt pour celle-ci soit au niveau du Saint-Siège, soit par l'intermédiaire de diverses organisations catholiques.[1]

---

1 [The relationship between the Church and the ILO is particularly close, not only because it stems from the beginning, and that Christians prepared the foundation, of the ILO, but because

The years covered in this chapter were largely troubled, and the work of the ILO has to be weighed against this. On the eve of another catastrophic war, though still hoping for peace, Harold Butler delivered a speech to the Trades Union Congress, Blackpool on 7 September 1938:

> When I look back over the record of the Office since its foundation, I am astonished not by the poverty but by the magnitude of its accomplishment. It has not had an easy passage. Its whole career up to date has been in a time of constant storm and stress. There have not been five years out of the twenty years of its existence during which the world can be said to have enjoyed anything like tranquillity, either political or economic. We have had to face the reaction against the liberal ideas which produced the foundation of the ILO and of the League [of nations]. We have had to make headway against all the obstructing influences which have always militated against any effort in the direction of social progress and international understanding.
>
> Yet, in spite of all these handicaps, the Organisation has gone steadily forward.[2]

Albert Thomas – pioneer

In examining the origins and early workings of the ILO, the enormous contribution to its development – not least to the ILO's bond with the Catholic Church – of its first Director-General, Albert Thomas is immediately evident. He held office from 1919 until his death in post aged 53 in 1932.[3] He was "a game changer in the relationship between the Holy See and the ILO".[4]

---

there exists a profound harmony between the two institutions and an astonishing convergence between their policies and goals upon social issues. The historic background to the creation of the ILO, its tripartite structure aimed at promoting dialogue between employers and workers, and its strategy envisioning the development of international labour legislation addressed perfectly the hopes of the Catholic community, hopes expressed in the social doctrine of the Church and amongst the Christian trade unions. That is why the Catholic community tended the close relationship with the ILO in two ways: for the one part, the Christian trade unions, a majority of which were Catholic and inspired by the social doctrine of the Church, participated directly in the activities of the Organisation; for the other, the Catholic Church in its own right expressed its interest in the Organisation, be that directly at the level of the Holy See or indirectly through a range of Catholic organisations.] Maurice Barbier, "Les Relations Entre l'Église Catholique et l'Organisation International du Travail" in *Politique étrangère*, Vol. 37, No. 3 (1972) (Institut Français des Relations Internationales) 351, 352, 355.

2 Harold Butler, *Peace through Social Justice* (Peace Book Company (London) Ltd., London, 1938) 4.

3 A short biography is available from the ILO at <www.ilo.org/global/about-the-ilo/how-the -ilo-works/ilo-director-general/former-directors-general/WCMS_192645/lang--en/index .htm> (accessed 17 October 2020).

4 Archbishop Paul Richard Gallagher, Secretary for Relations with States, Secretariat of State, the Holy See "The Holy See and the International Labour Organization: Common Pathways

In his first Report to the International Labour Conference, in 1933, Albert Thomas's successor as Director-General Harold Butler (who served from 1932 to 1938) wrote of

> the sudden death of Albert Thomas, to whose incomparable vision and driving force its development as a great international institution was mainly due. The magnitude of his achievement, the inspiration of his idealism, the versatility of the brilliant gifts which he brought to the last and greatest task of his life are abundantly witnessed by the tributes paid to his work and memory from men and women of every country and every shade of opinion with whom he came into contact. [...] [He was] the great architect of the Organisation as it is today.[5]

Albert Thomas' close colleague (and eventual successor, serving as Director-General 1941 to 1948)[6] Edward Phelan wrote of him:

> Albert Thomas came to be wholly identified with the International Labour Office. The object which it was designed to achieve, social justice, was the ruling and consuming passion of his life. The great instrument which he directed in such masterly fashion became in some sort a part of himself. As the years went by, and his leadership became more and more undisputed, the identity of the man and the institution became more and more complete. [...]

> He realised that the International Labour Organisation must develop as it were a personality of its own. And he sought the basis for such a personality on wider and deeper lines than those which its authors had commonly advanced. He rejected the theory that it existed mainly to secure equitable conditions of commercial competition, and he laid the major emphasis on the idea of the pursuit of social justice. [7]

> That belief was indeed the mainspring of his activity and he was untiring his effort to arouse and to spread the conviction that in the pursuit social justice lay the only road to an enduring peace; but he believed with equal intensity

---

on Labour" in *Rethinking Labour, Ethical Reflections on the Future of Work, Labour after Laudato Si'* 241–250, at 245 (The Caritas in Veritate Foundation Working Papers, FCIV, Chambésy, 2018) <https://futureofwork-labourafterlaudatosi.net/2018/11/14/rethinking -labour-ethical-reflections-on-the-future-of-work-14-november-2018-global/> © The Caritas in Veritate Foundation (accessed 17 October 2020).

5 Report of the Director-General to the 17th Session of the ILC 1933 5 <www.ilo.org/public/ libdoc/ilo/P/09383/09383(1933-17).pdf> (accessed 17 October 2020) © ILO.

6 A short biography is available from the ILO <www.ilo.org/global/about-the-ilo/how-the -ilo-works/ilo-director-general/former-directors-general/WCMS_192711/lang--en/index .htm> (accessed 17 October 2020).

7 E J Phelan, *Yes and Albert Thomas* (The Cresset Press, London, 1949) 57, 242.

that in the I.L.O. the world possessed for the first time an effective instrument through which the cause of social justice might be steadily advanced.[8]

Reiner Tosstorff sees Albert Thomas's appointment as having had "immense repercussions for the future of the ILO":

> The appointment of Thomas was decisive for the ILO's further development into an entirely autonomous form, which took the ILO beyond the letter of what the ILO Charter was intended to achieve and how this had presumably been envisaged by some of the most influential representatives of the Allied Powers. Thomas was to turn it from a purely socio-political appendage of the League of Nations into an international organization, with its own "political personality".[9]

The strategy of Albert Thomas according to Daniel Maul was "both diplomatic and technocratic in nature", and Albert Thomas sought to create a supporting network to provide the backing he needed in dealing with national Governments. Amongst these, as Maul reports were "religious groups, most prominently the Catholic trade unions and the Vatican itself".[10]

Edward Phelan himself was the quiet man whose own very considerable contribution to the creation and development of the ILO is far less prominent in the histories. He was an Irish Catholic, schooled as a teenager in Liverpool by Jesuits and described as "a social liberal rather than a socialist".[11] It was his contribution to the drafting of the ILO Constitution – the "Phelan Memorandum" – which introduced into workings of the International Labour Conference the distinctive tripartite structure of Government, employer and worker representatives.

This chapter is an account of gifted and highly motivated individual pioneers within the new organisation, of the contribution of the Catholic trade union movement, the role within the ILO of the Jesuit in residence and of a real though publicly unacknowledged diplomatic relationship between the ILO and the Holy See in the years leading up to World War Two.

---

8   Edward Phelan, "Some Reminiscences of the International Labour Organisation" in *Studies: An Irish Quarterly Review*, Vol. 43, No. 171 (Autumn, 1954) 241, 242.

9   Reiner Tosstorff, "Albert Thomas, the ILO and the IFTU: A Case of Mutual Benefit?" in International Institute of Social History Amsterdam (Jasmien Van Daele and others, eds), *ILO Histories: Essays on the International Labour Organization and Its Impact on the World during the Twentieth Century* (Peter Lang, Bern, 2010) 94.

10   Daniel Maul, *The International Labour Organization: 100 Years of Global Social Policy* (De Grutyer, Berlin, 2019) 37–38.

11   Emmet O'Connor, "Edward Phelan: A Biographical Essay" in *Edward Phelan and the ILO: The Life and Views of an International Social Actor* (International Labour Office, Geneva, 2009) 13–14.

Social, economic and political context: The year 1919

The year 1919 turns out on closer examination not to have been the sunlit peaceful uplands to which the world moved after the guns fell silent on 11 November 1918.

As Birte Förster observes: "Der Krieg war zwar beendet, aber die Erfahrung von Gewalt war 1919 noch längst keine Vergangenheit". War between Nation States Europe-wide was continued in the form of national revolutions. Self-styled but nonetheless functioning and law-giving Soviet republics (*Räterrepublik*) briefly held sway in the former German Reich in Munich and Bremen. The newly created Hungarian Republic formed in November 1918 was overthrown and replaced with a Soviet republic in March 1919 by the Hungarian Communist Party. Civil unrest in the form of mass strikes broke out in the United Kingdom in the docks of Glasgow and Liverpool (to which troops and tanks were swiftly despatched). A general strike originating in Barcelona paralysed Catalonia (again, ended by military intervention). In the former Russian Empire, Lenin's forces continued to advance against a hastily assembled White Army. Romania was at war with Hungary, Greece with Turkey, Turkey with Armenian nationals of the former Ottoman Empire and Poland with West Ukraine. In the newly created Baltic States of Latvia, Lithuania and Estonia, a mercenary army of German *Freikorps* fought not only the Red Army of Lenin but also the civilian population who had summoned them, and often each other. A war of independence had begun in Ireland. Demobbed service personnel returned to their homes in part traumatised and weakened, with no realistic prospect of finding employment at a time when social support systems were, if they existed at all, rudimentary.[12] "Recent statistics have shown that the total number of war disabled is at least ten millions, including eight millions who, in spite of their pensions, are forced to a varying extent to look for work".[13]

During the influenza pandemic of 1918–1919, between 25 and 50 million people fell victim to the disease, with the working-age population in their 20s to their 40s the most severely hit.[14]

It was a world suffering from an unemployment crisis of unexampled intensity, producers and consumers alike tossed about in a mad whirl of rising and falling prices, of alternate glut and famine, boom and slump. [...] It was a moment of reaction, of disillusion and of doubt.[15]

---

12 [The war was indeed over, but the experience of violence was in 1919 far from being confined to the past.] Birte Förster, *1919: Ein Kontinent erfindet sich neu* (Philipp Reclam jun. Verlag GmbH, Stuttgart, 2019) 31–55, 136, 191, 201.

13 G A Johnston, *International Social Progress: The Work of the International Labour Organisation of the League of Nations* (George Allen & Unwin Ltd., London, 1924) 177.

14 The Editors of Encyclopaedia Britannica *Influenza Pandemic of 1918–19* <www.britannica.com/event/influenza-pandemic-of-1918-1919> (accessed 17 October 2020).

15 G A Johnston, *International Social Progress: The Work of the International Labour Organisation of the League of Nations* (George Allen & Unwin Ltd., London, 1924) 111.

There was in consequence a deep and objectively well-founded concern on the part of those negotiating the Peace that Europe could be on the point of meltdown.

ILO: a beacon of hope

Contemporary commentators saw in the ILO a beacon of hope.

For G A Johnston, writing in 1924:

> [A]mid all the uncertainties of the post-war world, where all beliefs, all conventions, all standards are in flux, the brightest element of hope for the peace of the world seems to lie in the education of public opinion to a higher sense of social justice. It is with this conviction that the International Labour Office has adopted as its motto "*Si vis pacem, cole justitiam*". [*If you desire peace, cultivate justice*][16]

Johnston's fellow ILO official George Barnes wrote in the same vein in 1926:

> And there is a special reason at present why the International Labour Organisation should be supported by all those who want to see orderly and evolutionary progress in social and industrial betterment. The forces of disorder and anarchy are active and unscrupulous, especially in the international sphere. And internationalism has come to stay. [...] Is internationalism to be voiced by all in the interests of all? Or is it to be left to be voiced by violent revolutionists in the alleged interests of some? The I.L.O. stands for the former. It affords an opportunity for Governments, employers and employed to come together to advance common interests, it spreads knowledge from all for the benefit of all, and it helps to maintain peace by fostering the right spirit.[17]

Harold Butler had been an active member of the British delegation at Versailles concerned with the birth of the ILO. Writing in 1950 he recalled the swing from bleakness to optimism in 1919:

> As a civil servant, I saw the shadows creeping over the sun, as the political and social struggles of the Edwardian decade developed and the rising menace of Germany foreboded the end of peace in Europe. With the first world war came the first eclipse, out of which England and Europe emerged in a new shape. Their social foundations were loosened and their political

---

16 G A Johnston, *International Social Progress: The Work of the International Labour Organisation of the League of Nations* (George Allen & Unwin Ltd., London, 1924) 258–259.

17 George N Barnes, *History of the International Labour Office* (Williams and Norgate Limited, London, 1926) 80.

structure transformed, but with the creation of the League of Nations and the International Labour Organization the world began to grope back toward the light, filled with the hope of a new age which would herald a better social order and an assurance of world peace. [...]

The I.L.O. was thus brought to birth in a world of storm and travail. The old Europe had disappeared. [...] What new balance of forces might ultimately emerge, no-one could foretell. The continent was in the melting-pot, and with it the old order of its society. The slogan of class warfare mingled with the cries of national triumph or despair. The peacemakers went stumbling blindly forward, unable to contain the whirlwinds which the war had unloosed.[18]

Writing in 1931 Albert Thomas looked back on "the boldness of the solutions imagined in 1919":

We are beginning to see that the historian who a century later may analyse the facts of this memorable year will lay by far the greatest stress on the creation of international institutions. What he will find it necessary to explain will not be the timidity but the boldness of their constitutions, not the hesitations of certain States but the rapidity with which an organisation was set up which in many respects ran counter to the traditional conceptions of the law of nations.[19]

Edward Phelan writing in 1949 and reflecting on the conditions of 1919 provided at least one explanation for this "boldness":

[M]illions of men, trained in the use of arms, to whom extravagant promises had been freely made were about to be demobilised; the wave of unrest had spread even to such stable and peaceful democracies as the Netherlands and Switzerland. How gravely the situation was viewed may be indicated by the fact that during the Peace Conference itself, Clemenceau moved many thousands of troops into Paris as a precaution against rioting in the streets. The decision to give labour matters a prominent place in the Peace Treaty was essentially a reflection of this preoccupation. *The Peace Conference accepted the proposals of its Labour Commission without much concern either for the generalisations of the Preamble or for the details of the proposed organisation.* In other circumstances, it is indeed highly probable that some of the more daring innovations of the latter, such as the provision that non-Government delegates should enjoy equal voting power and equal status with Government

---

18 Harold Butler, *Confident Morning* (Faber and Faber, London, 1950) 12, 175.
19 Albert Thomas, *The International Labour Organisation: The First Decade* (George Allen & Unwin Ltd., London, 1931) 20.

delegates in the International Labour Conference would have been considered unacceptable.[20] [Emphasis added]

21st-century commentators see the creation of the ILO less in terms of idealism and more as a bulwark against Marxist revolution. Writing at the turn of the century Krzysztof Drzewicki comments:

> Thus the international community began dealing with labour issues in an organised and regular manner after World War I, largely for reasons attributable to neither a charity nor an enlightened rationality of governments, but clearly to their fears of further revolutionary unrest which were sweeping over virtually all of Europe at that time.[21]

Matthew Parish a decade later follows the same line, attributing its inception to the interplay between Marxism and socialism:

> There was a perhaps surprising level of acceptance within the international community of the demands of this [Marxist] movement because in the early twentieth century several countries, including Mexico, Russia, Ireland, Germany, Austria and Italy suffered either revolutions or severe civil disturbances instigated by organised labour movements. The internationalisation of labour rights was seen as a way of defusing this threat. Thus was the International Labour Office (ILO, now the International Labour Organisation) born, charged upon its inception in 1919 with promoting an international labour law. [...] [T]he workings of the ILO in this early stage are important, because they represent the internationalisation of individual rights. The category of economic and social rights, so important in contemporary human rights discourse, was a creation of the ILO and the early twentieth-century socialists who pushed for the organisation's creation.[22]

Steve Hughes and Nigel Haworth remind us that:

> The ILO was born within the capitalist system and remains firmly in that system. Its traditional role has been to challenge policy settings and outcomes within the system, in order to foster adaptation of the system. Its origins

---

20 Edward Phelan, "The Contribution of the ILO to Peace" in *International Labour Review* (ILO, Geneva, 1949) Vol. LIX, No. 6.
21 Krzysztof Drzewicki, "The Right to Work and Rights in Work" in Asbjørn Eide and others, eds, *Economic, Social and Cultural Rights* (2nd Revised edn, Martinus Nijhoff Publishers, Dordrecht, 2001) 223.
22 Matthew Parish, *Mirages of International Justice: The Elusive Pursuit of a Transnational Legal Order* (Edward Elgar Publishing Limited, Cheltenham, 2011) 187.

as an institution to contain revolutionary worker mobilization by providing a voice and presence in the capitalist system for workers should not be
forgotten.[23]

Few if any commentators in the present century have ranged beyond this Marxist/
socialist/capitalist stand-off. Few have acknowledged the role played by Catholic
Social Teaching in the creation and evolution of the ILO.

ILO Constitution 1919 and the Declaration of Philadelphia 1944

Commission on International Labour Legislation and the "Phelan Memorandum"

The ILO's Constitution was prepared by the Commission on International
Labour Legislation of the Peace Conference in 1919 and formed part of the
Treaty of Versailles. The members of the Commission were drawn from Belgium,
Cuba, Czechoslovakia, France, Italy, Japan, Poland, the United Kingdom and the
United States (with those States which had suffered defeat being excluded), under
the Chairmanship first of Samuel Gompers, head of the American Federation of
Labour and then of English socialist campaigner and member of the Second
(Socialist) International George Barnes.

The fundamentals of Catholic Social Teaching and its concept of labour rights
were not alien to the jurisprudence of a majority of these nations. Pope Pius XI
pinpointed the cross-fertilisation as having begun as part of the Versailles peace
process following World War One:

> Furthermore, after the terrible war, when the statesmen of the leading
> nations were attempting to restore peace on the basis of a thorough reform
> of social conditions, did not they, among the norms agreed upon to regulate
> in accordance with justice and equity the labour of the workers, give sanction
> to many points that so remarkably coincide with Leo's principles and instruc-
> tions as to seem consciously taken therefrom?[24]

For him, *Rerum novarum* was "the Magna Charta upon which all Christian activity in the social field ought to be based, as on a foundation".[25]

It was, however, the United Kingdom, in whose democracy confessional politics (in the sense of Christian democracy – primarily Catholic – as understood
in Continental Europe) was almost entirely absent that dominated the debate.
A think tank had been set up late in World War One by the United Kingdom

23 Steve Hughes and Nigel Haworth, *The International Labour Organisation (ILO): Coming
in from the Cold* (Routledge, London and New York, 2011) 43.
24 Pope Pius XI, *Quadragesimo anno* (1931) s 22 © Copyright – Libreria Editrice Vaticana.
25 Pope Pius XI, *Quadragesimo anno* (1931) s 39 © Copyright – Libreria Editrice Vaticana.

Ministry of Labour, the two principal actors in which were both future Directors-General of the ILO – Harold Butler and Edward Phelan. It was the "Phelan Memorandum"[26] which set out options for how the future ILO would be structured, all of which included the principle of tripartism. Olga Hidalgo-Weber concludes:

> Despite heated talks which almost broke down altogether on certain points, such as tripartism and the distribution of votes, if we compare the initial British draft with the final convention which created the ILO, it is clear that the British draft formed the matrix for it.[27]

Edward Phelan summarised the proposals put forward by the British Government in the "Phelan Memorandum", which:

> came down definitely in favour of the creation of special machinery for the treatment of international labour problems. It decided in favour of one organisation, that organisation to be permanent and to hold periodical meetings; it decided in favour of the representation of employers and workers as well as the representation of governments, and further that non-governmental representatives should have the same status as their governmental colleagues; it decided that the choice of these non-governmental representatives should be made in agreement with the most representative organisations of employers and workers as the case might be: it decided that periodical reports should be made on the application of the decisions taken, and that workers' organisations should have the right to draw attention to cases of non-observance.[28]

Emmet O'Connor attributes the promotion of tripartism to Edward Phelan:

> The concept of tripartism was more original to Phelan. Bipartite employer–labour councils for the improvement of industrial relations were being introduced in Britain, following the report of J.H. Whitley in 1917, but tripartism was a step beyond Whitleyism, and Phelan's memoirs make it clear that his thinking was dictated by the dynamics of the proposed ILO. Tripartism was

---

26 *Memorandum on the Machinery and Procedure Required for the International Regulation of Industrial Conditions, Prepared in the British Delegation, January 15–20, 1919* in J T Shotwell, *Origins of the International Labour Organization* Volume II (Columbia University Press, New York, 1934) Document 25 117–125.

27 Olga Hidalgo-Weber, "Social and Political Networks and the Creation of the ILO: The Role of British Actors" in Sandrine Kott and Joëlle Droux, eds, *Globalizing Social Rights: The International Labour Organization and Beyond* (ILO and Palgrave Macmillan, Basingstoke, 2013) 17, 20.

28 E J Phelan, "The Preliminaries of the Peace Conference, British Preparations" in J T Shotwell *Origins of the International Labour Organization* Volume I (Columbia University Press, New York, 1934) 110.

also controversial in its rejection of trade union demands for a body composed of delegates of governments and unions only, and in equal measure.
Offending the unions, Phelan was told by his colleagues, would be self-
defeating, the whole point of establishing the ILO being to appease the
social democratic left and keep workers out of communism. Again, from
Phelan's memoirs it is evident that he was prepared to dismiss political expe-
diency, convinced that an organization without the backing of all interested
parties could not deliver practical results.[29]

In this there is a striking parallel with Catholic Social Teaching, which rejects the
idea of a class struggle and advocates co-operation between "the wealthy and
the working men". The seminal pronouncement is that of Pope Leo XIII in his
Encyclical *Rerum novarum* (1891):

> 19. *The great mistake made in regard to the matter now under consideration
> is to take up with the notion that class is naturally hostile to class, and that the
> wealthy and the working men are intended by nature to live in mutual conflict.*
> So irrational and so false is this view that the direct contrary is the truth. Just
> as the symmetry of the human frame is the result of the suitable arrangement
> of the different parts of the body, so in a State is *it ordained by nature that
> these two classes should dwell in harmony and agreement, so as to maintain the
> balance of the body politic.* Each needs the other: capital cannot do without
> labour, nor labour without capital. Mutual agreement results in the beauty
> of good order, while perpetual conflict necessarily produces confusion and
> savage barbarity.[30] [Emphasis added]

Indeed, tripartism as a mechanism corresponds with the need not to promote the
atomised aspirations of the individual or interest group at the expense of their
fellow citizens but instead to promote "the common good" which is at the heart
of Catholic Social Teaching.

It is tempting to read into Edward Phelan's work influences having their origin in the fact that he was born in 1888 an Irish Catholic, schooled by Jesuits,
who for a student of his generation (it is not unreasonable to conjecture) would
have been well-versed in the concepts of Catholic Social Teaching in the wake
of Pope Leo XIII's Encyclical *Rerum novarum*. As a member of the Intelligence

---

29 Emmet O'Connor, "Edward Phelan: A Biographical Essay" in *Edward Phelan and the ILO:
The Life and Views of an International Social Actor* (International Labour Office, Geneva,
2009) 18. The still young Edward Phelan writing in 1925 was wholly self-effacing (border-
ing on disingenuous) as regards the tripartite mechanism: "The Conference thus provides a
rather startling example of vocational representation, and it is curious to note that so bold
an experiment should have been made in the international field". E J Phelan, "The International Labour Organisation: Its Ideals and Results" in *Studies: An Irish Quarterly Review*,
Vol. 14, No. 56 (December 1925) 611, 616.
30 Pope Leo XIII, *Rerum novarum* (1891) s 19 © Copyright – Libreria Editrice Vaticana.

Division of the Ministry of Labour responsible for the examination of foreign questions[31] he surely would have been aware of the 19th-century Catholic social initiatives tending to tripartism, particularly those of Bishop of Mainz, Wilhelm Emmanuel von Ketteler, Bishop Mermillod of Fribourg in Switzerland and the Fribourg Union.[32] Nothing however in the documentary records, at least in so far as these have come to light, supports this reading and *post hoc ergo propter hoc* has always been a sinkhole for the inductive researcher. Yet it is tempting.[33]

ILO Constitution 1919

The provisions of the Constitution are expressed in a language compatible not with the language of *rights*, which has dominated the justice discourse since the end of World War Two (though elements such as equal treatment for men and women and child labour were later absorbed into the canon of human rights), but of *welfare*. In this, they resonate more strongly with the principles of Catholic Social Teaching.[34]

The Preamble to the ILO Constitution 1919 states:

> Whereas universal and lasting peace can be established only if it is based upon social justice;

> And whereas conditions of labour exist involving such injustice, hardship and privation to large numbers of people as to produce unrest so great that the peace and harmony of the world are imperilled; and an improvement of those conditions is urgently required; as, for example, by the regulation of the hours of work, including the establishment of a maximum working day and week, the regulation of the labour supply, the prevention of unemployment, the provision of an adequate living wage, the protection of the worker against sickness, disease and injury arising out of his employment, the protection of children, young persons and women, provision for old age and injury, protection of the interests of workers when employed in countries other than their own, recognition of the principle of equal remuneration for

31 E J Phelan, "The Preliminaries of the Peace Conference, British Preparations" in J T Shotwell, ed, *Origins of the International Labour Organization* Volume I (Columbia University Press, New York, 1934) 106.

32 See Chapter 3.

33 This is not an interpretation currently in vogue with ILO historians. Kari Tapiola in his recent study focusses exclusively on the contribution of the ILO Workers' Group, specifically non-confessional trade unions, in the adoption and development of tripartism. It is apparent that the influence of any other value system was outside his brief. Kari Tapiola, *The Driving Force: Birth and Evolution of Tripartism – Role of the ILO Workers' Group* (ILO, Geneva, 2019) <www.ilo.org/actrav/info/pubs/WCMS_710908/lang--en/index.htm> (accessed 17 October 2020) © ILO.

34 For a discussion on the fundamental difference of approach between Catholic Social Teaching and human rights, see Chapter 2.

work of equal value, recognition of the principle of freedom of association, the organization of vocational and technical education and other measures;

Whereas also the failure of any nation to adopt humane conditions of labour is an obstacle in the way of other nations which desire to improve the conditions in their own countries;

The High Contracting Parties, moved by sentiments of justice and humanity as well as by the desire to secure the permanent peace of the world, and with a view to attaining the objectives set forth in this Preamble, agree to the following Constitution of the International Labour Organization:[35]

Within Section II, General Principles, of the ILO Constitution in its original form in 1919 (Part XIII of the Treaty of Versailles)[36] Article 427 provides:

The High Contracting Parties, recognising that the well-being, physical, moral and intellectual, of industrial wage-earners is of supreme international importance, have framed, in order to further this great end, the permanent machinery provided for in Section I and associated with that of the League of Nations.

They recognise that differences of climate, habits, and customs, of economic opportunity and industrial tradition, make strict uniformity in the conditions of labour difficult of immediate attainment. But, holding as they do, that labour should not be regarded merely as an article of commerce, they think that there are methods and principles for regulating labour conditions which all industrial communities should endeavour to apply, so far as their special circumstances will permit.

Among these methods and principles, the following seem to the High Contracting Parties to be of special and urgent importance:

First The guiding principle above enunciated that labour should not be regarded merely as a commodity or article of commerce.

Second The right of association for all lawful purposes by the employed as well as by the employers.

Third The payment to the employed of a wage adequate to maintain a reasonable standard of life as this is understood in their time and country.

Fourth The adoption of an eight hours day or a forty-eight hours week as the standard to be aimed at where it has not already been attained.

---

35 Preamble to the Constitution of the ILO (1919) <www.ilo.ch/dyn/normlex/en/f?p=1000
:62:0::NO:62:P62_LIST_ENTRIE_ID:2453907:NO> (accessed 17 October 2020) © ILO.
36 Treaty of Versailles 1919, Part XIII <www.ilo.org/public/libdoc/ilo/1920/20B09_18_e
ngl.pdf> (accessed 17 October 2020).

Fifth The adoption of a weekly rest of at least twenty-four hours, which should include Sunday wherever practicable.

Sixth The abolition of child labour and the imposition of such limitations on the labour of young persons as shall permit the continuation of their education and assure their proper physical development.

Seventh The principle that men and women should receive equal remuneration for work of equal value.

Eighth The standard set by law in each country with respect to the conditions of labour should have due regard to the equitable economic treatment of all workers lawfully resident therein.

Ninth Each State should make provision for a system of inspection in which women should take part, in order to ensure the enforcement of the laws and regulations for the protection of the employed.

Without claiming that these methods and principles are either complete or final, the High Contracting Parties are of opinion that they are well fitted to guide the policy of the League of Nations; and that, if adopted by the industrial communities who are members of the League, and safeguarded in practice by an adequate system of such inspection, they will confer lasting benefits upon the wage-earners of the world.

Given the avowedly secular context in which the Nine Articles were formulated, there is a pleasant irony in their description by Director-General Harold Butler (1932–1938) as the ILO's "Nine Articles of its faith, upon which Albert Thomas built a great body of doctrine with all the dialectic of a medieval theologian".[37]

Tripartism

Tripartism, as advocated in the "Phelan Memorandum", looked to practical work experience and to the effect on public opinion as justifying the necessity of its inclusion:

It would plainly be impossible for the Conference to arrive at a satisfactory agreement about labour questions without the participation of representatives of employers and workpeople in the discussion. Many of the questions discussed will relate to particular industries and could not be adequately treated without the assistance of employers and workpeople with a first-hand knowledge of the conditions. [...]

International public opinion could only be effectively created by allowing all parties to express their views freely and to vote if necessary. Moreover, if

37 Harold Butler, *Confident Morning* (Faber and Faber, London, 1950) 173.

the agreements arrived at are to be effectively observed when translated into terms of national legislation it is in the highest degree desirable that they should command the loyal adherence of trade unions and employers in the different countries. This is less likely to be secured unless those who speak for each party are fully accredited representatives, and are free to vote as such.[38]

Tripartism in the form in which it was subsequently adopted is embodied in Article 389 of the Treaty of Versailles:[39]

> The meetings of the General Conference of Representatives of the Members shall be held from time to time as occasion may require, and at least once in every year. It shall be composed of four Representatives of each of the Members, of whom two shall be Government Delegates and the two others shall be Delegates representing respectively the employers and the workpeople of each of the Members.
>
> Each Delegate may be accompanied by advisers, who shall not exceed two in number for each item on the agenda of the meeting. When questions specially affecting women are to be considered by the Conference, one at least of the advisers should be a woman.
>
> The Members undertake to nominate non-Government Delegates and advisers chosen in agreement with the industrial organisations, if such organisations exist, which are most representative of employers or workpeople, as the case may be, in their respective countries.
>
> [...] The names of the Delegates and their advisers will be communicated to the International Labour Office by the Government of each of the Members.
>
> The credentials of Delegates and their advisers shall be subject to scrutiny by the Conference, which may, by two-thirds of the votes cast by the Delegates present, refuse to admit any Delegate or adviser whom it deems not to have been nominated in accordance with this Article.

Reflecting on the significance of tripartism in the context of Catholic Social Teaching, Director-General Juan Somavia speaking in 2005 commented:

> There are some striking parallels, for example, between the ILO Constitution and the first social encyclical *Rerum Novarum* on the relations between

---

38 *Memorandum on the Machinery and Procedure Required for the International Regulation of Industrial Conditions, Prepared in the British Delegation, January 15–20, 1919* in J T Shotwell, *Origins of the International Labour Organization* Volume II (Columbia University Press, New York, 1934) Document 25, 117–125 at 118–120.

39 Treaty of Versailles 1919 <www.ilo.org/public/libdoc/ilo/1920/20B09_18_engl.pdf> (accessed 17 October 2020).

capital and work issued by Pope León XIII in 1891. The ILO Constitution reminds us that: "[…] universal and lasting peace can be established only if it is based upon social justice". And it created tripartism – dialogue between governments, workers and employers – as a fundamental vehicle for solving conflicts and maintaining peace. The encyclical says: "Let those in charge of States make use of the provision afforded by laws and institutions; let the rich and employers be mindful of their duties; let the workers, whose cause is at stake, press their claims for reason." *In both visions, peace and justice, justice and peace are inextricably woven together in tripartite dialogue.*[40] [Emphasis added]

In the present century, the trend towards individualism – the rise of a monad culture which conflicts so strikingly with the regard for the common good expressed in Catholic Social Teaching – has begun to impact adversely on tripartism. In his Report as Director-General to the 102nd Session of the ILC in 2013 Guy Ryder commented:

> 89. […] [T]he ILO's tripartite structure and methods have been the subject of criticism. Among the most familiar are the following: that at best they reflect past, but not contemporary, world of work realities; that the declining membership of some employers' and workers' organizations deprives them of the necessary representative legitimacy; and that such organizations are often unable to reach or speak for large segments of the working population, including those in the informal economy.

Referring to "a perceived trend in late-twentieth and early-twenty-first-century society away from the collective to the individual" he continued:

> 91. […] If there is a growing preference for advancing personal interests on an individual rather than collective basis, and an increased tendency to interact through technology-mediated networks rather than by joining formally constituted associative bodies, and if lifestyles are indeed eroding community and promoting the atomization of societies, then it is not surprising that the ILO should feel the effects.[41]

---

40 Juan Somavia, *The Challenge of a Fair Globalization*, Presentation at the Pontifical Lateran University on the Report of the World Commission on the Social Dimension of Globalization (Rome, 25 February 2005) <www.ilo.org/public/english/bureau/dgo/speeches/somavia/2005/rome.pdf> (accessed 17 October 2020) (c) ILO.

41 *Towards the ILO Centenary: Realities, Renewal and Tripartite Commitment*, Report of the Director-General, International Labour Conference 102nd Session 2013 Report 1(A) paras 89, 91 <www.ilo.org/public/libdoc/ilo/P/09383/09383(2013-102-1A).pdf> (accessed 17 October 2020) (c) ILO.

Social dialogue, and a corresponding diminution of class conflict, is at the heart of Catholic Social Teaching. The essence of tripartism is a dialogue between Governments, employers and workers. On the occasion of the ILO Centenary in 2019 Archbishop Bernardito Auza, Apostolic Nuncio and Permanent Observer of the Holy See to the United Nations wrote:

> The good practice and continued relevance of social dialogue, with its important contributions, is increasingly necessary, in a context of global developments, employment as well as in labour relations. Over the last century, we have had the pleasure to observe that, in order to promote a real social dialogue, the effective tripartite structure of the ILO, has been both an objective in itself and a means to achieve other objectives.[42]

Dialogue is inherent in tripartism, and dialogue has been placed at the forefront of CST by Pope Francis in his Encyclical *Fratelli tutti* (2020):

> 198. Approaching, speaking, listening, looking at, coming to know and understand one another, and to find common ground: all these things are summed up in the one word "dialogue". If we want to encounter and help one another, we have to dialogue. There is no need for me to stress the benefits of dialogue. [...]

> 211. In a pluralistic society, dialogue is the best way to realize what ought always to be affirmed and respected apart from any ephemeral consensus. Such dialogue needs to be enriched and illumined by clear thinking, rational arguments, a variety of perspectives and the contribution of different fields of knowledge and points of view.[43]

Declaration of Philadelphia 1944

The Declaration concerning the aims and purposes of the ILO (Declaration of Philadelphia) 1944[44] reaffirmed these *founding principles*:

---

42 Archbishop Bernardito Auza, Apostolic Nuncio and Permanent Observer of the Holy See to the United Nations, Address to the High-Level Meeting of the United Nations General Assembly to commemorate the 100th anniversary of the ILO (New York, 11 April 2019) <https://holyseemission.org/contents/statements/5cb0ae1bdd6e4.php> (accessed 13 September 2020). © 2015–2020 The Permanent Observer Mission of the Holy See to the United Nations. For a fuller discussion on the importance of dialogue within the ILO and as a principle of Catholic Social JTeaching, see Chapter 6.
43 Pope Francis, *Fratelli tutti* (2020) ss 198, 211 © Copyright – Libreria Editrice Vaticana.
44 Declaration of Philadelphia 1944 <www.ilo.ch/dyn/normlex/en/f?p=1000:62:0::NO:62 :P62_LIST_ENTRIE_ID:2453907:NO#declaration> (accessed 17 October 2020). The Declaration "continues to be fully relevant in the twenty-first century" – Declaration on Social Justice for a Fair Globalisation 10 June 2008 Preface <www.ilo.org/wcmsp5/g

- labour is not a commodity
- freedom of expression and of association are essential to sustained progress
- poverty anywhere constitutes a danger to prosperity everywhere
- the war against want requires to be carried on with unrelenting vigour within each nation, and by continuous and concerted international effort in which the representatives of workers and employers, enjoying equal status with those of governments, join with them in free discussion and democratic decision with a view to the promotion of the common welfare.

To make this a practical reality, the ILO was to promote *a ten point plan of action*:

(a) full employment and the raising of standards of living;
(b) the employment of workers in the occupations in which they can have the satisfaction of giving the fullest measure of their skill and attainments and make their greatest contribution to the common well-being;
(c) the provision, as a means to the attainment of this end and under adequate guarantees for all concerned, of facilities for training and the transfer of labour, including migration for employment and settlement;
(d) policies in regard to wages and earnings, hours and other conditions of work calculated to ensure a just share of the fruits of progress to all, and a minimum living wage to all employed and in need of such protection;
(e) the effective recognition of the right of collective bargaining, the cooperation of management and labour in the continuous improvement of productive efficiency, and the collaboration of workers and employers in the preparation and application of social and economic measures;
(f) the extension of social security measures to provide a basic income to all in need of such protection and comprehensive medical care;
(g) adequate protection for the life and health of workers in all occupations;
(h) provision for child welfare and maternity protection;
(i) the provision of adequate nutrition, housing and facilities for recreation and culture;
(j) the assurance of equality of educational and vocational opportunity.

Article V of the Declaration affirmed its universality, and also its progressive pragmatism:

> The conference affirms that the principles set forth in this Declaration are fully applicable to all peoples everywhere and that, while the manner of their application must be determined with due regard to the stage of social and economic development reached by each people, their progressive application

---

roups/public/---dgreports/---cabinet/documents/genericdocument/wcms_371208.pdf> (accessed 17 October 2020).

to peoples who are still dependent, as well as to those who have already achieved self-government, is a matter of concern to the whole civilized world.

It was in 1944 that the language of human rights, which was to be fully articulated four years later in the Universal Declaration of Human Rights, infiltrated (or, perhaps more charitably put, augmented) the ILO Constitution. Steve Hughes and Nigel Haworth observed of the Declaration of Philadelphia that:

> Critically it placed human rights at the center of the ILO's functions for the first time. [...] The inclusion of human rights at the center of the Philadelphia Declaration was significant. It was not only a key element in Phelan's [Edward Phelan, Director General 1941 to 1948] re-launch of the ILO and the reformulation of its constitution as it pushed for a place at the table of post-war planning, but also argued that labor standards were an indelible part of political democracy, bound up with a growing post-war emphasis on human rights and the pursuit of industrial prosperity.[45]

Gerry Rodgers and his co-authors writing in 2009 referring to the principles set out in the Declaration also see this as a turning point, where "the connection was made for the first time between economic and social development and basic human rights principles [...] the concept of universal social rights of the individual". Nevertheless, they strike a more cynical (albeit empirical) note. The principles "are, of course, regularly flouted":

> Labour is widely treated as a commodity, poverty persists alongside prosperity, equality and freedom of association are widely honoured in the breach, and peace and social justice still remain distant goals in many parts of the world. Realizing these principles therefore continues to frame the action of the ILO.[46]

The obvious convergence of the ILO Constitution and the Declaration of Philadelphia with Catholic Social Teaching was stated plainly by Archbishop Bertello, Observer of the Holy See, when addressing the 85th Session of the ILC in 1997:

> The Declaration of Philadelphia and the ILO Constitution with their solemn endorsements of the dignity of the human person and of labour have inspired the standards of this Organization. They constitute the essential

---

45 Steve Hughes and Nigel Haworth, *The International Labour Organisation (ILO): Coming in from the Cold* (Routledge, London and New York, 2011) 13.
46 Gerry Rodgers, Eddy Lee, Lee Swepston and Jasmien Van Daele,, *The ILO and the Quest for Social Justice 1919–2009* (Cornell University Press, Ithaca and International Labour Office, Geneva, 2009) 8, 44.

means for protecting, and if necessary, for reinterpreting the fundamental rights of workers in a world which is ever more complex and changing and which requires fresh thinking and the ability of governments, employers and workers to project themselves into the future in a spirit of constructive dialogue. In this connection the social doctrine of the Catholic Church is quite clear. The economy is to serve man, and not the reverse, and the rights of workers come before the rights of capital.[47]

Origins and Social Catholicism

In the same way that Pope Leo XIII's Encyclical *Rerum novarum* did not spring fully formed from the papal mind but was the summation of decades of Catholic social thinking, the ILO was a synthesis of its antecedents.[48] Albert Thomas wrote of this:

> The special treatment accorded to the social problem by the peace-makers of 1919 can be understood only in the light of the past. In the history of institutions thought has always preceded action. For a century, indeed, the movement of ideas had paved the way for the new organisation and had even before the War taken concrete form and provided lessons for the future.[49]

Writing in 1924 G A Johnston commented on the ILO's origins: "While it is a child of the War, its birth had already been prepared for by almost a century of effort".[50]

As former ILO Director-General David Morse (in office 1948–1970)[51] noted in an address to mark the 50th anniversary of the ILO, the Allied Governments

> had to take due account of the international workers' conferences, held during the war in Leeds, Stockholm and Berne, which had urged and resolved that the terms of peace should ensure to the workers minimum guarantees

---

47 Record of the Proceedings of the 85th Session of the ILC 1997 172–173 <www.ilo.org/public/libdoc/ilo/P/09616/09616(1997-85).pdf> © ILO (accessed 17 October 2020).

48 A comprehensive history of those antecedents, both secular and religious, is to be found in John W Follows, *Antecedents of the International Labour Organization* (Oxford University Press, London, 1951).

49 Albert Thomas, *The International Labour Organisation: The First Decade* (George Allen & Unwin Ltd., London, 1931) 22. The origin and evolution of those antecedents has been widely researched and a secular history is outside the scope of this book (though as rooted in the evolution of Catholic Social Teaching is explored in Chapter 3).

50 G A Johnston, *International Social Progress: The Work of the International Labour Organisation of the League of Nations* (George Allen & Unwin Ltd., London, 1924) 14 (this quotation is taken from Chapter II "The Origins of International Labour Legislation").

51 A short biography is available on the ILO's website at <www.ilo.org/global/about-the-ilo/how-the-ilo-works/ilo-director-general/former-directors-general/WCMS_192712/lang--en/index.htm> (accessed 17 October 2020).

in regard to labor legislation and trade union rights, in recognition of the signal services rendered during the war by the workers, both in the factories and on the battlefield.[52]

What was the underlying motivation, what was the cultural and religious context of the members of the Commission on International Labour Legislation which in early 1919 drafted the ILO Constitution? Was it primarily liberal or socialist secularism as Daniel Maul suggests?

> The organization's roots can be traced back to the crossroads of (social) liberal and Socialist aspirations in the nineteenth century. [...] [T]he ILO was a supreme expression of liberal traditions of internationalist thought and action. At the same time, it incorporated the central aims of the Second (Socialist) International (1889–1916) and the international trade union movement, which was an important – if not the most important – driver behind the ILO's founding.[53]

Daniel Maul's secularist view is shared by Jean-Michel Servais and Valérie Van Goethem, who go yet further than he by distancing those origins from any particular ideology and who see in the creation of the ILO in 1919

> a reaction to what was an almost exclusively economic perception of development and recalled that men, women and children deserving of respect and protection were involved. The Organization owes its very existence to the efforts of humanists and of well-intentioned men, particularly industrialists, and little in fact to any particular ideology.[54]

For the *founding* of the ILO this has in the historical canon been a largely unchallenged hypothesis, but as to the nature and content of the ILO Constitution, its tripartite form and the evolution of the workings of the ILO other equally important influences must be acknowledged. There was a Catholic dimension. Not all workers' organisations were rooted in socialism, something particularly

---

52 David A Morse, *The Origin and Evolution of the I.L.O. and Its Role in the World Community* (New York State School of Industrial and Labor Relations, Cornell University, Ithaca, New York, 1969) 7–8.

53 He does however see the connection to Catholicism when discussing the role of the International Association for Labour Legislation (IALL) formed in 1900 which "appealed to representatives of the social Christian (Catholic) doctrine" and had "significant lines of continuity" with the ILO. A majority of the members of the Commission on International Labour Legislation at the Peace Conference in Paris were known to each other through the IALL: Daniel Maul, *The International Labour Organization: 100 Years of Global Social Policy* (De Gruyter, Berlin, 2019) 4, 18–20.

54 Jean-Michel Servais and Valérie Van Goethem, *International Labour Organization* (Second edition) (Wolters Kluwer, Alphen aan den Rijn, 2016) para 218.

true of the Catholic trade union movement.[55] In a history of its own origins the ILO acknowledged this plurality:

> Politically it drew on the main European democratic political currents of its time, in particular social democracy, Christian democracy and social liberalism, and actors from each of these perspectives participated in its work and contributed to its development.[56]

What Albert Thomas described as "the movement of ideas" on a Catholic plane reached a focal point at the end of World War One. Alongside the socialist trade unions, the Catholic unions demanded the drawing up of international labour legislation. Calls for the inclusion in the Peace Treaty of such legislation were made at the conference at the Hague in June 1918 of the Belgian Christian and free trade unions. The French Federation of Catholic Workers made the same demand in December 1918 in a letter addressed to US President Wilson. At their international conference in Paris in March 1919 the Christian trade unions not only echoed these earlier demands but also put forward a detailed legislative programme; including a call for the creation of an international labour organisation tasked with promulgating labour laws with an international inspectorate to monitor their adoption and application. It was this conference that put forward the proposal which led directly to the tripartite structure of what was to become the ILO, albeit in a modified form – a call for each participating country to send two delegates each from Government, employers and workers.[57]

Writing in 1933, former (and the first) Jesuit in residence at the ILO André Arnou reflected on the psychology of the creation of the ILO:

> L'organisation internationale du Travail c'est plus qu'un moment de la conscience humaine: pour ses créateurs enthousiastes, ce doit être la conscience sociale du monde, vigilante, active, s'il le faut incisive et mordante. Après la guerre, en un de ces instants psychologiques où les peuples secoués, réveillés, même rapprochés par tant de malheurs, ont comme une intuition douloureuse de leurs devoirs et de leurs solidarités d'humanité, les nations ont voulu donner à cette conscience une voix qui ne s'éteigne point, qui ne se taise point.[58]

---

55 See Chapter 3.
56 Gerry Rodgers, Eddy Lee, Lee Swepston and Jasmien Van Daele, *The ILO and the Quest for Social Justice 1919–2009* (Cornell University Press, Ithaca and International Labour Office, Geneva, 2009) 2.
57 Maurice Barbier, "Les Relations Entre l'Église Catholique et l'Organisation International du Travail" in *Politique étrangère*, Vol. 37, No. 3 (1972) (Institut Français des Relations Internationales) 351, 353–354.
58 [The ILO is more than just a moment of human awareness: for its enthusiastic founders, this would be the social conscience of the world, vigilant, alert, and if necessary incisive and penetrating. After the war, in one of those psychological situations where shaken, roused

His later successor as Jesuit in residence Albert Le Roy (in office 1936 to 1955) writing in 1937 reflected on the mural in the entrance hall of the then premises of the ILO in Geneva, a scene depicting Christ in his workshop, surrounded by disciples and tradesmen, which had been donated to the ILO by the International Federation of Christian Trade Unions (J P S Serrarens, its secretary, and Gaston Tessier, secretary general of the Confédération Française des Travailleurs Chrétiens themselves feature in the mural, sitting in a corner and contemplating the scene):

> Mieux que de longs discours, cette fresque nous fait entendre clairement qu'entre le catholicisme social et l'Organisation internationale du Travail d'étroites et cordiales relations se sont nouées, fondées sur une estime réciproque. Dans l'institution de Genève, les catholiques ont su discerner une force puissante, capable de créer un peu plus de justice dans le monde. Et, d'autre part, le Bureau international du Travail, cherchant sincèrement à faire oeuvre universelle et à n'exclure personne de ceux qui acceptent de travailler avec lui à son oeuvre de progrès social, s'est toujours montré prêt à donner aux catholiques la place qui leur revenait.[59]

The most recent historian of the ILO records that from "the very first day" one question had to be answered: "whose organization, exactly, would and could it be; and what kinds of workers and what forms of work would it represent?"[60]

The ILO itself regards the "driving forces" for its creation as:

> security, humanitarian, political and economic considerations. The founders of the ILO recognized the importance of social justice in securing peace, against a background of the exploitation of workers in the industrializing nations of that time. There was also increasing understanding of the world's

---

peoples, so close in time to such misfortunes, become, as if through intuitive suffering, aware of their duties and of the obligations placed upon them by their common humanity; the nations desired to give to this conscience a voice which could not falter, which could not fall silent.] A Arnou, *L'Organisation internationale du Travail et les Catholiques* (Éditions Spes, Paris, 1933) 87.

59 [Better than an extended debate, this mural lets us clearly understand that social Catholicism and the ILO are bound together in a close and warm relationship, based upon mutual esteem. Catholics have identified in that institution in Geneva a powerful force, capable of creating a little more justice in the world. And, for its part, the International Labour Office, genuinely seeking to work universally and not to exclude anyone willing to work with it in its task of social progress, has always shown itself ready to accord to Catholics the role due to them.] Albert Le Roy, *Catholicisme social et organisation internationale due travail* (Éditions Spes, Paris, 1937) 7–9.

60 Daniel Maul, *The International Labour Organization: 100 Years of Global Social Policy* (De Grutyer, Berlin, 2019) 33.

economic interdependence and the need for cooperation to obtain similarity of working conditions in countries competing for markets.[61]

This self-assessment lends insufficient weight to the social, economic and political climate of 1919 in which the Treaty of Versailles was negotiated and concluded.

The ILO, the Holy See and Catholic organisations

Beyond mere political expedience another force was at play, one which has in the histories of the ILO received little attention; the interaction between the ILO, the Holy See and Catholic organisations.

Although during the course of its first decade this was to evolve rapidly, at the time of its formation the ILO as an institution had no formal association with the Vatican. Dominique Peccoud (Jesuit in residence at the ILO 1997–2008) comments:

> The ILO itself also had no specific links with the Catholic Church. It was, rather, very much shaped by two ethical axes that crossed each other in the ILO's origins: the first one involved the Freemasons and liberal Jews, the second a current that went from Catholics to liberal Protestants; all the four communities had developed major concerns about social justice and the development of the industrialized society from the beginning of the nine-teenth century.[62]

Albert Thomas: diplomatic initiatives 1926 to 1932

From 1926 until his death in 1932, Albert Thomas included in his annual Reports to the ILC an account of the relations of the ILO with "the Churches". It seems no coincidence that this innovation, seven years into the life of the ILO, came about as a result of the appointment in 1926 of the Jesuit in residence as spiritual director to the Director-General. It proved to be short-lived. With the appointment in 1932 of Harold Butler as his successor, and during the years leading to the Declaration of Philadelphia in 1944, with the sole exception of acknowledging in 1931 the Encyclical of Pope Pius XI *Quadragesimo anno*, the Reports to the ILCs of the Directors-General made almost no further reference to Catholicism or indeed to any religious dimension. During this secularised

61 *History of the ILO* <www.ilo.org/global/about-the-ilo/history/lang--en/index.htm> (accessed 17 October 2020).
62 *A Discussion with Dominique Peccoud, SJ* (Berkley Center for Religion, Peace and World Affairs, Georgetown University, 23 February 2011) <http://berkleycenter.georgetown.edu /interviews/a-discussion-with-dominique-peccoud-s-j> (accessed 17 October 2020) © 2020 Berkley Center for Religion, Peace & World Affairs.

period, various delegates to the ILCs did in their conference addresses emphasise the importance of Catholic principles of social justice as being fundamental elements in the laws of their own countries, but these individual expressions received no general endorsement either from the ILO as an institution or amongst the ILC delegates.

In his Report to the ILC 1926 Albert Thomas briefly addressed the topic of the ILO's relations with the churches, singling out the Catholic Church:

> Since the Encyclical of 1893 [*sic*] Catholic thought has not remained inert. The Church has not renounced the tradition which led it to occupy itself with international labour legislation. Perhaps it has not yet deliberately integrated in the corpus of its doctrines the new tendencies which have shown themselves in the field of industry and labour. But it follows with great interest an endeavour whose universal character cannot be misunderstood. One of the many proofs of this interest is the activity of the Catholics in the Christian trade unions. Another example is the "Social Week" movement, which for more than 20 years in France and various other countries has been the most active expression of educational activity on social problems.[63]

P J S Serrarens (International Federation of Christian Trade Unions) addressing the 8th Session of the ILC in 1926 reflected on this:

> Je suis heureux de pouvoir constater ici que le Directeur, dans le paragraphe qu'il a consacré aux relations avec les Eglises, a prouvé qu'il reconnaissait les grandes forces morales du christianisme. En effet, non seulement il n'y a aucune contradiction entre les bases de l'Organisation internationale du Travail et les principes énoncés par le Congrès des Eglises protestantes qui s'est tenu à Stockholm en 1925, mais j'ai pu exposer en plusieurs occasions que les principes de cette Organisation même peuvent être trouvés dans l'Encyclique *Rerum novarum*, de 1891, que le Directeur mentionne dans son Rapport. [...]
>
> [T]oute l'Encyclique est un appel éloquent aux Gouvernements, aux employeurs, aux travailleurs eux-mêmes, c'est-à-dire aux trois groupes représentés ici, en vue de l'amélioration du sort de la classe ouvrière. C'est un appel éloquent adressé à tous pour que règne enfin la justice sociale.
>
> [...] [L]e même esprit que celui des Encycliques de Léon XIII [...] doit être à la base de notre Organisation. . Je voudrais bien que la haute autorité de l'Eglise, qui a toujours exercé une si heureuse influence sur l'opinion publique, en faveur de la législation sociale et de la protection ouvrière, pût se

---

63 Albert Thomas, Report of the Director General to the 8th Session of the ILC 1926 172, para 93 <www.ilo.org/public/libdoc/ilo/P/09383/09383(1926-8).pdf> (accessed 17 October 2020) © ILO.

faire valoir d'une manière plus directe et plus efficace, au sein de cette assemblée où, parmi les considérations de politique nationale, parfois égoïstes, le but de notre Organisation, c'est-à-dire le bien-être physique, moral et intellectuel des travailleurs par l'application de la justice, est trop souvent oublié.[64]

In his Report to the 11th Session of the ILC in 1928, Albert Thomas went to great detail in discussing the correlation between Catholic teaching and the fundamental principles of the ILO.[65] He noted "The great movement, for example, which was originated in the Roman Catholic Church by the Encyclical "*Rerum Novarum*" continues to produce excellent results". He continued:

On assuming the pontificate (December, 1922) Pope Pius XI restated the catholic doctrine on moral, legal and social questions, and especially on "the right of ownership, the rights and duties of workmen, both agricultural and industrial, and relations between workers and employers". Pius XI protested energetically against those who, while recognising these principles, "acted throughout their lives exactly as if the teachings and orders so often reiterated had lost their initial value or had even been wholly repealed". The Pope therefore stated that these instructions should be again put into force, and specially emphasised the necessity of a "renaissance in the education of modern youth".

The Catholic Hierarchy has remained faithful to this spirit of the Encyclical "*Rerum Novarum*", and is intensifying its efforts to make the influence of

---

64 [I am pleased to be able to note at this point that the Director, in the paragraph which he devoted to relations with the churches, demonstrated his awareness of the great moral imperatives of Christianity. There is indeed not merely no contradiction between the basis of the International Labour Organisation and the principles proclaimed by the Congress of Protestant Churches held in Stockholm in 1925, but, as I have been able to demonstrate on many occasions, the principles themselves of this Organisation are to be found in the Encyclical *Rerum novarum* of 1891 to which the Director refers in his Report.

The entire Encyclical is an eloquent appeal to Governments, employers and workers themselves, that is, to the three groups represented here, with a view to improve the lot of the working class. It is an eloquent appeal to everyone that in the end social justice should prevail.

That same spirit which is found in the Encyclicals of Leo XIII should be the foundation of our Organisation. I sincerely wish that the high authority of the Church, which has always exercised such a favourable influence on public opinion as regards social legislation and worker protection, could bring this about in a way more direct and efficient, within this assembly, where, amongst issues of national politics, sometimes self-serving, the goal of our Organisation, that is to say the physical, moral and intellectual wellbeing of workers through the application of justice, is too often forgotten.] Record of the Proceedings of the 8th Session of the ILC 1926, 82–83 <www.ilo.org/public/libdoc/ilo/P/09616/09616(1926-8) V.1.pdf> (accessed 17 October 2020) © ILO.

65 Albert Thomas, Report of the Director-General to the 11th Session of the ILC 1928 56–59 <www.ilo.org/public/libdoc/ilo/P/09383/09383(1928-11).pdf> (accessed 17 October 2020) © ILO.

the Encyclical felt in everyday life. Provincial decrees, pastoral letters, collective manifestoes, and catechisms all reiterate and expand the teachings of Leo XIII on the rules of a really Catholic social organisation, on an adequate wage, legitimate strikes, conciliation, and the duties of the workman to assist his companions in joining "associations which support in a Christian manner the interests of the workers".

He then writes for three closely printed pages about the contemporary initiatives in matters of labour protection of the Catholic Church in a wide variety of countries, and the Church's approach (articulated in the Christmas message of Austrian Bishops in 1925) that "it is not with the devil of socialism that the demon of capitalism can be driven out". His approach is ambiguous: is he merely neutrally *reporting* developments in Catholic labour doctrine (if so, why, and why at such length?), is he as Director-General *endorsing* them or is there a higher diplomatic purpose? As a life-long socialist, Albert Thomas surely was not about to change horses and demonise the political philosophy which drove him. A clue lies in his concluding remarks:

> It has been considered important to give the above quotations here and so re-emphasise the Catholic doctrine enunciated in the Encyclical of 1891. In light of this doctrine it is not difficult to understand how, from the point of view of their own teachings, the Catholics can give their support not only to the programme of labour legislation defined in Part XIII but also to the aspirations from which that programme was formed.

Albert Thomas again warmed to his theme in his Report to the 12th Session of the ILC in 1929.[66]

> Last year an attempt was made to review the development of the social doctrine of Catholicism, particularly during the past ten years. This review was sympathetically received by the Catholic press, which appreciated the objective outlook from which it was written. It may therefore be desirable to carry the review somewhat further this year.

He continued:

> The Papal Encyclical and Episcopal messages, of which an account was given in last year's Report, were, in spite of their detailed character and the new contributions which they made to the subject, definitely not intended to establish any particular economic and social system. Their only object was

---

66 Albert Thomas, Report of the Director-General to the 12th Session of the ILC 1929 58–61 <www.ilo.org/public/libdoc/ilo/P/09383/09383(1929-12).pdf> (accessed 17 October 2020) © ILO.

to draw attention to the eternal principles of justice and charity and to give guidance to men of action who have to deal with the constantly changing circumstances of practical industrial life.

Specifically, he set out a short history of the International Catholic Social Union, focussing on "the essential principle of the Catholic Social movement":

> The principle of the legally organised trade, in which capital and labour are bound together by a solidarity of interests and by direct contact through permanent bodies to which certain powers of the public authorities are delegate and which are responsible for maintaining order at all stages of production and distribution, and for reconciling the autonomy of the trade corporations with the general prosperity of the community.

Though he did not expressly discern a parallelism in the programme of Catholic Social doctrine and the structure and principles of the ILO itself, this conclusion cannot fail to be drawn from the inclusion at such length of such an exposition in his Report. He set out his motivation:

> It has been thought necessary to give the above brief outline of the Catholic Social doctrine; not only is it unexpectedly acquiring an immediate practical interest owing to the action of a number of States, but it explains the active interest which is taken in the Office by the Catholic Social movement. It explains why the Paris Social Week, which was held in 1928 and was even more largely attended than usual, cordially welcomed the representative of the Office; why the Catholic Workers' Congress sent a pressing invitation to the Director, and why the "Caritas catholica", both at the Social Service Congresses and at its Basle Conference, was anxious to get into closer touch with the Office.

P J S Serrarens addressing the 12th Session of the ILC in 1929, commenting on Albert Thomas' Report to the ILC, again stressed the importance of the moral force found in the Catholic Church and other religious organisations for the success of the ILO:

> C'est pour cette raison qu'il sera inevitable, dans l'intérêt du succès de notre oeuvre, de faire appel à toutes les forces morales qui peuvent exercer une grande influence sur l'opinion publique. Je constate avec satisfaction que le Directeur du Bureau international du Travail a bien compris l'importance de l'appui que des forces morales comme l'église catholique et autres communautés religieuses peuvent représenter pour le succès de l'oeuvre de notre Organisation, et j'espère qu'il trouvera les moyens de rendre les relations avec les églises encore plus fructueuses que par le passé.

> Il ne rentre, en effet, pas dans la tâche de l'Eglise de faire une oeuvre de propagande directe pour chaque convention adoptée par notre Conférence,

mais les grands principes, qui sont à la base même de notre Organisation, les grands principes de justice et de charité, qui exigent qu'il soit fait droit aux revendications légitimes de la classe ouvrière, le principe de la protection nécessaire à accorder à la dignité humaine de tous les travailleurs, de toutes races et de toutes couleurs, nous les reconnaissons comme des principes essentiellement chrétiens et nous ne pouvons, du point de vue chrétien, que desirer leur réalisation complète.[67]

By 1930 the inclusion in the Reports of the Director-General to the ILC of notes on "the social tendencies of religious movements" had begun to attract criticism but Albert Thomas in his Report to the 14th Session of the ILC in 1930[68] had no doubt of the benefits:

> As a matter of fact, the more the Office endeavours to understand them, the deeper becomes its conviction that, in its difficult struggle for the creation of a real international life and for the protection of the workers, the great currents of thought and faith can aid and sustain it, and that these big movements will to an increasing degree have to take account of the daily realities of industrial life.

In that same Report he gave full weight to the "social spirit" of Catholicism, the importance of the Encyclical of Pope Leo XIII *Rerum novarum* – "the Christian Labour Charter for all Catholics, employers or workers" – and the impact of Catholicism on secular political institutions:

> This "current doctrine" provides, in labour matters, a common basis for the various political parties which while not denominational are nevertheless

67 [It is on this ground that there is no other course of action in the interests of the success of our work but to call upon those moral forces which have the power to exercise a strong influence over public opinion. I am pleased to note that the Director of the International Labour Office has well understood the importance of the support which moral forces such as the Catholic Church and other religious communities embody for the success of the work of our Organisation, and I hope that he will find the means whereby relations with the churches may become even more fruitful than hitherto. It does not indeed form part of the duties of the Church to engage in direct propaganda for each Convention which has been promulgated by our Conference, but the fundamental principles which form the basis itself of our Organisation, the fundamental principles of justice and charity, which require that effect be given to the rightful claims of the working class, to the principal of appropriate protection for the grant of human dignity for all workers, of all races and of all colours, these we understand as principles which are in essence Christian and from a Christian standpoint we can do no other than wish for their complete realisation.] Record of the Proceedings of the 12th Session of the ILC 1929 148 <www.ilo.org/public/libdoc/ilo/P/09616/09616(1929-12). pdf> (accessed 17 October 2020) © ILO.

68 Albert Thomas, Report of the Director-General to the 14th Session of the ILC 1930 59–62 <www.ilo.org/public/libdoc/ilo/P/09383/09383(1930-14).pdf> (accessed 17 October 2020) © ILO.

associated with Catholicism. It forms a rallying point and serves as a means of *rapprochement*.

Commenting on the relationship between the ILO and international Catholic organisations, Albert Thomas wrote in 1931:[69]

> The International Labour Office has followed in a spirit of wide sympathy the activities of religious bodies, on whose attention social problems have a strong claim.
>
> The great movement which was originated in the Roman Catholic Church by the Encyclical *Rerum Novarum* of 1891 has proved extremely fruitful. This Catholic labour charter has inspired a number of associations, which aim at establishing social equity. [...] Catholics as such have been able to participate in the work of labour protection defined by Part XIII [Treaty of Paris] and in the aspirations of which it is the outcome. In May 1929, in the course of the ceremony in which the Catholics of Rome celebrated the anniversary of the Encyclical *Rerum Novarum,* Father Balduzzi, Director and secretary of the Catholic Institute, referred to the results obtained by Leo XIII's denunciation of the rising tide of individualism and added that the principles of justice then laid down had been adopted in the social legislation of the various nations in turn and formed one of the most striking instances of the intervention of the State in connection with labour. The same ideas after the War had brought about the setting up of a permanent international organisation attached to the League of Nations, for the extension and universal adoption of labour legislation.
>
> The International Labour Organisation has received frequent proofs of the sympathy of Catholic Organisations in the work they have carried out, the researches they have made and their social propaganda.

Albert Thomas following this passage referred specifically to the "Social Weeks" of France,[70] an educational movement whose aim was "to deepen the doctrine of the Catholic Church on social questions", to which the ILO sent a representative, his close colleague Paul Devinat (who went on to represent the ILO at the Social Weeks for years to come).[71] Albert Thomas himself had sent a greeting to the delegates in 1929 as "strong moral forces" praising their readiness to assist the ILO in carrying out its task. He listed other Catholic organisations with

---

69 Albert Thomas, *The International Labour Organisation: The First Decade* (George Allen & Unwin Ltd., London, 1931) 360–362.
70 The Semaines Sociales de France, formed in 1904, continues its work to this day <www .ssf-fr.org/page/336239-decouvrir-les-semaines-sociales-de-france> (accessed 17 October 2020).
71 Paul Droulers, *Le Père Desbuquois at l'Action Populaire 1919–1946* (Les Éditions Ouvrières and Presses de l'Université Grégorienne, Paris and Rome, 1980) 125.

whom the ILO had a close collaborative relationship: the Association of Catholic Students; the International Bureau of Catholic Journalists; the International Catholic Association for the Protection of Girls; a permanent centre for the documentation and joint action set up by Catholic institutions of various countries interested in charitable work, hygiene and social service, the *Caritas Catholica*; the International Catholic Social Services Union; and the Catholic Union of International Studies.[72]

He singled out the support of Catholic organisations for the draft of what became the Forced Labour Convention 1930,[73] noting that the Catholic Union of International Studies had declared this to be "the effective means [...] of extending to all workers of the world the rules of law that establish labour protection and that [...] in most cases merely apply to labour legislation the principles of Christian social morality".[74]

Albert Le Roy writing in 1937[75] (and then in post as the Jesuit in residence) saw in the principles espoused by the ILO no impediment to collaboration between it and Catholic Social Teaching – on the contrary, such principles were a standing invitation for Catholics to join forces with the proponents of such beneficial legislation. It was through membership of workers' or employers' organisations and through Christian trade unions that Catholics could take their seats as ILC delegates or as experts. Nevertheless, one had to face the truth: a Catholic majority amongst the membership of employers' associations did exist in France, Belgium and the Netherlands, but these countries were exceptions, and on top of this the Catholic presence was confined to small and medium enterprises, and had yet done no more than begin to penetrate big business ("grand patronat"). That was not to exclude the possibility that amongst employers' representatives

---

72 In his Report to the ILC in 1927 Albert Thomas had referred to these Catholic organisations, which "extending and developing their international activities, have come still more closely in touch with the work of the Office, and cordial and sustained collaboration has naturally resulted". Albert Thomas, Report of the Director-General to the 10th Session of the ILC 1927 52 <www.ilo.org/public/libdoc/ilo/P/09383/09383(1927-10).pdf> (accessed 17 October 2020) © ILO.

73 Forced Labour Convention 1930 (C29) <www.ilo.org/dyn/normlex/en/f?p=NORM LEXPUB:12100:0::NO:12100:P12100_INSTRUMENT_ID:312174:NO> (accessed 17 October 2020).

74 Maurice Barbier credits the Catholic Union of International Studies as, amongst the Catholic organisations, having exercised the greatest influence on the ILO. It had been formed in 1917 in Fribourg with the aim of studying international issues in the light of Christian doctrine, and went on to represent specifically Catholic principles at the League of Nations – embracing within this role the activities of the ILO. Following its successful piloting of the Forced Labour Convention, it presented papers to the ILC in 1934 and 1935 on the rights of women at work, in 1936 on manual labour and in 1938 and 1939 on indigenous people in those regions under colonial administration. Maurice Barbier, "Les Relations Entre l'Église Catholique et l'Organisation International du Travail" in *Politique étrangère*, Vol. 37, No. 3 (1972) (Institut Français des Relations Internationales) 351–387, at 366–368.

75 Albert Le Roy, *Catholicisme social et organisation internationale du travail* (Éditions Spes, Paris, 1937) 7–9, chapter 5 "La collaboration des catholiques" 65–74.

there were not to be found leading Catholics, members of active religious organisations and speakers at Social Weeks, but it was not generally the case that these
had been chosen as delegates on the basis of such characteristics. If Catholic
employers and Christian trade unions were disadvantaged by being in a minority
in their home States (though as had been demonstrated in 1921 in the case of
the Netherlands, this was not an insuperable problem)[76] their remedy lay not with
the ILO itself but in enlarging their own national presence and political effectiveness. As for Catholic representation at a Government level, that this was possible
had already been demonstrated by the appointment as President of the ILC in
1926 of Mgr Nolens (a serving Government Minister in the Netherlands) and
the Abbé Brauns (former Employment Minister in Germany). He saw cooperation as extending however beyond mere participation in the ILC or within the
International Labour Office: there were also the Catholic organisations:

> Ici, nous sommes en présence de relations multiples et quotidiennes avec les
> groupements catholiques et toutes ont toujours été empreintes de la plus
> grand cordialité. On peut dire qu'il n'existe pas de groupement catholoque
> tant soit peu intéressé aux questions sociales qui ne soit entré en rapports
> avec le Bureau et qui n'ait eu à s'en féliciter.[77]

In May 1931 the 40th anniversary of the proclamation of Pope Leo XIII's
Encyclical *Rerum novarum* was celebrated in Rome. Albert Thomas, in a message read at the commemoration, acknowledged the Catholic contribution to the
establishment of the ILO:

> Chargée, par la confiance des peuples, au lendemain de la catastrophe mon-
> diale, d'établir, dans un but de paix et d'harmonie universelle un régime de
> travail véritablement humain, l'Organisation internationale du Travail a entre-
> pris cette tâche immense avec une ardeur pleine d'assurance. C'est qu'elle
> était consciente de n'être point une génération spontanée, l'explosion d'un
> enthousiasme subit, mais l'aboutissement d'initiatives déjà anciennes, d'une
> entente étroite et active de toutes les bonnes volontés ainsi que toutes les
> forces d'idéal. La semence était jetée dans une terre féconde, soigneusement

---

76 n 100.
77 [Here we enjoy contact on a daily basis with many Catholic associations and all have at all
    times had impressed upon them the warmest of welcomes. One can say that there does not
    exist a single Catholic association no matter how indirectly engaged with social issues which
    has not connected with the International Labour Office and which has not expressed its sat-
    isfaction in having done so.] Albert Le Roy gives as examples *les Semaines sociales de France,
    la Jeunesse Ouvrière Chrétienne*, the international association of students *Pax Romana*, the
    seafarers' welfare organisation *Apostolatus Maris*, the *Bureau international des journalistes
    catholiques*, the *National Catholic Welfare Conference* in Washington DC, as well as Catholic
    social and trade union movements in Canada and South America n 75.

préparée depuis des années par des ouvriers tenaces de la justice sociale, entre autres par ceux qui se réclament de l'Encyclique "Rerum Novarum".

He concluded:

> Dans ces assises de l'humanité du travail, tenues pour mettre un terme à l'injustice, à la misère, aux privations, nous entendons des syndicalistes, des hommes politiques, des Ministres du Travail critique l'*Encyclique Rerum Novarum* et, sous l'inspiration active de ses principes, nous apporter leur collaboration. Ainsi, la force morale de l'Église catholique et son esprit de conciliation qui peuvent aider puissamment à l'oeuvre de la justice et de la concorde internationale.[78]

A contemporary commentator, Stephen J Brown, himself a Jesuit, writing about the ILO in 1932 observed:

> [T]he best part of the activities of this organisation is directed towards embodying in people's ways of thinking, in manners, and in institutions reforms which, for the most part, are simply the confirmation of the explicit requirements of Christian morality. On several occasions, moreover, the Director of the ILO [Albert Thomas] has, without finding his views controverted, paid a tribute to the beneficial activities of Catholics, and, in particular, has pointed out the services rendered by the Christian workingmen's organisations, the international federation of which counts some four million adherents. He has not hesitated to reject the unjustifiable claims of the Socialists who, in certain countries, arrogate to themselves as a sort of monopoly the right to speak in the name of the working classes.[79]

---

78 [Charged, with the trust of the people, on the morrow of the global catastrophe, to establish, with the aim of securing universal peace and harmony, a truly humane labour organisation, the ILO enthusiastically undertook this immense responsibility full of confidence. It was conscious that this was no mere spontaneous growth, no sudden burst of enthusiasm, but the fulfilment of initiatives, themselves already well-established; the culmination of a close and active understanding of all the goodwill as well as of all the imperatives of idealism. The seed was sown in fertile soil, carefully tended for years by workers steadfast for social justice, amongst whom were those who called in aid the Encyclical "Rerum Novarum". In these gatherings of the world of labour, held to put an end to injustice, to misery, to deprivation, we hear trade unionists, politicians, Ministers of Labour critiquing the Encyclical *Rerum Novarum* and, inspired by its precepts, offering us their sincere collaboration. In this way, the moral authority of the Catholic Church and its spirit of conciliation can powerfully assist in the work of justice and international understanding.] Quoted in A Arnou, *L'Organisation internationale du Travail et les Catholiques* (Éditions Spes, Paris, 1933) 20, 95.

79 Stephen J Brown, *International Relations from a Catholic Standpoint* (Browne and Nolan Limited, Dublin, 1932) 194–195.

Why therefore has this interaction in its formative years between the ILO, the Holy See and Catholic organisations and its contribution to the development of the ILO not become more widely known?

Death of Albert Thomas – the curtain falls

Following Albert Thomas' death in 1932 the discussion about that interaction ceased, at least as reflected in the Reports of the Directors General and in the Proceedings of the ILO, as if a curtain had fallen. Save for very few passing references, Catholicism, Catholic Social Teaching and even Christianity itself was never again to feature in those Reports.[80] Individual delegates to the ILC would on occasion base their submissions on the Catholic traditions embodied in their domestic legal systems, and refer to Encyclicals which they felt best expressed the principles they wished to highlight, but nothing was heard from the ILO administration itself. The discussion was not to resume until decades later, and then only spasmodically, set in motion by the appointment by the Holy See in 1968 of a formal Observer of the ILC and by the high-profile address of Pope St Paul VI to the ILC on the occasion of the 50th anniversary of the founding of the ILO in 1969 – matters explored in Chapter 6.

It is perhaps just one of many information lacunae which are a result of the traditionally understated way in which the ILO has promoted itself, particularly during those formative years in which its bond with the Holy See was forged.

George Barnes in 1926 referred to the ILO's "quiet unostentatious work for the workers of the world".[81] Kathleen Gibberd in 1937 called the ILO "the unregarded revolution", its work a "remarkable yet largely unobserved advance in the direction of social justice" in a period of "political distrust, cynicism and despair".[82] A decade, and a further World War, later, R J P Mortished (retired Chief of the ILO Maritime Service) regretted that "In a vague way the British public does know something about the ILO, but it does not know nearly enough" and urged the ILO to "engage in more and more effective publicity".[83]

It also stemmed from the reluctance of the Holy See to engage publicly with the ILO, as Pope Pius XI continued to distance himself from secular political institutions; a reluctance which would last until the engagement of Pope St John XXIII with human rights at the dawn of the 1960s.

---

80 The Reports of the Directors-General and the Records of the Proceedings of the ILC for the period 1919 to 2019 (the 2020 ILC having been postponed due to the Covid-19 crisis) are available online from the ILO at <http://libguides.ilo.org/documentation> (accessed 17 October 2020).

81 George N Barnes, *History of the International Labour Office* (Williams and Norgate Limited, London, 1926) 78.

82 Kathleen Gibberd, *I.L.O.: The Unregarded Revolution* (J M Dent and Sons Limited, London, 1937) v–vi, 7.

83 R J P Mortished, *The World Parliament of Labour: A Study of the I.L.O.* (Fabian Publications Limited, London, 1946) 28–29.

By the 21st century the ILO's benign self-effacement had become something of a handicap. As the then Director-General Juan Somavia acknowledged in his Report to the ILC in 2004:

> The Organization and its activities are not well known even within the international networks of employers' and workers' organizations. *ILO publications are not widely cited in the literature on development, labour economics, industrial relations or social policy, and do not figure prominently in students' reading lists.* The ILO is mentioned quite frequently in debates and articles about globalization, but few of those referring to ILO standards in the context of corporate social responsibility display much knowledge of the standards themselves or of the system that backs them up.
>
> Although the ILO cannot be said to be secretive, *we can be criticized as inward looking, preoccupied with procedure, relatively slow in response, and having a style of expression that deters all but the most enthusiastic from discovering our ideas.* The Organization might therefore be wise to reflect on how it could become more outward looking, better able to express and communicate its messages and faster in responding to demands of individual constituents.[84] [Emphasis added]

The cumulative effect of the absence of discussion following the death of Albert Thomas coupled with this tendency towards self-effacement amounts in our times to collective amnesia on the part of the ILO as regards the role of Catholic Social Teaching in its formation and development.

Christian trade unionism and the ILO

In 1931 under the editorship of Albert Thomas, the ILO published an assessment of its first decade, and within that assessment is a first-hand account both of the close working relationship between the ILO and the International Federation of Christian Trade Unions and of the influence on the work of the ILO of Catholic Social Teaching and contemporary international Catholic organisations.[85]

In June 1920 a congress of Christian trade unions held at The Hague founded an International Federation as a continuation of an international secretariat based before World War One in Köln. By 1922 the membership base was substantial (in the region of three million) in Austria, Belgium, Czechoslovakia, France, Germany, Hungary, Italy, Luxembourg, the Netherlands, Poland, the Kingdom

---

84 ILO, *A Fair Globalisation: The Role of the ILO, Report of the Director-General on the World Commission on the Social Dimension of Globalisation,* Report of the Director-General to the International Labour Conference, 92nd Session, Geneva 2004 53 <www.ilo.org/public/l ibdoc/ilo/2004/104B09_112_engl.pdf> (accessed 17 October 2020).

85 Albert Thomas, *The International Labour Organisation: The First Decade* (George Allen & Unwin Ltd., London, 1931).

(later State) of the Serbs, Croats and Slovenes (later, Yugoslavia), Spain and Switzerland. As this clearly implies, "Christian" in this context denoted predominantly Catholic.[86] The founding principle of the International Federation of Christian Trade Unions was to defend on Christian principles the interests of workers. Amongst its objects was "To defend the social and economic interests of the workers, especially in the International Labour Organisation and the Economic Organisation of the League of Nations."[87]

The influence and even the internal cohesion (undermined by the Christian trade unions having taken a nationalist stance during the World War One)[88] of the newly formed Federation of Christian Trade Unions must not however be overstated. Efren Cordova describes it as being at the outset largely overshadowed by the communist-dominated World Federation of Trade Unions and the International Confederation of Free Trade Unions and so it seemed "doomed to play a secondary, gray and inconspicuous role", derided by its competitors as "the midget organisation" and "the faithful servant of the Vatican". Furthermore, Christian trade unionism was limited in terms of political geography, being largely confined to Europe. There was particular indifference towards it in the Anglo-American community "where no significant confessional trade unions have ever existed".[89] Patrick Pasture attributes this to the differing hierarchical structures of the Catholic Church and those of the Protestant Communion which lacked clerical authority.[90]

The relationship at this time between the Federation of Christian Trade Unions and the ILO was symbiotic.

Aurelien Zaragori records

> how the International Federation of Christian Trade Unions tried to organise itself, to act as an international body and an international force, though its participation in the activities of the International Labour Organization

86 See Chapter 3.
87 League of Nations Search Engine, *International Federation of Christian Trade Unions* <www .lonsea.de/pub/org/456> (accessed 5 July 2020).
88 For an account of the personal hostilities which emerged between members of Christian labour unions in the wake of the First World War, and how these were overcome in the formation of the Federation of Christian Trade Unions, see Paul Misner, *Catholic Labor Movements in Europe: Social Thought and Action 1914–1965* (The Catholic University of America Press, Washington, DC, 2015) 41–45.
89 Efren Cordova, "The Changing Character of the Christian International" in *Industrial Relations* Volume 23, Number 1, 1968 70.
90 Patrick Pasture, "The ILO and the Freedom of Association as the Ideal of the Christian Trade Unions" in International Institute of Social History Amsterdam (Jasmien Van Daele and others, eds), *ILO Histories: Essays on the International Labour Organization and Its Impact on the World during the Twentieth Century* (Peter Lang, Bern, 2010) 119.

[...] [I]t tried to coordinate its actions, to lessen its divisions and to issue common resolutions.[91]

As Misner points out, thus co-ordinated

the Christian labor unions (with their predominantly Catholic component) were able to present themselves as an organized international federation in short order so as not to leave the international discussion of labor issues in the ILO entirely in the hands of socialist labor leaders and those of the American Federation of Labor.[92]

At the first two sessions of the International Labour Conference, in Washington and Genoa, several delegations included representatives of the Christian trade unions as advisors. The movement was already gaining power. The International Labour Office sent a representative to The Hague Congress in 1920, as well as to the congress of the most important branch of the new Federation – the Federation of German Christian Trade Unions – held in Essen. After a delegation of the International Federation had visited the Office in May 1921, the Director appointed a special official to maintain regular relations with the Christian trade union movement.[93] The International Labour Office was thus in a position to draw the attention of the Christian unions to the International Labour Organisation and its work.

[...] Few congresses of Christian unions have been held without touching on the International Labour Organisation. They have passed resolutions in favour of the ratification of Conventions, or demanded the inclusion of certain special questions in the agenda of the Conference, or expressed demands more or less closely connected with the work and aims of the Organisation. [94]

B W Schaper stressed the importance to Albert Thomas of his relationship with the Christian trade unions:

91 Aurelien Zaragori, "Acting Internationally: The Consolidation of the International Federation of Christian Trade Unions Through Its Participation in the International Labour Organization" in Steven Parfitt, Lorenzo Costaguta, Matthew Kidd, and John Tiplady, eds, *Working-Class Nationalism and Internationalism until 1945: Essays in Global Labour History* (Cambridge Scholars Publishing, Newcastle-upon-Tyne, 2018) chapters 4, 89.

92 Paul Misner, *Catholic Labor Movements in Europe: Social Thought and Action 1914–1965* (The Catholic University of America Press, Washington, DC, 2015) 41.

93 This was Hermann Henseler, a German Christian trade unionist: Aurelien Zaragori, "Acting Internationally: The Consolidation of the International Federation of Christian Trade Unions Through Its Participation in the International Labour Organization" in Steven Parfitt, Lorenzo Costaguta, Matthew Kidd, and John Tiplady, eds, *Working-Class Nationalism and Internationalism until 1945: Essays in Global Labour History* (Cambridge Scholars Publishing, Newcastle-upon-Tyne, 2018) chapters 4, 92.

94 Albert Thomas, *The International Labour Organisation: The First Decade* (George Allen & Unwin Ltd., London, 1931) 336–337.

Il importe de noter que Thomas non seulement a toujours reconnu pleine-ment le syndicalisme chrétien, mais même l'a hautement apprécié. Il a manifesté cette appréciation par des visites aux Congrès internationaux du mouvement et par l'engagement au Bureau de plusieurs de ses membres. Mentionnons à ce propos le R. P. jésuite Arnou, qui fut depuis 1928 un col-laborateur enthousiaste due B.I.T. et qui loua au plus haut degré le grand intérêt, la "sympathie objective" que portait Thomas à ce qui se passait dans les milieux religieux.[95]

There had been a sea change in the attitude of the Holy See to Catholic trade unions with the ascension of Pope Benedict XV in 1914. As weighed in the bal-ance by Paul Misner, Pope Benedict XV was "an aristocrat of more secure and distinguished lineage than Leo XIII [who] firmly believed in *noblesse oblige*, the duty of the upper classes to attend to the needs of their social inferiors". He abhorred the notion of class struggle and the holding in contempt of figures placed in authority – and railed against these in his first Encyclical *Ad beatissimi apostolorum* (Appealing for Peace) proclaimed on 1 November 1914:

5. For ever since the precepts and practices of Christian wisdom ceased to be observed in the ruling of states, it followed that, as they contained the peace and stability of institutions, the very foundations of states necessarily began to be shaken. Such, moreover, has been the change in the ideas and the mor-als of men, that unless God comes soon to our help, the end of civilization would seem to be at hand. Thus we see the absence from the relation of men of mutual love with their fellow men; the authority of rulers is held in con-tempt; injustice reigns in relations between the classes of society; the striving for transient and perishable things is so keen, that men have lost sight of the other and more worthy goods they have to obtain.[96]

As Paul Misner observes:

Given this diagnosis of the predicament of contemporary society, one might not expect Benedict XV to show any favour to the highly controversial Christian labor unions formed under Catholic auspices in Italy, Germany

---

95 [It is important to note that Thomas always not only accorded full recognition to Catholic trade unionism, he also greatly esteemed it. His appreciation made itself known through his attendances at international Congresses of the movement, and though his engaging with the administrative bodies of many of its members. In this context it merits mentioning Fr. Arnou who from 1928 [*actually,* 1926] made an enthusiastic contribution to the ILO, and who commended at the highest level the great interest taken, that "objective sympathy" which Thomas displayed in that which was happening in religious circles.] B W Schaper, *Albert Thomas:Trente ans de réformisme social* (Van Gorcum & Comp. N.V., Assen, 1959) 250.
96 Pope Benedict XV, *Ad Beatissimi Apostolorum* (1914) s 5 © Copyright – Libreria Editrice Vaticana.

and elsewhere. But he did. [...] To be sure, Catholic workers needed their own separate Christian unions, apart from the unions whose socialist leaders propagated false and unacceptable principles. Christian unions deserved the backing of church leaders, he felt, as long as they upheld religion, the family, and private property rights while claiming the rights of workers.[97]

In his Report to the ILC in 1925, Albert Thomas singled out the contribution made to the work of the ILO by the Christian trade unions:

> The Christian trade unions devote particular attention to labour legislation, and are constantly endeavouring to bring influence to bear on the legislative authorities. Both in the national and international sphere they have done much to stem re-action and to hasten further progress. At their congresses and other meetings they have repeatedly manifested their sympathy and interest for the International Labour Organisation. They have carried on an energetic campaign for the ratification of the Conventions. [...]
>
> It may once more be emphasised—and this is a matter for great satisfaction that the differences of opinion which may exist between the various sections in the trade union movement, and indeed the claims which the Christian trade unions have constantly put forward for fuller representation in the International Labour Organisation, have not prevented them from giving constant assistance to the work of the Organisation. It is confidently believed that the cordial relations between the International Labour Organisation and the Christian trade unions will continue to be proof against all difficulties. This is a most fortunate omen for the future of the Organisation.[98]

In September 1928 speaking at the Fourth Congress of the International Federation of Christian Trade Unions in Munich, Albert Thomas sought their support as one of the major social forces in the modern world. Specifically, he emphasised that this ought in no way to compromise their religious principles and faith – recognising that it was this which drew into membership of the Christian trade unions large numbers of believers, and that this was their unique contribution to the ILO communal enterprise:

> Ce n'est pas, en tentant de réduire et de restraindre prudemment et presque honteusement nos actions particulières, ce n'est pas en violant les principes qui nous animent dans l'intimité de nos âmes, bien au contraire, c'est en nous efforçant d'élever aus plus haut nos idéals respectifs, en les dévoilant

97 Paul Misner, *Catholic Labor Movements in Europe: Social Thought and Action 1914–1965* (The Catholic University of America Press, Washington, DC, 2015) 16–17.
98 Albert Thomas, Report of the Director General to the 7th Session of the ILC 1925 164 <www.ilo.org/public/libdoc/ilo/P/09383/09383(1925-7).pdf> (accessed 17 October 2020) © ILO.

dans leur pureté, dans leur intégrité, en cherchant à comprendre chaque jour davantage les nobles aspirations qui nous les ont fait concevoir, que nous pourrons le mieux les assembler et les unir, et que nous creérons la possibilité de concentrer nos regards vers des pensées et des actions qui nous soient communes à tous.[99]

"Not rewarded as they had deserved"

The impression must not be given that the influence of the Catholic trade unions within the ILO in the inter-war years went unchallenged or was adequately acknowledged.

An early example of the predominance of Catholic trade unions in certain Member States of the ILO finding themselves regarded as a lower-ranking minority in the ILO is illustrated by the dispute at the 1921 Session of the ILC, at which the Government of the Netherlands appointed as workers' delegate Petrus Josephus Servatius Serrarens, General Secretary of the Federation of Christian Trade Unions in the Netherlands. This union ranked in terms of membership third out of five (the first ranked being the socialist Netherlands Federation of Trade Unions, which strongly opposed the appointment; the remaining four all being Christian trade unions). The dispute escalated, and was referred to the Permanent Court of International Justice, which ruled in favour of the appointment.[100] The Court's decision was based on *headcount, not confession*: a Government should strive to make a choice best calculated to ensure the representation of the workers of the country (and so try to reach an agreement with all workers' organisations), failing which it would not be acting against the terms of the 1919–1920 Peace

99 [It is in no way tempting to diminish and constrain, guardedly or even shamefacedly, our own particular ways, it is not in violation of those principles which animate us in the recesses of our souls; quite the opposite. It is in our endeavouring to raise to the highest level our respective ideals, in revealing them in their purity of form, in their integrity, in searching more each day to understand the high-minded aspirations to which these have given rise in us, that we can the better combine and unite them, and which creates in us the ability to focus our gaze on those concepts and actions which are common to us all.] Quoted in Maurice Barbier, "Les Relations Entre l'Église Catholique et l'Organisation International du Travail" in *Politique étrangère*, Vol. 37, No. 3 (1972) (Institut Français des Relations Internationales) 351, 357. Commenting on this some years later, Jesuit in residence Albert Le Roy wrote: "Dans un telle clarté, loin de toute équivoque, il est facile de travailler ensemble, la main dans la main, à une oeuvre devant laquelle aucun homme de coeur ne peut rester indifférent". [In light of such unambiguous lucidity, it is easy to work together hand in hand at a task towards which no-one great-hearted could remain indifferent.] Albert Le Roy, *Catholicisme social et organisation internationale due travail* (Éditions Spes, Paris, 1937) 74.

100 G A Johnston, *International Social Progress: The Work of the International Labour Organisation of the League of Nations* (George Allen & Unwin Ltd., London, 1924) 236–239. A detailed account of the arguments raised in favour of and against the appointment of P J S Serrarens is found in the Record of the Proceedings of the 3rd Session of the ILC 1921 614–631 <www.ilo.org/public/libdoc/ilo/P/09616/09616(1921-3).pdf> (accessed 17 October 2020).

Treaties if it nominated the worker's delegate in agreement with the organisations which, taken together, represented the majority of the organised workers of the country.[101] "Numbers are not the only test of the representative character of the organisations, but they are an important factor; other things being equal, the most numerous will be the most representative".[102] The battle had been won, but the effect on the relationship between the Catholic trade unions and their secular equivalents within the ILO was toxic: given the minority status of the former, this accounts for much of the subsequently focussed and effective resistance on the part of the secular trade union membership of the ILO to the advancement of Catholic trade unions within the organisation.

The Catholic trade unions may have had majority status in some countries, such as the Netherlands, but nevertheless were in a minority within the ILO, as the events of 1921 had shown. They ranked in numbers behind the socialist International Trade Union Federation and in consequence often lost out when workers' delegates were being nominated by their home Governments or when positions of authority within the ILO became available.[103]

In his Report to the ILC in 1926 Albert Thomas, whilst acknowledging the desire of the Christian trade unions for a greater representation within the ILO, including the ILO Governing Body, and confirming that "The Directorate of the International Labour Office will always do, as it has done in the past, everything in its power to assure to the representatives of the Christian organisations an influence and an authority worthy of their strength and of their will to collaborate in the common work" nevertheless urged them to take the initiative and to seek an agreement with "the Trade Unions of other tendencies" or to lobby for the rules of the ILC or of the Peace Treaty itself to be amended.[104]

Addressing the ILC in 1928 P J S Serrarens did not mince his words:

101 Advisory Opinion 31 July 1922 (Series B., No. 1) *Appointment of Workers' Delegate to the International Labour Conference* in *The Permanent Court of International Justice 1922 2012* (Registry of the International Court of Justice, The Hague, 2012) 69 <www.icj-ci j.org/files/permanent-court-of-international-justice/serie_other/cpji-pcij.pdf> (accessed 17 October 2020).

102 (This extract from the judgment of the Court is quoted by the Credentials Committee in its Sixth Report to the ILC in 1946.) Record of the Proceedings of the 28th Session of the ILC 1946 200 <www.ilo.org/public/libdoc/ilo/P/09616/09616(1946-28).pdf> (accessed 17 October 2020) © ILO.

103 "It clearly had the ambition to play a major role in the ILO, but was perhaps overly optimistic in this respect. Labour representation was de facto monopolized by the much larger IFTU, which represented up to 22,703,103 affiliated members, compared to only 3,366,400 for the CISC [International Federation of Christian Trade Unions]". Patrick Pasture, "The ILO and the Freedom of Association as the Ideal of the Christian Trade Unions" in International Institute of Social History Amsterdam (Jasmien Van Daele and others, eds) *ILO Histories: Essays on the International Labour Organization and Its Impact on the World during the Twentieth Century* (Peter Lang, Bern, 2010) 122.

104 Albert Thomas, Report of the Director-General to the 8th Session of the ILC 1926 186/187 <www.ilo.org/public/libdoc/ilo/P/09383/09383(1926-8).pdf> (accessed 17 October 2020) © ILO.

Je dois toutefois vous dire, Messieurs, que les syndicalistes chrétiens ne pensent pas a accepter un rôle de Cendrillon. Nous avons protesté avec vous et nous lutterons même sans vous contre toute atteinte à la liberté syndicale. Nous rejetons comme vous le joug du fascisme, aussi bien que celui du bolchévisme. Nous voulons que partout les ouvriers aient le droit de s'associer, et [...] de s'associer dans les organisations de leur choix. Mais nous exigeons que nos syndicats chrétiens, que nous avons fondé en vertu de notre liberté, liberté aussi sacrée que la vôtre, nous exigeons que nos syndicats chrétiens soient traités sur un pied d'égalité avec les vôtres.[105]

In his Report to the 14th Session of the ILC in 1930 Albert Thomas whilst acknowledging their "sincere collaboration and energetic support of the Office's work" again reflected on the institutional difficulties within the ILO faced by the Christian trade unions:

The working of the constitution of the Organisation may sometimes, it is true, prevent them from exercising as much influence as they would wish in all the phases of the development of international labour legislation. It is also true that any action which the Office itself may take will not remove their grievances or satisfy their claims. Their support is, nevertheless, often of the highest value and has always been forthcoming when efforts are made to give effect to reforms on which agreement has been reached at the International Labour Conference or when Draft Conventions are submitted to parliament.[106]

Maurice Barbier was of the view that during the first 20 years of the existence of the ILO, despite their close relationship with it and their loyal cooperation, the Catholic unions failed to achieve that status within the ILO which they had hoped for, and which would have enabled them to participate more fully and to bring their viewpoint more directly to bear in the decision-making process: "leur

---

105 [Nevertheless, gentlemen, I must say to you that the Christian trade unions have no intention of playing the part of Cinderella. We have protested alongside you and we have fought even without you against every attack on the liberty of trade unionism. Like you, we throw off the yoke of fascism as well as that of bolshevism. Our wish is that workers everywhere should have the right of association and to associate within organisations of their choice. But we demand that our Christian trade unions – which we have established in pursuance of our freedom, freedom just as sacred as your own – we demand that our Christian trade unions be treated on a footing equal with your own.] Record of the Proceedings of the 11th Session of the ILO 1928 195 <www.ilo.org/public/libdoc/ilo/P/09616/09 616(1928-11).pdf> (accessed 17 October 2020) © ILO.
106 Albert Thomas, Report of the Director-General to the 14th Session of the ILC 1930 73–74 <www.ilo.org/public/libdoc/ilo/P/09383/09383(1930-14).pdf> (accessed 17 October 2020) © ILO.

attachement et leur fidélité à l'O.I.T. furent donc loin d'être recompense comme ils le méritait".[107]

The Jesuit presence at the ILO[108]

There has been a Jesuit in residence, on the full-time staff of the ILO as special ecclesiastical advisor to the Director-General, since 1926.[109] At the time of its formation, this was not pre-ordained.

According to Dominique Peccoud, the first director of the ILO, Albert Thomas was struck by the eloquence of the head of the Netherlands delegation of the time, the priest Mgr Nolens[110] at the opening International Labour Conference (ILC) in Washington in 1919. On Monday 10 November 1919 the Conference contin-

---

107 [Their participation in and loyalty to the ILO had far from produced the rewards which they had deserved.] Maurice Barbier, "Les Relations Entre l'Église Catholique et l'Organisation International du Travail" in *Politique étrangère*, Vol. 37, No. 3 (1972) (Institut Français des Relations Internationales) 351–387, at 361.

108 The material in this section is taken in part from *Eighty Years of Jesuit Presence in the International Labour Movement* by Joseph Joblin, SJ (published by the Social Justice and Ecology Secretariat of the Jesuit Curia in Rome, 1981) <www.sjweb.info/sjs/pjold/pj_show.cfm?PubTextID=1544> (accessed 17 October 2020) © 2020 SJES and from *A Discussion with Dominique Peccoud, SJ* (Berkley Center for Religion, Peace and World Affairs, Georgetown University, 23 February 2011) <http://berkleycenter.georgetown.edu/interviews/a -discussion-with-dominique-peccoud-s-j> (accessed 17 October 2020) © 2020 Berkley Center for Religion, Peace & World Affairs.

109 Fr Andre Arnou 1926–1932, Fr Achille Danset 1933–1936, Fr Albert Le Roy 1936–1955, Fr Joseph Joblin 1956–1981, Fr John Lucal 1981–1986, Fr Louis Christiaens 1987–1995, Fr Dominique Peccoud 1997–2008, and Fr Pierre Martinot-Lagarde 2008 to date.

110 Mgr Nolens would go on to make a hugely important contribution to the evolution of the ILO. Edward Phelan painted a picture of the man: "Though not himself a Minister he was a great, if not the greatest, personal influence in the Catholic party, which held the balance of power in his country. As such he was reputed to have made and unmade Cabinets. He was personally a very progressive man with a passion for social reform. He was also a man of keen intelligence and original mind who was destined to play a considerable role in succeeding International Labour Conferences". E J Phelan, *Yes and Albert Thomas* (The Cresset Press, London, 1949) 97. Albert Thomas in 1932, shortly before his own death, had marked the death of Mgr Nolens on 27 August 1931, calling him one of the "most influential members and wisest counsellors" of the ILC, praising the quality of his contributions to debate "compounded of learning and humour" by which "he would bring the discussion back to essentials, unravel the tangled skein of the debate, and decide between the amendments proposed. No one had given more thought than he to the principles of international law and the Constitution of the Organisation. [...] A statesman in the true sense of the word, i.e. with a firm attachment to a consistent doctrine and principles, he had made social justice the objective of all his political activity. [...] [H]e furnished the most striking proof that men of differing religious and political opinions can work together wholeheartedly in the Conference for bringing about just reforms for the protection of the workers without having to make mutual concessions or abandon any of their ideas or convictions". Report of the Director-General to the 16th Session of the ILC 1932 1, 2 <www.ilo.org/public/l ibdoc/ilo/P/09383/09383(1932-16).pdf> (accessed 17 October 2020) © ILO.

ued its debate on the proposition that an eight-hour day should be adopted. The session had been extended to permit Mgr Nolens to expand on his proposals. His contribution was greeted with applause from the other delegates. He said:

> [A]lready we realise, as a matter of incalculable moral importance, that whatever our differences, we have here for the first time the expression, the synthesis, may I say, of international public opinion; not only of the workers, but also of the employers and Government representatives, in favour of limiting the duration of adult labour.

> It may be observed that a long time – too long a time – passed before the public conscience was awakened. I need only mention the fact that it was nearly 30 years ago that the papal encyclical "Rerum Novarum" contributed so considerably and powerfully toward changing public opinion that it may be said to have made contributions which cannot be expressed in mathematical terms, but which can be appraised and appreciated by those who, like myself, have been able these 30 years to follow the changes of opinion, not only of Catholic employers but of everybody concerned with the labour question. [...]

> [He referred to the need to conserve the physical health and strength of workers, and continued] There exists another motive, of a social and ethical character, which in these days has been raised to the first place. There was a period during which in almost all countries it seemed to be forgotten both in economic life and in the Government of the country that man was not a machine to be worked, but a rational, moral and intellectual being, made in the image of God, and having, by his nature and destiny, faculties and requirements which need time and leisure for their development, improvement and satisfaction.

> To quote the words of the peace treaty, it has been forgotten "that labour should not be regarded merely as a commodity or article of commerce". It also seems to have been forgotten [...] that our economic life, in no matter what shape, exists for the express benefit of man, including the worker in modern industry, and that economic work in the widest sense of the word, as well as manual labour itself, is a means to an end and not an end in itself. [...]

> At the present time, thanks to the influence of the teachings of the papal encyclical "Rerum Novarum" first spread among the Catholics, a general conviction is prevalent that the worker should have the necessary time and leisure not only to maintain health, but also to do his duty and exercise his rights as an intelligent, religious, intellectual, moral and social being.[111]

---

111 Record of the Proceedings of the 1st Session of the ILC 1919 69 <www.ilo.org/public/l ibdoc/ilo/P/09616/09616(1919-1).pdf> (accessed 17 October 2020) © ILO.

This impression was reinforced at the second ILC in Genoa in 1920 when Mgr Nolens spoke of the social objectives of the ILO. On Saturday 10 July 1920 the debate concerned conditions of work at sea. Mgr Nolens spoke on this occasion in French. The draft before the Conference had come to the closing vote, and Mgr Nolens reminded the delegates that their decision would have "profound global repercussions", be those repercussions ones which tended towards peace and benevolence or in the alternative would be fatally destructive. He continued:

> Et quant à moi-même, permettez-moi de le dire, comme catholique, que j'ai l'intime conviction à ce moment, comme déjà depuis 25 ans dans la politique sociale de mon pays [...] que je suis en parfait accord avec les principes catholiques, répétés et appliqués à la situation actuelle de la vie économique moderne, entre autres dans l'Encyclique "Rerum Novarum". [...].

> En acceptant ce project, vous contribuez à mettre un peu de calme dans le monde ouvrier qui en a tant besoin, de calme et d'ordre qui sont indispensables pour la véritable progrès.

> En le rejetant [...] vous plantez et fomentez la défiance dans le coeur non seulement des marins, mais des ouvriers en général la défiance aux promesses et aux principes de justice sociale solennellement proclamés et énoncés par vos Gouvernements.

> En l'acceptant [...] vous êtes appelés à faire dans les relations modernes de la vie économique par la justice sociale.[112]

In the succeeding year Albert Thomas researched the social thinking of the Catholic Church "and found himself profoundly in agreement with the social approach that he found in the doctrine".

Dominique Peccoud recounts that Albert Thomas told Mgr Nolens "that it was clearly vital that he, Thomas, go to the Vatican".

Albert Thomas' future successor as ILO Director-General Juan Somavia speaking in Rome at the Pontifical Lateran University on 25 February 2005 reflected on the significance of Albert Thomas' initiative.

---

112 [As for myself, allow me to say, as a Catholic, that I hold the deep conviction both now and after 25 years' involvement in the social politics of my country, that I am in full agreement with those principles of Catholicism applied time and again to the present state of modern economic life, among others the Encyclical "Rerum Novarum". In voting for this draft, you make your contribution to establishing a little peace of mind in the world of work, which it so badly needs; a calm and order which are themselves essential to real progress. In rejecting it, you plant and promote suspicion not only in the hearts of seamen but of workers in general; a mistrust in the promises and principles of social justice which have been solemnly promulgated and declared by your Governments. In voting for it you heed the call to promote in economic life modern relationships based on social justice.] Record of the Proceedings of the 2nd Session of the ILC 1920 471 <www.ilo.org/public/libdoc/ilo/P/09616/09616(1920-2).pdf> (accessed 17 October 2020) © ILO.

Our meeting today reflects the long and strong bonds between the Holy See and the ILO which date back from our earliest days. In 1920, at the second International Labour Conference, Monsignor Nolens, delegate of the Netherlands as President of the Dutch Roman Catholic State Party, member of Parliament, and later Minister of State (1923–31), made a speech emphasizing the need for common shared values in building the Organization, in order to reconcile the opposing interests of workers and employers.

Impressed by his speech, the first Director of the ILO, Albert Thomas, said to him: "All that remains to be done is to go to the Vatican!" The very next day he visited Nolens at his home, telling him: "You probably thought I was joking. This is not the case. I would be very happy if the Office and our Conferences could establish relations with the Vatican in order to ensure moral collaboration". [quoting from a letter of Mgr Nolens to the Holy See sent in September 1921][113]

Daniel Maul believes Albert Thomas' interest to have been long-standing:

Thomas had shown an early interest in Catholic social doctrine, which had long played a strong role in the French social reformist milieu. He saw the Holy See as a key ally in building good relations not only with various governments and the Christian trade union federations but also with some members of the Employers group, who were committed Catholics.[114]

Daniel Maul sees this as being a further aspect of Albert Thomas's diplomatic networking initiative, something which is borne out by Dominique Peccoud:

Part of the background was that Thomas was afraid that his agency, the ILO, instead of being an international agency producing international law, would be reduced to the role of simply controlling here and there minimum social standards that each country could adopt, but that it would have no power to produce international legal instruments. He thus asked Nolens how he could get in contact with the Vatican State and the Pope. He saw the potential to breathe a new spirit and direction into the ILO.

The Holy See, under Pope Benedict XV – notwithstanding that he had attempted (in vain) to act as peace broker between the warring Sates during World War

---

113 Juan Somavia, *The Challenge of a Fair Globalization*, Presentation at the Pontifical Lateran University on the Report of the World Commission on the Social Dimension of Globalization (Rome, 25 February 2005) <www.ilo.org/public/english/bureau/dgo/speeches/somavia/2005/rome.pdf> (c) ILO.

114 Daniel Maul, *The International Labour Organization: 100 Years of Global Social Policy* (De Gruyter, Berlin, 2019) 53.

One[115] – had been excluded from the Versailles Peace Conference of 1919, though not from choice; its public denials at the time of wanting a place at the table having proved false in light of subsequent historical enquiry.[116] The Holy See had not become a member state of the ILO. Daniel Maul attributes this to the fact that "the Vatican, as a state entity, did not have any organizational link to, or representation of, trade unions and employers. Consequently it did not fit in the tripartite structure of the ILO".[117] Albert Thomas solved the difficulty by creating the post of Jesuit in residence.

Meeting in private over a five-year period,[118] Albert Thomas and firstly Pope Benedict XV and then Pope Pius XI negotiated the appointment of a senior officer to be proposed by the Holy See to the ILO Director-General, to serve as a special adviser to the ILO for socio-religious affairs. B W Schaper outlined the process:

> Dès 1924, Thomas, à titre strictement privé et a l'insu de ses plus proches collaborateurs, avait rendu visite au Vatican. Le pape Pie XI lui fit alors l'impression de se tenir hors de la politique. Depuis lors, Thomas s'efforça constamment d'établir, sous une forme ou sous une autre, des relations avec le monde catholique, comme "force moral". Des personnalités comme le nonce en France, Mgr Ceretti, le délégué syndical catholique Serrarens et sans nul doute Mgr Nolens prêtèrent leurs bons offices. [...] [C]es démarches aboutirent à la nomination du père Arnou comme agent de liaison au B.I.T.[119]

---

115 Pope Benedict XV had pursued a peace initiative from July 1915 with the issue of his Exhortation "To the Belligerent Peoples and their Rulers", culminating in the delivery in August 1917 of his Peace Note. It met with no positive response, and in some quarters – including Italy itself where he was denounced as "the German Pope" – with hostility. John F Pollard, *The Unknown Pope: Benedict XV (1914–1922) and the Pursuit of Peace* (Geoffrey Chapman, London, 1999) 117–128.

116 "In the event, exclusion was no great diplomatic defeat because *none* of the neutral powers, including Spain, Holland and Switzerland [...] were admitted to the conference, thus saving the Holy See a major loss of face". John F Pollard, *The Unknown Pope: Benedict XV (1914–1922) and the Pursuit of Peace* (Geoffrey Chapman, London, 1999) 142.

117 Daniel Maul, *The International Labour Organization: 100 Years of Global Social Policy* (De Grutyer, Berlin, 2019) 53.

118 Dominique Peccoud comments that Albert Thomas "who had been a member of the first socialist international, was not really a person who could be seen publically and officially to be in contact with the Vatican. Thomas was never officially received by the Pope but he did meet him in private".

119 [As early as 1924, on a purely personal basis and without the knowledge of his closest colleagues, Thomas paid visits to the Vatican. Pope Pius XI however gave Thomas to understand that he held himself above politics. From then on, Thomas pressed unrelentingly for the establishment, in one form or another, of relations with the Catholic world, as a "moral imperative". Individuals such as the Papal Nuncio in France, Archbishop Ceretti, Serrarens the representative of the Catholic trade unions and, without any doubt, Mgr Nolens all played their part. This lobbying resulted in the nomination of Father Arnou as liaison

The creation of the appointment, if mentioned at all, and in particular the choice of Father Arnou and what experience he brought to the post, has received little attention in the admittedly sparse secular histories of the ILO. In his seminal work on l'Action Populaire Paul Droulers filled in those missing details.[120] The following account is drawn largely from his study, which attributes the initiative not to Albert Thomas in the first instance but to Mgr Nolens himself.

Mgr Nolens at the Washington Conference of the ILO in 1919 drew attention both in his public addresses and in private to the absence of a moral imperative, principally religious, which to him was the indispensable element in securing the dynamism and success of the ILO. He saw the delegates of both the employers and the workers as driven primarily by their respective self-interests, and the Government representatives as mere functionaries acting, speaking and voting according to the instructions given to them.

During the Genoa Conference of the ILO in 1920 Mgr Nolens successfully lobbied both Albert Thomas and the president of the ILO administrative council, Arthur Fontaine. Albert Thomas, convinced by Mgr Nolens of the benefits this would bring, urged him to engage with the Holy See with a view to establishing a relationship between it and the ILO which would itself be the means of creating a more solid basis of co-operation on the part of Catholic workers and employers with the ILO.

In advance of the Geneva Conference of the ILO in 1921 Mgr Nolens wrote at length to the Vatican Secretary of State, Cardinal Gasparri, with whom he had been in correspondence about the ILO since the autumn of 1920. The difficulty faced by the Holy See was that it had not been invited to participate in the Conference of Versailles and that the ILO was an organisation within the framework of the League of Nations of which the Holy See was not a member;[121] and so, lacking – and not seeking – the characteristics of a secular Government, the Holy See itself could not be a decisive presence within the ILO.

Mgr Nolens suggested to Cardinal Gasparri a middle way – "un adjoint spécial auprès du Bureau à Genève".[122]

This initiative found further support at the Social Week[123] in 1920 at which the faith of French Social Catholics in the necessity and future of the ILO was

---

officer within the ILO.] B W Schaper, *Albert Thomas:Trente ans de réformisme social* (Van Gorcum & Comp. N.V., Assen, 1959) 292.

120 Paul Droulers, *Le Père Desbuquois at l'Action Populaire 1919–1946* (Les Éditions Ouvrières and Presses de l'Université Grégorienne, Paris and Rome, 1980) 124–130. L'Action Populaire was founded in 1903 by Father Henri-Joseph Leroy with the aim of "aimer le monde" [loving the world] through the application in French social politics of the principles of Pope Leo XIII's Encyclical *Rerum novarum* (1891). Its work continues into the modern era as Le Centre de recherche et d'actions sociales (CERAS) <http://ceras-projet.org/> (accessed 17 October 2020)

121 <www.britannica.com/topic/League-of-Nations/Members-of-the-League-of-Nations> (accessed 17 October 2020).

122 A special deputy attached to the [International Labour Office] in Geneva.

123 n 70.

resolved. Beginning in October 1923 Paul Devinat[124] corresponded with Eugène Duthoit, president of the Social Weeks, which led directly to Albert Thomas and Eugène Duthoit being received in the Vatican in May 1924 by Mgr Borgongini-Duca, Secretary for Ecclesiastical Relations.[125] As B W Schaper in the passage quoted above remarked, Pope Pius XI held himself above politics; and furthermore did not wish the Holy See to become a member of the League of Nations. Albert Thomas sought and won the support of Gaston Tessier, general secretary of the International Federation of Catholic Trade Unions, and they determined on a strategy of having a clerical appointee at the ILO who would not have the status of an official delegate of the Holy See. Gaston Tessier closed the circle, approaching Father Desbuquois of l'Action Populaire and it was he who nominated from the ranks of the Social Weeks a man regarded as highly qualified for the task, Father Arnou:

> Simple conseiller ecclésiastique, sans aucune mission du Saint-Siège ni officielle ni officieuse, autorisé seulement à prêter au B.I.T. le concours que celui-ci lui demande pour donner au besoin son avis à titre consultatif.[126]

This arrangement had a tentative beginning – Father Arnou's contract was at first renewed on a rolling monthly basis – but it soon settled down, and Father Arnou's brief was broadened. He became Albert Thomas's conference representative at a numerous national and international Catholic institutions, including the Social Weeks, Caritas,[127] and the international Conference of the Federation of Catholic Workers.

The arrangement was not uncontroversial, and aroused opposition from some of the workers' representatives, but as Edward Phelan recalled:

124   n 71.
125   Albert Thomas was received in the Vatican again in November 1925. His brief memoire of the visit is found in ILO Archives, Cabinets des Directeurs généraux, Cabinet d'Albert Thomas, Voyage en Italie (1925), CAT 1/25/13/2 which is reproduced (in an English translation) in Liliosa Azara, "The Holy See and the International Labour Organisation: The Origins of a Special Relationship" in Jean-Dominique Durand, ed, *Christian Democrat Internationalism: Its Action in Europe and Worldwide from Post World War II until the 1990s Vol. II* (P.I.E. Peter Lang S.A., Brussels, 2013) 41–56, at 50–51. It was on this visit that Albert Thomas, noting that the Holy See had neither employers nor workers, speculated (not entirely seriously?) whether the Swiss Guards and gardeners constituted the Holy See's "working class".
126   [an ordinary clerical adviser, with no commission from the Holy See either formal or official, charged only with providing assistance to the ILO at its request, giving his advice in a purely consultative capacity] Paul Droulers, *Le Père Desbuquois at l'Action Populaire 1919–1946* (Les Éditions Ouvrières and Presses de l'Université Grégorienne, Paris and Rome, 1980) 126.
127   <www.caritas.org/> (accessed 17 October 2020).

[Albert Thomas] never made himself the mere mouthpiece of the workers' aspirations and demands. [...] [H]e ran counter to the wishes of a majority of them when he paid his visit to the Pope and instituted a collaboration with the Church. [...] He had to weigh his hold on the workers against the necessity for giving the Organisation its widest scope. The Organisation must become a real power. No movement or State that could add to its strength, or support the cause of social justice, must be alienated or kept at arm's length.[128]

Paul Droulers describes the contribution which Father Arnou made, as he in effect created his own job description:

Très vite accepté, pour son caractére ouvert et sa compétence, en un milieu où dominent socialistes et agnostiques, protestants et juifs, d'abord étonnés de la présence de ce prêtre et jésuite, et où les instances administratives lui sont peu favorables, Arnou déploie une intense activité de documentation, de correspondence, de relations, établit des dossiers, dont l'essentiel est repris dans les rapports du Directeur devant l'assembleé annuelle de l'O.I.T.[129]

Albert Thomas himself explained the decision to seek the appointment of a Jesuit in residence more prosaically in his Report to the 12th Session of the ILC in 1929:

It is clear that the moral authority of the Catholic Church can do much to help in the establishment of social justice. Does this imply that an organic connection should be created between the Church and the International Labour Organisation? This question has recently been raised in connection with the Lateran agreements. Certain publicists have alleged that in recent years the Office proposed that the Vatican should become a Member of the International Labour Organisation, and that the Vatican replied that it could not enter any organisation except as its leader and head. All this is pure invention. What really happened was that the Director considered how the important moral collaboration which has been described above could be further developed, either by the application of Article 404 of the Treaty or by some other means. It was finally agreed that a priest might be authorised

---

128 E J Phelan, *Yes and Albert Thomas* (The Cresset Press, London, 1949) 247.
129 [Very soon accepted because of his openness and ability, finding himself in a situation dominated by socialists and agnostics, protestants and Jews, who were at first astonished at the presence of this Jesuit priest, and where the administrative authorities did not favour him, Arnou was intensely active in the creation of documentation, correspondence, networking and case reports, the essence of which found its way into the annual reports of the Director to the ILO Conference.] Paul Droulers, *Le Père Desbuquois at l'Action Populaire 1919–1946* (Les Éditions Ouvrières and Presses de l'Université Grégorienne, Paris and Rome, 1980) 127.

by his Bishop to join the staff of the Office, and to maintain the necessary contact. This has been done, and, it is noted with satisfaction, with complete success.[130]

When it was suggested to Albert Thomas in May 1932 that Father Arnou be retired from the ILO and returned to his former duties, Albert Thomas said he had an absolute need of him, and, perhaps not entirely in jest, said he would contest this at the Holy See itself. Albert Thomas died the following day.

Under pressure from the French and Italian Governments, who opposed the services of a Jesuit in any branch of the League of Nations, Father Arnou was indeed retired in 1932. Almost two years of protracted negotiations led by Father Desbuquois then led to the appointment of Father Achille Danset (himself also active in l'Action Populaire) in 1933, whose term of office was cut short by his premature death in 1936. At the request of Albert Thomas's successor as Director-General, Harold Butler, following the death of Father Danset there was appointed Father Albert Le Roy. By 1938 it was clear that the role of the Jesuit in Residence had developed into more than a counsellor and had taken on a diplomatic, almost missionary, character: "Father Le Roy made an extensive journey in Brazil, Uruguay, Argentina and Chile, which enabled him to explain the work of the Office in Catholic circles interested in social questions".[131] Albert Le Roy served until 1955 and provided the stability and continuity which consolidated the role and which has led to this arrangement being continued to the present day.

A Protestant opposite number (Georges Thelin) was briefly in post before World War Two, but when the ILO relocated to Canada in 1940 during the hostilities, he did not go with them, and his post fell into desuetude. After the war, the suggestion was made in 1956 that the post be restored but the Director-General refused to create any new posts with religious links, citing the multiplicity of religions by then represented amongst the members of the ILO. Joseph Joblin (Jesuit in residence 1956–1981) explained this: "The Director General felt that Catholicism had one clear spokesman, the Pope, and adding one representative from each religion to the Bureau would not be possible".[132]

---

130   Albert Thomas, Report of the Director-General to the 12th Session of the ILC 1929 61 <www.ilo.org/public/libdoc/ilo/P/09383/09383(1929-12).pdf>(accessed 17 October 2020) © ILO.

131   Harold Butler, Report of the Director-General to the 24th Session of the ILC 1938, 63 <www.ilo.org/public/libdoc/ilo/P/09383/09383(1938-24).pdf> (accessed 17 October 2020) © ILO.

132   Not that this was consciously the death of ecumenism or the handing of an exclusive prize to the Holy See. Joseph Joblin comments: "Their job was not to discuss the merits of the various social doctrines but to join efforts to produce concrete results on a commonly recognised objective: the good of the poorest of the poor. From this perspective, the Jesuit at the [ILO] is not there to promulgate the social doctrine of the Church, but to help Christian movements to come together for realising the goal of a progressive social policy".

Joseph Joblin defined the post:

> Rather than being a representative of the Holy See or a sort of chaplain to the personnel of the institution, the "ILO Jesuit" has been a bureaucrat of the institution. He has not performed any pastoral role in the post-Conciliar sense of the word. If he has rendered some priestly assistance to a colleague or delegate, this must be considered as something purely private and occasional. He is in the institution to fulfil the tasks assigned to him by the Director General, and consequently has the same obligations as any official in this capacity. He is at the service of the organisation. A further clarification may be in order. He has been called to be a functionary of the Organisation because he is a priest with an intellectual and spiritual formation capable of providing expert assistance to the General Director in policy matters regarding religious affairs.
>
> [...] The Jesuit at the ILO is there to help judge what is possible at a given moment by making known the Christian reaction to a given proposal. He can be an engine to solve development issues, and a break against certain demographic policies.

Why a Jesuit? Joseph Joblin explained

> the Jesuit is expected to understand the concept of justice in a way that is free from any political or partisan influence, and as one that flows from the logic of faith. He makes it possible for others to discover the existence of a world unknown to them; this is another way of articulating the problems of life to the ILO. This perception of his role has been particularly strong since the publication of *Pacem in Terris (1963)*.[133]

The work of the Jesuit in residence is not on a purely spiritual plane. Joseph Joblin gave examples of his own field work, and in doing so gives credence to the proposition that the Catholic Church is, in the areas of the world in which its influence remains strong, a potent collaborator with which the ILO can better guarantee the successful application of its policies:

> As long as I remained a functionary in charge of relations with Christian trade unions I helped them to organise themselves in Africa, Vietnam and Latin America. Circumstances forced me to turn my attention to indigenous populations, especially in South America. I took part in the first Convention where a text on the living and working conditions of aboriginal populations was discussed. A number of aid projects were implemented. Though the majority of those responsible at the ILO were not Christians, they were

---

133   Pope St John XXIII, *Pacem in terris* (1963) © Copyright – Libreria Editrice Vaticana.

persuaded that these projects could not succeed in Latin America without the support and participation of the Church.

Lobbied for and then created largely through the use of back-channels of the ILO and of the Holy See, the consequent establishment of virtual diplomatic relations[134] between the two institutions as well as the work of the Jesuit in Residence was not the least factor in bringing about a closeness which had been far from evident when the first tentative approaches were made in 1919.

Conclusions

The period between the formation of the ILO in 1919 and World War Two, and more particularly the years up to the early death of Director-General Albert Thomas in 1932, are the most crucial in the forging of the bond between the ILO and the Holy See.

It was during this time that what Maurice Barbier referred to as a profound harmony between the Holy See and the ILO and a convergence between their policies and goals on social issues became apparent to Albert Thomas and became a driving force in his diplomatic initiatives.

The immediate post-War period was one of hardship and despair, revolution and social meltdown, and in 1919 called for the bold solutions which the ILO pioneers, led by Albert Thomas, were to employ. That the contribution of the Holy See remained very much under the radar is no indication of a lack of support. The agreement of Pope Pius XI in 1926 to the appointment of a Jesuit to the staff of the ILO to act as spiritual director to the Director-General, and to provide a personal connection with that "*force morale*", the moral imperative which Social Catholicism embodied, is proof enough. That role continues to the present day.

The structure of the ILO itself, promoting dialogue between Governments, employers and workers in its tripartite system, was and remains in perfect accord with Catholic social teaching on the need to avoid class conflict and to promote co-operation between what Pope Leo XIII had referred to in his Encyclical *Rerum novarum* (1891) as "the wealthy and the working men".[135] Tripartism

---

134 The presence within the ILO of the Jesuit in residence did not of itself constitute a substantive diplomatic relationship. That emerged forty years after the appointment of André Arnou, when in August 1967 official relations between the Holy See and the ILO were formally established with the appointment of a Dominican priest, Henri de Riedmatten, as Permanent Observer to the ILO (whilst also serving as Permanent Observer of the Holy See to the United Nations in Geneva). Charles R Gallagher, "Religion and International Labour: The Roman Catholic Church, the ILO and the Search for Social Justice" in Jean-Dominique Durand, ed, *Christian Democrat Internationalism: Its Action in Europe and Worldwide from Post World War II until the 1990s Vol II* (P.I.E. Peter Lang S.A., Brussels, 2013) 35–39, at 37.

135 See Chapter 3.

corresponds with the need to promote the common good which is at the heart of Catholic Social Teaching.

Both the ILO Constitution of 1919 and the Declaration of Philadelphia 1944 in the words of Archbishop Bertello at the 85th Session of the ILC in 1997 correspond "with their solemn endorsements of the dignity of the human person and labour" exactly with the social teaching of the Catholic Church that "the economy is to serve man, and not the reverse, and the rights of workers come before the rights of capital".[136]

Though in a minority, and ultimately not rewarded as they had deserved in terms of numbers of delegates accredited to the International Labour Conferences and of representation on the ILO Governing Body, the International Federation of Christian Trade Unions, whose membership was overwhelmingly Catholic, was vocal and unrelenting in its support for the ILO's objectives precisely because, in the words of P J S Serrarens at the 8th Session of the ILC in 1926, the same spirit found in the Encyclicals of Pope Leo XIII should be regarded as the foundation of the ILO.[137]

Though following Albert Thomas' death in 1932 it was as if a curtain had fallen on the public debate, at least in the records of the ILO itself, the bond between the Holy See and the ILO was not broken, and continued to develop through and beyond World War Two to the point where Pope St John XXIII incorporated formally in the Magisterium of the Catholic Church what was to prove to be the first of many references to the ILO, in his Encyclical *Mater et magistra* (1961).[138]

The secular histories of the formation and early evolution of the ILO are numerous and by sheer weight of those numbers have tended to dominate the narrative. The historical records, however, are far broader than the secular narrative will admit and are unambiguous. The secular approach far from tells the whole story.

Bibliography

The Holy See

Encyclicals, Apostolic letters, Exhortations (in chronological order)

Pope Leo XIII, *Rerum novarum* (1891).
Pope Benedict XV, *Ad Beatissimi Apostolorum* (1914).
Pope Pius XI, *Quadragesimo anno* (1931).
Pope St John XXIII, *Pacem in terris* (1963).
Pope Francis, *Fratelli tutti* (2020).

136 n 47.
137 n 64.
138 See Chapter 3.

Other materials (in chronological order)

Archbishop Bernardito Auza, Apostolic Nuncio and Permanent Observer of the Holy
  See to the United Nations, Address to the High-Level Meeting of the United
  Nations General Assembly to Commemorate the 100th Anniversary of the ILO
  (New York, 11 April 2019) <https://holyseemission.org/contents/statements
  /5cb0ae1bdd6e4.php> (accessed 13 September 2020).

International Labour Organisation

Conventions and recommendations

Forced Labour Convention 1930 (C29).

International Labour Conferences (in chronological order)

Record of the Proceedings of the 1st Session of the ILC 1919 69 <www.ilo.or
  g/public/libdoc/ilo/P/09616/09616(1919–1).pdf> (accessed 17 October
  2020).
Record of the Proceedings of the 2nd Session of the ILC 1920 471 <www.ilo.org/
  public/libdoc/ilo/P/09616/09616(1920–2).pdf> (accessed 17 October 2020).
Record of the Proceedings of the 3rd Session of the ILC 1921 614–631 <www.ilo
  .org/public/libdoc/ilo/P/09616/09616(1921–3).pdf> (accessed 17 October
  2020).
Record of the Proceedings of the 8th Session of the ILC 1926, 82–83 <www.ilo.or
  g/public/libdoc/ilo/P/09616/09616(1926–8)V.1.pdf> (accessed 17 October
  2020).
Record of the Proceedings of the 11th Session of the ILO 1928 195 <www.ilo.or
  g/public/libdoc/ilo/P/09616/09616(1928–11).pdf>(accessed 17 October
  2020).
Record of the Proceedings of the 12th Session of the ILC 1929 148 <www.ilo.or
  g/public/libdoc/ilo/P/09616/09616(1929–12).pdf> (accessed 17 October
  2020).
Record of the Proceedings of the 28th Session of the ILC 1946 200 <www.ilo.or
  g/public/libdoc/ilo/P/09616/09616(1946–28).pdf> (accessed 17 October
  2020).
Record of the Proceedings of the 85th Session of the ILC 1997 172–173 www.i
  lo.org/public/libdoc/ilo/P/09616/09616(1997–85).pdf © ILO (accessed
  17 October 2020).

Reports (in chronological order)

Albert Thomas, Report of the Director General to the 7th Session of the ILC 1925
  164 <www.ilo.org/public/libdoc/ilo/P/09383/09383(1925–7).pdf> (accessed
  17 October 2020).
____, Report of the Director General to the 8th Session of the ILC 1926 172, para
  93 <www.ilo.org/public/libdoc/ilo/P/09383/09383(1926–8).pdf> (accessed
  17 October 2020).

____, Report of the Director-General to the 10th Session of the ILC 1927 52 <www.ilo.org/public/libdoc/ilo/P/09383/09383(1927–10).pdf>   (accessed 17 October 2020).

____, Report of the Director-General to the 11th Session of the ILC 1928 56–59 <www.ilo.org/public/libdoc/ilo/P/09383/09383(1928–11).pdf>   (accessed 17 October 2020).

____, Report of the Director-General to the 12th Session of the ILC 1929 58–61 www.ilo.org/public/libdoc/ilo/P/09383/09383(1929–12).pdf>   (accessed 17 October 2020).

____, Report of the Director-General to the 14th Session of the ILC 1930 59–62 <www.ilo.org/public/libdoc/ilo/P/09383/09383(1930–14).pdf>   (accessed 17 October 2020).

Report of the Director-General to the 16th Session of the ILC 1932 1,2 <www.ilo .org/public/libdoc/ilo/P/09383/09383(1932–16).pdf> (accessed 17 October 2020).

Report of the Director-General to the 17th Session of the ILC 1933 5 <www.ilo.org/ public/libdoc/ilo/P/09383/09383(1933–17).pdf> (accessed 17 October 2020).

Harold Butler, Report of the Director-General to the 24th Session of the ILC 1938, 63 <www.ilo.org/public/libdoc/ilo/P/09383/09383(1938-24).pdf> (accessed 17 October 2020).

ILO, *A Fair Globalisation: The Role of the ILO, Report of the Director-General on the World Commission on the Social Dimension of Globalisation*, Report of the Director-General to the International Labour Conference, 92nd Session, Geneva 2004 53 <www.ilo.org/public/libdoc/ilo/2004/104B09_112_engl.pdf> (accessed 17 October 2020).

Towards the ILO Centenary: Realities, Renewal and Tripartite Commitment, Report of the Director-General, International Labour Conference 102nd Session 2013 Report 1(A) paras 89, 91 <www.ilo.org/public/libdoc/ilo/P/09383/09 383(2013-102–1A).pdf> (accessed 17 October 2020).

Other materials (in chronological order)

Treaty of Versailles 1919, Part XIII <www.ilo.org/public/libdoc/ilo/1920/20B09 _18_engl.pdf> (accessed 17 October 2020).

Preamble to the Constitution of the ILO (1919).

ILO Archives, Cabinets des Directeurs généreaux, Cabinet d'Albert Thomas, Voyage en Italie (1925), CAT 1/25/13/2.

Declaration of Philadelphia 1944 <http://www.ilo.ch/dyn/normlex/en/f?p=100 0:62:0::NO:62:P62_LIST_ENTRIE_ID:2453907:NO#declaration> (accessed 17 October 2020).

Somavia, Juan, *The Challenge of a Fair Globalization*, Presentation at the Pontifical Lateran University on the Report of the World Commission on the Social Dimension of Globalization (Rome, 25 February 2005) <www.ilo.org/public/ english/bureau/dgo/speeches/somavia/2005/rome.pdf> (accessed 17 October 2020).

Declaration on Social Justice for a Fair Globalisation, 10 June 2008, Preface <www .ilo.org/wcmsp5/groups/public/---dgreports/---cabinet/documents/genericd ocument/wcms_371208.pdf> (accessed 17 October 2020).

History of the ILO <www.ilo.org/global/about-the-ilo/history/lang--en/index
.htm> (accessed 17 October 2020).

International documents

Advisory Opinion 31 July 1922 (Series B., No. 1) *Appointment of Workers' Delegate
to the International Labour Conference in The Permanent Court of International
Justice 1922 2012* (Registry of the International Court of Justice, The Hague,
2012) 69 <www.icj-cij.org/files/permanent-court-of-international-justice/serie
_other/cpji-pcij.pdf> (accessed 17 October 2020).

Secondary sources

Arnou, A, *L'Organisation internationale du Travail et les Catholiques* (Éditions Spes,
Paris, 1933).
Azara, Liliosa, "The Holy See and the International Labour Organisation: The Origins
of a Special Relationship" in Jean-Dominique Durand, ed, *Christian Democrat
Internationalism: Its Action in Europe and Worldwide from Post World War II
Until the 1990s Vol II* (P.I.E. Peter Lang S.A., Brussels, 2013).
Barbier, Maurice, "Les Relations Entre l'Église Catholique et l'Organisation
International du Travail" in *Politique étrangère*, Vol. 37, No.3 (1972) (Institut
Français des Relations Internationales) 351.
Barnes, George N *History of the International Labour Office* (Williams and Norgate
Limited, London, 1926)
Brown, Stephen J, *International Relations from a Catholic Standpoint* (Browne and
Nolan Limited, Dublin, 1932).
Butler, Harold, *Peace Through Social Justice* (Peace Book Company (London) Ltd.,
London, 1938).
____, *Confident Morning* (Faber and Faber, London, 1950).
Cordova, Efren, "The Changing Character of the Christian International" in
Industrial Relations, Vol. 23, No. 1 (1968) 70.
A Discussion with Dominique Peccoud, SJ (Berkley Center for Religion, Peace and
World Affairs, Georgetown University, 23 February 2011) <http://berkleyc
enter.georgetown.edu/interviews/a-discussion-with-dominique-peccoud-s-j>
(accessed 17 October 2020).
Droulers, Paul, *Le Père Desbuquois at l'Action Populaire 1919–1946* (Les Éditions
Ouvrières and Presses de l'Université Grégorienne, Paris and Rome, 1980).
Drzewicki, Krzysztof, "The Right to Work and Rights in Work" in Asbjørn Eide,
Catarina Krause and Allan Rosas, eds, *Economic, Social and Cultural Rights* (2nd
revised edn, Martinus Nijhoff Publishers, Dordrecht, 2001) 223.
The Editors of Encyclopaedia Britannica, *Influenza Pandemic of 1918–19* <www.b
ritannica.com/event/influenza-pandemic-of-1918-1919> (accessed 17 October
2020).
Follows, John W, *Antecedents of the International Labour Organization* (Oxford
University Press, London, 1951).
Förster, Birte, *1919: Ein Kontinent erfindet sich neu* (Philipp Reclam jun. Verlag
GmbH, Stuttgart, 2019).

Gallagher, Charles R, "Religion and International Labour: The Roman Catholic Church, the ILO and the Search for Social Justice" in Jean-Dominique Durand, ed, *Christian Democrat Internationalism: Its Action in Europe and Worldwide from Post World War II until the 1990s Vol II* (P.I.E. Peter Lang S.A., Brussels, 2013).

Gallagher, Archbishop Paul Richard, Secretary for Relations with States, Secretariat of State, the Holy See, "The Holy See and the International Labour Organization: Common Pathways on Labour" in *Rethinking Labour, Ethical Reflections on the Future of Work, Labour After Laudato Si'* 241–250, at 245 (The Caritas in Veritate Foundation Working Papers, FCIV, Chambésy, 2018) <https://futureofwork -labourafterlaudatosi.net/2018/11/14/rethinking-labour-ethical-reflections-on -the-future-of-work-14-november-2018-global/> (accessed 17 October 2020).

Gibberd, Kathleen, *I.L.O.: The Unregarded Revolution* (J M Dent and Sons Limited, London, 1937).

Hidalgo-Weber, Olga, "Social and Political Networks and the Creation of the ILO: The Role of British Actors" in Sandrine Kott and Joëlle Droux, eds, *Globalizing Social Rights: The International Labour Organization and Beyond* (ILO and Palgrave Macmillan, Basingstoke, 2013) 17.

Hughes, Steve and Haworth, Nigel, *The International Labour Organisation (ILO): Coming in from the Cold* (Routledge, London and New York, 2011).

Joblin SJ, Joseph, *Eighty Years of Jesuit Presence in the International Labour Movement* by (published by Social Justice and Ecology Secretariat of the Jesuit Curia in Rome, 1981) <http://www.sjweb.info/sjs/pjold/pj_show.cfm?PubTextID=1 544> (accessed 17 October 2020).

Johnston, G A, *International Social Progress: The Work of the International Labour Organisation of the League of Nations* (George Allen & Unwin Ltd., London, 1924).

Le Roy, Albert, *Catholicisme social et organisation internationale du travail* (Éditions Spes, Paris, 1937).

Maul, Daniel, *International Labour Organization: 100 Years of Global Social Policy* (De Grutyer, Berlin, 2019).

Misner, Paul, *Catholic Labor Movements in Europe: Social Thought and Action 1914– 1965* (Catholic University of America Press, Washington, DC, 2015).

Morse, David A, *The Origin and Evolution of the I.L.O. and Its Role in the World Community* (New York State School of Industrial and Labor Relations, Cornell University, Ithaca, NY, 1969).

Mortished, R J P, *The World Parliament of Labour: A Study of the I.L.O.* (Fabian Publications Limited, London, 1946).

O'Connor, Emmet, "Edward Phelan: A Biographical Essay" in Gerry Rodgers (ed) *Edward Phelan and the ILO: The Life and Views of an International Social Actor* (International Labour Office, Geneva, 2009).

Parish, Matthew, *Mirages of International Justice: The Elusive Pursuit of a Transnational Legal Order* (Edward Elgar Publishing Limited, Cheltenham, 2011).

Pasture, Patrick, "The ILO and the Freedom of Association as the Ideal of the Christian Trade Union" in International Institute of Social History Amsterdam, Jasmien Van Daele and others, eds, *ILO Histories: Essays on the International Labour Organization and Its Impact on the World during the Twentieth Century* (Peter Lang, Bern, 2010).

Phelan, E J, "The International Labour Organisation: Its Ideals and Results" in *Studies: An Irish Quarterly Review*, Vol. 14, No. 56 (1925) 611.

____, "The Preliminaries of the Peace Conference, British Preparations" in J T Shotwell, *Origins of the International Labor Organization* Volume I (Columbia University Press, New York, 1934) 110.

____, *Yes and Albert Thomas* (Cresset Press, London, 1949).

____, "The Contribution of the ILO to Peace" in *International Labour Review* (ILO, Geneva, 1949) Vol. LIX, No. 6.

____, "Some Reminiscences of the International Labour Organisation" in *Studies: An Irish Quarterly Review*, Vol. 43, No. 171 (Autumn, 1954) 241.

Pollard, John F, *The Unknown Pope: Benedict XV (1914–1922) and the Pursuit of Peace* (Geoffrey Chapman, London, 1999).

Rodgers, Gerry, Lee, Eddy, Swepston, Lee and Van Daele, Jasmien, *The ILO and the Quest for Social Justice 1919–2009* (Cornell University Press, Ithaca and International Labour Office, Geneva 2009).

Schaper, B W, *Albert Thomas: Trente ans de réformisme social* (Van Gorcum & Comp. N.V., Assen, 1959).

Servais, Jean-Michel and Van Goethem, Valérie, *International Labour Organization* (Second edition) (Wolters Kluwer, Alphen aan den Rijn, 2016).

Shotwell, J T, *Origins of the International Labor Organization* Volume II (Columbia University Press, New York, 1934) Document 25 *Memorandum on the Machinery and Procedure Required for the International Regulation of Industrial Conditions, Prepared in the British Delegation*, January 15–20 (1919) 117–125.

Tapiola, Kari, *The Driving Force: Birth and Evolution of Tripartism – Role of the ILO Workers' Group* (ILO, Geneva, 2019) <www.ilo.org/actrav/info/pubs/WCMS _710908/lang--en/index.htm> (accessed 17 October 2020).

Thomas, Albert, *The International Labour Organisation: The First Decade* (George Allen & Unwin Ltd., London, 1931).

Tosstorff, Reiner, "Albert Thomas, the ILO and the IFTU: A Case of Mutual Benefit?" in *International Institute of Social History Amsterdam* (Jasmien Van Daele and others, eds), *ILO Histories: Essays on the International Labour Organization and Its Impact on the World during the Twentieth Century* (Peter Lang, Bern, 2010) 94.

Zaragori, Aurelien, "Acting Internationally: The Consolidation of the International Federation of Christian Trade Unions Through Its Participation in the International Labour Organization" in Steven Parfitt, Lorenzo Costaguta, Matthew Kidd, and John Tiplady, eds, *Working-Class Nationalism and Internationalism until 1945: Essays in Global Labour History* (Cambridge Scholars Publishing, Newcastle-upon-Tyne, 2018).

6   The Holy See and the
ILO 1946 to 2020

Introduction

On the eve of World War Two, Catholic Social Teaching was part of the warp and weft of the ILO; but that great conflict proved in the decades which followed to have been a watershed in the relations between the ILO, the Holy See and the Christian trade unions.

A review of the ILO's relations with the churches which had featured so prominently in Reports of the Director-General to the ILC during Albert Thomas' tenure had ended on his death in 1932, never to resume. There were to be milestone events when the mutual influence and respect between the ILO and the Holy See was officially acknowledged – the visits to the ILO in 1969 of Pope St Paul VI and in 1982 of Pope St John Paul II – but never again was any ILC debate initiated by the International Labour Office. What voices there were, calling for the principles of Catholic Social Teaching to be applied to the work of the ILO, came from the floor in the ILC. These were increasingly few, and their domestic political context often confessional – many of them delegates from South American Member States. Their citations across the years of various Encyclicals said a great deal about the profound influence of Catholic Social Teaching in their respective nations, but have no bearing on the relationship between the ILO and the Holy See. By the beginning of the 1970s the voices of such delegates were largely stilled, and commentary was left to the Observers of the Holy See.

Maurice Barbier points to the inversion in the relationship between the ILO on the one hand and the Holy See and the Christian trade unions on the other after World War Two:

> Ainsi, entre les deux guerres, tout un réseau de relations se tissa progressivement entre les milieux catholiques et l'O.I.T., surtout sous l'impulsion d'Albert Thomas. D'une part, ce réseau se déployait à tous les niveaux, celui du Saint-Siège, de certaines personnalités catholiques et de diverses O.I.C. D'autre part, ces relations étaient réciproques, car, si les milieux catholiques s'intéressaient beaucoup aux travaux de l'O.I.T., inversement celle-ci suivait de près leurs activités dans le domaine social. A cette période d'organisation progressive des relations – plus laborieuses pour les syndicats chrétiens et

plus faciles pour l'Eglise catholique – devait succéder, après la seconde guerre mondiale, une période caractérisée par une collaboration plus critique pour les syndicats chrétiens et plus engagée pour l'Eglise catholique.[1]

Did the relative silence within the ILO betoken that the stream of inspiration from the Holy See to the ILO had ceased to flow? Or was it evidence that the ILO was formed in accordance and infused with Catholic Social Teaching; something so axiomatic as not to need mentioning? Had the flow in fact not stopped, but instead reversed and had the ILO become a source of inspiration for the Holy See, such that the Holy See was assuming a protective stance towards it? This accords with Maurice Barbier's analysis:

> Tandis que l'intérêt des O.I.C. pour l'organisation genevoise stagnait, les rapports de l'Eglise avec celle-ci avaient tendance à se centraliser et à se personnaliser au niveau du Saint-Siège et du pape lui-même.

> Depuis plus de cinquante ans, les milieux catholiques, nourris de la doctrine sociale de l'Eglise, ont voulu collaborer étroitement avec une organisation dont l'idéologie réformiste répondait à leurs aspirations profondes. Malgré de constantes difficultés de représentation, les syndicats chrétiens ont participé loyalement à ses activités, mais devant sa sclérose et son inefficacité, ils sont devenus de plus en plus critiques et exigeants à son égard. Inversement, les relations de l'Eglise catholique avec l'O.I.T., qui furent d'abord assez discrètes, se sont ensuite progressivement développées et centralisées au niveau du Saint-Siège, qui lui a apporté un appui moral croissant, tandis que les O.I.C. ne lui manifestaient qu'un intérêt limité.[2]

---

1 [Thus, between the two wars, a whole network of relationships gradually was woven between the Catholic milieu and the ILO, above all driven by Albert Thomas. On the one hand, this network extended to all levels – the Holy See itself, specific Catholics and a variety of international Catholic organisations. On the other, these relationships were reciprocal because, if the Catholic milieu took a great interest in the work of the ILO, conversely the latter closely followed the former's activity in the social sphere. This period of gradual establishment of relations – more arduous for the Catholic trade unions and easier for the Catholic Church – would be followed after the Second World War by a period characterised by a collaboration more critical on the part of the Christian trade unions and more committed on the part of the Catholic Church.] Maurice Barbier, "Les Relations Entre l'Église Catholique et l'Organisation International du Travail" in *Politique étrangère*, Vol. 37, No. 3 (1972) (Institut Français des Relations Internationales) 351–387, at 368.
2 [Notwithstanding that the interest of international Catholic organisations for the Genevan institution was stagnating, the relationship between it and the Church had a tendency to become centred upon and personalised at the level of the Holy See and of the Pope himself. […] For more than fifty years, the Catholic milieu, feeding on the social doctrine of the Church, had wished to cooperate closely with an organisation whose reformist ideology corresponded to their own deepest desired. In spite of constant difficulties in obtaining representation, the Christian trade unions loyally took part in its activities, but faced with its lack of adaptability and its ineffectiveness became more and more critical and demanding. The rela-

Daniel Maul assesses the relationship between the ILO and the Catholic Church as having "obviously fluctuated over time" but adds "on more than one occasion it has served as a broker of ILO politics in the Catholic world" and gives as examples the involvement of the Holy See in the ILO's Andean Indian Programme in the 1950s, engagement by Pope St John XXIII to overcome Cold War impasses with American trade unions in the 1960s and Pope St John Paul II's engagement with the independent trade union Solidarność in Poland in the 1980s.[3]

As part of the ILO's Centenary Project, the then Director-General Juan Somavia interviewed his predecessor Francis Blanchard on 11 February 2008.[4] Neither was in any doubt that Catholic Social Teaching had played – and continued to play – a role of fundamental importance within the ILO:

> Je pense que, si l'on observe les phénomènes qui ont mené à la création de l'OIT, je pense que Rerum Novarum et l'affirmation de la doctrine sociale de l'Eglise et la dénonciation par Rerum Novarum des conditions de travail de la fin du XIXe siècle ont joué un rôle, un rôle très important. C'était une dénonciation éthique et morale de situations inacceptables, cela a joué un rôle, je pense, dans la création de l'institution et cela continue. Moi-même, en tant que Directeur général, j'ai été reçu par Jean-Paul II, par Benoît XVI et, disons, la relation continue, c'est un aspect très important de la base sur laquelle l'OIT travaille, les valeurs de l'OIT, non?[5] [Juan Somavia]

In that same interview, Francis Blanchard recalled the support which he as Director-General had received from the Holy See, in the person of Pope St John Paul II, in the context of the efforts on the part of Francis Blanchard to encourage official recognition by the then communist government in Poland of Solidarność. Cardinals Casaroli and Etchegaray were sent on mission to the ILO in Geneva,

---

tions of the Catholic Church and the ILO, on the other hand, which had begun so discretely, then developed progressively, centred on the Holy See, which accorded it increasing moral support, even though the International Labour Office evinced only a limited interest in the Holy See.] Maurice Barbier, "Les Relations Entre l'Église Catholique et l'Organisation International du Travail" in *Politique étrangère*, Vol. 37, No. 3 (1972) (Institut Français des Relations Internationales) 351–387, at 381, 386.

3 Daniel Maul, *The International Labour Organization: 100 Years of Global Social Policy* (ILO and De Grutyer, Berlin, 2019) 54.

4 *Transcription de l'entrevue de Francis Blanchard, Directeur Général de 1974 à 1989, par Juan Somavia, Directeur Général depuis 1999, Pré Bailly, Gex, France, 11 février 2008* © ILO The transcript (not itself online) is available on request from the ILO Library.

5 [I think that, if one examines the phenomena which led to the founding of the ILO, Rerum Novarum and the statements contained in the social doctrine of the Church and the condemnation by Rerum Novarum of working conditions at the close of the 19th century played a part, a very important part. It was an ethical and moral condemnation of objectionable conditions which itself played a part, I think, in the foundation of the organisation, and that continues to be the case. For myself, as Director-General, I have been received by John Paul II, by Benedict XVI and, let us say, the relationship continues; it is a very important aspect of the basis upon which the ILO operates, of the values of the ILO, is it not?]

meeting Francis Blanchard, in his words, "many times". The discussions ranged wider than the Polish question, and Pope St John Paul II in a personal audience with Francis Blanchard stressed the importance of the USSR, saying "Il faut tenir le choc contre l'Union soviétique",[6] which was to be the next step. Francis Blanchard recalled: "Oui, il m'a beaucoup encouragé. C'était extraordinaire".[7]

The history of the post-War interaction between the Holy See and the ILO is to be found not only within the confines of the ILO, its Reports and Records of Proceedings at the ILC, but also in this wider diplomatic context – diplomatic channels which had first been opened by Director-General Albert Thomas in the 1920s.

The shift to human rights

The language of international human rights first entered the mass consciousness in 1948 with the proclamation by the United Nations of the Universal Declaration of Human Rights.[8] ILO historian Daniel Maul locates the ILO's "ideological point of departure" in its human rights work as the Declaration of Philadelphia 1944[9] which constituted its "rebirth".

> [T]he Declaration of Philadelphia's focus on human rights served both as an intellectual (and propagandistic) weapon and as a means of self-assurance for the democratic states of the wartime alliance as well as representing the promise of a new democratic and socially just post-war order based on clearly defined social rights of citizenship. As a basis on which the ILO formulated an overriding social objective that was to be the goal of all economic policy, *human rights ultimately also provided the International Labour Office with* both legitimation for extending the Organization's own field of activity and influence and *a strong moral foundation* to its claim "to examine and consider all international economic and financial policies and measures in the light of this fundamental objective" [quoting ILO Constitution, paragraph 4].
>
> [...] [T]he ILO proposed an integrated approach to development in which *human rights standards were promoted not just as a goal but as a method of development*, claiming that such standards helped to ease the consequences of the development process and paved the way for the transition to a modern society.[10]

6 [One must stand firm against the Soviet Union.]
7 [Yes, he greatly encouraged me. It was remarkable.]
8 <www.un.org/en/universal-declaration-human-rights/> (accessed 17 October 2020).
9 See Chapter 5.
10 Daniel Roger Maul, "The 'Morse Years': The ILO 1948–1970" in International Institute of Social History Amsterdam (Jasmien Van Daele and others, eds) *ILO Histories: Essays on*

Daniel Maul himself does not make the connection, but this secularisation of moral values marks the shift in the ILO away from the "*force morale*" of Catholic Social Teaching as being the expressly acknowledged guiding principle behind its work, driven by Albert Thomas and Mgr Nolens in the immediate post–World War One period.[11] After World War Two, the "strong moral foundation" and "method of development" of the ILO was to be human rights.

After almost 20 years, during which international human rights rhetoric was strong but its political application less so, the United Nations promulgated in 1966 the International Covenant on Economic, Social and Cultural Rights[12] and the International Covenant on Civil and Political Rights.[13] The United Nations designated the year 1968 to be the International Year for Human Rights, and the ILC at its 50th Session in 1966 passed the following Resolution:

> The General Conference of the International Labour Organisation,
>
> Considering that the International Labour Organisation *has pioneered in the field of human rights and has adopted a number of instruments concerning fundamental principles of human rights*, such as the Conventions concerning freedom of association and protection of the right to organise, abolition of forced labour, discrimination in respect of employment and occupation, and equal remuneration for men and women workers for work of equal value, [...]
>
> Considering that *the protection and advancement of human rights*, as proclaimed by the Universal Declaration of Human Rights adopted by the United Nations General Assembly in 1948, *are of fundamental importance for the fulfilment of the objectives of the International Labour Organisation*, [...]
>
> 7. Invites the Governing Body of the International Labour Office to take the following action with respect to human rights questions falling within the competence of the International Labour Organisation:
>
> (a) to promote the observance of fundamental human rights in all member States;
> (b) to review and assess the role, objectives and activities of the International Labour Organisation in the field of human rights, including the possibilities of extending standard-setting activities in this field;

---

the International Labour Organization and Its Impact on the World during the Twentieth Century (Peter Lang, Bern, 2010) 365, at 391–392.

11 See Chapter 5.

12 International Covenant on Economic, Social and Cultural Rights 1966 <www.ohchr.org/en/professionalinterest/pages/cescr.aspx> (accessed 17 October 2020).

13 International Covenant on Civil and Political Rights 1966 <www.ohchr.org/en/professionalinterest/pages/ccpr.aspx> (accessed 17 October 2020).

(c) to encourage technical co-operation projects and advisory missions designed to promote human rights objectives everywhere;

(d) to consider the possibility of co-ordinating research, publicity, technical co-operation projects, advisory missions and standard setting activities into a significant concerted programme, and of allocating adequate financial resources and staff to carry it out.[14]

ILO Director-General David Morse made international human rights the central theme of his Report to the 52nd Session of the ILC in 1968. In it, he saw the ILO as having been a human rights organisation ahead of its time:

> The activities of the International Labour Organisation in the field of human rights will henceforth be guided both by the Universal Declaration and the two Covenants on human rights, and by the Organisation's own past work and experience in the discharge of its special responsibilities.
>
> In the first place, the adoption of the Universal Declaration and the Covenants constitutes a recognition of the general trend towards inclusion among human rights of all forms of protection that can free man from fear and want – not only civil and political freedoms but economic, social and cultural rights as well. This has brought the human rights aspect of all the ILO's activities into particularly sharp relief. *The clear recognition in the Universal Declaration that economic and social rights are the corollary of civil freedoms is largely due to the existence of the Constitution of the ILO, which preceded it by nearly 30 years and of the Declaration of Philadelphia, which did so by nearly five years.* As the Organisation also took an active part in their preparation, the same can be said of the Covenants. [...]
>
> *One of the objectives assigned to the ILO under its Constitution is to encourage formal recognition of the human rights that lie within its field and of the conditions for their realisation.* From the beginning it set itself the task of building up a body of international labour standards and of achieving their widest possible acceptance throughout the world.[15] [Emphasis added]

There are two ways of looking at this use of language; descriptive and attributive. As a description of the achievements of the ILO using contemporary human rights terminology, there is not much to which to object. However, to use human rights technology to attribute to secular human rights the basis of those achievements,

---

14 Resolutions Adopted by the International Labour Conference at Its 50th Session 1966, Resolution III <www.ilo.org/public/libdoc/ilo/P/09734/09734(1966-50).pdf> © ILO (accessed 17 October 2020). The Resolution was passed on 20 June 1966 by 232 votes to 4, with no abstentions.

15 Report of the Director-General to the 52nd Session of the ILC 1968 3, 11 <www.ilo.org/public/libdoc/ilo/P/09383/09383(1968-52-part-1).pdf> (accessed 17 October 2020) © ILO.

where this could not have been the case, is illicit. What flows from this attributive approach is a reinterpretation of the basis upon which the ILO was created and its subsequent development before World War Two, applying anachronistic human rights terminology to achievements of the ILO which no contemporary would have been in a position to describe in these terms; which terms are absent from the contemporary record precisely because their articulation lay in the future. It "blue washes"[16] the contribution of Catholic Social Teaching.

The immediate post-War years: 1946 to 1963

The 29th Session of the ILC in 1946 was held in Montreal, hosted by the French Catholic University, whose Rector Mgr Maurault praised the resilience of the ILO:

> Perhaps not all your recommendations have been put into practice, but your very existence and the tenacity of your survival for twenty-five years show the will of the world for a social justice which is of the Kingdom of Heaven. In your building in Geneva there is a picture, the gift of the Christian trade unions, of Jesus speaking to the workers. Today through the leaders of the Church He still speaks, and no one can fail to recognise the Papal Encyclicals as embodying the Charter of Labour today.[17]

Even if this resonated with the University internally, this was not a view articulated at the Conference by the International Labour Office or by any of the delegates. The voices of the Observers of the Holy See to the Conferences would not be heard until their first accreditation in 1967, and throughout the late 1940s, the 1950s and early 1960s Catholic Social Teaching featured almost not at all at the Conferences. If there can be said to have been a dominant moral narrative during those years, it was in the realm of secular human rights.

At the 34th Session of the ILC in 1951, marking the 60th anniversary of *Rerum novarum* and the twentieth of *Quadragesimo anno*, stalwart from the pioneering days of the ILO Gaston Tessier, now President of the International Federation of Christian Trade Unions, spoke of "many analogies", but was a lone voice:

> A few weeks ago, in many places, a great anniversary was celebrated, that of the promulgation of the Encyclical Rerum novarum by which on 15 May

16 "Blue washing" is jargon used by contemporary human rights commentators where the United Nations is credited with achievements properly belonging to others (which, I argue, is the case here), or where individuals and organisations pay lip service to United Nations principles in order to "blue wash" (in the sense of cloak) their own fundamentally human rights abusive practices. For a discussion of the fundamental differences between secular human rights and Catholic Social Teaching, see Chapter 2.

17 Record of the Proceedings of the 29th Session of the ILC 1946 1 <www.ilo.org/public/l ibdoc/ilo/P/09616/09616(1946-29).pdf> (accessed 17 October 2020) © ILO.

1891 Pope Leo XIII proclaimed the rights of the workers. He reiterated that wages must be sufficient to allow the worker to live soberly and honestly, authoritatively sketched the essential lines of a peaceful organisation of social reform, and called for structural reforms for the true progress of the workers. *Many analogies exist between this high resolve and the principles which are the basis of our international institution.* Let us all resolve how, not only sentimentally, but practically, to be faithful to our ideal and, by the true observance of freedom of association, to accomplish this task of mutual information which, by dissipating prejudice and drawing together minds, hearts and wills in a common search for economic prosperity and social progress, will contribute greatly to internal peace and to international tranquillity.[18] [Emphasis added]

Pope Pius XII and a threshold crossed

The Holy See itself in the reign of Pope Pius XII as World War Two drew to a close was still to make an overt reference to the ILO, but remained concerned with the extent to which a trade union should expand its operations beyond the representation of workers and promote its own *political* objectives. Kevin Quinn refers to those concerns and to a striking parallel with the ILO:

> The fullest expression of the thought of Pius XII is given in his allocution to the A.C.L.I. [*Associazioni Cristiane Lavoratori Italiani*] in March 1945. He laid down as a fundamental condition for the participation of Catholics in a unified Italian trade union movement, "that the trade union remain within the limits of its essential object of representing and defending the interests of the workers in their contracts of work. Within the ambit of this task the union will naturally exercise an influence on politics and public opinion. But it cannot go beyond this limit without doing grave harm to itself. If the trade union as a result of political and economic developments should come to possess the power or right of freely disposing of the worker and of his energies and goods, as happens elsewhere, the very concept of a trade union – which is a union for self-help and defence – would be altered or destroyed".

> The validity and timeliness of Pius XII's doctrine was confirmed by a resolution passed by the International Labour Conference in 1952. Confronted with the growing power of the state in economic matters, the members of the I.L.O. felt it necessary to determine more precisely the relation of trade union freedom to political authority and political parties.[19]

---

18 Record of the Proceedings of the 34th Session of the ILC 1951 138 <www.ilo.org/public/l ibdoc/ilo/P/09616/09616(1951-34).pdf> (accessed 17 October 2020) © ILO.
19 Kevin Quinn, "Trade Unions in 'Mater et Magistra'" in *Gregorianum*, Vol. 43, No. 2 (1962) (Gregorian Biblical Press, 1962) 268, 286.

The text of that resolution passed by the ILC at its 35th Session in 1952 reads:

1. The fundamental and permanent mission of the trade union movement is the economic and social advancement of the workers.
2. The trade unions also have an important role to perform in cooperation with other elements in promoting social and economic development and the advancement of the community as a whole in each country.
3. To these ends it is essential for the trade union movement in each country to preserve its freedom and independence so as to be in a position to carry forward its economic and social mission irrespective of political changes.
4. A condition for such freedom and independence is that trade unions be constituted as to membership without regard to race, national origin or political affiliations and pursue their trade union objectives on the basis of the solidarity and economic and social interests of all workers.
5. *When trade unions in accordance with national law and practice of their respective countries and at the decision of their members decide to establish relations with a political party or to undertake constitutional political action as a means towards the advancement of their economic and social objectives, such political relations or actions should not be of such a nature as to compromise the continuance of the trade union movement or its social and economic functions irrespective of political changes in the country.*
6. Governments in seeking the co-operation of trade unions to carry out their economic and social policies should recognise that the value of this co-operation rests to a large extent on the freedom and independence of the trade union movement as an essential factor in promoting social advancement and *should not attempt to transform the trade union movement into an instrument for the pursuance of political aims,* nor should they attempt to interfere with the normal functions of a trade union movement because of its freely established relationship with a political party.[20] [Emphasis added]

Whether this resolution was in direct response to Pope Pius XII's allocution or whether it was merely a coincidental response to a problem which was of concern independently to the Holy See and to the ILO, a threshold had been crossed. There soon followed the first *public* acknowledgement by the Holy See of the work of the ILO. On 19 November 1954 Pope Pius XII addressed[21] in Rome a delegation from the ILO "which certainly represents a vast number of workers, with their cares, their difficulties, and especially their aspirations for a better, a

---

20 Record of the Proceedings of the 35th Session of the ILC 1952 Appendix IV 451 <www .ilo.org/public/libdoc/ilo/P/09734/09734(1952-35).pdf> (accessed 17 October 2020) © ILO.
21 Discorso di Sua Santità Pio PP. XII ai partecipanti alla 127a sessione del Consiglio 'd'Amministrazione dell'Organizzazione Internazionale del Lavoro 19 November 1954 <www.vatican.va/content/pius-xii/en/speeches/1954/documents/hf_p-xii_spe_195 41119_lavoro.pdf> (accessed 17 October 2020) © Copyright – Libreria Editrice Vaticana.

more just world" and conferred on them "and on all who collaborate with the International Labour Organisation" his apostolic blessing.

> For more than thirty years you have patiently, untiringly built up a work of which you are justly proud, not only because you have contributed to forwarding social legislation in different States, but especially because you have brought together governments, employers and workers in courageous and productive collaboration. You have led them to rise above passion, above feelings of bitter vindictiveness, above the obstinate refusal to acknowledge unavoidable change in order to listen to one another, to weigh calmly the givens of an extremely complex problem and. with common accord, to propose needed improvements. [...]

> At the present time, the human factor, its role too long neglected – but not, however, in Catholic social doctrine – is attracting attention, especially of sociologists, and we know that you want to place it in the forefront of your considerations. The authority and effectiveness of your institution arises in the main from its respect for the high ideal animating those who press for a civilization completely open to the just aspirations of workers. The International Labour Organization has no desire to represent only one social class or to become an expression of any exclusive bias. It welcomes everything constructive, everything that responds to the real needs of a harmoniously formed society; *because of this, our predecessor Pius XI did not hesitate to call attention to the remarkable coincidence of the principles set forth in the Labour Code with those in the encyclical Rerum Novarum.* [Emphasis added]

In his lengthy opening address to the 43rd Session of the ILO in 1959[22] on the 40th anniversary of its foundation, reviewing the history of the ILO, the Chairman of the Governing Body of the International Labour Office Julio Barboza-Carneiro (Brazil) made one passing reference to Pope Pius XII's observation that "The International Labour Organisation has not tried to represent one social class alone, or to become the vehicle of any single trend. It welcomes whatever is constructive, whatever meets the real needs of a balanced society"[23] – but made no mention of the influence of Catholic Social Teaching or of the part played by Catholic actors in the creation and development of the ILO.

Pope St John XXIII introduces the ILO into the Magisterium

Pope St John XXIII succeeded Pope Pius XII in 1958 and it was in his reign that for the first time a reference to the ILO and its achievements entered the

---

22 Record of the Proceedings of the 43rd Session of the ILC 1959 7 <www.ilo.org/public/l ibdoc/ilo/P/09616/09616(1959-43).pdf> (accessed 17 October 2020) © ILO.
23 The official Vatican translation differs slightly.

Magisterium. In his Encyclical *Mater et magistra* (1961) Pope St John XXIII expressed his praise and appreciation for the ILO:

> 100. It is Our prerogative to be a Father, and there is a special place in Our thoughts and in Our heart for those professional groups and Christian associations of workers which exist and operate in so many parts of the world. We know the nature and extent of the difficulties under which these dearest sons of Ours are labouring, as they strive continually and effectually to promote in their own countries and throughout the world the material and moral interests of the working people. [...]

> 103. We must also express here Our heartfelt appreciation of the work that is being done by the International Labor Organization – popularly known in various countries as the O.I.L. or I.L.O. or O.I.T. For many years now it has been making an effective and valued contribution to the establishment in the world of an economics and social order marked by justice and humanity, an order which recognizes and safeguards the lawful rights of the workingman.[24]

There was far more to this expression of support than perhaps met the eye, for the stakes were high.

David Morse (ILO Director-General 1948–1970) recounts that:

> When the Soviet Union and other Eastern European Countries renewed their active participation in the work of the ILO in 1954, the Organization was brought to the brink of crisis. It was widely felt in employers' and workers' circles that the social system in Socialist countries of Eastern Europe was incompatible with membership of the ILO, and that the presence of these countries in the Organization would shatter its very foundations.[25]

Writing from an American perspective, John F Cronin in his near-contemporary commentary[26] on *Mater et magistra* saw this as "significant, not only as a direct approval of the magnificent work of this group, but also as an implied rebuke to those who have tried to destroy it". He gave as an example the fact that in the late 1950s there was pressure on the government of the United States of America

---

24 Pope St John XXIII, *Mater et magistra* (1961) 101, 103 © Copyright – Libreria Editrice Vaticana.
25 David A Morse, *The Origin and Evolution of the I.L.O. and Its Role in the World Community* (New York State School of Industrial and Labor Relations, Cornell University, Ithaca, NY, 1969) 40. The USSR, having effectively suspended its membership of the ILO in 1939 fully re-joined in 1954. The ILO/USSR negotiations are recorded in the ILO archives: ILOA-MF, Z 5/1/64/1: Re-admission USSR: 1954, 1961© ILO.
26 John F Cronin, *Christianity and Social Progress: A Commentary on Mater et Magistra* (Helicon, Baltimore, 1965) 63–64.

to withdraw from membership of the ILO because communist States participated in its deliberations. David Morse, himself an American and known for his anti-communist convictions, became the whipping boy of the American right wing and personally came under attack during the anti-communist McCarthy era. Within the US, not least in Congress, ran strong anti-internationalist currents.[27] The then Republican administration rejected the call for withdrawal, reasoning that there was far more chance to continue the good work from within the ILO than externally.[28]

The death of Pope St John XXIII in 1963 elicited at the 47th Session of the ILC a brief but nonetheless sincere tribute from the Chairman of the Governing Body of the International Labour Office Alexandre Parodi (France) stressing the common cause of the late Pope and of the ILO, the pursuit of peace:

> I know that you will consider it right that in speaking to you here, just after the very great loss which has been suffered, I should say a few words to express the grief we feel at the death of Pope John XXIII. I am not speaking in the name of a religion but, I am sure, in the name of all the spiritual families represented here. The work of this most eminent man has had a profound effect on religious life during the last few years and has opened up new possibilities for the coming together of the peoples. *In the two great texts which he left behind him, he underlined the part which the International Labour Organisation should play in promoting and ensuring social peace.* Profoundly attached to the cause of peace among men, he stated his conviction that the world ought to enter without delay on the path of a real international community. Because that ideal is our own, it is my duty to pay a tribute to his memory.[29] [Emphasis added]

Under-representation of the Christian trade unions resolved

One last loose end from the pre-War years – the under-representation of the Christian trade unions at the ILC – still needed to be tied. In 1921 this had escalated to a hearing before the Permanent Court of International Justice,[30] but after

---

27 Daniel Roger Maul, "The 'Morse Years': The ILO 1948–1970" in International Institute of Social History Amsterdam (Jasmien Van Daele and others, eds) *ILO Histories: Essays on the International Labour Organization and Its Impact on the World during the Twentieth Century* (Peter Lang, Bern, 2010) 365, 372–375.

28 President Dwight D Eisenhower (1953–1961) had no doubts on that score, when asked if the US should restrict its appropriations in support of the ILO: "But I do believe, I do believe we should be bona fide members of the ILO". The President's News Conference 9 May 1956 *The American Presidency Project* <www.presidency.ucsb.edu/documents/the-pr esidents-news-conference-302> (accessed 17 October 2020).

29 Record of the Proceedings of the 47th Session of the ILC 1963 <www.ilo.org/public/l ibdoc/ilo/P/09616/09616(1963-47).pdf> (accessed 17 October 2020) © ILO.

30 See Chapter 5.

World War Two much of the heat seems to have gone out of the debate. The matter was raised at the 29th Session of the ILC in 1946 by another prominent veteran from the dawn of the ILO, P J S Serrarens:

> [T]he International Confederation of Christian Trade Unions, of which I happen to be the General Secretary, fully adheres to the fundamental principles of this Organisation, though it resents the position of often being left on the door-mat. This is not a question which depends on the Director. I feel confident that, as far as it will be within his power, he will try to find solutions for a better contact between the International Labour Organisation and the Christian labour movement than is possible at the moment.[31]

This issue was quietly resolved at the 31st Session of the ILC which on 19 June 1948 adopted the following somewhat dry resolution, establishing "consultative relations" and amended the Standing Orders of the ILC so as to classify bodies such as the International Federation of Christian Trade Unions as "non-governmental international organisations" with the right to "make or circulate statements for the information of the Conference on questions which are being considered by the Conference other than administrative and financial questions":

> The Governing Body approves in principle the establishment of consultative relationships with the International Confederation of Christian Trade Unions and the Inter-American Confederation of Workers and the consultative relationships with these two organisations will become operative as soon as they have communicated to the Director-General the information concerning their Constitutions, officers, membership and annual reports as required by paragraph 4 of the resolution adopted by the Governing Body on 14 June 1948.[32]

They duly communicated the required information, and the matter was never again to be raised.[33]

---

31 Record of the Proceedings of the 29th Session of the ILC 1946 97 <www.ilo.org/public/l ibdoc/ilo/P/09616/09616(1946-29).pdf> (accessed 17 October 2020) © ILO.

32 Record of the Proceedings of the 31st Session of the ILC 1948 323 <www.ilo.org/public/l ibdoc/ilo/P/09616/09616(1948-31).pdf> (accessed 17 October 2020) © ILO.

33 The International Federation of Christian Trade Unions became the World Confederation of Labour in October 1968, and no longer nominally confessional. It was formally dissolved on 31 October 2006 when it merged with the International Confederation of Free Trade Unions to form the International Trade Union Confederation. <www.ituc-csi.org/> (accessed 17 October 2020).

Address of Pope St Paul VI to the 53rd Session of the ILC 1969[34]

In 1969 the ILO celebrated its 50th anniversary, and on 10 December was to be awarded the Nobel Peace Prize.[35] Pope St Paul VI addressed the 53rd Session of the ILC on 10 June.

In a speech in which he referred again and again to the common cause of the ILO and the Holy See, he first acknowledged their separate spheres of expertise:

> We do not belong to this international body, We are extraneous to the specific questions which have here their offices of study and halls of discussion, and Our spiritual mission is not intended to intervene in matters outside its proper domain.

In this there were shades of an earlier time, when Pope Pius XI resolutely held that the Holy See was above the political sphere, but clearly this was not his intention. The speech was crafted to show the interdependent, symbiotic nature of the relationship which had in the first 50 years of its existence grown up between the ILO and the Holy See. "Without any particular competence in the technical discussions on the defence and promotion of human labour, We are nevertheless no stranger to this great cause of labour for which this Organisation exists and to which you dedicate your energies".

He stated definitively that the work of the Church and that of the ILO were inextricably linked, in their common goal of universal peace through social justice, and quoted from "The International Labour Organisation: The First Decade"[36] in saying that "the great movement which was originated in the Roman Catholic Church by the Encyclical Rerum Novarum of 1891 has proved extremely fruitful". He stressed "the sympathy of the Church towards your organisation, and for the whole world of labour", "unceasingly manifested" in the Encyclicals and "most particularly" *Quadragesimo anno, Mater et magistra, Gaudium et Spes* and *Populorum progressio*.

> In other words, We are an attentive observer of the work you accomplish here, and more than that, a fervent admirer of the activity you carry on, and also a collaborator who is happy to have been invited to celebrate with you the existence, functions, achievements and merits of this world institution, and to do so as a friend. [...]

34 Record of the Proceedings of the 53rd Session of the ILC 1969 77–81 <www.ilo.org/public/libdoc/ilo/P/09616/09616(1969-53).pdf> (accessed 17 October 2020) © ILO.
35 <www.nobelprize.org/prizes/peace/1969/summary/> and <www.un.org/en/sections/nobel-peace-prize/international-labor-organization-ilo/index.html> (each accessed 17 October 2020).
36 Albert Thomas, *The International Labour Organisation: The First Decade* (George Allen & Unwin Ltd, London, 1931).

To Us, Who belong to an institution exposed to the wear of time for two thousand years, the fifty years untiringly dedicated to the International Labour Organisation are a source of fruitful meditation. [...]

With all Our heart We rejoice with you at the vitality of your fifty-year-old but still young institution, ever since its birth in the Peace Treaty of Versailles in 1919. Who can recount the work, the toil, the night watches so fruitful in courageous decisions of benefit to all workers as well as for the life of mankind, performed by all those who with great merit dedicated their talent and activity to this organisation ? Among all of these, We cannot omit to mention the first Director, Albert Thomas, and his present successor, David Morse. *Nor can We omit to mention that at their request, and almost from the very beginning, a priest has always been included among those who constituted, constructed, sustained and served this outstanding institution.* We are grateful to all for the work they have accomplished, and We express the wish that it may happily continue its complex and difficult mission which is truly providential for the greater good of modern society. [Emphasis added]

He praised the "modern concept" of work "of which you are the heralds and defenders":

It is based on a fundamental principle which has been brought out conspicuously by Christianity: in labour, it is man who comes first. Whether he be an artist or an artisan, contractor, peasant or labourer, manual or intellectual, it is man who works, it is for man that he works. An end has been put to the priority of labour over the labourer, to the supremacy of technical and economic necessities over human needs.

He saw the vocation of the ILO as having

a single aim: not money, not power, but the good of man. It is more than an economic concept, it is better than a political concept: it is a moral and human concept which inspires you, namely social justice, to be built up, day by day, freely and of common accord. [...] Thus you ensure a permanent passage from the ideal order of principles to the juridical order, that is, to positive law. In a word, you gradually refine and improve the moral conscience of mankind. This is an arduous and delicate task indeed, but it is so lofty and so necessary, and calls for the collaboration of all true friends of man. How then could We not give it Our adherence and Our support?

This convergence of ideas and of ideals between the Church and the ILO was summed up by Mr Migone (Representative of the Organisation of American States) focussing on the spiritual:

What is more, this great effort will not suffice if it is not accompanied by an all-out mobilisation of spiritual forces. In this respect His Holiness Pope Paul VI and the Director-General, Mr Morse, have expressed identical views, because it is obvious that those conflicts of interest which are hampering the progress of social justice will be resolved that much more swiftly and to the general satisfaction if a collective moral conscience develops – a collective moral conscience which is the inescapable responsibility of all of us.[37]

and by Mr Bury (Minister for Labour and National Service, Australia) emphasising the practical:

The words of His Holiness the Pope pointed to the spiritual nature and sanctity of the task. It is for us to devise and apply the necessary practical measures.[38]

It was a message which continued to resonate within the ILO in the succeeding decades. In his opening address to the Third Sitting of the 92nd Session of the ILC in 2004, ILO President Ray Guevara commented:

In 1969, the year in which the ILO received the Nobel Peace Prize, His Holiness Pope Paul VI stated before this very Conference that this Organization was more than an economic conception and better than a political conception and that rather it was a moral and human conception that inspired the establishment of social justice on a day-to-day basis, freely and by mutual agreement. In sum, His Holiness the Pope said that the Organization was fine-tuning and promoting the moral conscience of humanity. I think that, in the twenty-first century, it is our duty and our responsibility, more than ever before, to be this moral conscience that humankind needs so badly.[39]

Address of Pope St John Paul II to the 68th Session of the ILC 1982[40]

Introducing Pope St John Paul II, the Secretary-General commented, recalling that the Pope had once worked as a stonemason and in a chemicals factory and "had worked face to face with the realities of the working world":

Ninety years ago Pope Leo XIII published the encyclical *Rerum novarum* in which he condemned the unmerited poverty of the workers. You, Your

37 Record of the Proceedings of the 53rd Session of the ILC 1969 312 <www.ilo.org/public/l ibdoc/ilo/P/09616/09616(1969-53).pdf> (accessed 17 October 2020) © ILO.
38 Record of the Proceedings of the 53rd Session of the ILC 1969 212 <www.ilo.org/public/l ibdoc/ilo/P/09616/09616(1969-53).pdf> (accessed 17 October 2020) © ILO.
39 Record of the Proceedings of the 92nd Session of the ILC 2004 10/3 <www.ilo.org/public /libdoc/ilo/P/09616/09616(2004-92).pdf> (accessed 17 October 2020) © ILO.
40 Record of the Proceedings of the 68th Session of the ILC 1982 21/1/–21/6 <www.ilo.org /public/libdoc/ilo/P/09616/09616(1982-68).pdf> (accessed 17 October 2020) © ILO.

Holiness, wished to commemorate this anniversary by publishing the encyclical *Laborem exercens*, entirely concerned with the promotion of the dignity of labour and of the worker. [...] *Before you speak, may I emphasise the convergence that exists between the aims and purposes of the ILO and the human values which you tirelessly and unceasingly affirm. We work for a common cause:* the promotion of human rights and the dignity and freedom of the worker. The ILO, from the outset, has known how to heed the voices of the valuable forces represented by the social movements, and it must continue to heed them if it is to progress. It is its duty to do so because this is the place where mankind forges a common conscience. [Emphasis added]

In his address Pope St John Paul II focussed on his recently published Encyclical *Laborem exercens*[41] and noted that such texts "were respectfully and favourably received by the ILO, attuned as it always has been, throughout the various historic stages of its existence and its activities, to the varied aspects of all the complex problems associated with human work". He stressed however the difference between the mission of the Church, "which is primarily and essentially a religious and moral one" and that of the ILO, but confirmed that "[...] the Church and the Holy See share [the ILO's] concern for its basic objectives". As with his predecessor Pope St Paul VI in 1969, Pope St John Paul II stressed the interconnectivity of the Church and the ILO, which he had mentioned expressly in *Laborem exercens*:

> If I have ventured to mention the International Labour Organisation in my Encyclical *Laborem exercens*, I did so to draw attention to its many achievements and to encourage it to strengthen its activities aimed at making work more human. *I also sought to highlight the fact that in efforts to give human labour a truly moral basis – which is consistent with the objective principles of social ethics – the aims of the International Labour Organisation are very close to those which the Church and the Apostolic See are pursuing in their own sphere with means adapted to their mission.* [...] [T]he Church and the Apostolic See take great joy in their excellent co-operation with your Organisation, co-operation which has already lasted for half a century and which culminated in the formal accrediting in 1967 of a permanent observer to the International Labour Office. In this way the Holy See sought to give stable expression to its desire for co-operation and to the lively interest of the Catholic Church in labour problems, stemming from its concern for the true good of man. [Emphasis added]

He lauded the tripartite structure of the ILO, its "community spirit", "a spirit of universalism". *Laborem exercens* highlights the need for solidarity and Pope St John Paul II, referring to the intuitive need for solidarity, commented:

---

41 Pope St John Paul II, *Laborem exercens* (1981) © Copyright – Libreria Editrice Vaticana.

This fundamental intuition which the founders of the ILO so strongly emphasised in the structure of the Organisation itself and the corollary of which is that the objectives it pursues can be achieved only through community and solidarity, reflects the reality of human work.

The summation of his address is an unqualified, unlimited endorsement of the ILO and its "tremendous record of achievement within its field".

The feeling of the ILO delegates towards the issues raised in Pope St John Paul II's address and towards the significance of the address itself were expressed by Mr Di Giesi (Minister of Labour and Social Welfare, Italy):

> This event constitutes undoubtedly and in the truest sense a consecration of the universal vocation of the ILO. Also, as explicitly and significantly outlined in the last Encyclical *Laborem exercens*, there can be no doubt that the ILO constitutes today a rallying point for the aspirations which were at the centre of the Pope's message, namely the desire for the balanced development of ethical and social relations and the relations between our respective national economies founded upon respect, which is not merely formal, for the dignity of the human person, as well as upon freedom of the individual from anxiety and humiliation due to the failure to satisfy basic needs.[42]

Lech Wałęsa as a Workers' delegate representing Poland at the ILC in 1990 emphasised the synthesis between the ILO and Catholic Social Teaching inherent in *Laborem exercens*:

> Struggling for working people's rights, we realise that there will be no real freedom, democracy or peace without social justice, as stated by the ILO Constitution and the Declaration of Philadelphia, and by Pope John Paul II's encyclical *Laborem exercens*. The achievement of peace and security throughout the world has never depended as much as it does today on the building of a democratic and just social system concerned with development, progress and international order in the world of labour.[43]

At the 79th Session of the ILC in 1992 in his opening address[44] Mr Chotard (Chairman of the Governing Body of the International Labour Office) read out the greeting given by Pope St John Paul II at an audience granted to the Governing Body of the ILO on 30 May 1992, at which the delegates presented

---

42 Record of the Proceedings of the 68th Session of the ILC 1982 23/6 <www.ilo.org/public /libdoc/ilo/P/09616/09616(1982-68).pdf> (accessed 17 October 2020) © ILO.

43 Record of the Proceedings of the 77th Session of the ILC 1990 17/3 <www.ilo.org/public /libdoc/ilo/P/09616/09616(1990-77).pdf> (accessed 17 October) © ILO.

44 Record of the Proceedings of the 79th Session of the ILC 1992 7/12 <www.ilo.org/public /libdoc/ilo/P/09616/09616(1992-79).pdf> (accessed 17 October 2020) © ILO.

him with two volumes on the social teachings of the Catholic Church and the world of work and on the commemoration of the 100th anniversary of *Rerum novarum*.[45] Referring to the ILO as an "illustrious Organisation" the Pope continued:

> I am pleased that the Organisation pays special attention to the teachings of the Church, and I perceive similarities between its approach and the social doctrine of the Church. Quite recently the colloquium on work, culture and religion highlighted their common interests and concern for modern social issues. [...]
>
> The slow and laborious development of many countries which have chosen to follow the rules of market economics and the path of democratisation clearly has reinforced the mission of the International Labour Organisation and the need for it to be vigilant. *Indeed, it is sometimes said that you are the social conscience of the world.* [Emphasis added]

Addressing that same Conference, Mr Vittori, representing Pax Christi International,[46] referred to those two presentation volumes and saw in them evidence of convergence:

> Pax Christi International has read with great interest the two recent publications of the ILO. One gathers together summaries of the major documents of the Catholic Church in relation with the world of labour, and the other highlights – regarding Rerum Novarum and the publication of the encyclical Centesimus Annus, in 1991 – *the convergence of the perspectives of the social teachings of the Catholic Church and those of the ILO.* My organisation welcomes the fact that the ILO is envisaging the publication of other documents which will highlight the wealth of the reflection of other religions and ways of thinking about labour. *This can only contribute to reinforcing the ILO as the social conscience of the world.*[47] [Emphasis added]

ILO Commemoration of the Centenary of *Rerum novarum* 1991

It was noted by delegates to the 78th Session of the ILC in 1991 – albeit the observations were mainly those of delegates from South America[48] – that no

---

45 n 51.
46 Details of Pax Christi International are available at <https://paxchristi.net/about-us/> (accessed 17 October 2020).
47 Record of the Proceedings of the 79th Session of the ILC 1992 16/40 <www.ilo.org/public /libdoc/ilo/P/09616/09616(1992-79).pdf> (accessed 17 October 2020) © ILO.
48 Record of the Proceedings of the 78th Session of the ILC 1991 Argentina (8/11), Guatemala (17/10), Paraguay (13/38), Peru (6/21) and the International Federation of Trade

formal tribute was paid in Conference to commemorate the centenary of the Encyclical of Pope Leo XIII *Rerum novarum*. This was described by the representative of the Latin American Central of Workers, Mr Marius, as "a regrettable sign of social and political insensitivity".[49]

It was left to Archbishop Justo Mullor García, the Apostolic Nuncio and Permanent Observer of the Holy See to highlight in his address to the ILC[50] both *Rerum novarum* and the Encyclical of Pope St John Paul II *Centesimus annus* (1991). He recalled the strong social tensions between capital and labour which had existed in 1891, with colonialism and forced labour exacerbating this and commended the century-long role of the ILO:

> Such injustice posed a serious challenge to the conscience of the world and that of the Church. There have been many responses to this challenge. From the legal point of view, the least one can say is that the majority of workers in most parts of the world are no longer at the mercy of their employers. Tenacious and far-sighted action has been undertaken on a large scale under the auspices of the ILO. [...]
>
> The need for interdependence which makes the global economy is closely connected with universal standards of human rights and you can find this expressed in the Constitution of the International Labour Organisation, in the Declaration of Philadelphia and in the international labour Conventions.

Looking outside the confines of the Conference itself, however, the ILO did not fail to mark the anniversary. The Jesuit in residence Louis Christiaens edited and himself contributed to a collection of extracts from early ILO records, corresponding passages from the social Encyclicals and Papal addresses to the ILC, together with observations and endorsements from Member States which was published by the ILO under the title *L'Organisation internationale du Travail et l'encyclique sociale de Jean-Paul II Centesimus annus: Commémoration du centième anniversaire de Rerum novarum (1891–1991)*. It drew strong parallels between the work of the ILO and that of the Holy See.[51]

Unions of Transport Workers (9/25) <www.ilo.org/public/libdoc/ilo/P/09616/09 616(1991-78).pdf> (accessed 17 October 2020) © ILO.

49 Record of Proceedings of the 78th Session of the ILC 1991 8/14 <www.ilo.org/public/l ibdoc/ilo/P/09616/09616(1991-78).pdf> (accessed 17 October 2020) © ILO.

50 Record of Proceedings of the 78th Session of the ILC 1991 8/146–8/18 <www.ilo.org/ public/libdoc/ilo/P/09616/09616(1991-78).pdf> (accessed 17 October 2020) © ILO.

51 (Louis Christiaens, ed), *L'Organisation internationale du Travail et l'encyclique sociale de Jean-Paul II Centesimus annus: Commémoration du centième anniversaire de Rerum novarum* (ILO, Geneva, 1991). Available online at <www.worldcat.org/title/organis ation-internationale-du-travail-et-lencyclique-sociale-de-jean-paul-ii-centesimus-annus-co mmemoration-du-centieme-anniversaire-de-rerum-novarum-1891-1991-documents/oclc /463513912> (accessed 17 October 2020) © ILO.

In his Introduction, Louis Christiaens wrote that to celebrate the centenary of *Rerum novarum* would fulfil what he called the "vow" of Albert Thomas as first Director-General to come to know and understand the social dynamism of Christianity and its contribution to the aims of the ILO:

> L'Église catholique, comme elle le rappelle fréquemment dans ses documents officiels, n'a pas de solutions techniques ni de 'modèle' à proposer pour résoudre les difficiles problèmes économiques et sociaux que les responsables gouvernmentaux, les chefs d'entreprises et les travailleurs de ce temps ont à affronter quotidiennement. Par contre, il convient de s'accorder à reconnaître le solide et précieux apport des orientations intellectuelles et éthiques de son enseignement social.

> Aux yeux de tous, en effet, y compris des non-croyants, le christianisme apparaît bien porteur d'une efficacité sociale originale et, à ce titre déjà, son apport ne peut manquer de concerner l'avenir du monde internationale, c'est à dire l'avenir de l'homme. Les interventions des papes en cette matière gagnent par conséquent à être entendues, reçues et situées pour être, selon les missions spécifiques des organisations internationales et les fonctions propres des organisations d'employeurs et des syndicats intéressés, interprétées et mises en oeuvre avec profit. [...]

> L'enseignement de l'Église se déploie essentiellement dans une contexte universel qui recoupe précisément le cadre international des Etats Members de l'OIT.

> En second lieu, l'accent des analyses proposées dans les encycliques, à l'instar de celles organisations internationales, porte également sur la description objective de l'existence de travailleurs et de travailleuses, de responsables économiques et politiques.[52]

---

52 [The Catholic Church, as it often repeats in its official documents, has no technical solutions or "plan" to put forward which would resolve the difficult social and economic problems which face contemporary government officials, business leaders and workers on a daily basis. That said, it is appropriate to give recognition to the substantial and valuable contribution made by the intellectual and ethical guidance contained in its social teaching. In fact, in everyone's eyes, including those of non-believers, it is clear that Christianity comports a unique social effectiveness and, just on these grounds alone, its contribution cannot fail to affect the future of the international world, which is to say, the future of mankind itself. The involvement of the Popes in such matters benefits as a result from being heard, received and positioned (according to the specific functions of international organisations and the respective duties of employers and relevant trade unions) so as to be construed and implemented to advantage. [...] Fundamentally, the teaching of the Church unfurls universally and overlaps exactly the international footprint of the ILO Member States. Furthermore, the weight of the arguments, made in the manner of such international organisations, put forward in the Encyclicals bears equally an objective account of the lives of working men and women and of answerable political and economic institutions.]

This was not simply an in house publication or souvenir issue for the tripartite representatives of governments, employers and workers. It was clearly purposed for the Holy See and the Catholic Church in general, and was just as powerful a signal of the desire for mutual co-operation and support as those given "under the radar" to Pope Pius XI by Albert Thomas and Mgr Nolens in the 1920s.[53]

If proof were needed, it was this collection which the following year was presented in a bound volume to Pope St John Paul II when he granted an audience to the Governing Body of the ILO on 30 May 1992.

Commentaries on the work of the ILO made by the Holy See through its Observers

Commentaries in context

The cross influence not just of Catholic Social Teaching on the workings of the ILO but of those workings on Catholic Social Teaching itself can be discerned through the comments of the various Observers representing the Holy See at International Labour Conferences.

First accredited in 1967, the Observers have engaged in an increasingly technical and pragmatic debate with the Conference, whilst at the same time emphasising the priority of the spiritual and moral mission of the Church. They appear however to have been speaking in gatherings which, though not hostile, were apparently largely indifferent to them. Save at the milestone events which were the appearances at the ILC of Pope St Paul VI and Pope St John Paul II, delegates to the ILC throughout the past 50 years have rarely commented on Catholic Social Teaching and hardly ever in their own contributions to the debates have they made any reference to what was said by the Observers. The Reports of the Directors-General to the ILCs are equally devoid of comment.

The contributions in debate of the Observers over the past 20 years have sometimes been brief to the point of simply expressing support for a given initiative, and on occasions when setting out principles of Catholic Social Teaching have been generalisations, didactic rather than connecting with a specific Conference topic, but their significance does not lie in this.

What then is the value of the Observers' commentaries? They represent a running assessment and as such are amongst the clearest indications of thinking of the Holy See on the development of labour rights. More than this, they subject those seemingly silent Reports to an exegesis based on the principles of Catholic Social Teaching and in so doing identify what on a purely secular reading are hidden similarities in philosophy and approach. They speak with the authority of the Holy See. They are the embodiment of a continuing dialogue between the Holy See and the ILO.

---

53 See Chapter 3.

The commentaries have varied in their approach, but distinct themes have emerged. These have ranged from general endorsements by the Holy See of the activities of the ILO to specific observations on the necessity for dialogue, on poverty, on the plight of rural workers and migrants, on employment, on the need for vocational training, on child labour and on environmental issues.

Endorsement

Addressing the 57th Session of the ILC in 1972[54] Mgr Luoni stressed the importance of the relationship between the Holy See and the ILO, something which was to be referred to often by the Observers in the succeeding decades. Anything which strengthened the ILO "is a motive of satisfaction to this delegation":

> Although the Holy See is not a Member of the ILO, it has always wished to co-operate with the Organisation because of the existence of common interests between the ILO and the Holy See, both of which aim at improving the conditions of the workers in a human sense. The presence of Pope Paul VI in this hall at the time of the fiftieth anniversary of the ILO was not only an expression of friendship and esteem but also bore witness to the moral support of the Church for ILO action in favour of social justice. [...] You may be certain that any initiative on the part of the ILO aimed at promoting and protecting the fundamental rights of the individual, such as justice and freedom, will be welcomed and supported by the Holy See.

Three years later, addressing the 60th Session of the ILC in 1975[55] Mgr Luoni returned to this theme even more forcefully. He noted that the Holy See was not a Member of the ILO:

> but that does not prevent us from closely following the work of the Organisation with the greatest interest and sympathy. Nor does it prevent the Holy See from making its contribution to the Organisation's activities for the promotion of social justice with an original approach based on a comprehensive, harmonious and profound conception of the human being and of society.

> A contribution from the doctrinal standpoint first of all – the documents on the subject are innumerable – but also from a practical standpoint by lending discreet and effective support for the ILO's activities whenever possible.

---

54 Record of the Proceedings of the 57th Session of the ILC 1972 294–295 <www.ilo.org/public/libdoc/ilo/P/09616/09616(1972-57).pdf> (accessed 17 October 2020) © ILO.
55 Record of the Proceedings of the 60th Session of the ILC 1975 408–409 <www.ilo.org/public/libdoc/ilo/P/09616/09616(1975-60).pdf> (accessed 17 October 2020) © ILO.

The "Worker Pope" Pope St John Paul II had acceded in 1978. His milestone address to the ILC still lay two years in the future when Archbishop Jean-Éduard-Lucien Rupp addressed the 65th Session of the ILC in 1980:[56]

> Labour problems and the problems of workers are of profound concern to the Church, as evidenced by the frequent references made by the Holy Father to these matters in Mexico, Paris, Poland and Rome. The Holy See is glad to note the commitment of the ILO to the solution of those problems and to see its universality becoming more and more complete.

Addressing the 67th Session of the ILC in 1981,[57] Archbishop Edoardo Rovida emphasised the importance of the social Encyclicals and the compatibility of the social doctrine of the Church and international institutions such as the ILO:

> The influence of the social encyclicals on the programmes of human solidarity and advancement justifies the statement that it is mostly social movements which lead history, and they have lost nothing of their importance. The slow but sure progress of social legislation has been possible only after the social conscience of the various countries considered certain injustices and inequalities to be unacceptable. Any innovation as regards individual interests has no chance of being accepted and entering into our way of life unless it seems to be a solution to some problem of justice.
>
> The Church has the right and duty to participate in this task of increasing sensitivity because it is required by its mission to unmask selfishness, cupidity and thirst for power. It must also show human beings the path to integral liberation and development and offer them the means of taking it. [...]
>
> The international institutions are one of the places where people search for and formulate the common principles of social life. My delegation is happy to see that the ILO is particularly aware of the requirements of a dialogue with all the forces concerned.

Addressing the 70th Session of the ILC in 1984,[58] Rev Fr Roch congratulated the ILO:

> on its 65th anniversary and on the 40th anniversary of the Declaration of Philadelphia. This Declaration is basically still as ethically and morally valid

56 Record of Proceedings of the 66th Session of the ILC 1980 27/8–27/9 <www.ilo.org/public/libdoc/ilo/P/09616/09616(1980-66).pdf> (accessed 17 October 2020) © ILO.
57 Record of the Proceedings of the 67th Session of the ILC 1981 35/17–35/18 <www.ilo.org/public/libdoc/ilo/P/09616/09616(1981-67).pdf> (accessed 17 October 2020) © ILO.
58 Record of the Proceedings of the 70th Session of the ILC 1984 25/4–25/5 <www.ilo.org/public/libdoc/ilo/P/09616/09616(1984-70).pdf> (accessed 17 October 2020) © ILO.

as ever for the world of labour on the threshold of the twenty-first century and remains a source of vital inspiration for all of us. Indeed, its principles are fully applicable to all the peoples of the world. […]

The activities of the ILO until now, including the many programmes and strategies for technical cooperation, have indeed been worthy of the praise and interest of all those who attach importance to people, national communities and their harmony with the universal common good. That is why the Holy See, in its spiritual mission, feels solidarity with an effort which is making such a great contribution towards the establishment and development of justice and peace in the human family.

Rev Fr Roch also spoke of the distinct competences of the Holy See and the ILO. The Holy See "would not venture to make a scientific analysis of changing conditions and their influence on the life of society" but it would fulfil its mission to remind the world of the dignity and rights of the workers and to condemn violations of such dignity and rights. Satisfying the need for international labour standards however was not something with which the Holy See was charged to achieve, but was:

an arduous task that is also the responsibility of the ILO. On the one hand it must uphold firmly the fundamental rights of the individual, and the common weal that guarantees these rights, that is to say, this ideal of justice which springs from the legal conscience of a civilised world and is based on a natural law inspired by God the creator. On the other hand, the ILO must be realistic in that these principles must be suitable for concrete and effective application and accordingly have regard, in particular, to different legal systems, obtain the consent of States, take into account new and unforeseen events such as the rapid succession of developments in technological, sociological, economic or political conditions, etc.

This division of competences was again explored in the address given by Fr Giuseppe Bertello to the 71st Session of the ILC in 1985.[59] Whilst giving unqualified support to the ILO, he was nevertheless aware that the principles of Catholic Social Teaching to which he referred in his address "might appear to be no more than abstract principles and a manifestation of superficial solidarity" but was nevertheless "convinced that these principles, far from being abstract theories, constitute the ethical basis without which the problems of the economy would either become insoluble or would cast a shadow on the dignity of man".

59 Record of the Proceedings of the 71st Session of the ILC 1985 22/24 – 22/26 <www.ilo .org/public/libdoc/ilo/P/09616/09616(1985-71).pdf> (accessed 17 October 2020) © ILO.

Collaboration was further emphasised by Archbishop Jean-Louis Tauran addressing the 81st Session of the ILC in 1994,[60] which was another milestone:

> It is a particularly pleasant duty for me to convey to you the wishes of His Holiness Pope John Paul II as you celebrate the 75th anniversary of the ILO and the 50th anniversary of the Declaration of Philadelphia. The Holy Father calls down divine blessing upon you all and on your labours.

> Since 1919, the collaboration between your Organisation and the Holy See has been constant: the numerous messages from the Holy Father, as well as the visits made by Pope Paul VI and John Paul II to the Organisation's Geneva headquarters show the high esteem in which the Catholic Church holds the fundamental inspiration that lies behind the work done by the ILO: improving workers' conditions of life through genuine social dialogue, freedom of association, abolition of child labour and reconciling work with family life.

Emphasising that fundamental problems could not be resolved merely by "ready-made, over-simplistic solutions", that "work too needs a 'moral' dimension" he concluded:

> On the eve of the twenty-first century, the ILO must more than ever act *as the world's social conscience.*[Emphasis added]

Addressing to 100th Session of the ILC in 2011 Archbishop Silvano Tomasi drew attention to a particular strength and consequent importance of the ILO:

> In this 100th Session of the International Labour Conference we must reaffirm the importance of a new governance, based on the principles of subsidiarity and tripartism that *give the ILO an edge in integrating real-world knowledge about employment and work.* In a globally integrated financial system that is characterized by speed, mobility and flexibility, the voice and advocacy of those who protect and promote the rights of workers and the dignity of labour is essential.[61] [Emphasis added]

In his address to the 104th Session of the ILC in 2015 Archbishop Tomasi emphasised the importance to trade agreements of ILO Standards and the full support given to these by the Holy See:

60 Record of Proceedings of the 81st Session of the ILO 1994 9/8–9/7 <www.ilo.org/public/libdoc/ilo/P/09616/09616(1994-81).pdf> (accessed 17 October 2020) © ILO.
61 Record of the Proceedings of the 100th Session of the ILC 2011 9/9 <www.ilo.org/public/libdoc/ilo/P/09616/09616(2011-100).pdf> (accessed 17 October 2020) © ILO.

Labour provisions are increasingly included in bilateral and regional trade agreements. [...] There is however the risk that labour provisions contained in preferential trade agreements may divert trade towards less demanding partners, with an unintended belittling of ILO standards. The Holy See underscores the necessity that the ILO Standards should not be weakened but serve as a basis for all current and future bilateral and plurilateral agreements.[62]

Nor must sight be lost of the wider context. The ILO sits within the United Nations and here too the voice of the Holy See in support of the ILO is to be heard. On 11 April 2019 Archbishop Bernardito Auza, Apostolic Nuncio and Permanent Observer of the Holy See to the United Nations, addressed the High-Level Meeting of the United Nations General Assembly to commemorate the 100th anniversary of the ILO:[63]

We consider this celebration an opportunity to renew the necessary commitment to work together in order to achieve the goal of a social justice available to all, leaving no one behind, while moving forward into the second century of the Organization. [...]

The good practice and continued relevance of social dialogue, with its important contributions, is increasingly necessary, in a context of global developments, employment as well as in labour relations. Over the last century, we have had the pleasure to observe that, in order to promote a real social dialogue, the effective tripartite structure of the ILO, has been both an objective in itself and a means to achieve other objectives.

We wish to commend the ideals that, 100 years ago, presided over its creation and reaffirm that "the ILO possesses the moral compass to guide its decisions, and the values by which it must assess all changes in the world of work. The task is to shape the emerging realities of our time into conformity with those values, and not the reverse".[64] The Holy See confidently looks for-

---

62 Quoted in *Rethinking Labour, Ethical Reflections on the Future of Work, Labour after Laudato Si'* 333–338, at 336 (The Caritas in Veritate Foundation Working Papers, FCIV, Chambésy, 2018) <https://futureofwork-labourafterlaudatosi.net/2018/11/14/rethinking-labour-ethical-reflections-on-the-future-of-work-14-november-2018-global/> © The Caritas in Veritate Foundation (accessed 17 October 2020).

63 Archbishop Bernardito Auza, Apostolic Nuncio and Permanent Observer of the Holy See to the United Nations, address to the High-Level Meeting of the United Nations General Assembly 11 April 2019 <https://holyseemission.org/contents/statements/5cb0ae1bdd6e4.php> © 2015–2020. The Permanent Observer Mission of the Holy See to the United Nations (accessed 17 October 2020).

64 Quoting the Opening Statement of Director-General Guy Ryder for the ILO 100th Anniversary, Geneva 22 January 2019 <https://www.ilo.org/global/about-the-ilo/how-the-ilo-works/ilo-director-general/statements-and-speeches/WCMS_665184/lang--en/index.htm> (c) ILO (accessed 17 October 2020).

ward to a continued collaboration, as the International Labour Organization
addresses the theme of labour and of its impact on the economy and society,
in the best interest of every human person and for the just progress of every
country.

Dialogue

Speaking at the 56th Session of the ILC in 1971[65] Rev Fr de Riedmatten highlighted the strong similarities between the Report to the Conference of the
newly appointed Director-General Clarence Wilfred Jenks (who served from
1970 until his death in 1973)[66] entitled "Freedom by Dialogue: Economic
Development by Social Progress, the ILO Contribution"[67] and the provisions of
the Apostolic Letter of Pope St Paul VI *Octogesima Adveniens*[68] published shortly
before the Conference opened. He admitted that his background knowledge of
previous Reports of Directors-General to the ILC was limited and that he did
"not therefore know whether many of them have tackled, either directly or by
repeated references, so many questions ranging from metaphysics to the most
concrete challenge, from general social ethics to any particular Convention or
Recommendation of the ILO" but he recognised the striving of each for actions
and not mere words:

> it is not enough to recall principles, to affirm intentions and underline glar-
> ing injustices and to offer prophetic denunciations: these words will not have
> real weight unless they are accompanied by an awareness on the part of each
> one of us, a stronger awareness of his own responsibility and effective action.

Specifically, Rev Fr de Riedmatten referred to section 5 of the Report headed
"Technical Progress and Human Values":

> More wealth and more equal distribution of wealth are not the whole of the
> good things of life or the whole of social policy. The material basis for social
> progress is not to be despised. Nor is it likely to be – too much of life has
> been for too long a perpetual struggle for survival, dominated by the over-
> riding concern to produce the goods and services which make life at least
> tolerable and the future at least reasonably secure. [...]

---

65 Record of the Proceedings of the 56th Session of the ILC 1971 411–413 <www.ilo.org/
    public/libdoc/ilo/P/09616/09616(1971-56).pdf> (accessed 17 October 2020) © ILO.
66 A short biography is available from the ILO at <www.ilo.org/global/about-the-ilo/how
    -the-ilo-works/ilo-director-general/former-directors-general/WCMS_192713/lang--en/
    index.htm> (accessed 17 October 2020).
67 Report of the Director-General to the 56th Session of the ILC 1971 *Freedom by Dialogue:
    Economic Development by Social Progress, the ILO Contribution* <www.ilo.org/public/libdoc
    /ilo/P/09383/09383(1971-56-Part_1).pdf> (accessed 17 October 2020) © ILO.
68 Pope St Paul VI, *Octogesima adveniens* (1971) © Copyright – Libreria Editrice Vaticana.

Yet there is an ever-widening recognition and increasing insistence that this is not all, and that a society which places the whole emphasis on the production and distribution of wealth, ignoring that man does not live by bread alone and paying scant attention to the effect of technological and material progress on human welfare and on the physical, social and moral environment, is less than human.

He observed that this coincided with the Apostolic Letter:

[T]he Letter states that the quality and truth of human relations, the degree of participation and of responsibility are no less significant and important for the future of society than the quantity and variety of goods produced and consumed. It also puts the question: Is not true progress to be found in the development of the moral conscience which leads us to engage in wider solidarity and to open ourselves more freely to others and to God?

There were in his view "two major spheres of agreement between the Apostolic Letter and the Director-General's Report" – the sections headed "More Equal Enjoyment" and "The Graver Inequalities", which he summarised as discussing "the place of young people and of women, who are victims of present changes, discrimination, the promotion of workers, the right to emigrate and the status of emigrants, the creation of employment":

so many points on which once again we say that sound co-operation, which exists already and which we hope will be strengthened between Christians and their institutions at all levels and the ILO, will have to be harmonious and fruitful. May it help to combat this 'kind of fatalism which is overcoming even our leaders', to use the terms of the Apostolic Letter, in favour of this bold effort 'of social imagination' to which the Letter calls us.

There was yet another meeting of minds:

The Director-General proposes dialogue as a method of seeking better conditions of freedom, and he sees in the procedures devised by the ILO in the course of its history and embodied in its instruments the elements of sound and fruitful dialogue. One single fact will indicate the extent to which this appeal for dialogue is in line with the preoccupations of the Supreme Authority of the Church. The first great text published by Pope Paul VI after his election was also devoted to dialogue.[69]

He hoped in conclusion

that such a spirit of dialogue will spread throughout the world, in particular where the ILO has to carry out its own tasks. These are referred to at

---

69 Though not mentioned by name by Rev Fr de Riedmatten, this is the Encyclical of Pope St Paul VI, *Populorum progressio* (1967) © Copyright – Libreria Editrice Vaticana.

the beginning of the Director-General's Report by some forceful questions which are not mere figures of speech. The Church will not cease to ask similar questions.

Poverty

The Report of Director-General David Morse to the 54th Session of the ILC in 1970 was entitled "Poverty and Minimum Living Standards: The Role of the ILO",[70] a title and a subject which in his address[71] Rev Fr de Riedmatten said "cannot fail to touch a chord in the Church and every Christian conscience". He noted that David Morse "pleads in the specific terminology of the ILO" for a qualitative (as opposed to quantitative) conception of human development, something which coincided with the Christian perspective.

Addressing the 80th Session of the ILC in 1993 Archbishop Paul Fouad Naïm Tabet unreservedly endorsed the conclusions drawn in the ILO Director-General's Report *Social insurance and social protection*, in which access to social protection was framed in terms of human rights "as well as a measure of social welfare".[72] Archbishop Tabet himself blended the spiritual and the secular in terms of a common task between the Holy See and the ILO:

> The Holy See appreciates the fact that the criteria proposed for the protection of families, the unemployed, the sick, the elderly or handicapped people, or anyone who finds himself in a situation of vulnerability, extend beyond that of economic profitability.
>
> In this respect, in the century elapsed between the *Rerum novarum* and *Centesimus annus* encyclicals, whose importance has been highlighted by many Members of your Organization, successive Popes have emphasized that each human being must be able to benefit in all circumstances from a living standard in keeping with his human dignity.
>
> The slow but successful creation of social protection systems in certain countries, and the beginnings of such systems in other countries, despite a fragile economic situation, are remarkable efforts for the effective application of human rights. [...]

---

70 Report of the Director-General to the 54th Session of the ILC 1970, *Poverty and Minimum Living Standards: The Role of the ILO* <www.ilo.org/public/libdoc/ilo/P/09383/09383(1970-54-part1).pdf> (accessed 17 October 2020) © ILO.

71 Record of the Proceedings of the 54th Session of the ILC 1970 360–362 <www.ilo.org/public/libdoc/ilo/P/09616/09616(1970-54).pdf> (accessed 17 October 2020) © ILO.

72 Report of the Director-General to the 80th Session of the ILC 1993 *Social Insurance and Social Protection* 5 <www.ilo.org/public/libdoc/ilo/P/09383/09383(1993-80-part-1).pdf> (accessed 17 October 2020) © ILO.

The twentieth century has witnessed the discovery and the most wide-ranging formulation of human rights. Our task, at the threshold of the twenty-first century, appears to be that of furthering the compliance of States, of all the bodies which compose States, and of all men and women with their social duties.[73]

The Report of the Director-General to the 91st Session of the ILC in 2003 was entitled *Working out of poverty*.[74] The Report itself provides an in depth account of the efforts of the ILO to eradicate poverty, and makes no reference to any spiritual or religious contribution within the ILO to that struggle. This total secularisation on the part of the Director-General notwithstanding, in his address, Archbishop Giampaolo Crepaldi was wholly supportive – "the role that the ILO has played, plays and must continue to play to integrate the objectives of employment and decent work in strategies to reduce poverty is fundamental" – and he performed a masterly exercise in exegesis.[75]

> Working out of poverty, which translates from the French version as 'Freeing oneself from poverty through work', is a very significant and evocative title for the Holy See. This is the theme of this 91st Session of the International Labour Conference, and we find it evocative for three reasons.

> Freeing oneself is a strong word: it means to free the human being, in this particular instance, from poverty; poverty being a phenomenon which one could virtually call slavery, because it affects mankind deeply in his very dignity. The human being who is deprived of what is necessary to survive is a humiliated being, who has been denied his economic and social rights and, in extreme cases, even the right to life. But poverty is not an inevitability. That is why freeing man from poverty is an ethical imperative, which the conscience of humanity cannot ignore (John Paul II, Message for the Annual World Day of Peace, 1993). And the Catholic Church, whose mission is essentially that of serving mankind, all of mankind, being concerned also with the demands of daily life (*Mater et magistra*, No. 2), must be at the front lines of the fight against poverty.

> Moreover, freeing oneself from poverty indicates that the poor themselves are active players in this process of liberation. They are supposed to participate in their own liberation from poverty. We must therefore give up the

73 Record of the Proceedings of the 80th Session of the ILC 1993 20/8–20/9 <www.ilo.org/public/libdoc/ilo/P/09616/09616(1993-80).pdf> (accessed 17 October 2020) © ILO.
74 Report of the Director-General to the 91st Session of the ILC 2003 *Working Out of Poverty* <www.ilo.org/public/libdoc/ilo/P/09383/09383(2003-91)106.pdf> (accessed 17 October 2020) © ILO.
75 Record of the Proceedings of the 91st Session of the ILC 2003 18/7–18/8 <www.ilo.org/public/libdoc/ilo/P/09616/09616(2003-91).pdf> (accessed 17 October 2020) © ILO.

mentality that considers the poor – both individuals and peoples – as a burden (*Centesimus annus*, No. 28).

And, finally, the Holy See cannot fail but to agree with the existence of a direct link between poverty, work and lack of work. The Catholic Church, which considers itself the church of the poor, and has made them its preferred choice, knows very well that they appear in many different aspects and, in many cases, as the result of a violation of the dignity of human work, either because possibilities for human work are limited, which is the scourge of unemployment, or because the value of work and the rights which flow from it are underestimated, particularly the right to an equitable wage and to the security of the individual and his family (*Laborem exercens*, No. 8).

Rural workers and migrants

Amongst the issues considered in the Report of Director-General Francis Blanchard (1974 to 1989)[76]entitled "Problems and Prospects"[77] to the 59th Session of the ILC in 1974 were the difficulties being faced by rural workers and the growing exploitation of economic migrants. The inclusion of these themes was, said Fr Silvio Luoni,[78] noted by the Holy See "with especial satisfaction":

> We are now witnessing the inevitable consequences of unbalanced industrial development: agriculture in most countries is experiencing a major crisis, world food stocks are at the point of exhaustion, the countryside is emptied of the peasants and workers who, as Pope John XXIII said in the encyclical *Mater et magistra*, are desperately anxious to escape from the narrow horizons of an existence which offers them no future and are flooding into town and city, there to swell the tide of that subproletariat which subsists on the outskirts of our cities. [...]

> Hence we note with gratification that the ILO intends to devote greater attention to this sector of the world of labour, namely the rural workers who constitute, one might say, the under-developed section of the poorer classes.

As concerns migrant workers, Fr Luoni listed the many initiatives undertaken by the Catholic Church working "for equitable solutions to the numerous problems involved" and said that it was therefore "easy to understand the extent to which

---

76 A short biography is available from the ILO at <www.ilo.org/global/about-the-ilo/how-the-ilo-works/ilo-director-general/former-directors-general/WCMS_192714/lang--en/index.htm> (accessed 17 October 2020).

77 Report of the Director-General to the 59th Session of the ILC 1974 *Problems and Prospects* <www.ilo.org/public/libdoc/ilo/P/09383/09383(1974-59).pdf> (accessed 17 October 2020) © ILO.

78 Record of the Proceedings of the 59th Session of the ILC 1974 264–266 <www.ilo.org/public/libdoc/ilo/P/09616/09616(1974-59).pdf> (accessed 17 October 2020) © ILO.

the Holy See shares the concern felt by the ILO on the problem of migrant workers" and also for what he called the "black market" in clandestine migration:

> I shall conclude by recalling the hopes expressed by Pope Paul VI, on 17 October of last year, on the occasion of the meeting on the problem of migrant workers: "We hope that a healthily fostered solidarity towards migrant workers will accelerate the advent of a genuine statute for migrant workers". May this wish for a better guarantee of the rights of migrant workers soon become a reality, thanks to the ILO's decisions.

In his address to the 60th Session of the ILC in 1975[79] Fr Luoni again stressed the common approach of the ILO and the Holy See to the problems of rural workers and economic migrants, concluding in secular mode by quoting the Declaration of Philadelphia: "Poverty anywhere constitutes a danger to prosperity everywhere".[80]

The issue of migrant workers was again prominent in the Report of the Director-General to the 63rd Session of the ILC in 1977.[81] Fr Luoni saw in this another welcome parallel with Catholic Social Teaching:

> [T]he Director-General's Report quotes studies to determine the scope and modalities for "taking work to the workers" as an alternative to manpower movements from the developing to industrialised countries.
>
> This problem has preoccupied the Church's social doctrine for a long time. Already in 1963, the Supreme Pontiff declared in the Encyclical *Pacem in terris* that "whenever possible, the capital should be taken to the workers, not vice versa; in this way, a possibility of a better future is offered to many persons, without their being forced to leave their own environment in order to seek residence elsewhere". [...]
>
> In concluding these few remarks, the delegation of the Holy See would like to stress that it is submitting them with the firm conviction that they correspond to the hopes placed in the work of the ILO. These hopes were voiced in June 1969 when Pope Paul VI, in his address in Geneva to the ILO session, stated that the modern concept of which this Organisation is a defender

---

79 Record of the Proceedings of the 60th Session of the ILC 1975 408–409 <www.ilo.org/ public/libdoc/ilo/P/09616/09616(1975-60).pdf> (accessed 17 October 2020) © ILO.

80 Declaration of Philadelphia 1944 <www.ilo.org/public/libdoc/ilo/1944/44B09_10_e_f .pdf> (accessed 17 October 2020).

81 Report of the Director-General to the 63rd Session of the ILC 1977 *Technical Co-operation: New Prospects and Dimensions* <www.ilo.org/public/libdoc/ilo/P/09383/09383(1977-63-part-1).pdf> (accessed 17 October 2020) © ILO.

and a herald is based on a fundamental principle which Christianity, for its part, has singularly illuminated: that in labour it is man who comes first.[82]

Employment

Archbishop Paul Fouad Naïm Tabet addressing the 82nd Session of the ILC in 1995,[83] in response to the Report of the Director-General *Promoting employment*,[84] recalled principles found in the Encyclical of Pope St John Paul II *Centesimus annus* "that each man, each woman and especially each young person, would be able to exercise his or her right to self-fulfilment. In other words the right to live in dignity, in honesty and in humanity" and remarked on similar sentiments in the Report. This philosophical parallelism was for him however not enough, and the remainder of his address dealt with practical, technical and political initiatives intended to prevent the goals in the Report being a "purely utopian and unachievable wish", initiatives which he said "draw their inspiration from the philosophy and pragmatism of your own Organisation". Archbishop Tabet consciously adopted the informal rhetoric of the political economist:

> The social dialogue the world's workers are waiting for is, we would like to emphasize, not confined to defending the interests of a limited number of categories. It concerns all those men and women whose only aspiration is to become active players in economic and social life. It seems to us that the ILO's mandate is specifically to facilitate this.

Vocational training

At the 65th Session of the ILC in 1980, one element in the Report of the Director-General that year[85] was vocational training, and Archbishop Jean-Éduard-Lucien Rupp saw common ground with the Church:

> Its importance is evident to all those who have to deal with the future of mankind. The delegation of the Holy See has studied the Report with gratitude and esteem for the Director-General, who has proposed the consideration of

82 Record of the Proceedings of the 63rd Session of the ILC 1977 340–341 <www.ilo.org/public/libdoc/ilo/P/09616/09616(1977-63).pdf> (accessed 17 October 2020) © ILO.

83 Record of the Proceedings of the 82nd Session of the ILO 1995 12/24–12/25 <www.ilo.org/public/libdoc/ilo/P/09616/09616(1995-82).pdf> (accessed 17 October 2020) © ILO.

84 Report of the Director-General to the 82nd Session of the ILC 1995 *Promoting Employment* <www.ilo.org/public/libdoc/ilo/P/09383/09383(1995-82).pdf> (accessed 17 October 2020) © ILO.

85 Report of the Director-General to the 65th Session of the ILC 1980 *Part 1 Training* <www.ilo.org/public/libdoc/ilo/P/09383/09383(1980-66)3-50.pdf> (accessed 17 October 2020) © ILO.

this vital and fundamentally important subject for the future of mankind and has developed it with depth and competence. The Church has always followed closely the problems of human training. [...] The Director-General begins his Report with these important words: "People are the wealth of nations". This concern for man is a credit to him and the delegation of the Holy See congratulates him on it. Pope John-Paul II has often dealt with this matter.

Child labour

The Report of the Director-General to the 69th Session of the ILC in 1983 was entitled "Child Labour" and in noting that this had first been addressed by the ILC in 1919[86] acknowledged that "Child labour is still a widespread and perhaps even growing phenomenon in much of the world today".[87] This drew a strongly supportive response from the Holy See. Fr Giuseppe Bertello addressed the delegates:

> This problem has been at the centre of the preoccupations of the Catholic Church from the dawn of the industrial era, and thus it was that Pope Leo XIII, echoing the aspirations manifested by a large number of bishops and practising Catholics, said in his Encyclical *Rerum novarum* in 1891 that children in particular, and this requires to be observed strictly, should not be allowed on the shop floor until age has developed them sufficiently, and particularly their physical, intellectual and moral capacities, otherwise like a young and tender blade of grass they will wilt under the pressures of unduly precocious work and their education will be lost. [...]
>
> It will have escaped no one that the problems involved are not purely legal ones; there are also moral ones and they imply a conception of man to which no one can remain indifferent in the search for solutions. All activity must be placed in the service of life; it should in no case violate the laws and dignity, especially in the case of the poor.[88]

Environment

The theme of the Director-General's Report to the 77th Session of the ILC in 1990 was "Environment and the world of work". Archbishop Justo Mullor

---

86 Minimum Age (Industry) Convention 1919 (No. 5) <www.ilo.org/dyn/normlex/en/f?p =NORMLEXPUB:55:0::NO::P55_TYPE,P55_LANG,P55_DOCUMENT,P55_NODE :CON,en,C005,/Document> © ILO (accessed 17 October 2020).

87 Report of the Director-General to the 69th Session of the ILC 1983 *Child Labour* 3 <www .ilo.org/public/libdoc/ilo/P/09383/09383(1983-69-part-1).pdf> (accessed 17 October 2020) © ILO.

88 Record of the Proceedings of the 69th Session of the ILC 1983 25/11–25/12 <www.ilo .org/public/libdoc/ilo/P/09616/09616(1983-69).pdf> (accessed 17 October 2020) © ILO.

García noted that Director-General Michel Hansenne (1989 to 1999)[89] in the Introduction had cited Pope St John Paul II:

> As His Holiness Pope John Paul II stated in his message celebrating the World Day of Peace on 1 January 1990: 'In our day, there is a growing awareness that world peace is threatened not only by the arms race, regional conflicts and continued injustices among people and nations, but also by a lack of due respect for nature, by the plundering of natural resources and by a progressive decline in the quality of life'.[90]

Archbishop Mullor García saw this as evidence of the convergence of the ILO and the Holy See, each from its own perspective:

> The delegation of the Holy See is pleased about this significant convergence. The eyes of the Pope discern the spiritual and ethical aspects of the problem, while the eyes of the Director-General of the ILO and those participating in this assembly are mainly directed towards the questions that environmental considerations pose to all those involved in industrial production. The same question is considered from different angles, but the resulting analyses are complementary, and can contribute together towards the search for global solutions which must be found.

> The specific approach of the ILO – that of tripartism – does not exclude this [spiritual] dimension. It has often been mentioned in this forum that the first centre of interest of governments, employers' organisations and trade unions should always be man – the bearer of spiritual and moral values.[91]

Pope Francis' messages to the ILO

There is a strong argument to assert that integration of the principles promoted by ILO into Catholic Social Teaching had by the reign of Pope Francis become axiomatic.

A clear example of this came in September 2013 when Pope Francis, speaking through the Secretary of State of the Holy See Cardinal Tarcisio Bertone, sent his greetings to representatives, labourers and their families involved in the Mining

---

89 A short biography is available from the ILO at <www.ilo.org/global/about-the-ilo/how-the-ilo-works/ilo-director-general/former-directors-general/WCMS_192715/lang--en/index.htm> © ILO (accessed 17 October 2020).

90 Report of the Director-General to the 77th Session of the ILC 1990 *Environment and the World of Work* 4 <www.ilo.org/public/libdoc/ilo/P/09383/09383(1990-77-part-1).pdf> (accessed 17 October 2020) © ILO.

91 Record of the Proceedings of the 77th Session of the ILC 1990 13/28–13/29 <www.ilo.org/public/libdoc/ilo/P/09616/09616(1990-77).pdf> © ILO (accessed 17 October 2020).

Industry on the occasion of a Vatican organised conference focussing on the ethical issues involved in the sector.

> The participants at this meeting are aware that, so as not to repeat grave errors of the past, decisions today cannot be taken solely from geological perspectives or the possible economic benefits for investors and for the states in which the companies are based. A new and more profound decision-making process is indispensable and inescapable, one which takes into consideration the complexity of the problems involved, in a context of solidarity. *Such a context requires, first of all, that workers be assured of all their economic and social rights, in full accordance with the norms and recommendations of the International Labour Organization.*[92] [Emphasis added]

At the Ninth Sitting of the 103rd Session of the ILC in 2014, the Observer of the Holy See, Archbishop Silvano Tomasi, delivered a message from Pope Francis.[93] It began by acknowledging the contribution of the ILO:

> At the dawn of creation, God made man the steward of his handiwork and charged him to cultivate and protect it. Human labour is part of that creation and continues God's creative work. This truth leads us to consider work as both a gift and a duty. Indeed, labour is not a mere commodity but has its own inherent dignity and worth. The Holy See expresses its appreciation of the ILO's contribution to upholding the dignity of human work in the context of social and economic development through discussion and cooperation between governments, labourers and employers. Such efforts serve the common good of the human family and promote the dignity of workers everywhere.

Pope Francis singled out unemployment and mass migration as particular evils of what he termed the "globalization of indifference" contrasting this with the sustainable development goals proposed by the United Nations,[94] and concluded:

---

92 *Pope Hopes Day of Reflection on Mining Ethics Will Benefit Industry, Workers* (Vatican Radio 9 September 2013) <www.archivioradiovaticana.va/storico/2013/09/09/pope_hopes_day_of_reflection_on_mining_ethics_will_benefit_industry,/en1-726839> (accessed 17 October 2020) © Copyright – Libreria Editrice Vaticana.
93 Record of the Proceedings of the 103rd Session of the ILC 2014 18/139 <www.ilo.org/public/libdoc/ilo/P/09616/09616(2014-103).pdf> © ILO and also available at <http://w2.vatican.va/content/francesco/en/messages/pont-messages/2014/documents/papa-francesco_20140522_messaggio-ilo.html> © Copyright – Libreria Editrice Vaticana (accessed 17 October 2020).
94 Details of the UN's 17 Sustainable Development Goals are at <www.un.org/sustainabledevelopment/sustainable-development-goals/> (accessed 17 October 2020).

Dear Friends, the social teaching of the Catholic Church supports the initiatives of the ILO which aim to promote the dignity of the human person and the nobility of human labour. I encourage you in your efforts to face the challenges of today's world in fidelity to these lofty goals. At the same time, I invoke God's blessing on all that you do to defend and advance the dignity of work for the common good of our human family. [Emphasis added]

On the occasion of its centenary in 2019, Pope Francis again addressed a message to the ILO, delivered to the 108th Session of the ILC by the Observer of the Holy See Cardinal Peter Kodwo Appiah Turkson:

The theme of his address was "Work and personal and socio-ecological fulfilment" and he posed the question "what kind of work should we defend, create and promote?"

This is a complex issue. In today's interconnected world, responding to the complexity of 'labour' issues requires a thorough and interdisciplinary analysis. I welcome the ILO's approaches in this regard, especially its present attempt to redefine work in light of the *new* socio-economic and political realities, particularly those that are affecting the poor. *Thank you also for allowing the Church to be part of this initiative through the role of the Permanent Observer of the Holy See at the ILO.* [...]

In the current context of the fourth industrial revolution, characterized by this rapid and refined digital technology, robotics and artificial intelligence, the world needs institutions like the ILO. You have the capacity to challenge a widespread toxic mentality for which it does not matter if there is social or environmental degradation; for which it does not matter what or who is used and discarded; for which it does not matter if there is forced labour of children or unemployment of youth. [...]

A global institution like the ILO is well equipped to promote, alongside the Church, such a mentality of care, inclusion and real human development. [...]

In today's interconnected and complex world, we need to highlight the importance of good, inclusive and decent work. It is part of our human identity, necessary for our human development, and vital for the future of the planet. Therefore, while I commend the work the ILO has done in the last century, I encourage all who serve the institution to continue to address the issue of work in all its complexities. We need people and institutions that defend the dignity of workers, the dignity of everyone's work, and the well-being of the earth, our common home![95] [Emphasis added]

95 Record of the Proceedings of the 108th Session of the ILC 2019 271 <www.ilo.org/wcm sp5/groups/public/---ed_norm/---relconf/documents/meetingdocument/wcms_7262 21.pdf> © ILO (in an abridged form) also available in full at <www.vatican.va/content/ francesco/en/messages/pont-messages/2019/documents/papa-francesco_20190610

Conclusions

In the years following World War Two the ILO perceived its underlying moral imperative, its "*force morale*" which, in the years following World War One had been Catholic Social Teaching, now to be international human rights. So total was this realignment and commitment to human rights that the ILO itself came to be regarded as the world's oldest human rights organisation. Yet at its foundation and in its early years this could not have been the case, for the simple reason that the articulation of human rights terminology lay far in the future.

Until the late 1960s Catholic Social Teaching was almost entirely absent from International Labour Conference debates, and appeared not at all in the annual Reports of the Directors-General.

This was, however, the story only from the perspective of the ILO.

If the period following World War One had been a time when Catholic Social Teaching exerted a strong influence on the work of the ILO and the colour and scope of its Conventions and Recommendations, then the period following World War Two saw the flow reversed. Labour rights in Catholic Social Teaching themselves began to absorb and so be augmented by the principles adopted by the ILO.

The Holy See broke its silence and began publicly to praise the ILO and, as the 1960s dawned, to include the ILO in the Magisterium itself. The relatively low key allocution given by Pope Pius XII in 1954 marked the point in time where a threshold was crossed. Going forward, the Holy See felt able more and more to express its appreciation of and even its enthusiasm for the ILO – Pope St John XXIII in his Encyclical *Mater et magistra*, Pope St Paul VI in his milestone address to the International Labour Conference in 1969 where he pledged his fervent support as a friend and collaborator, Pope St John Paul II addressing the Conference in 1982 focussing on shared moral objectives within the "means adapted to their mission".

From their first accreditation in 1967 the Observers of the Holy See to the International Labour Conference diligently presented their contributions. The ILC delegates made hardly a reference to them, the Reports of Directors-General were it seemed blind to them, but the voice of the Holy See in a running commentary on the work of the ILO was to be heard, and by its endorsement was not merely impliedly but actually expressly by a process of exegesis absorbing the principles espoused by the ILO into the Magisterium itself.

There is a strong argument to assert that integration of the principles promoted by ILO into Catholic Social Teaching had by the reign of Pope Francis become axiomatic.

As the 20th century came to an end, the ILO introduced the first of its overarching policy initiatives, the Decent Work Agenda, followed in the run up to the ILO

_messaggio-labourconference.html> © Copyright – Libreria Editrice Vaticana (accessed 17 October 2020).

Centenary by the Future Work Initiative. If the years leading to these could charitably be described as a companionable silence on the part of the ILO, the introduction of these initiatives was to reignite the dialogue, as the following chapter shows.

Bibliography

The Holy See

Encyclicals, Apostolic letters, Exhortations (in chronological order)

Pope St John XXIII, *Mater et magistra* (1961).
Pope St Paul VI, *Octogesima adveniens* (1971).
Pope St John Paul II, *Laborem exercens* (1981).

Other materials (in chronological order)

Discorso di Sua Santità Pio PP, XII ai partecipanti alla 127a sessione del Consiglio d'Amministrazione dell'Organizzazione Internazionale del Lavoro 19 November 1954 <www.vatican.va/content/pius-xii/en/speeches/1954/documents/hf_p-xii_spe_19541119_lavoro.pdf> (accessed 17 October 2020).
Pope Hopes Day of Reflection on Mining Ethics Will Benefit Industry, Workers (Vatican Radio, 9 September 2013) <www.archivioradiovaticana.va/storico/2013/09/09/pope_hopes_day_of_reflection_on_mining_ethics_will_benefit_industry,/en1-726839> (accessed 17 October 2020).
Archbishop Bernardito Auza, Apostolic Nuncio and Permanent Observer of the Holy See to the United Nations, Address to the High-Level Meeting of the United Nations General Assembly, 11 April 2019 <https://holyseemission.org/contents/statements/5cb0ae1bdd6e4.php> (accessed 17 October 2020).

International Labour Organisation

Conventions and recommendations

Minimum Age (Industry) Convention 1919 (No. 5).

International Labour Conferences (in chronological order)

Record of the Proceedings of the 29th Session of the ILC 1946 1 <www.ilo.org/public/libdoc/ilo/P/09616/09616(1946–29).pdf> (accessed 17 October 2020).
Record of the Proceedings of the 31st Session of the ILC 1948 323 <www.ilo.org/public/libdoc/ilo/P/09616/09616(1948–31).pdf> (accessed 17 October 2020).
Record of the Proceedings of the 34th Session of the ILC 1951 138 <www.ilo.org/public/libdoc/ilo/P/09616/09616(1951–34).pdf> (accessed 17 October 2020).
Record of the Proceedings of the 35th Session of the ILC 1952 Appendix IV 451 <www.ilo.org/public/libdoc/ilo/P/09734/09734(1952–35).pdf> (accessed 17 October 2020).

Record of the Proceedings of the 43rd Session of the ILC 1959 7 <www.ilo.org/pub lic/libdoc/ilo/P/09616/09616(1959–43).pdf> (accessed 17 October 2020).

Record of the Proceedings of the 47th Session of the ILC 1963 3 <www.ilo.org/pub lic/libdoc/ilo/P/09616/09616(1963–47).pdf> (accessed 17 October 2020).

Resolutions Adopted by the International Labour Conference at Its 50th Session 1966, Resolution III <www.ilo.org/public/libdoc/ilo/P/09734/09734(1966-50).pdf> (accessed 17 October 2020).

Record of the Proceedings of the 53rd session of the ILC 1969 77–81 <www.ilo .org/public/libdoc/ilo/P/09616/09616(1969–53).pdf> (accessed 17 October 2020).

Record of the Proceedings of the 54th Session of the ILC 1970 360–362 <www.ilo .org/public/libdoc/ilo/P/09616/09616(1970–54).pdf> (accessed 17 October 2020).

Record of the Proceedings of the 56th Session of the ILC 1971 411–413 <www.ilo .org/public/libdoc/ilo/P/09616/09616(1971–56).pdf> (accessed 17 October 2020).

Record of the Proceedings of the 57th Session of the ILC 1972 294–295 <www.ilo .org/public/libdoc/ilo/P/09616/09616(1972–57).pdf> (accessed 17 October 2020).

Record of the Proceedings of the 59th Session of the ILC 1974 264–266 <www.ilo .org/public/libdoc/ilo/P/09616/09616(1974–59).pdf> (accessed 17 October 2020).

Record of the Proceedings of the 60th Session of the ILC 1975 408–409 <www.ilo .org/public/libdoc/ilo/P/09616/09616(1975–60).pdf> (accessed 17 October 2020).

Record of the Proceedings of the 63rd Session of the ILC 1977 340–341 <www.ilo .org/public/libdoc/ilo/P/09616/09616(1977–63).pdf> (accessed 17 October 2020).

Record of Proceedings of the 66th Session of the ILC 1980 27/8–27/9 <www.ilo .org/public/libdoc/ilo/P/09616/09616(1980–66).pdf> (accessed 17 October 2020).

Record of the Proceedings of the 67th Session of the ILC 1981 35/17–35/18 <www.ilo.org/public/libdoc/ilo/P/09616/09616(1981–67).pdf> (accessed 17 October 2020).

Record of the Proceedings of the 68th Session of the ILC 1982 21/1/–21/6 <www.ilo.org/public/libdoc/ilo/P/09616/09616(1982–68).pdf> (accessed 17 October 2020).

Record of the Proceedings of the 69th Session of the ILC 1983 25/11–25/12 <www.ilo.org/public/libdoc/ilo/P/09616/09616(1983–69).pdf> (accessed 17 October 2020)

Record of the Proceedings of the 70th Session of the ILC 1984 25/4–25/5 <www .ilo.org/public/libdoc/ilo/P/09616/09616(1984–70).pdf> (accessed 17 October 2020)

Record of the Proceedings of the 71st Session of the ILC 1985 22/24–22/26 <www.ilo.org/public/libdoc/ilo/P/09616/09616(1985–71).pdf> (accessed 17 October 2020)

Record of the Proceedings of the 77th Session of the ILC 1990 17/3 <www.ilo.org/ public/libdoc/ilo/P/09616/09616(1990–77).pdf> (accessed 17 October)

Record of the Proceedings of the 78th Session of the ILC 1991 Argentina (8/11), Guatemala (17/10), Paraguay (13/38), Peru (6/21) and the International Federation of Trade Unions of Transport Workers (9/25) <www.ilo.org/public/l ibdoc/ilo/P/09616/09616(1991–78).pdf> (accessed 17 October 2020).

Record of the Proceedings of the 79th Session of the ILC 1992 7/12 <www.ilo.org/ public/libdoc/ilo/P/09616/09616(1992–79).pdf> (accessed 17 October 2020).

Record of the Proceedings of the 80th Session of the ILC 1993 20/8–20/9 <www .ilo.org/public/libdoc/ilo/P/09616/09616(1993–80).pdf> (accessed 17 October 2020).

Record of Proceedings of the 81st Session of the ILO 1994 9/8–9/7 <www.ilo.org/ public/libdoc/ilo/P/09616/09616(1994–81).pdf> (accessed 17 October 2020).

Record of the Proceedings of the 82nd Session of the ILO 1995 12/24–12/25 <www.ilo.org/public/libdoc/ilo/P/09616/09616(1995–82).pdf> (accessed 17 October 2020).

Record of the Proceedings of the 91st Session of the ILC 2003 18/7–18/8 <www.ilo .org/public/libdoc/ilo/P/09616/09616(2003–91).pdf> (accessed 17 October 2020).

Record of the Proceedings of the 92nd Session of the ILC 2004 10/3 <www.ilo.org/ public/libdoc/ilo/P/09616/09616(2004–92).pdf> (accessed 17 October 2020).

Record of the Proceedings of the 100th Session of the ILC 2011 9/9 <www.ilo.or g/public/libdoc/ilo/P/09616/09616(2011–100).pdf> (accessed 17 October 2020).

Record of the Proceedings of the 103rd Session of the ILC 2014 18/139 <www.ilo.org /public/libdoc/ilo/P/09616/09616(2014–103).pdf> and also available at <http: //w2.vatican.va/content/francesco/en/messages/pont-messages/2014/docum ents/papa-francesco_20140522_messaggio-ilo.html> (accessed 17 October 2020).

Record of the the the Proceedings of the 108th Session of the ILC 2019 271 <www.i lo.org/wcmsp5/groups/public/---ed_norm/---relconf/documents/meetingdoc ument/wcms_726221.pdf> (in an abridged form) also available in full at <www .vatican.va/content/francesco/en/messages/pont-messages/2019/documents /papa-francesco_20190610_messaggio-labourconference.html> (accessed 17 October 2020).

Report of the Director-General to the 52nd Session of the ILC 1968 3, 11 <www .ilo.org/public/libdoc/ilo/P/09383/09383(1968-52-part-1).pdf> (accessed 17 October 2020)

Reports (in chronological order)

Report of the Director-General to the 54th Session of the ILC 1970 *Poverty and Minimum Living Standards: The Role of the ILO* <www.ilo.org/public/libdoc/ ilo/P/09383/09383(1970-54-part1).pdf> (accessed 17 October 2020).

Report of the Director-General to the 56th Session of the ILC 1971 *Freedom by Dialogue: Economic Development by Social Progress, the ILO Contribution* <www .ilo.org/public/libdoc/ilo/P/09383/09383(1971-56-Part_1).pdf> (accessed 17 October 2020).

Report of the Director-General to the 59th Session of the ILC 1974 *Problems and Prospects* <www.ilo.org/public/libdoc/ilo/P/09383/09383(1974–59).pdf> (accessed 17 October 2020).

Report of the Director-General to the 63rd Session of the ILC 1977 *Technical Co-operation: New Prospects and Dimensions* <www.ilo.org/public/libdoc/ilo/P/09383/09383(1977-63-part-1).pdf> (accessed 17 October 2020).

Report of the Director-General to the 65th Session of the ILC 1980 *Part 1 Training* <www.ilo.org/public/libdoc/ilo/P/09383/09383(1980–66)3-50.pdf> (accessed 17 October 2020).

Report of the Director-General to the 69th Session of the ILC 1983 *Child Labour* 3 <www.ilo.org/public/libdoc/ilo/P/09383/09383(1983-69-part-1).pdf> (accessed 17 October 2020).

Report of the Director-General to the 77th Session of the ILC 1990 *Environment and the World of Work* 4 <www.ilo.org/public/libdoc/ilo/P/09383/09383(1990-77-part-1).pdf> (accessed 17 October 2020).

Report of the Director-General to the 80th Session of the ILC 1993 *Social Insurance and Social Protection* 5 <www.ilo.org/public/libdoc/ilo/P/09383/09383(1993-80-part-1).pdf> (accessed 17 October 2020).

Report of the Director-General to the 82nd Session of the ILC 1995 *Promoting Employment* <www.ilo.org/public/libdoc/ilo/P/09383/09383(1995–82).pdf> (accessed 17 October 2020).

Report of the Director-General to the 91st Session of the ILC 2003 *Working Out of Poverty* <www.ilo.org/public/libdoc/ilo/P/09383/09383(2003–91)106.pdf> (accessed 17 October 2020).

Other materials (in chronological order)

Louis Christiaens, ed, *L'Organisation internationale du Travail et l'encyclique sociale de Jean-Paul II Centesimus annus: Commémoration du centième anniversaire de Rerum novarum* (ILO, Geneva, 1991). <www.worldcat.org/title/organisation-internationale-du-travail-et-lencyclique-sociale-de-jean-paul-ii-centesimus-annus-commemoration-du-centieme-anniversaire-de-rerum-novarum-1891-1991-documents/oclc/463513912> (accessed 17 October 2020).

Transcription de l'entrevue de Francis Blanchard, Directeur Général de 1974 à 1989, par Juan Somavia, Directeur Général depuis 1999, Pré Bailly, Gex, France, 11 février 2008.

Opening Statement of Director-General Guy Ryder for the ILO 100th Anniversary, Geneva, 22 January 2019 <www.ilo.org/global/about-the-ilo/how-the-ilo-works/ilo-director-general/statements-and-speeches/WCMS_665184/lang--en/index.htm> (accessed 17 October 2020).

International documents

Universal Declaration of Human Rights 1948.

United Nations, 17 Sustainable Development Goals <www.un.org/sustainabledevelopment/sustainable-development-goals/> (accessed 17 October 2020).

Secondary sources

Barbier, Maurice, "Les Relations Entre l'Église Catholique et l'Organisation International du Travail" in *Politique étrangère*, Vol. 37, No. 3 (1972) (Institut Français des Relations Internationales) 351.

Caritas in Veritate Foundation, *Rethinking Labour, Ethical Reflections on the Future of Work, Labour after Laudato Si'* (The Caritas in Veritate Foundation Working Papers, FCIV, Chambésy, 2018) <https://futureofwork-labourafterlaudatosi.net /2018/11/14/rethinking-labour-ethical-reflections-on-the-future-of-work-14-november-2018-global/> (accessed 17 October 2020).

Cronin, John F, *Christianity and Social Progress: A Commentary on Mater et Magistra* (Helicon, Baltimore, 1965).

Quinn, Kevin, "Trade Unions in 'Mater et Magistra" in *Gregorianum*, Vol. 43, No. 2 (1962) (Gregorian Biblical Press, 1962) 268.

Maul, Daniel Roger, "The 'Morse Years': The ILO 1948–1970" in International Institute of Social History Amsterdam, Jasmien Van Daele, Magaly Rodríguez García, Geert Van Goethem and Marcel van der Linden , eds, *ILO Histories: Essays on the International Labour Organization and Its Impact on the World During the Twentieth Century* (Peter Lang, Bern, 2010) 365.

____, *The International Labour Organization: 100 Years of Global Social Policy* (ILO and De Grutyer, Berlin, 2019).

Morse, David A, *The Origin and Evolution of the I.L.O. and Its Role in the World Community* (New York State School of Industrial and Labor Relations, Cornell University, Ithaca, NY, 1969).

The President's News Conference, 9 May 1956, *The American Presidency Project* <www.presidency.ucsb.edu/documents/the-presidents-news-conference-302> (accessed 17 October 2020).

Thomas, Albert, *The International Labour Organisation: The First Decade* (George Allen & Unwin Ltd, London, 1931).

7   Common pathways

Introduction

Under Directors-General Michel Hansenne (1989–1999), Juan Somavia (1999–2012) and his successor Guy Ryder, who took office on 1 October 2012 the ILO broke the bounds of Conventions and Recommendations, and formulated overarching policies on the quality of work itself and on the future evolution of work as a concept.

Those policies are the Decent Work Agenda and the Future of Work Initiative.

The "common pathways" of the title of this chapter are those on which the Holy See and the ILO have found themselves when weighing those policies. Over the past 20 years, each has openly acknowledged their shared ethical values which, even if not always explicitly documented, show a convergence between the principles espoused by the ILO and the social teaching of the Catholic Church.

The Decent Work Agenda[1]

Michel Hansenne, ILO Director-General 1989 to 1999,[2] came from a Christian Democratic background in Belgian politics, and took office at a time when globally the trend towards liberalisation meant that anti-regulatory governments were less eager to adopt international standards of any kind. According to Daniel Maul, Michel Hansenne in introducing the Decent Work Agenda in 1998 was following a strategy "to save the ILO from falling into irrelevance" and "to focus instead on a few basic principles". Daniel Maul sees this as a purely secular initiative:

---

1 The ILO maintains a running commentary on its Decent Work Agenda, with national examples of its implementation, at <www.ilo.org/global/topics/decent-work/lang--en/index.ht m> (accessed 17 October 2020). The concept is now embodied in the ILO Declaration on Social Justice for a Fair Globalization 2008 <www.ilo.org/wcmsp5/groups/public/---dgre ports/---cabinet/documents/genericdocument/wcms_371208.pdf> (accessed 17 October 2020).
2 A short biography is available from the ILO at <www.ilo.org/global/about-the-ilo/how-the -ilo-works/ilo-director-general/former-directors-general/WCMS_192715/lang--en/index .htm> (accessed 17 October 2020).

Inspiration came also from post-Cold War human rights discourses, which emphasised liberal rights of the individual over social and economic rights to support political democratisation and the rule of law.[3]

This human rights analysis is supported by Colin Fenwick:

> The ILO's insistence on the necessity for a general climate of civil liberties shows it reaching beyond "mere" labour rights and into broader matters of economic and social rights. Indeed, in this area it plays a role in the broader realm of civil and political rights, thus showing its acceptance (even if only implicitly) of the principle of the indivisibility of all human rights.[4]

That is not, however, the only working hypothesis, and was not solely how the initiative was to be regarded in the following two decades.

The Decent Work Agenda was given its first expression in the Declaration on Fundamental Principles and Rights of Work,[5] adopted at the 86th Session of the ILC in 1998. Setting aside the fact that many ILO Members had not ratified all ILO Conventions, the Declaration is overarching, its policy universal as set out in the Preamble:

> Whereas the ILO was founded in the conviction that social justice is essential to universal and lasting peace; Whereas economic growth is essential but not sufficient to ensure equity, social progress and the eradication of poverty, confirming the need for the ILO to promote strong social policies, justice and democratic institutions; [...]

> Whereas, in seeking to maintain the link between social progress and economic growth, the guarantee of fundamental principles and rights at work is of particular significance in that it enables the persons concerned, to claim freely and on the basis of equality of opportunity, their fair share of the wealth which they have helped to generate, and to achieve fully their human potential; [...]

> Whereas it is urgent, in a situation of growing economic interdependence, to reaffirm the immutable nature of the fundamental principles and rights embodied in the Constitution of the Organization and to promote their universal application;

---

3 Daniel Maul, *The International Labour Organization: 100 Years of Global Social Policy* (ILO and De Gruyter, Berlin, 2019) 249–250.

4 Colin Fenwick, "The International Labour Organisation" in Malcolm Langford, ed, *Social Rights Jurisprudence* (Cambridge University Press, Cambridge, 2008) 598.

5 ILO Declaration on Fundamental Principles and Rights at Work 1998 (revised to 2010) <www.ilo.org/wcmsp5/groups/public/---ed_norm/---declaration/documents/normat iveinstrument/wcms_716594.pdf> (accessed 17 October 2020).

The fundamental principles themselves are all the more powerful for being brief and to the point:

THE INTERNATIONAL LABOUR CONFERENCE

1.   Recalls: (a) that in freely joining the ILO, all Members have endorsed the principles and rights set out in its Constitution and in the Declaration of Philadelphia, and have undertaken to work towards attaining the overall objectives of the Organization to the best of their resources and fully in line with their specific circumstances; (b) that these principles and rights have been expressed and developed in the form of specific rights and obligations in Conventions recognized as fundamental both inside and outside the Organization.

2.   Declares that all Members, even if they have not ratified the Conventions in question, have an obligation arising from the very fact of membership in the Organization to respect, to promote and to realize, in good faith and in accordance with the Constitution, *the principles concerning the fundamental rights which are the subject of those Conventions, namely: (a) freedom of association and the effective recognition of the right to collective bargaining; (b) the elimination of all forms of forced or compulsory labour; (c) the effective abolition of child labour; and (d) the elimination of discrimination in respect of employment and occupation.* [Emphasis added]

Building on this foundation Juan Somavia in his first Report to the ILC as Director-General in 1999 *Decent Work* set out his strategy for a Decent Work Agenda. In his preliminary remarks, he stresses the need to "give a human face to the global economy":

The call to give a human face to the global economy is coming from many – and very different – quarters. *Pope John Paul II has emphasized the 'need to establish who is responsible for guaranteeing the global common good and the exercise of economic and social rights. The free market by itself cannot do it, because in fact there are many human needs that have no place in the market'.* [Emphasis added]

This was a straw in the wind, the first indication of what was soon to become massive support by the Holy See for the Decent Work Agenda.

The goal of the Decent Work Agenda is to secure decent work for people everywhere:

The ILO's mission is to improve the situation of human beings in the world of work. Today, that mission finds resonance in the widespread preoccupation of people at times of great change: to find sustainable opportunities for decent work.

The primary goal of the ILO today is to promote opportunities for women and men to obtain decent and productive work, in conditions of freedom, equity, security and human dignity. [His emphasis]

This is the main purpose of the Organization today. Decent work is the converging focus of all its four strategic objectives: the promotion of rights at work; employment; social protection; and social dialogue. It must guide its policies and define its international role in the near future.

In Juan Somavia's definition of "decent work" there are not merely economic elements but also spiritual aspects (although not expressed in these terms) to be found in "the quality of employment" and "feelings of value and satisfaction":

> The goal is not just the creation of jobs, but the creation of jobs of acceptable quality. The quantity of employment cannot be divorced from its quality. All societies have a notion of decent work, but the quality of employment can mean many things. It could relate to different forms of work, and also to different conditions of work, as well as feelings of value and satisfaction.[6]

The argument for the exclusivity of a purely secular interpretation of decent work was proving to be false, and exclusive secularisation did not go unchallenged, as Juan Somavia went on to demonstrate by his acknowledgement of the contribution of Catholic Social Teaching.

Speaking at the Pontifical Lateran University in Rome in 2005 Juan Somavia elaborated further on what he referred to as "the shared ethical values" on which the Decent Work Agenda was founded and which, "even if not explicitly stated", "converge with the social teaching of the Catholic Church". The Decent Work Agenda:

> represents the ILO's twenty-first century vision of our mandate [...] *has much in common with the social doctrine of the Catholic Church.*

> When we speak of decent work, we mean work on which women and men can raise their family and send their children to school. Work in which people

---

6 Report of the Director-General to the 87th Session of the ILC 1999 *Decent Work* 2 – 4 <www .ilo.org/public/libdoc/ilo/P/09383/09383(1999-87).pdf> (accessed 17 October 2020) © ILO. Gerry Rodgers and his fellow contributors sound a word of caution: "The word decent is rather subjective and does not always translate easily into other languages than its original English. [...] There are also a number of empirical and conceptual difficulties. The notion of decent work includes many issues that are not usually covered in existing statistical systems, and some of them – for example freedom of association or economic security – are very hard to measure unambiguously". On the other hand, "decent work is a flexible concept which can be adapted to the aspirations of different actors". Gerry Rodgers, Eddy Lee, Lee Swepston and Jasmien Van Daele, *The ILO and the Quest for Social Justice 1919–2009* (Cornell University Press, Ithaca and International Labour Office, Geneva, 2009) 233, 235.

are respected, can organize and have a voice. Work that will provide for a reasonable pension at the end of a working life. Policies that generate quality work throughout society. We call it decent work because we know work is a source of dignity. Work is fundamental to family stability. Work is linked with peace. A community that works well is a community in peace. Decent work recognizes you cannot have stable societies based on persistent social inequality, as there can be no social development based on unstable economies.

Decent work is not an international standard, it is a legitimate human goal in every society. It is based on job creation and the enabling environment for investment and enterprise development together with rights at work and social protection within the possibilities of each economy, all facilitated by dialogue among governments, employers, workers, and international solidarity. [...]

Understood in this way, the concept of decent work is not limited to a mere material dimension. *It also includes the properly spiritual dimension of work.* As the ILO's Philadelphia Declaration of 1944 states: 'all human beings – irrespective of race, creed or sex – have the right to pursue both their material well-being and their spiritual development in conditions of freedom and dignity, of economic security and equal opportunity'.

The social teaching of the Catholic Church insists on the fundamental ethical fact that 'work [...] is not only good in the sense that it is useful or something to enjoy; it is also good as being something worthy [...] something that corresponds to personal dignity and increases it [...] through work one achieves fulfilment as a human being and indeed [...] becomes "more a human being".[7] [Emphasis added]

Nor has the Decent Work Agenda remained external to the principles of Catholic Social Teaching itself.[8] As early as 2000 at the Jubilee for Workers both decent work and – expressly – the role played by Juan Somavia and the ILO had received the full approbation of Pope St John Paul II.

---

7 Juan Somavia, *The Challenge of a Fair Globalization*, Presentation at the Pontifical Lateran University on the Report of the World Commission on the Social Dimension of Globalization (Rome, 25 February 2005) <www.ilo.org/public/english/bureau/dgo/speeches/somavia/2005/rome.pdf> (c) ILO [Quoting from the Encyclical of Pope St John Paul II, *Laborem exercens* (1981)] (accessed 17 October 2020).
8 For a succinct comparative analysis of the Decent Work Agenda and corresponding provisions of Catholic social justice see Dominique Peccoud, "Decent Work: A Catholic Perspective" in Dominique Peccoud, ed, *Philosophical and Spiritual Perspectives on Decent Work* (ILO, World Council of Churches, ILO International Institute for Labour Studies, Geneva, 2004) 129.

Pope St John Paul II: Jubilee of Workers, Greeting after Mass on 1 May 2000 – "*Decent work*"[9]

At the close of the Jubilee of Workers on 1 May 2000, an event convened by the Holy See, Juan Somavia in his statement *Work for All: Path of Solidarity and Justice*[10] addressed the participants, calling upon them to unite in pursuit of "a global coalition for decent work":

> Those of us gathered here today represent different dimensions of the world of work. Yet, beyond our various perspectives, we share a common responsibility to expand the frontiers of decent work for all in today's troubling global economy. We have to redress the enormous sense of insecurity that invades the home of so many families worldwide. It is a global struggle for human dignity.
>
> *I come to you from the International Labour Organization with a secular appeal to all people of faith:* we need action now, right away, urgently. To begin with, for each of us to live our values, to integrate principles of justice, fairness, equality and compassion into our daily lives, from the intimacy of our homes to our interaction with the world. To consciously use our moral compass to take decisions, to influence decisions. To make our voices heard. To promote solidarity without frontiers.
>
> [...] Holy Father, you have said it very clearly. 'Perhaps the time has come for new and deeper reflections on the nature of the economy and its purposes'.
>
> Following your wise guidance, I believe we should re-examine the rules and policies that govern our global economy.
>
> We should develop the political will to recast those rules so that globalization benefits the many, not just the few. So we can expand to more people the advantages of open markets and open societies. So that the promise of the information society reaches the excluded and does not create new inequalities. So that globalization acquires a widespread social legitimacy that it lacks today. [...]
>
> *I call for a global coalition for decent work. [...]*
>
> The hope for decent work around the world, of our families and the families of our children, can become a reality. The resources and the knowledge are

9 *Jubilee of Workers, Greeting of the Holy Father John Paul II after Mass 1 May 2000* <www .vatican.va/content/john-paul-ii/en/speeches/2000/apr-jun/documents/hf_jp-ii_spe_2 0000501_jub-workers.html> (accessed 17 October 2020) © Copyright – Libreria Editrice Vaticana.

10 Juan Somavia, *Work for All: Path of Solidarity and Justice* (Rome, 1 May 2000) <www.ilo.org /global/about-the-ilo/newsroom/news/WCMS_007886/lang--en/index.htm> (accessed 17 October 2020) © ILO.

available, but the will and policies are not. *The social doctrine of the Church has helped many to find the right pathways.*

[...] Holy Father,

Those of us gathered here today are a sample of the "global family", as you called the whole of humanity in your last message for the celebration of the World Day of Peace. We are here to receive your guidance, your inspiration and your indefatigable energy. [Emphasis added]

The concept of decent work had found immediate acceptance within the principles of Catholic Social Teaching. In his Homily for the Jubilee of Workers Pope St John Paul II looked to the meaning and value of work:

Therefore the Jubilee Year calls for *a rediscovery of the meaning and value of work.* It is also an invitation to address the economic and social imbalances in the world of work by re-establishing the right hierarchy of values, giving priority to the dignity of working men and women and to their freedom, responsibility and participation. It also spurs us to redress situations of injustice by safeguarding each people's culture and different models of development.[11] [His emphasis]

In his Greeting after Mass, Pope St John Paul II thanked Juan Somavia, and wholeheartedly endorsed his call for a global coalition for decent work:

2. The festival of work brings to mind the industriousness of men and women who, in accordance with the command of the Lord of life, desire to work for a future of hope, justice and solidarity for all humanity. Today on this path of civilization, thanks to new technologies and global computerized communications, fresh possibilities of progress are emerging. However, there is no shortage of new problems, which combine with already existing ones and give rise to legitimate preoccupation. Realities such as unemployment, exploitation of minors and low wages persist, and are even getting worse in some parts of the world. It must be recognized that the organization of labour does not always respect the dignity of the human person, and the universal destination of resources is not always given due consideration.

The commitment to resolve these problems in all parts of the world involves everyone. It concerns you, owners and management, you, financiers, and you, craftsmen, tradespeople and workers. *All must work so that the economic system in which we live does not upset the fundamental order of the priority of*

---

11 *Homily of His Holiness Pope John Paul II, Jubilee of Workers 1 May 2000* <www.vatican.va/content/john-paul-ii/en/homilies/2000/documents/hf_jp-ii_hom_20000501_jub-workers.html> (accessed 17 October 2020) © Copyright – Libreria Editrice Vaticana.

work over capital, of the common good over private interest.12 *It is ever more necessary, as Mr Juan Somavia said a short while ago, to establish a global coalition in favour of 'decent work'.* [Emphasis added]

Such unqualified support is unsurprising, given the striking parallels between the Encyclical of Pope St John Paul II *Laborem exercens* (1981)[13] together with his Message for the World Day of Peace 1996 and the four fundamental principles of decent work.[14] In *Laborem exercens* he illustrated the problem when reflecting on the conflicts which were "marked and in a sense symbolized by the publication of the Encyclical *Rerum novarum*" and which remained contemporary:

> 11. Throughout this period, which is by no means yet over, the issue of work has of course been posed on the basis of a great *conflict* that in the age of, and together with, industrial development emerged *between "capital" and "labour"*, that is to say between the small but highly influential group of entrepreneurs, owners and holders of the means of production, and the broader multitude of people who lacked these means and who shared in the process of production solely by their labour. The conflict originated in the fact that the workers put their powers at the disposal of the entrepreneurs, and these, following the principle of maximum profit, tried to establish the lowest possible wages for the work done by the employees. In addition there were other elements of exploitation, connected with the lack of safety at work and of safeguards regarding the health and living conditions of the workers and their families. [His emphasis]

Laborem exercens and the four fundamental principles of Decent Work

(a) freedom of association and the effective recognition of the right to collective bargaining

Paragraph 20 of *Laborem exercens* deals with the "Importance of Unions":

> All these rights, together with the need for the workers themselves to secure them, give rise to yet another right: the right of association, that is

---

12 This sentence was highlighted by Director General Juan Somavia in his Report to the 100th Session of the ILC in 2011 *A New Era of Social Justice* para 26 <www.ilo.org/public/libdoc /ilo/P/09383/09383(2011-100).pdf> (accessed 17 October 2020) © ILO.
13 Pope St John Paul II, *Laborem exercens* (1981) © Copyright – Libreria Editrice Vaticana.
14 . Matthew Irunnaya Ezea subjects the principles of Christian ethics as a basis for decent work to close analysis, and compares and contrasts what he sees as the three main themes of *Laborem exercens* with the four strategic objectives of decent work in his published thesis *The ILO's Concept of Decent Work in the Light of the Social Teaching of the Church and Its Relevance to Nigeria* (LIT Verlag GmbH & Co. KG, Vienna, 2011) 93–118, 137–159.

to form associations for the purpose of defending the vital interests of those employed in the various professions. These associations are called labour or trade unions. [...] Their task is to defend the existential interests of workers in all sectors in which their rights are concerned. The experience of history teaches that organizations of this type are an indispensable element of social life, especially in modern industrialized societies. [...] They are indeed a mouthpiece for the struggle for social justice, for the just rights of working people in accordance with their individual professions. [...] [L]abour and capital are indispensable components of the process of production in any social system – it is clear that, even if it is because of their work needs that people unite to secure their rights, their union remains a constructive factor of social order and solidarity, and it is impossible to ignore it.

(b) the elimination of all forms of forced or compulsory labour

Paragraph 9 of *Laborem exercens* deals with "Work and personal Dignity":

Remaining within the context of man as the subject of work, it is now appropriate to touch upon, at least in a summary way, certain problems that more closely define the dignity of human work, in that they make it possible to characterize more fully its specific moral value. [...] Again, it is well known that it is possible to use work in various ways against man, that it is possible to punish man with the system of forced labour in concentration camps, that work can be made into a means for oppressing man, and that in various ways it is possible to exploit human labour, that is to say the worker. All this pleads in favour of the moral obligation to link industriousness as a virtue with the social order of work, which will enable man to become, in work, 'more a human being' and not be degraded by it.

(c) the effective abolition of child labour

In his Message for the World Day of Peace 1996 Pope St John Paul II focussed on children:

5. [...] In some countries children are forced to work at a tender age and are often badly treated, harshly punished, and paid absurdly low wages. Because they have no way of asserting their rights, they are the easiest to blackmail and exploit. In other circumstances children are bought and sold, so that they can be used for begging or, even worse, forced into prostitution, as in the case of so-called 'sex tourism'. This utterly despicable trade degrades not only those who take part in it but also those who in any way promote it.[15]

---

15 Pope St John Paul II, *Message for the 1996 World Day of Peace "Let Us Give Children a Future of Peace"* para 5 <https://w2.vatican.va/content/john-paul-ii/en/messages/

(d) the elimination of discrimination in respect of employment and occupation

As expressed in *Laborem exercens*, gender discrimination in the workplace, in the home and in society at large is anathema to Catholic Social Teaching.

> 9. [...] Toil is something that is universally known, for it is universally experienced. [...] It is familiar to women, who, sometimes without proper recognition on the part of society and even of their own families, bear the daily burden and responsibility for their homes and the upbringing of their children. [...]

> 19. [...] [O]n a more general level, the whole labour process must be organized and adapted in such a way as to respect the requirements of the person and his or her forms of life, above all life in the home, taking into account the individual's age and sex. It is a fact that in many societies women work in nearly every sector of life. But it is fitting that they should be able to fulfil their tasks *in accordance with their own nature*, without being discriminated against and without being excluded from jobs for which they are capable, but also without lack of respect for their family aspirations and for their specific role in contributing, together with men, to the good of society. The *true advancement of women* requires that labour should be structured in such a way that women do not have to pay for their advancement by abandoning what is specific to them and at the expense of the family, in which women as mothers have an irreplaceable role. [His emphasis]

As is any form of discrimination against those suffering a disability:

> 22. [...] The disabled person is one of us and participates fully in the same humanity that we possess. It would be radically unworthy of man, and a denial of our common humanity, to admit to the life of the community, and thus admit to work, only those who are fully functional. To do so would be to practise a serious form of discrimination, that of the strong and healthy against the weak and sick. Work in the objective sense should be subordinated, in this circumstance too, to the dignity of man, to the subject of work and not to economic advantage.

---

peace/documents/hf_jp-ii_mes_08121995_xxix-world-day-for-peace.html> (accessed 17 October 2020) © Copyright – Libreria Editrice Vaticana. In the context of modern slavery Pope Francis has addressed child labour in his Encyclical *Fratelli tutti* (2020), discussed in Chapter 3.

Decent Work Agenda and the Observers of the Holy See

The voice of the Holy See in its continuing support for the Decent Work Agenda has been heard in the contributions made to the ILC by its Observers.

The Report of Director-General Juan Somavia[16] to the 89th Session of the ILC in 2001 was entitled *Reducing the Decent Work Deficit: A Global Challenge.*[17] Archbishop Diarmuid Martin addressing that Session indicated the full support of the Holy See for the issues raised in the Report, emphasising its convergence with both *Laborem exercens* and the Greeting after Mass; and reflected on the "pioneering and painstaking efforts" of the ILO in promoting decent work:

> The ILO is one of the oldest members of the family of international organizations. Its mandate, however, remains always pertinent and of vital interest. Its activities continue to affect the lives and the future of all the citizens of the world. [...]

> The theme of work needs to become even more central in the international reflection of our day, when human aspirations have to be realized within a dramatically changed situation of economic and political interdependence. It is within this broad context that the theme of decent work has emerged as an overarching theme of the ILO's policy, a policy which stresses the qualitative aspects of work and its deepest connection with human dignity. Just over one year ago, at the Jubilee Gathering of Workers in Rome, Pope John Paul II said 'it is ever more necessary to establish a global coalition in favour of decent work'. Twenty years earlier, he had published an encyclical letter on work – *Laborem Exercens* – which placed the human person at the centre of his reflections. Many of the elements of that document have been taken up in the Director-General's Report, especially in his reflections on the significance of work. [...]

> The International Labour Organization, with its important network of Conventions and Recommendations, has made pioneering and painstaking efforts in this area, building up a wide consensus. We must ensure that consensus now becomes universal.[18]

In his address to the 92nd Session of the ILC in 2004 Archbishop Silvano M Tomasi commented:

> The task of building a society which respects the human person and its work gives priority to the human ordering of social relationships over technical

---

16 A short biography is available from the ILO at <www.ilo.org/global/about-the-ilo/how-the-ilo-works/ilo-director-general/former-directors-general/WCMS_192716/lang--en/index.htm> © ILO (accessed 17 October 2020).

17 Report of the Director-General to the 89th Session of the ILC 2001 *Reducing the Decent Work Deficit: A Global Challenge* <www.ilo.org/public/libdoc/ilo/P/09383/09383(2001-89)76.pdf> (accessed 17 October 2020) © ILO.

18 Record of the Proceedings of the 89th Session of the ILC 2001 7/4 <www.ilo.org/public/libdoc/ilo/P/09616/09616(2001-89).pdf> (accessed 17 October 2020) © ILO.

progress, necessary as the latter is. [...] In his call for a rediscovery of the meaning and value of work, Pope John Paul II has extended an invitation to address the economic and social imbalances in the world of work by re-establishing the right hierarchy of values, giving priority to the dignity of working men and women and to their freedom, responsibility and participation [...] (and) to redress situations of injustice by safeguarding each people's culture and different models of development. [...]

The interconnectedness of economic variables and actors on the global scene has been underlined in the important conclusions of the World Commission on the Social Dimension of Globalization. The Commission supports the ILO's strategic objectives and these, in turn, serve as a base for decent work. In this way, securing employment, with social protection, with adequate standards and rights at work, in a constructive tripartite social dialogue opened to others and to new forces of civil society, recognizes that work is an expression of each person's dignity and identity, and that it goes far beyond any quantitative measurable economic value.[19]

The accession of Pope Benedict XVI resulted in no diminution of that support. In his address to the 93rd Session of the ILC in 2005 Archbishop Silvano M Tomasi commented:

Speaking on 1 May 2005 to many workers attending his first Sunday audience, the new Holy Father Pope Benedict XVI said 'I hope that work will be available, especially for young people, and that working conditions may be ever more respectful of the dignity of the human person'. *The creation of decent work for all in a sustainable world has been a longstanding common base for a fruitful dialogue between the ILO and the social doctrine of the Church.* The dignity of every human person requires access to work in conditions of personal security, health, fair remuneration and safety. Work is a right and the expression of human dignity.[20] [Emphasis added]

The Holy See was not, however, beyond offering constructive criticism of the effectiveness of the Decent Work Agenda or the way in which it was to be implemented. In his address to the 95th Session of the ILC in 2006 Archbishop Silvano M Tomasi commented:

The delegation of the Holy See notices with satisfaction that decent work, not only as a notion, but as a strategic agenda, is now at the forefront of any discussion on the eradication of poverty, and that a convergence of efforts is

19 Record of the Proceedings of the 92nd Session of the ILC 2004 11/28 <www.ilo.org/pub lic/libdoc/ilo/P/09616/09616(2004-92).pdf> (accessed 17 October 2020) © ILO.

20 Record of the Proceedings of the 93rd session of the ILC 2005 11/26–11/27<www.ilo.org /public/libdoc/ilo/P/09616/09616(2005-93).pdf> (accessed 17 October 2020) © ILO.

under way for its implementation. The task, however, is far off from reaching its target. [...]

If the measure of decent work is adopted, it becomes clear that too many people remain excluded from enjoying it because they are indecently exploited or are altogether out of work. People not sufficiently qualified to board the globalization train, or whose capacity and talents are utilized to propel forward the global economy without their sharing in the accruing benefits, are in the tens of millions: undocumented migrants working in agriculture, in manufacturing, in domestic service; women in textile industry working in unhealthy conditions and with miserable salaries; workers labelled by their race, caste or religion that are relegated to the marginal jobs of society without a chance for upward mobility; exploited workers in export processing zones and all over the world, workers being paid less and less who must work more and more to earn a decent salary.[21] [Emphasis added]

Archbishop Tomasi stressed the "shared objectives" in decent work of the Holy See and ILO in his address to the 96th Session of the ILC in 2007:

Even today, the pursuit of social justice remains a most challenging ideal and an operational task for the International Labour Organization as it continues to develop up to date standards and to influence policy in the world of work within the evolving global economy. *In this regard, the delegation of the Holy See acknowledges shared objectives with the ILO. It fully supports the combined action of workers, employers and governments to make decent work for sustainable development a collective goal within the international community, as well as a priority in national programmes.* Much of the restlessness and many of the conflicts that torment our society are rooted in the lack of jobs.[22] [Emphasis added]

Coinciding with the economic crash of 2008, though issued just before it impacted, the ILC had adopted at its 97th Session in June 2008 the *ILO Declaration on Social Justice for a Fair Globalisation*, expressed by Juan Somavia in its Preface to be

the third major statement of principles and policies adopted by the International Labour Conference since the ILO's Constitution of 1919. It builds on the Philadelphia Declaration of 1944 and the Declaration on Fundamental Principles and Rights at Work of 1998. The 2008 Declaration

21 Record of the Proceedings of the 95th Session of the ILC 2006 14/24–14/25 <www.ilo.org/public/libdoc/ilo/P/09616/09616(2006-95).pdf≥ (accessed 17 October 2020) © ILO.
22 Record of the Proceedings of the 96th Session of the ILC 2007 19/10 <www.ilo.org/public/libdoc/ilo/P/09616/09616(2007-96).pdf> (accessed 17 October 2020) © ILO.

expresses the contemporary vision of the ILO's mandate in the era of globalization

and was "the most important renewal of the Organization since the Declaration of Philadelphia". The Declaration functions as a restatement of the Decent Work Agenda with a key additional principle set out in Article I.B:

> *The four strategic objectives are inseparable, interrelated and mutually supportive. The failure to promote any one of them would harm progress towards the others.* To optimize their impact, efforts to promote them should be part of an ILO global and integrated strategy for decent work. Gender equality and non-discrimination must be considered to be cross-cutting issues in the abovementioned strategic objectives.[23] [Emphasis added]

Steve Hughes and Nigel Haworth describe its immediate impact:

> The 2008 declaration positioned the ILO as the pretender to the pre-eminent role in the creation of global social justice and a fair globalization. It also positioned the Decent Work agenda as the key delivery mechanism to achieve those ends.[24]

In 2008 Archbishop Silvano Tomasi called for the definition of "decent work" to be widened. Addressing the 97th Session of the ILC that year he commented:

> For some time, the ILO has provided effective leadership in promoting decent work, consistent with human dignity, in both developed and developing countries. *In this context, care should be taken not to reduce the concept of decency to simply better-paid jobs and healthier working conditions. Human dignity calls for a wider concept,* work is an opportunity for a person to discover herself in action and to develop the web of relationships she is inserted in, allowing her to fulfil her vocation by fully exploiting her talents. In other words, a decent job is one that allows an expression of personal freedom and

---

23 ILO Declaration on Social Justice for a Fair Globalisation (2008) 1, 4, 11 <www.ilo.org/wcmsp5/groups/public/---dgreports/---cabinet/documents/genericdocument/wcms_371208.pdf> © ILO (accessed 17 October 2020). The ILO maintains a running commentary on the Declaration at <www.ilo.org/global/meetings-and-events/campaigns/voices-on-social-justice/WCMS_099766/lang--en/index.htm> © ILO (accessed 17 October 2020). The Declaration had its origins in the Report of the ILO Director-General Juan Somavia on the World Commission on the Social Dimension of Globalization presented to the 92nd Session of the ILC in 1994, stating in his Preface that "decent work should become a global goal, not just an ILO goal". <www.ilo.org/public/english/standards/relm/ilc/ilc92/pdf/adhoc.pdf> © ILO (accessed 17 October 2020).

24 Steve Hughes and Nigel Haworth, *The International Labour Organisation (ILO): Coming in from the Cold* (Routledge, London and New York, 2011) 80.

the responsibility for self-realization that will lead to an integral development of the human being.[25] [Emphasis added]

The global financial crisis of 2008 gave the issue of decent work, in a world of diminishing employment opportunities, an even sharper edge. What relevance does decent work have if there is no work to be had? In his address to the 98th Session of the ILC in 2009 Archbishop Tomasi emphasised the equal importance of personal dignity and decent work:

> Over the years, the ILO has placed much emphasis on the notion of decent work. We can say that decent work is at the centre of ILO policy and initiatives. *However, in ILO jargon, decency is mainly related to the provision and realization of standards* in terms of safety, wages, health, environment and similar rights. *Whilst the Holy See praises all the efforts that are aimed at improving working conditions,* especially of the poor, as well as the introduction of new standards, like the proposed instrument for the protection of domestic workers, *it stresses the need to recognize that a work-centred strategy has to put the person, not the task, in the centre of the production process. If this is done, then decency acquires a new importance and a more profound meaning because it is linked directly to the person and his dignity. In fact, it is the dignity of the person that provides the basis for setting standards that make a job decent.* As a result of this approach, when losing his job, an individual can experience economic difficulties and hardships, but does not lose his dignity.[26] [Emphasis added]

Pope Benedict XVI – Caritas in veritate

The concept of "decent work" is in these same words embodied also in the Encyclical of Pope Benedict XVI *Caritas in Veritate* (2009),[27] in which he also drew on the work of Pope St John Paul II in *Laborem exercens* and the Jubilee of Workers, Greeting after Mass on 1 May 2000:[28]

> 63. No consideration of the problems associated with development could fail to highlight the direct link between poverty and unemployment. In many cases, poverty results from a violation of the dignity of human work, either

25 Record of the Proceedings of the 97th Session of the ILC 2008 17/44 <www.ilo.org/public /libdoc/ilo/P/09616/09616(2008-97).pdf> (accessed 17 October 2020) © ILO.

26 Record of the Proceedings of the 98th Session of the ILC 2009 8/25 <www.ilo.org/public /libdoc/ilo/P/09616/09616(2009-98).pdf> (accessed 17 October 2020) © ILO.

27 Pope Benedict XVI, *Caritas in veritate* (2009) © Copyright – Libreria Editrice Vaticana.

28 *Jubilee of Workers, Greeting of the Holy Father John Paul II after Mass 1 May 2000* <www .vatican.va/content/john-paul-ii/en/speeches/2000/apr-jun/documents/hf_jp-ii_spe_2 0000501_jub-workers.html> (accessed 17 October 2020) © Copyright – Libreria Editrice Vaticana.

because work opportunities are limited (through unemployment or under-employment), or 'because a low value is put on work and the rights that flow from it, especially the right to a just wage and to the personal security of the worker and his or her family' [*Laborem exercens*]. For this reason, on 1 May 2000 on the occasion of the Jubilee of Workers, my venerable predecessor Pope John Paul II issued an appeal for "a global coalition in favour of decent work" [*Greeting after Mass*], *supporting the strategy of the International Labour Organization*. In this way, he gave a strong moral impetus to this objective, seeing it as an aspiration of families in every country of the world. What is meant by the word "decent" in regard to work? It means work that expresses the essential dignity of every man and woman in the context of their particular society: work that is freely chosen, effectively associating workers, both men and women, with the development of their community; work that enables the worker to be respected and free from any form of discrimination; work that makes it possible for families to meet their needs and provide schooling for their children, without the children themselves being forced into labour; work that permits the workers to organize themselves freely, and to make their voices heard; work that leaves enough room for rediscovering one's roots at a personal, familial and spiritual level; work that guarantees those who have retired a decent standard of living.[29] [Emphasis added]

This is explained by Dominique Peccoud (Jesuit in residence at the ILO 1997–2008) as being no coincidence. Confirming he was involved in making the links, he comments:

> [B]ut more important the convergence of ideas and their articulation reflect the deep convergence, the resonance between the social doctrine of the Church and the foundational principles that underlie the ILO. *The influence goes both ways, but to my mind I see a greater weight of influence from the ILO towards the practical issues the Catholic Church deals with in its social doctrine than vice versa.* There are active and continuing bilateral relationships between the two.

> It is telling that when an ILO colleague read the decent work language in the Encyclical, his comment was 'bravo!' and noted that the ideas behind decent work had never been presented in such a lyrical way, with such persuasive force.[30] [Emphasis added]

---

29 Pope Benedict XVI, *Caritas in veritate* (2009) s 63 © Copyright – Libreria Editrice Vaticana.
30 *A Discussion with Dominique Peccoud, SJ* (Berkley Center for Religion, Peace and World Affairs, Georgetown University, 23 February 2011) <http://berkleycenter.georgetown.edu /interviews/a-discussion-with-dominique-peccoud-s-j> © 2020 Berkley Center for religion, Peace & World Affairs (accessed 27 June 2020). This was already evident in the first decade of the ILO – "[T]he Catholic hierarchy, faced with the changed and unforeseen conditions

In his Address on 11 April 2019 to a High-Level Meeting of the United Nations General Assembly to commemorate the 100th anniversary of the ILO, Archbishop Bernadito Auza (Apostolic Nuncio and Permanent Observer of the Holy See to the United Nations) set decent work within an ecological paradigm:

> First of all, access to decent work for all is an essential condition for development. During the last decades, the world economy has not been able to create sufficient decent work opportunities for all. 'While the earnings of a minority are growing exponentially, so too is the gap separating the majority from the prosperity enjoyed by those happy few' [Pope Francis, Apostolic Exhortation Evangelii Gaudium, 2013, paragraph 56.]. [...] Secondly, as repeatedly underlined by Pope Francis, decent work must fully integrate the ecological paradigm, rather than being based on a selfish and outdated growth model. The three 'T' motto used by Pope Francis in his mother language – Tierra Land, Techo Housing, and Trabajo Work – push us to reassert the inner value of developmental principles based on the dignity of the human person.

He continued, evidencing the full support of the Holy See for the Decent Work Agenda:

> Rights and benefits should not be disposable. The Decent Work Agenda today is part and parcel of the global development agenda and it is universally applicable, regardless of countries' economic, social or political status. *Labour should have its legal and political framework based on just ethical principles that bear real political, legal and economic consequences. A labour contract, by definition, involves a transaction between human beings, it cannot, thus, be considered as a mere commercial relationship. As clearly stated by the ILO Constitution, 'Labour is not a commodity'.*[31] [Emphasis added]

---

of the last few years and the economic conflicts of the War and post-War periods, has applied itself to completing and expanding the traditional teaching on such questions as an adequate wage, social insurance, the intervention of the law, trade unionism and mutual understanding between capital and labour". Albert Thomas, *The International Labour Organisation: The First Decade* (George Allen & Unwin Limited, London, 1931) 359 and see generally 359–362. And see Dominique Peccoud, ed, *Philosophical and Spiritual Perspectives on Decent Work* (ILO, Geneva, 2004).

31 Archbishop Bernardito Auza, Apostolic Nuncio and Permanent Observer of the Holy See to the United Nations, address to the High-Level Meeting of the United Nations General Assembly 11 April 2019 <https://holyseemission.org/contents/statements/5cb0a e1bdd6e4.php> © 2015–2020. The Permanent Observer Mission of the Holy See to the United Nations (accessed 17 October 2020). The Global Commission on the Future of Work, formed under the auspices of the ILO and chaired jointly by Stefan Löfven (Prime Minister of Sweden) and Matamela Cyril Ramaphosa (President of the Republic of South Africa) issued its Report *Work for a Brighter Future* on 22 January 2019 as part of the ILO centenary celebrations. In it the Global Commission expresses itself in terms wholly com-

The concept of decent work now finds its international expression beyond the confines of the ILO and has become Goal 8 of the 17 Sustainable Development Goals of the United Nations' 2030 Agenda for Sustainable Development adopted in 2015.[32]

The Future of Work Initiative

On 18 November 2013 ILO Pope Francis received the current Director-General Guy Ryder[33] in a private audience at the Vatican. They discussed the dignity of work, and the ILO press release of the event records Guy Ryder as saying that "the dignity of work is a common concern for the ILO and the Catholic Church, particularly the situation of the most vulnerable, child labourers, domestic workers and migrants". The press release also noted that the ILO works closely with different institutions of the Catholic Church, including the Pontifical Council for Justice and Peace, which oversees with the Secretary of State the commitment of the Church to social justice, as well as the Pontifical Council for the Care of Migrants and Itinerant People.[34]

As that press release acknowledged, co-operation between the ILO and the Holy See was already well developed, and the private audience was in no sense the inception of a relationship. Yet history requires milestones, and this audience serves as such. Within six years, culminating in the ILO centenary in 2019, the ILO and the Holy See would jointly declare themselves to have common pathways on labour.

It was in his first Report as Director-General to the 102nd session of the ILC in 2013[35] that Guy Ryder introduced seven ideas for ILO centenary initiatives, the seventh of which was "the future of work". This was the focus of his Report to the 104th Session of the ILC in 2015, its stated ambition being "not to mark

patible with developmental principles based on the dignity of the human person advocated by Archbishop Bernadito Auza, yet makes no express reference to any confessional institution or philosophy. The Report calls for the world economy to be re-orientated towards "a human-centred agenda for the future of work" in the struggle to create decent work. Global Commission on the Future of Work *Work for a Brighter Future* (ILO, Geneva, 2019) 24 <www.ilo.org/global/topics/future-of-work/publications/WCMS_662410/lang--en/index.htm> (accessed 17 October 2020) (c) ILO.

32 United Nations' 2030 Agenda for Sustainable Development 2015 Goal 8 <https://sdgs.un.org/goals/goal8≥ (accessed 17 October 2020).

33 Guy Ryder was elected Director-General in May 2012. A short biography is available from the ILO at <www.ilo.org/global/about-the-ilo/how-the-ilo-works/ilo-director-general/WCMS_205241/lang--en/index.htm> © ILO (accessed 17 October 2020).

34 <www.ilo.org/global/about-the-ilo/newsroom/news/WCMS_229924/lang--en/index.htm> © ILO (accessed 17 October 2020).

35 Report of the Director-General to the 102nd Session of the ILC 2013 *Towards the ILO Centenary: Realities, Renewal and Tripartite Commitment* <www.ilo.org/public/libdoc/ilo/P/09383/09383(2013-102-1A).pdf> (accessed 17 October 2020) © ILO.

the ILO's centenary in a purely ceremonial way, but with a process that will help to guide its work for social justice into its second centenary".

> 5. The rationale underpinning the future of work initiative stems from the fact that it is difficult for the ILO (or any comparable international organization) to address all the implications of transformational change in its regular day-to-day activities. While all such activities are relevant, even taken together they are not enough. This is because, by their nature, they tend to be short-term and specific: necessary responses to immediate policy challenges.
>
> 6. Rarely does the opportunity arise to step back and to look at the broader picture or the longer term, overall dynamics and direction of change and to think through what they require of an organization. The centenary provides that opportunity and through this initiative it can be taken.
>
> 7. It follows that the initiative needs to operate at a high level of ambition. *It needs to involve its tripartite constituency fully and universally, but has also to reach beyond them to the academic world, and indeed to all other relevant and interested actors.* That implies no threat to tripartism; a greater threat would lie in failure to connect with that wider public. [Emphasis added]

The Report does not underestimate the magnitude of the task:

> 32. Universal respect for fundamental principles and rights at work remains a distant prospect. While there have been considerable advances, there have also been setbacks in recent years. Half of the world's workers are in countries that have not yet ratified the Freedom of Association and Protection of the Right to Organise Convention, 1948 (No. 87); there are still 168 million child labourers and 21 million victims of forced labour; and the world of work is still affected by deeply ingrained discrimination, on the grounds of gender – as already noted – but also on other grounds, including ethnicity, religion and disability.

Though not referring directly to Catholic Social Teaching, the Report in recalling the ILO's mandate perhaps subconsciously reflects its influence in language reminiscent of the Social Encyclicals:

> 42. […] The Declaration of Philadelphia refers to the need to act to ensure that workers 'can have the satisfaction of giving the fullest measure of their skill and attainments and make their greatest contribution to the common wellbeing' and refers to *the right to pursue 'their spiritual development' as well as 'their material well-being'.* Embedded in the ILO's mandate is the idea that work should be an act of self-realization, imbued with the notion of personal and collective purpose. *Work must certainly meet material needs, but it must also respond to an individual's quest for personal development and*

the instinctive desire to contribute to something larger than one's own or one's family's welfare.[36] [Emphasis added]

"Sustainable Development and the Future of Work in the Context of the Jubilee of Mercy" 2016

From 2 to 5 May 2016 there was held in Rome under the auspices of the ILO, the Pontifical Council for Justice and Peace and Caritas Internationalis a Global Seminar "Sustainable Development and the Future of Work in the Context of the Jubilee of Mercy",[37] coinciding with the celebration of the Feast of Saint Joseph the Worker. It was attended by Catholic organisations, trade union and co-operative movements and associations of business leaders.[38] The opening address was given by Cardinal Peter Kodwo Appiah Turkson, in which he focussed on the Decent Work Agenda and the need for sustainable development and concluded:

So the mission of Justice and Peace,[39] the Constitution of the I.L.O. and the social teaching of the Church coincide in linking development, justice, sustainability and peace with decent work.

Guy Ryder gave an address in which he acknowledged the contribution made by Catholic Social Teaching to the origins and development of the ILO:

I'm going to start by underlining something which I think is probably familiar to everybody in the room, but I do want to underline, and that is the community of values which exists between the Catholic Church and its social teaching, and the International Labour Organization. Indeed, as we approach the centenary of the International Labour Organization in just three years' time and look forward to the future of work that we want to create together.

We at the same time look back over our history, and when we do that we understand very well that the origins of the International Labour

---

36 Report of the Director-General to the 104th Session of the ILC 2015, *The Future of Work Centenary Initiative* iii, 1–2, 6–7, 10 <www.ilo.org/public/libdoc/ilo/P/09383/09 383(2015-104-I).pdf> (accessed 17 October 2020) © ILO. Ongoing coverage of the Future of Work initiative is on the ILO's website at <www.ilo.org/global/topics/future-of -work/lang--en/index.htm> (accessed 17 October 2020).

37 Global Seminar, *Sustainable Development and the Future of Work in the Context of the Jubilee of Mercy* (Rome, 2 to 5 May 2016) <www.iustitiaetpax.va/content/giustiziaepace/en/att ivital/presidente/2016/_sustainable-development-and-the-future-of-work--in-the-contex t-.html> © Pontificum Consilium De Iustitia Et Pace (accessed 17 October 2020).

38 <www.ilo.org/global/about-the-ilo/newsroom/statements-and-speeches/WCMS_4795 20/lang--en/index.htm> © ILO (accessed 17 October 2020).

39 www.iustitiaetpax.va (accessed 17 October 2020).

Organization have much to do with the social teaching of The Church all the way from *Rerum Novarum* through to the present day. I think this intertwining of history and this community of values is what truly places us in a very good and strong position to work together to address the issues that we have before us today. [...]

I think it is right to say that all faiths as well as preaching justice. All faiths value work. This is very important, and I was looking at the very impressive extracts from *Laudato Si* as colleagues were speaking in the panel this morning. And there is a great truth in *Laudato Si* which says that, "Man" – men and women – I would say, "Are created with a vocation to work, and work is a fundamental part, not just of material existence, but of the realization of the human being".

I think this is something that in some ways has been lost from sight in the current policy environment and amongst other things needs to be put very securely back at the centre of our discussions.[40]

In language strikingly similar to that used at the dawn of the ILO by Albert Thomas and Mgr Nolens, when they called for a "*force morale*" to underpin the work of the ILO,[41] Guy Ryder decried the absence of value-based international policy decisions:

What it means is that by trying to, I would say almost sanitize the international policy agenda, make it value-free, because of the needs to respond to the technocratic vision of how markets work, and what markets needs to be more effective, policy makers are actually missing the point of the objective of policy making.

He recalled a phrase used by Pope Francis: "It was a phrase that struck me with particular effect when he spoke about the globalization of indifference, and this indifference is perhaps our biggest enemy as we seek to advance our values". He acknowledged the launch by Pope St John Paull II in 2000 during the Jubilee of the Worker (as echoed in the Encyclical of Pope Benedict XVI *Caritas in veritate*) of a call for a global coalition for decent work, and concluded:

We have an extraordinary opportunity to move forward *with the values and objectives that we share*, and what better way to do it than by putting into real action in a qualitatively new way, a response to that call in the year 2000 for a global coalition for decent work. [Emphasis added]

---

40 <www.ilo.org/global/about-the-ilo/newsroom/statements-and-speeches/WCMS_4808
23/lang--en/index.htm> © ILO (accessed 17 October 2020).
41 See Chapter 5.

A Joint Statement of Commitment and Action[42] was issued by the participants at the end of the Global Seminar on 5 May 2016. Declaring themselves "inspired by the Social Doctrine of the Catholic Church", they cited "respect for and enhancement of human dignity, solidarity, subsidiarity and sustainability" as being "congruent with the principles and international standards that ground the tripartite processes and activities" of the ILO. They pointed to the common ground between the Declaration of Philadelphia 1944, the Declaration on Fundamental Principles and Rights at Work 1998 (the Decent Work Agenda) and the Declaration on Social Justice for a Fair Globalisation 2008 on the one hand, and the Encyclical of Pope Francis *Laudato Si'* on the other. They commended the process of dialogue as being "one of the strong values held in common by both the Social Doctrine of the Church and the ILO". Channelling the need for a moral imperative (though without articulating this) they declared:

> Promotion of exchanges between and among countries of the South and the North, as well, is urgently needed, in particular, to identify and reinforce best practices, *and to search for alternative models of socio-economic integration based on the principles underlying the Social Doctrine of the Catholic Church and the standards set in ILO Conventions and Recommendations.* We sincerely hope that such dialogue and advocacy will result in the formulation, strengthening, enforcement and monitoring of public policies by States, in order to guarantee decent work, equitable compensation, and social protection for all workers and their families. [Emphasis added]

ILO Centenary Declaration for the Future of Work 2019

On 21 June 2019 at the 108th Session of the International Labour Conference there was adopted the *ILO Centenary Declaration for the Future of Work*.[43] It is a powerful recapitulation of the fundamental principles developed within the ILO over a century, recalling and reaffirming the purpose, principles and mandate set out in its Constitution 1919 and in the Declaration of Philadelphia 1944, and underlining the importance of the ILO Declaration on Fundamental Principles and Rights at Work (1998) and the ILO Declaration on Social Justice for a Fair Globalisation (2008).

Inevitably, therefore, though without making an express connection – perhaps at this point in time without needing to make a conscious effort, so embedded are they – the Centenary Declaration reflects the precepts of Catholic Social Teaching which have contributed to the ILO's development.

42 <www.ilo.org/global/about-the-ilo/newsroom/statements-and-speeches/WCMS_4795 20/lang--en/index.htm> © ILO (accessed 17 October 2020).

43 *ILO Centenary Declaration for the Future of Work 2019* <www.ilo.org/wcmsp5/groups /public/@ed_norm/@relconf/documents/meetingdocument/wcms_711674.pdf> (accessed 17 October 2020) © ILO.

The ILO is "moved by the imperative of social justice", recognises "that social dialogue contributes to the overall cohesion of societies", reaffirms "that labour is not a commodity".

At its heart is the clarion call that there must be a *human-centred* approach:

> I.D. The ILO must carry forward into its second century with unrelenting vigour its constitutional mandate for social justice by further developing its human-centred approach to the future of work, which puts workers' rights and the needs, aspirations and rights of all people at the heart of economic, social and environmental policies.

It declares that policies must be developed "aimed at generating full, productive and freely chosen employment and decent work opportunities for all", with vocational training for young people, optimising the opportunities for older workers "to work in good-quality, productive and healthy conditions until their retirement, and to enable active ageing", "ensuring equal opportunities and treatment in the world of work for persons with disabilities, as well as for other persons in vulnerable situations" and "eradicating forced and child labour".

It is a rejection of what Pope Francis in his Encyclical *Fratelli tutti* (2020) has called "a 'throwaway' world" in which:

> some parts of our human family, it appears can be readily sacrificed for the sake of others considered worthy of a carefree existence. Ultimately, persons are no longer seen as a paramount value to be cared for and respected, especially when they are poor and disabled, "not yet useful" – like the unborn, or "no longer needed" – like the elderly.[44]

Common pathways

The idea of a common path was introduced in 2005 by Director-General Juan Somavia in his address to the Pontifical Lateran University in Rome:

> The ILO and the Holy See began their collaboration some 85 years ago. Over the years, the Catholic Church has enriched its social teachings, while we have developed the international legal framework for a better society, built, through tripartite dialogue, on the ideal of work being more and more decent and available to all. To move sustainably in that direction the voice of the Church can be so significant. [...]
>
> Our paths have not diverged during this history of relations. The values embodied in the *Compendium* [of the Social Doctrine of the Church][45] and

44 Pope Francis, *Fratelli tutti* (2020) s 18 © Copyright – Libreria Editrice Vaticana.
45 *Compendium of the Social Doctrine of the Church* (2004) <www.antoniano.org/carbajo/ FST/Readings/Magisterium/EN_Compendium_CST.pdf> (accessed 17 October 2020).

in the Decent Work Agenda as well as the report of the World Commission bode extremely well for even closer relations between us in the future, and *we will continue our work along what is clearly a common path.*[46] [Emphasis added]

On 14 November 2018 The Caritas in Veritate Foundation published *Rethinking Labour, Ethical Reflections on the Future of Work, Labour After Laudato Si'.*[47] The second half of this Working paper is concerned with "The Church and Labour", specifically the relationship between the Holy See and the ILO. It reproduces at length contributions to debates at the ILC made by Observers from the Holy See in the 21st century, considered earlier in this chapter. Many of those contributions had been largely unremarked by the remaining ILC delegates, at least in so far as reported in the Records of Proceedings. Their significance lay elsewhere. Their prominence in *Rethinking Labour* is compelling evidence, both of their importance to the Holy See and of the Holy See's integration of the work of the ILO within labour rights in Catholic Social Teaching.

The Holy See and the ILO acknowledge that they are on *common pathways* on labour.

The opening Editorial in *Rethinking Labour* was contributed by Guy Ryder, who recalled the ILO's origins and set out contemporary economic and ethical challenges:

There are times – and especially times of upheaval – when it is essential to reflect on broad social and economic developments and the direction they are taking. At one such time of transformation in the late XIXth century, the Encyclical Letter "*Rerum Novarum*" reflected on the condition of labour.

Less than two decades later, in 1919, the ILO itself was established to address working conditions "involving such injustice, hardship and privation to large numbers of people so as to produce unrest so great that the peace and harmony of the world are imperilled". [...]

Today, we are at another crossroads. We are reminded of the call in '*Centesimus Annus*', issued on the centenary of '*Rerum Novarum*' to look back, to look around, to look at new things and to look to the future. [...]

46 Juan Somavia, *The Challenge of a Fair Globalization*, Presentation at the Pontifical Lateran University on the Report of the World Commission on the Social Dimension of Globalization (Rome, 25 February 2005) <www.ilo.org/public/english/bureau/dgo/speeches/somavia/2005/rome.pdf> (accessed 17 October 2020) (c) ILO.

47 *Rethinking Labour, Ethical Reflections on the Future of Work, Labour after Laudato Si'* (The Caritas in Veritate Foundation Working Papers, FCIV, Chambésy, 2018) <https://futureofwork-labourafterlaudatosi.net/2018/11/14/rethinking-labour-ethical-reflections-on-the-future-of-work-14-november-2018-global/> © The Caritas in Veritate Foundation (accessed 17 October 2020).

The Encyclical Letter '*Laudato Si*' speaks of bringing the whole human family together to seek a sustainable and integral development. Doing so will be facilitated by a shared ethical framework anchored in the values of solidarity and inclusion that can generate creative and innovative thinking on policies that yield better outcomes for all and, in so doing, counter visions of the future as a zero sum game and the resulting policies of exclusion and individualism.[48]

It was echoed in 2018 by Archbishop Paul Richard Gallagher, Secretary for Relations with States, Secretariat of State, the Vatican[49] in his essay titled *The Holy See and the International Labour Organization: Common Pathways on Labour*.[50] Recalling the origin of the ILO in the Treaty of Versailles, he comments: "Even though the Holy See was, at first, excluded from participation in the new organisation – because of the same bias that challenged its presence in the League of Nations – it followed with deep interest the work of the ILO" and credits first Director-General Albert Thomas as being "a game changer in the relationship between the Holy See and the ILO". He sees the appointment of the French Jesuit Father André Arnou as first Jesuit in residence at the ILO in 1926, "the first official of the ILO charged with the management of the relationship with Catholic institutions", as the start of "a hundred-year-old partnership between the Holy See and the International Labour Office".[51] This relationship

48 Guy Ryder, "Editorial" in *Rethinking Labour, Ethical Reflections on the Future of Work, Labour after Laudato Si'* 9–11 (The Caritas in Veritate Foundation Working Papers, FCIV, Chambésy, 2018) <https://futureofwork-labourafterlaudatosi.net/2018/11/14/rethinki ng-labour-ethical-reflections-on-the-future-of-work-14-november-2018-global/> © The Caritas in Veritate Foundation (accessed 17 October 2020).
49 His position in the Catholic Hierarchy is set out at <www.catholic-hierarchy.org/bishop/ bgalla.html> (accessed 17 October 2020). Archbishop Gallagher is an almost exact contemporary of current ILO Director-General Guy Ryder, both men born in Liverpool, the Archbishop in 1954 and Guy Ryder in 1956. No particular significance should be attributed to this, but such coincidences are always intriguing.
50 Archbishop Paul Richard Gallagher, Secretary for Relations with States, Secretariat of State, the Vatican, "The Holy See and the International Labour Organization: Common Pathways on Labour" in *Rethinking Labour, Ethical Reflections on the Future of Work, Labour after Laudato Si'* 241–250, at 245–247 (The Caritas in Veritate Foundation Working Papers, FCIV, Chambésy, 2018) <https://futureofwork-labourafterlaudatosi.net/2018/11/14/ rethinking-labour-ethical-reflections-on-the-future-of-work-14-november-2018-global/> © The Caritas in Veritate Foundation (accessed 17 October 2020). Archbishop Gallagher returned to his theme of common pathways on 25 February 2019, addressing in Geneva a Special Event "Rethinking Labour and the Future of Work – An Interreligious Perspective" as part of the ILO centenary programme, with the title "Holy See and ILO: Common Pathways on Labour", quoting extensively from his essay in the Working Paper <www.jesuites.ch /images/2019/News/Province/25Feb19_SpecialEventRethinkingLabour_ArchbishopG allagher.pdf> (accessed 17 October 2020).
51 See Chapter 5.

he describes as "mutual and close", as recognised by the official visits to the ILO of Pope St Paul VI and Pope St John Paul II:

> It has always been rooted in the common priority of the Holy See and the ILO: upholding human dignity. As reiterated in the 1919 ILO Constitution, the values of human dignity, solidarity and social justice represent the core activities of the ILO. As a matter of fact, all the activities of the ILO stem from the idea first expressed in the 1944 Declaration of Philadelphia, in which the ILO reformulated its guiding principles and called on member States to develop policies and financial structures that would favour the 'material development and spiritual progress' of each and every person.

> As highlighted before, at the heart of the Catholic Social Teaching is the dignity of the human person: "No man may with impunity outrage that human dignity which God himself treats with great reverence, nor stand in the way of that higher life which is the preparation of the eternal life of heaven".[52]

> True dignity concerns all the components of the world of work, without exclusion: "The great mistake made in regard to the matter now under consideration is to take up with the notion that class is naturally hostile to class, and that the wealthy and the working men are intended by nature to live in mutual conflict. So irrational and so false is this view that the direct contrary is the truth".[53] This reality is evident in the tripartite structure of the ILO that today finds a new implementation in the actions foreseen by the development cooperation strategies that require the participation of the different components: governments, civil society and the private sector.

Looking at both the ILO Constitution and Catholic Social Teaching, "from Pope Leo XIII to Pope Francis", he finds "an opportunity for a continued and positive dialogue" and that "a positive future of work will be the result of our common efforts to realise a common vision".

Conclusions

The promotion of two overarching policies by the ILO, the Decent Work Agenda and the Future of Work Initiative, caused the fog of collective amnesia which had descended on the ILO for decades, blanking out debate on the early foundational contribution made by Catholic Social Teaching and on its continuing influence, to lift. A wholly refreshed dialogue began, with a newly rediscovered awareness that the Holy See and the ILO were on common pathways.

After decades of scholarly exegesis by Observers of the Holy See to the International Labour Conferences, unremarked upon in the Records of Proceedings

---

52 Quoting Pope Leo XIII, *Rerum novarum* (1891) para 40.
53 Quoting Pope Leo XIII, *Rerum novarum* (1891) para 9.

or in the Reports of Directors-General,[54] suddenly that process of exegesis was being carried out by the ILO itself in explaining the presence – express or implied – of the principles of Catholic Social Teaching in the two overarching principles.

The concept of decent work was acknowledged by Juan Somavia as not limited to a mere *material* dimension, but to include the *properly spiritual* dimension of work. Just when a secular human rights analysis of the ILO's work and character seemed to have won the day, having been (at least within the walls of the ILO) an unchallenged axiom since World War Two, the metaphysical has come storming back.

In the reigns of Pope St John Paul II, Pope Benedict XVI and Pope Francis the concept of decent work originated by Michel Hansenne and Juan Somavia has been integrated in the Magisterium of the Catholic Church.

The Holy See and the ILO not only follow common pathways, they share a common vision and employ means in common to make that vision a reality.

Bibliography

The Holy See

Encyclicals, Apostolic letters, Exhortations (in chronological order)

Pope Leo XIII, *Rerum novarum* (1891).
Pope St John Paul II, *Laborem exercens* (1981).
Pope Benedict XVI, *Caritas in veritate* (2009).
Pope Francis, *Fratelli tutti* (2020).

Other materials (in chronological order)

Pope St John Paul II, *Message for the 1996 World Day of Peace "Let Us Give Children a Future of Peace"* para 5 <https://w2.vatican.va/content/john-paul-ii/en/messages/peace/documents/hf_jp-ii_mes_08121995_xxix-world-day-for-peace.html> (accessed 17 October 2020).
Homily of His Holiness Pope John Paul II, Jubilee of Workers 1 May 2000 <www.vatican.va/content/john-paul-ii/en/homilies/2000/documents/hf_jp-ii_hom_20000501_jub-workers.html> (accessed 17 October 2020).
Jubilee of Workers, Greeting of the Holy Father John Paul II after Mass 1 May 2000 <www.vatican.va/content/john-paul-ii/en/speeches/2000/apr-jun/documents/hf_jp-ii_spe_20000501_jub-workers.html> (accessed 17 October 2020).
Compendium of the Social Doctrine of the Church (2004) <www.antoniano.org/carbajo/FST/Readings/Magisterium/EN_Compendium_CST.pdf> (accessed 17 October 2020).
Global Seminar Sustainable Development and the Future of Work in the Context of the Jubilee of Mercy (Rome, 2 to 5 May 2016) <www.iustitiaetpax.va/content/giustiziaepace/en/attivita1/presidente/2016/_sustainable-development-and-the-future-of-work--in-the-context-.html> (accessed 17 October 2020).

---

54 Discussed in Chapter 6.

Archbishop Bernardito Auza, Apostolic Nuncio and Permanent Observer of the Holy
    See to the United Nations, Address to the High-Level Meeting of the United
    Nations General Assembly, 11 April 2019 <https://holyseemission.org/contents
    /statements/5cb0ae1bdd6e4.php>.

International Labour Organisation

International Labour Conferences (in chronological order)

Record of the Proceedings of the 89th Session of the ILC 2001 7/4 <www.ilo.or
    g/public/libdoc/ilo/P/09616/09616(2001–89).pdf> (accessed 17 October
    2020).
Record of the Proceedings of the 92nd Session of the ILC 2004 11/28 <www.ilo
    .org/public/libdoc/ilo/P/09616/09616(2004–92).pdf> (accessed 17 October
    2020).
Record of the Proceedings of the 93rd session of the ILC 2005 11/26–11/27<www
    .ilo.org/public/libdoc/ilo/P/09616/09616(2005–93).pdf>   (accessed   17
    October 2020)
Record of the Proceedings of the 95th Session of the ILC 2006 14/24–14/25
    <www.ilo.org/public/libdoc/ilo/P/09616/09616(2006–95).pdf> (accessed 17
    October 2020).
Record of the Proceedings of the 96th Session of the ILC 2007 19/10 <www.ilo
    .org/public/libdoc/ilo/P/09616/09616(2007–96).pdf> (accessed 17 October
    2020).
Record of the Proceedings of the 97th Session of the ILC 2008 17/44 <www.ilo
    .org/public/libdoc/ilo/P/09616/09616(2008–97).pdf> (accessed 17 October
    2020).
Record of the Proceedings of the 98th Session of the ILC 2009 8/25 <www.ilo.org/
    public/libdoc/ilo/P/09616/09616(2009–98).pdf> (accessed 17 October 2020).

Reports (in chronological order)

Report of the Director-General to the 87th Session of the ILC 1999 *Decent Work* 2 –
    4 <www.ilo.org/public/libdoc/ilo/P/09383/09383(1999–87).pdf> (accessed
    17 October 2020).
Report of the Director-General to the 89th Session of the ILC 2001 *Reducing the
    Decent Work Deficit: A Global Challenge* <www.ilo.org/public/libdoc/ilo/P/093
    83/09383(2001–89)76.pdf> (accessed 17 October 2020).
Report of the Director-General to the 100th session of the ILC 2011 *A New Era of
    Social Justice* para 26 <www.ilo.org/public/libdoc/ilo/P/09383/09383(2011–
    100).pdf> (accessed 17 October 2020).
Report of the Director-General to the 102nd Session of the ILC 2013 *Towards the
    ILO Centenary: Realities, Renewal and Tripartite Commitment* <www.ilo.org/
    public/libdoc/ilo/P/09383/09383(2013-102-1A).pdf> (accessed 17 October
    2020).
Report of the Director-General to the 104th Session of the ILC 2015 *The Future of
    Work Centenary Initiative iii*, 1–2, 6–7, 10 <www.ilo.org/public/libdoc/ilo/P
    /09383/09383(2015-104-I).pdf> (accessed 17 October 2020).

Other materials (in chronological order)

Somavia, Juan, *Work for All: Path of Solidarity and Justice* (Rome, 1 May 2000) <www.ilo.org/global/about-the-ilo/newsroom/news/WCMS_007886/lang--en/index.htm> (accessed 17 October 2020).

ILO Declaration on Fundamental Principles and Rights at Work 1998 (revised to 2010) <www.ilo.org/wcmsp5/groups/public/---ed_norm/---declaration/documents/normativeinstrument/wcms_716594.pdf> (accessed 17 October 2020).

Somavia, Juan, *The Challenge of a Fair Globalization*, Presentation at the Pontifical Lateran University on the Report of the World Commission on the Social Dimension of Globalization (Rome, 25 February 2005) <www.ilo.org/public/english/bureau/dgo/speeches/somavia/2005/rome.pdf> (accessed 17 October 2020).

Declaration on Social Justice for a Fair Globalization 2008 <www.ilo.org/wcmsp5/groups/public/---dgreports/---cabinet/documents/genericdocument/wcms_371208.pdf> (accessed 17 October 2020).

Global Commission on the Future of Work, *Work for a Brighter Future* (ILO, Geneva, 2019) 24 <www.ilo.org/global/topics/future-of-work/publications/WCMS_662410/lang--en/index.htm> (accessed 17 October 2020).

ILO Centenary Declaration for the Future of Work 2019 <www.ilo.org/wcmsp5/groups/public/@ed_norm/@relconf/documents/meetingdocument/wcms_711674.pdf> (accessed 17 October 2020).

International documents

United Nations' 2030 Agenda for Sustainable Development 2015 Goal 8 <https://sdgs.un.org/goals/goal8> (accessed 17 October 2020).

Secondary sources

Caritas in Veritate Foundation, *Rethinking Labour, Ethical Reflections on the Future of Work, Labour after Laudato Si'* (The Caritas in Veritate Foundation Working Papers, FCIV, Chambésy, 2018) <https://futureofwork-labourafterlaudatosi.net/2018/11/14/rethinking-labour-ethical-reflections-on-the-future-of-work-14-november-2018-global/> (accessed 17 October 2020).

A Discussion with Dominique Peccoud, SJ (Berkley Center for Religion, Peace and World Affairs, Georgetown University, 23 February 2011) http://berkleycenter.georgetown.edu/interviews/a-discussion-with-dominique-peccoud-s-j.

Ezea, Matthew Irunnaya, *The ILO's Concept of Decent Work in the Light of the Social Teaching of the Church and Its Relevance to Nigeria* (LIT Verlag GmbH & Co. KG, Vienna, 2011).

Fenwick, Colin, "The International Labour Organisation" in Malcolm Langford, ed, *Social Rights Jurisprudence* (Cambridge University Press, Cambridge, 2008) 598.

Gallagher, Archbishop Paul Richard, Secretary for Relations with States, Secretariat of State, the Vatican, "The Holy See and the International Labour Organization: Common Pathways on Labour" in *Rethinking Labour, Ethical Reflections on the Future of Work, Labour after Laudato Si'* 241–250, at 245–247 (The Caritas in Veritate Foundation Working Papers, FCIV, Chambésy, 2018) <https://futureofwork-labourafterlaudatosi.net/2018/11/14/rethinking-labour-ethical-reflect

ions-on-the-future-of-work-14-november-2018-global/> (accessed 17 October 2020).

____, Address "Holy See and ILO: Common Pathways on Labour", to an ILO Special Event "Rethinking Labour and the Future of Work – An Interreligious Perspective" (Geneva, 25 February 2019). <www.jesuites.ch/images/2019/Ne ws/Province/25Feb19_SpecialEventRethinkingLabour_ArchbishopGallagher.p df> (accessed 17 October 2020).

Hughes, Steve and Haworth, Nigel, *The International Labour Organisation (ILO): Coming in from the Cold* (Routledge, London and New York, 2011).

Maul, Daniel, *International Labour Organization: 100 Years of Global Social Policy* (ILO and De Grutyer, Berlin, 2019).

Peccoud, Dominique, "Decent Work: A Catholic Perspective" in Dominique Peccoud, ed, *Philosophical and Spiritual Perspectives on Decent Work* (ILO, World Council of Churches, ILO International Institute for Labour Studies, Geneva, 2004) 129.

Rodgers, Gerry , Lee, Eddy, Swepston, Lee and Van Diele, Jasmien , *The ILO and the Quest for Social Justice 1919–2009* (Cornell University Press, Ithaca and International Labour Office, Geneva 2009).

Ryder, Guy, "Editorial in *Rethinking Labour, Ethical Reflections on the Future of Work, Labour After Laudato Si*" 9–11 (The Caritas in Veritate Foundation Working Papers, FCIV, Chambésy, 2018) <https://futureofwork-labourafterlaudatosi.net /2018/11/14/rethinking-labour-ethical-reflections-on-the-future-of-work-14-november-2018-global/> (accessed 17 October 2020).

Thomas, Albert, *The International Labour Organisation: The First Decade* (George Allen & Unwin Limited, London, 1931).

8   Afterword

The Catholic Church had engaged in a critical examination of workers' rights and employers' duties long before the ILO was formed. The concept of an international standard of protection was already present in the work of mid-19th-century Catholic clerics such as Archbishop Ketteler, Bishop Mermillod and Cardinal Manning who laid the foundations of Social Catholicism. Pope Leo XIII in his Encyclical *Rerum novarum* consolidated the Church's teaching, and this continues to evolve.

Yet Social Catholicism in the abstract without a political and institutional delivery mechanism may have little impact on society. André Arnou had recognised this in the earliest years of the ILO when in 1933 he wrote:

> Car si pour vivre en ce monde sensible, l'âme a besoin d'un corps, l'esprit de justice et de charité agira-t-il sur la Société des hommes sans des lois, sans des organismes? Et c'est pourquoi a été créée, forgée, mise au point, une technique et une institution de la Paix sociale internationale: l'Organisation internationale du Travail.[1]

Fifty years later, the Holy See had continued to acknowledge that:

> Naturally the Church has neither the competence nor the means to propose technical solutions in regard to structural change due to economic and technical innovations. [...] However, [...] the Church feels that an essential part of its mission is to indicate the ethical principles – and that is its specific contribution to the solution of economic problems – according to which

1 [For just as in order to live in this tangible world, the soul needs a body, could the spirit of justice and of charity bring their influence to bear on mankind without laws, without institutions? And it is for this reason that there has been established, wrought, put in place, an engine and agency for international social Peace: the International Labour Organisation.] A Arnou, *L'Organisation internationale du Travail et les Catholiques* (Éditions Spes, Paris, 1933) 20.

such solutions should be contemplated, if they are to be in keeping with man's needs, to act not against man but for him.[2]

John A Coleman presents the same case in the 21st century:

> [I]deas have impact on history and on society through a distinctive institutionalization and carrier units. [...] If the older forms of these have been lost, eclipsed or secularized, there is no way that a mere evocation of the splendid Catholic anthropology will have much contemporary impact on politics or social policy. Like liberalism, critical theory, feminism, and other political viewpoints, social Catholicism will need vehicles that bring it, with legitimacy and credibility, into the policy arenas. Only through a set of institutions will contemporary Catholicism generate the sort of middle axioms to guide social policy that flow from its unique anthropological legacy.[3]

Under its first Director-General Albert Thomas, and the influence of Mgr Nolens, the young ILO sought a "*force morale*", a moral imperative to underpin the principles contained in its Conventions and Recommendations. It turned to Social Catholicism and to the Holy See, which appointed in 1926 the first of what was to become an unbroken succession of Jesuits in residence at the ILO. To the Christian trade unions, Albert Thomas declared in 1928:

> [C]'est en nous efforçant d'élever aus plus haut nos idéals respectifs, en les dévoilant dans leur pureté, dans leur intégrité, en cherchant à comprendre chaque jour davantage les nobles aspirations qui nous les ont fait concevoir, que nous pourrons le mieux les assembler et les unir, et que nous creérons la possibilité de concentrer nos regards vers des pensées et des actions qui nous soient communes à tous.[4]

That this proved to have been enduring was remarked upon by Director-General Juan Somavia in 2005:

---

2 Mgr Bertello, Observer of the Holy See, Record of Proceedings of the 71st Session of the ILC 1985 22/24–22/26 <www.ilo.org/public/libdoc/ilo/P/09616/09616(1985-71).pdf> © ILO (accessed 17 October 2020).

3 John A Coleman, *The Future of Catholic Social Thought in Modern Catholic Social Teaching* (Second edition) (Kenneth R Himes, ed) (Georgetown University Press, Washington, DC, 2018) 610, 617.

4 Albert Thomas, Address to the Fourth Congress of the International Federation of Christian Trade Unions in Munich 1928. [It is in our endeavouring to raise to the highest level our respective ideals, in revealing them in their purity of form, in their integrity, in searching more each day to understand the high-minded aspirations to which these have made us conceive them, that we can the better combine and unite them, and be able to focus our gaze on those concepts and actions which are common to us all.] Quoted in Maurice Barbier, 'Les Relations Entre l'Église Catholique et l'Organisation International du Travail' in *Politique étrangère*, Vol. 37, No. 3 (1972) (Institut Français des Relations Internationales) 351, 357.

The ILO and the Holy See began their collaboration some 85 years ago. Over the years, the Catholic Church has enriched its social teachings, while we have developed the international legal framework for a better society, built, through tripartite dialogue, on the ideal of work being more and more decent and available to all. To move sustainably in that direction the voice of the Church can be so significant. [...] Our paths have not diverged during this history of relations, [...] and we will continue our work along what is clearly a common path.[5]

Yet in the inter-War years there was no official acknowledgement on the part of the Holy See that it had any form of relationship with the ILO; the Holy See holding itself above politics. Then for decades after World War Two there had been silence on the part of the ILO when it came to any form of relationship with the Holy See; commentators on the ILO adopting a human rights narrative and projecting this retrospectively in analysing its origin and evolution.

Looking back across the chapters in this book, which analogy best fits the bond between the Holy See and the ILO? The ebb and flow of a tide? Warp and weft?

The relationship has not been tidal, because that implies advance and retreat, and the evidence overwhelmingly points to it having only advanced.

Labour rights in Social Catholicism and the principles embodied in the Conventions and Recommendations of the ILO have been subject to such mutual influence that they can be spoken of as the warp and weft of one cloth. The labour rights of the one have become, in substance if not in form, the labour rights of the other.

The Holy See and the ILO of course remain distinct: they readily acknowledge that they are on common pathways, but this does not mean that they tread the *same* path. The stages of their diplomatic approaches have been formal and measured, but if this has seemed at times like a shy dance, they at least danced to the same music, and that shyness wore off.

That this bond between them has not always been apparent to the casual observer is due perhaps in part to the ILO's reluctance to explain itself, or in its not feeling the need to do so, and in part to a general decline in awareness of Social Catholicism and of the transcendent. There has been a shift to legalism, with all which that implies. Costas Douzinas put it succinctly: "Legal thinking has abandoned transcendence, has condemned natural law to the history of ideas, has tamed justice and has become an accountancy of rules".[6]

As this book has shown, the reclassification of the history and development of the ILO in exclusively secular terms is not supported by the contemporary evidence.

---

5 Juan Somavia, *The Challenge of a Fair Globalization*, Presentation at the Pontifical Lateran University on the Report of the World Commission on the Social Dimension of Globalization (Rome, 25 February 2005) <www.ilo.org/public/english/bureau/dgo/speeches/somavia/2005/rome.pdf> (accessed 17 October 2020) (c) ILO.
6 Costas Douzinas, *The End of Human Rights* (Hart Publishing, Oxford, 2000) 374.

Throughout the lifetimes of the current generation of ILO commentators, analysts and historians the human rights narrative within a secular social historic framework has informed the discussion. That narrative is insufficient. In Tony Judt's words:

> The Enlightenment vision – with or without God as its first mover and moral arbiter – no longer convinces: we need reasons to choose one policy or set of policies over another. What we lack is a moral narrative: an internally coherent account that ascribes purpose to our actions in a way that transcends them.[7]

In 2008 ILO historian Jasmien Van Daele wrote:

> Within the broader network of transnational actors a lot has been said about labour and to a lesser extent liberal internationalism. On the side of Catholic social organizations, research on the ILO and the Christian working class is far less popular. One reason is the dominance of the socialist International Federation of Trade Unions in the ILO's Workers' Group in the first half of the twentieth century. In this light it would be interesting to know more about the (development of the) relationship between the ILO and the Catholic Church, after all both universal international organizations.[8]

This book has told that story.

Bibliography

The Holy See

Encyclicals, Apostolic letters, Exhortations (in chronological order)

Pope Leo XIII, *Rerum novarum* (1891).

International Labour Organisation

International Labour Conferences

Mgr Bertello, Observer of the Holy See, Record of Proceedings of the 71st Session of the ILC 1985 22/24–22/26 <www.ilo.org/public/libdoc/ilo/P/09616/09 616(1985-71).pdf>.

---

7 Tony Judt, *Ill Fares the Land* (Allen Lane, London, 2010) 183.
8 Jasmien Van Daele, 'The International Labour Organization (ILO) in Past and Present Research' in *International Review of Social History*, Vol. 53, No. 3 (December 2008) 485, 510.

Other materials

Somavia, Juan, *The Challenge of a Fair Globalization*, Presentation at the Pontifical Lateran University on the Report of the World Commission on the Social Dimension of Globalization (Rome, 25 February 2005) <www.ilo.org/public/e nglish/bureau/dgo/speeches/somavia/2005/rome.pdf>.

Secondary sources

Arnou, A, *L'Organisation internationale du Travail et les Catholiques* (Éditions Spes, Paris, 1933).
Barbier, Maurice, "Les Relations Entre l'Église Catholique et l'Organisation International du Travail" in *Politique étrangère*, Vol. 37, No.3 (1972) (Institut Français des Relations Internationales) 351.
Coleman, John A, *The Future of Catholic Social Thought in Modern Catholic Social Teaching* (Second edition) (Kenneth R Himes, ed) (Georgetown University Press, Washington, DC, 2018) 610.
Douzinas, Costas, *The End of Human Rights* (Hart Publishing, Oxford, 2000).
Judt, Tony, *Ill Fares the Land* (Allen Lane, London, 2010).
Van Daele, Jasmien, "The International Labour Organization (ILO) in Past and Present Research" in *International Review of Social History*, Vol. 53, No. 3 (December 2008) 485.

Index

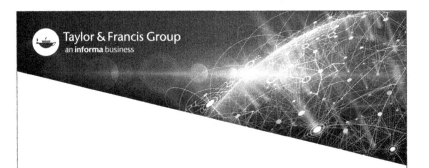